Translational Computing Pedagogies for Interdisciplinary Classrooms

Aquil Mirza Mohammed
https://orcid.org/0000-0001-7756-4363
The Hong Kong Polytechnic University, Hong Kong

IGI Global
Scientific Publishing
Publishing Tomorrow's Research Today

Vice President of Editorial	Melissa Wagner
Director of Acquisitions	Mikaela Felty
Director of Book Development	Jocelynn Hessler
Production Manager	Mike Brehm
Cover Design	Jose Rosado

Published in the United States of America by
IGI Global Scientific Publishing
701 East Chocolate Avenue
Hershey, PA, 17033, USA
Tel: 717-533-8845 | Fax: 717-533-7115
Website: https://www.igi-global.com E-mail: cust@igi-global.com

Library of Congress Cataloging-in-Publication Data

LCCN: 2026030944 (CIP Data Pending)
ISBN13: 979-8-2600-1811-8
Isbn13Softcover: 979-8-2600-1812-5
EISBN13: 979-8-2600-1813-2
British Cataloguing in Publication Data
A Cataloguing in Publication record for this book is available from the British Library.

Table of Contents

Detailed Table of Contents

This chapter establishes the framework of translational computing pedagogy within higher education. As computing becomes a universal academic literacy across non-technical domains, traditional instructional modes fail to support diverse interdisciplinary cohorts. The authors map a complex problem landscape characterized by cognitive, linguistic, representational, psychological, disciplinary, and assessment barriers that induce student anxiety. To bridge these gaps without diluting conceptual integrity, this chapter introduces an architecture structured on cognitive visibility, translational explanation, adaptive support, psychological safety, output conversion, and evidence-informed refinement to systematically drive student retention, self-efficacy, and active contribution.

This chapter develops a multi-theoretical framework for translational pedagogy in cross-disciplinary computer science education, addressing the limitation that single educational theories fail to support learners from diverse disciplinary backgrounds. The authors integrate learning, cognitive, motivation-identity and cross-disciplinary translation theories to validate six core components of translational pedagogy: cognitive explicitation, translational explanation, adaptive scaffolding, psychological safety, output transformation and evidence-based optimization. By synthesizing constructivism, cognitive load theory and self-efficacy theory, this chapter clarifies mechanisms of knowledge construction, cognitive burden control, learner motivation improvement and cross-domain knowledge transfer. It verifies translational pedagogy as a rigorous and inclusive instructional model, providing solid theoretical support for cross-disciplinary computer education practice and guiding tailored teaching for heterogeneous learners to promote sustainable knowledge transfer.

This chapter, per the authors, addresses the persistent invisibility problem in computing education, where expert reasoning remains hidden behind polished code and correct outputs, leading novices and interdisciplinary learners to guess, imitate, or disengage. The chapter introduces and defines cognitive visibility as a deliberate translational practice that externalizes hidden thinking processes such as logic sequencing, debugging, and state tracking into observable and learnable forms. The chapter distinguishes cognitive visibility from general explanation and positions it within a broader translational pedagogy. Six major forms of visibility are examined, including verbalized reasoning, paper-based tracing, flowcharts, state-change diagrams, debugging narratives, and think-aloud protocols. Pedagogical design strategies such as pre-coding tasks, live coding with intentional errors, slow demonstration, and student explanation routines are presented.

Effective teaching in interdisciplinary computing classrooms requires more than technical accuracy; it requires translational explanation, a pedagogical process that renders computational concepts intelligible across disciplinary boundaries while preserving rigor. This chapter argues that explanation must bridge the formal structures of computing and the diverse disciplinary worlds students inhabit. A five-step framework is proposed for constructing translational explanations, and discipline-specific models are provided for engineering, health sciences, design, business, linguistics, and biology students. Attention is given to language, multimodal representation, and visual design, alongside guidelines for evaluating explanation quality and building institutional capacity for translational teaching. The chapter concludes by positioning translational explanation as a foundational form of interdisciplinary bridgework.

This chapter per the authors argues for deliberate, design-driven support in multidisciplinary computing classrooms, articulating how scaffolded challenge and psychologically safe environments enable rigorous learning for diverse student cohorts. It outlines how support structures; low-stakes checks, guided examples, visible reasoning, progressive tasks, and flexible consultation; can reduce cognitive load while maintaining high standards, thereby promoting belonging and persistence. The chapter integrates theory from motivation and social-cognitive perspectives with practical guidance on assessment, feedback, governance, and ethical considerations, and offers design principles and evaluative prompts to inform researchers and practitioners aiming to foster equitable, high-quality learning across disciplines.

This chapter examines the limitations of conventional computing assessments that prioritize syntactic correctness over deep comprehension, arguing that such models fail to measure knowledge transfer or cognitive reasoning. To address these gaps within interdisciplinary university cohorts, this chapter per the authors proposes a "translational outcomes" framework. This model expands evaluative scope to capture conceptual portability, metacognitive awareness, and learner self-efficacy across diverse domain applications without sacrificing technical rigor. By unpacking structural methodologies like process-oriented milestones, multi-tiered transfer tasks, and neutral linguistic variations, this text demonstrates how to dismantle construct-irrelevant barriers that isolate non-technical students. Finally, this chapter per the authors explores "output conversion," detailing how scaffolded classroom capstones can be converted into tangible external contributions, including academic publications, industry competitions, and functional startup prototypes.

This chapter investigates how adaptive learning technologies can advance translational and interdisciplinary computing education in diverse, large-scale classrooms. It presents a framework in which adaptive systems tailor access, explanation, progression, and support while preserving shared learning outcomes. The discussion covers ALTS (Adaptive Learning and Teaching Systems), CAT (Computerized Adaptive Testing), instructor dashboards, background-aware question banks, and personalized learning pathways, illustrating how mass personalization can occur without fragmenting the curriculum. It also addresses ethical considerations, data privacy, and bias, and outlines scalable design principles, including governance, staffing, assessment, and sustainability. By linking pedagogy to infrastructure, the chapter outlines concrete pathways for institutions to deploy adaptive technologies to improve engagement, equity, and transfer, with examples and guiding questions to aid researchers and practitioners in evaluation and implementation of adaptive learning strategies.

This chapter introduces systematic approaches to improve cross-disciplinary computing teaching using multi-source evidence collection, triangulation verification and continuous quality improvement. Per the authors, teaching evidence falls into five categories: quantitative statistics, qualitative feedback, student coursework, in-class performance data and long-term follow-up records, preventing biased evaluation from sole test scores or surveys. A four-dimensional triangulation model verifies teaching results via varied data sources, research methods, stakeholder opinions and different teaching periods to avoid one-sided assessment. Combined with iterative CQI, the chapter demonstrates how teachers adjust curricula, classroom arrangements and grading standards based on verified empirical evidence. It also summarizes practical teaching difficulties and optimization advice to support instructional reform and quality control for interdisciplinary computing education.

This chapter argues that translational pedagogy, developed in computing education, offers a broadly applicable model for higher education. Its core principles are making expert reasoning visible, translating abstract concepts into learner-accessible forms, scaffolding challenge without lowering standards, converting coursework into authentic outputs, and refining teaching through evidence. The chapter shows how these principles can be adapted in engineering, design, health sciences, business, the built environment, and the social sciences and humanities, while preserving disciplinary integrity. It frames computing as a pedagogical laboratory for broader educational problems and concludes that effective transfer depends on identifying hidden barriers, aligning assessment with teaching, and redesigning learning environments to support participation, identity, and meaningful contribution.

This chapter argues for expanding translational and interdisciplinary learning from classroom practice to a university-wide ecosystem that supports scalable, impactful pedagogy. It outlines how translation of expert cognition into accessible explanations, combined with a creation-oriented culture, can surface student thinking, foster belonging, and promote transfer across disciplines. The discussion centers on design principles for scale, including governance, staffing, space, funding, and evaluation, and presents a cohesive framework linking pedagogy, curriculum, assessment, and policy. Drawing on theoretical foundations and illustrative contexts, the chapter examines how institutional structures can reward, sustain, and extend classroom innovations while addressing equity, sustainability, and stakeholder alignment. The text integrates perspectives from leadership and organizational change to articulate actionable implications for policy-makers, academics, and practitioners seeking to cultivate lasting, interdisciplinary learning ecosystems.

Preface

Higher education is undergoing a profound pedagogical transition. Computing, once treated as a specialist discipline largely confined to computer science and engineering programs, has increasingly become a cross-disciplinary academic literacy. Students in biology, health sciences, architecture, business, design, media, linguistics, construction, mathematics, and the social sciences now encounter computation not as a peripheral technical curiosity but as part of their intellectual and professional formation. Data analysis, automation, algorithmic reasoning, digital systems, intelligent technologies, and computational tools are now embedded across fields in ways that have transformed what it means to be educated for contemporary practice. Yet while the presence of computing across disciplines has expanded rapidly, pedagogical approaches have not always evolved at the same pace. Too often, computing is still taught through assumptions of technical familiarity, disciplinary homogeneity, and linguistic fluency that no longer reflect the realities of today's classrooms.

This book, *Translational Computing Pedagogies for Interdisciplinary Classrooms*, emerges from that pedagogical tension. Its central premise is that if computing is now being taught as a shared academic literacy across diverse fields, then its pedagogy must also become more translational, more inclusive, and more attentive to the varied intellectual worlds from which students enter the classroom. Computing education can no longer be understood solely as the transmission of syntax, tools, and canonical problem-solving methods to self-identified technical learners. It must increasingly be understood as the work of helping students from varied disciplinary backgrounds gain access to computational reasoning, conceptual confidence, practical transfer, and meaningful forms of contribution. This requires more than simplified explanation. It requires a pedagogical framework capable of preserving conceptual rigor while opening multiple pathways into understanding.

The present volume addresses this need by developing the concept of **translational computing pedagogy**. The book argues that teaching computing in interdisciplinary settings requires several interconnected moves: making expert reasoning visible to novices; translating abstract concepts across disciplinary languages and examples;

scaffolding challenge without diluting standards; creating psychologically safe conditions for trial, error, and growth; supporting students in transforming coursework into authentic outputs; and refining teaching through systematic evidence. These elements are not treated as isolated techniques but as components of a coherent pedagogical model designed for contemporary higher education.

The subject matter of this book therefore sits at the intersection of computing education, interdisciplinary pedagogy, higher education studies, learning sciences, and curriculum design. It is concerned with what happens when students who do not necessarily see themselves as "computer people" are nevertheless expected to engage deeply with computational ideas. It is concerned with the pedagogical implications of disciplinary diversity, variable prior knowledge, uneven confidence, and large-scale teaching. It is concerned with how students move from uncertainty to capability, from passive completion to active reasoning, and from classroom participation to meaningful contribution. Most importantly, it is concerned with how educators and institutions can design environments in which this transformation becomes more likely, more equitable, and more sustainable.

The topic of this volume is particularly timely. Across the world, universities are rethinking graduate capabilities in relation to artificial intelligence, automation, digital infrastructures, global uncertainty, and interdisciplinary problem solving. In many sectors, graduates are expected not merely to consume knowledge but to work across disciplinary boundaries, interpret complex systems, collaborate with technical specialists, and create new forms of value. At the same time, higher education is under pressure to widen participation, support increasingly diverse learners, and maintain standards in large and complex teaching environments. These pressures make the pedagogical questions addressed in this book especially urgent. How should computing be taught when it is no longer only for future computer scientists? How can rigor be preserved while access is widened? How can learning be designed not only for assessment performance, but for transfer, identity development, and contribution? And how can such work be sustained beyond isolated classroom innovation?

This book is written for a broad but identifiable readership. Its primary audience includes computing educators working with mixed or interdisciplinary cohorts, whether in foundational programming, data literacy, digital methods, systems teaching, or application-oriented computational modules. It also speaks to higher education teachers in non-computing disciplines who are integrating digital, analytical, or computational elements into their own programs. Educational developers, curriculum designers, assessment specialists, and learning scientists may also find value here, particularly those interested in inclusive pedagogy, cognitive visibility, feedback systems, interdisciplinary transfer, and evidence-informed teaching improvement. In addition, the volume is intended for academic leaders and policy-minded readers concerned with the future of university teaching in increasingly complex and digitally mediated environments. While the book is grounded in computing education, its broader contribution lies in offering a pedagogical model that can travel into other disciplines where difficult knowledge must be made accessible across diverse learner backgrounds.

This volume reflects a common conceptual architecture emerging from my work on translational computing pedagogy. The contributing authors, representing diverse disciplinary backgrounds, were invited to extend, interpret, and contextualize this model through the lenses of their own fields, experiences, and intellectual trajectories. The chapters were developed through sustained editorial dialogue within this shared pedagogical framework. Although each chapter addresses a distinct dimension of the book's overall argument, the volume is united by a common concern: how to teach difficult, high-value knowledge in ways that are conceptually rigorous, humanly responsive, and educationally generative.

CHAPTER OVERVIEW

Chapter 1, **"Translational Computing Pedagogy for Interdisciplinary Classrooms: Scope, Need, and Framework,"** establishes the central argument of the volume. It explains why computing must now be regarded as a cross-disciplinary literacy rather than a specialist enclave, identifies the pedagogical gap that emerges when traditional technical teaching models meet diverse learner populations, and introduces the translational pedagogy framework that guides the rest of the book. The chapter is foundational because it names the problem clearly and provides the conceptual vocabulary through which the subsequent chapters can be read as parts of a coherent whole.

Chapter 2, **"Theoretical Foundations of Translational Pedagogy in Computing Education,"** provides the scholarly grounding for the book's pedagogical model. Drawing on constructivism, situated learning, cognitive apprenticeship, schema theory, transfer theory, self-efficacy, belonging, boundary crossing, and related traditions, the chapter explains why translational pedagogy is not merely practical improvisation but theoretically defensible educational design. Its importance lies in demonstrating that the book's model stands within an established intellectual lineage while also integrating those theories in a way specifically responsive to interdisciplinary computing contexts.

Chapter 3, **"Making Thinking Visible: Cognitive Visibility as a Translational Practice,"** addresses one of the most important practical problems in computing education: the invisibility of expert reasoning. Students often see polished solutions but not the thought processes that produce them. This chapter explores how making reasoning visible—through tracing, think-alouds, partial modeling, explicit debugging, and interpretive articulation—can improve conceptual understanding and reduce the false perception that expertise is effortless. Its significance lies in translating theoretical ideas about apprenticeship and cognitive access into a pedagogical principle with broad practical value.

Chapter 4, **"Translational Explanation: Explaining Computing Concepts Across Disciplines,"** focuses on the challenge of explanation itself. It asks how core concepts such as iteration, abstraction, conditionals, data structures, and systems logic can be explained in ways that remain rigorous while becoming more intelligible to students from different fields. This chapter is particularly important because interdisciplinary teaching often fails not at the level of content, but at the level of representational access. By examining analogy, recontextualization, discourse, and disciplinary framing, the chapter clarifies how explanation becomes a serious scholarly and pedagogical act rather than a mere presentation skill.

Chapter 5, **"Adaptive Support, Scaffolded Challenge, and Psychological Safety in Multidisciplinary Computing Classrooms,"** addresses the developmental and emotional dimensions of learning. It argues that rigorous computing education requires not only conceptual clarity but also environments in which students can engage uncertainty without humiliation, receive support without stigma, and grow through challenge rather than be defeated by it. This chapter is important because it links pedagogy to persistence, belonging, and learner identity—areas often underestimated in technical education despite their central influence on who continues, who disengages, and who comes to see computing as part of their intellectual repertoire.

Chapter 6, **"From Assessment to Translational Outcomes: Measuring Understanding, Transfer, and Contribution,"** turns to a central question in higher education: how do we know whether translational pedagogy is working? The chapter argues that assessment must move beyond narrow correctness measures and engage broader outcomes such as conceptual understanding, cross-context transfer, reflective reasoning, and contribution-oriented learning. Its importance lies in showing that if the aims of pedagogy change, then the logic of assessment must also change. The chapter therefore bridges instructional intention and educational accountability.

Chapter 7, **"Adaptive Learning Technologies and Pedagogy: Personalization for Interdisciplinary Computing Education,"** explores the role of adaptive systems, personalized learning pathways, and digitally mediated support in complex computing classrooms. Rather than treating technology as inherently transformative, the chapter positions it within pedagogical purpose. Its significance lies in asking how personalization can be achieved ethically and effectively in diverse cohorts without surrendering teaching design to technical systems. In a period where AI and educational technology are rapidly expanding, this chapter helps readers distinguish between pedagogy-led adaptation and technology-led solutionism.

Chapter 8, **"Evidence, Triangulation, and Continuous Quality Improvement in Cross-Disciplinary Computing Teaching,"** examines how teaching quality can be improved through systematic evidence gathering rather than intuition alone. By discussing triangulation across student feedback, performance trends, help-seeking patterns, outputs, and observation, the chapter develops a disciplined framework for pedagogical refinement. Its importance lies in reinforcing that high-quality teaching, particularly in interdisciplinary and large-class contexts, is not static. It depends on continuous interpretation, revision, and ethical use of evidence.

Chapter 9, **"Student Transformation Across Disciplines: Case Studies of Learning, Identity, and Transfer,"** moves from framework to lived experience. Through case-based and narrative approaches, it explores how students from different disciplinary backgrounds transform through translational pedagogy. Rather than reducing success to grades, the chapter considers changes in confidence, belonging, reasoning, transfer, and professional imagination. Its contribution is to humanize the pedagogy discussed in earlier chapters and to show that educational transformation often occurs through identity shifts as much as cognitive gain.

Chapter 10, **"Teaching Computing at Scale in Interdisciplinary Settings: Design, Delivery, and Sustainability,"** addresses one of the most pressing practical challenges facing contemporary educators: how to maintain quality in classes of 200 to 350 students without collapsing into impersonal instruction. The chapter considers large-class architecture, scalable routines, layered support systems, teaching-team coordination, and sustainable workload design. Its importance lies in demonstrating that translational pedagogy is not confined to small, idealized teaching environments. It can be designed for scale, though only through deliberate structure and systems thinking.

Chapter 11, **"Beyond Computing: Generalizing Translational Pedagogy Across Disciplines,"** extends the argument of the volume outward. It asks what aspects of the pedagogical model are specific to computing and what aspects can travel into engineering, design, health sciences, business, the built environment, and the humanities. This chapter is important because it positions the book not only as a contribution to computing education, but as a broader intervention in higher education pedagogy. It suggests that translational teaching may serve as a general model wherever difficult knowledge must be made accessible across disciplinary difference.

Chapter 12, **"Cultivating a Creation-Oriented Culture in Higher Education: Institutional Ecosystems for Translational and Interdisciplinary Learning,"** concludes the volume by zooming out from classrooms to institutions. It argues that pedagogy alone is not enough if universities wish to sustain contribution-oriented learning. Curriculum structures, mentoring systems, research pathways, innovation ecosystems, service-learning, faculty recognition, and policy alignment all matter.

This chapter is particularly significant because it reframes the entire discussion as an institutional challenge rather than only a classroom one. If students are to move from learning to contribution, higher education must cultivate ecosystems in which such movement is possible, recognized, and ethically supported.

Taken together, these chapters offer more than a set of isolated discussions. They build a cumulative argument. The volume begins by identifying a pedagogical problem in contemporary higher education: the mismatch between the growing importance of computing and the limited suitability of traditional pedagogy for diverse interdisciplinary learners. It then develops a theoretical foundation, practical framework, evidence logic, and broader institutional vision in response. In this sense, the book is both analytical and constructive. It diagnoses a problem and also proposes a model.

The contribution of this volume to the field is threefold. First, it contributes to computing education by addressing an under-theorized but increasingly central challenge: how to teach computing effectively when many learners do not primarily identify with computing as a field. Second, it contributes to higher education pedagogy by showing how difficult knowledge can be taught in ways that are rigorous, scalable, inclusive, and contribution-oriented. Third, it contributes to interdisciplinary pedagogy by reframing translation not as a secondary accommodation, but as a primary act of educational design.

More broadly, the book argues for a shift in how we think about university learning itself. It suggests that higher education should not be satisfied with helping students merely survive difficult subjects or reproduce content in assessed form. Instead, students should be supported to understand deeply, transfer meaningfully, and create responsibly. In computing education, this may involve moving from code imitation to conceptual reasoning, from fear to confidence, from course tasks to authentic outputs. In institutional terms, it means building cultures where learning is not only acquired but converted into contribution.

If this book succeeds, it will do so not because it offers a final answer, but because it helps open a more serious conversation about the future of teaching in interdisciplinary higher education. Computing is becoming everyone's concern. The pedagogies we use to teach it must therefore become more humane, more flexible, more evidence-informed, and more intellectually generous. This volume is offered in that spirit.

Chapter 1
Translational Computing Pedagogy for Interdisciplinary Classrooms:
Scope, Need, and Framework

Aquil Mirza Mohammed
http://orcid.org/0000-0001-7756-4363
Department of Computing, The Hong Kong Polytechnic University, Hong Kong

ABSTRACT

This chapter establishes the framework of translational computing pedagogy within higher education. As computing becomes a universal academic literacy across non-technical domains, traditional instructional modes fail to support diverse interdisciplinary cohorts. The authors map a complex problem landscape characterized by cognitive, linguistic, representational, psychological, disciplinary, and assessment barriers that induce student anxiety. To bridge these gaps without diluting conceptual integrity, this chapter introduces an architecture structured on cognitive visibility, translational explanation, adaptive support, psychological safety, output conversion, and evidence-informed refinement to systematically drive student retention, self-efficacy, and active contribution.

DOI: 10.4018/979-8-2600-1811-8.ch001

1. INTRODUCTION

1.1 The Rise of Computing as a Universal Academic Literacy

Computing is no longer confined to computer science departments or specialist technical programs. Across higher education, the ability to think computationally, work with data, understand algorithmic logic, and engage critically with digital systems has become increasingly relevant to students in engineering, business, health sciences, design, construction, linguistics, media, biology, and the social sciences (Denning, 2017; Wing, 2006). This shift has been driven by several converging forces: the digitization of professional practice, the expansion of artificial intelligence and automation, the datafication of nearly every field, and the expectation that graduates will operate confidently within technologically mediated environments (Bers, 2020; Guzdial, 2008; National Academies of Sciences, Engineering, and Medicine [NASEM], 2018).

In earlier decades, students could progress through university with little direct engagement with programming, systems thinking, or digital analysis unless they were enrolled in computing-related disciplines. That is no longer typical. A biology student may need to automate data cleaning or analyze genomic datasets; a designer may need to engage generative tools and interactive systems; an architecture student may model environments computationally; a linguistics student may analyze corpora; and a business student may need to interpret analytics platforms and algorithmic decision systems (Jasanoff et al., 2021; NASEM, 2018). Even when students do not become programmers by profession, they increasingly require sufficient computational literacy to navigate contemporary industrial frameworks, such as those governing smart infrastructures and automated safety analytics (Mohammed et al., 2026), and understand how algorithmic infrastructures shape their own fields (Denning, 2017; Wing, 2006).

As a result, introductory and intermediate computing courses now often enroll students who do not identify as computer scientists and who may not have chosen computing as a central academic identity. This development is educationally significant. It means that computing instruction now functions less as a specialist gatekeeping mechanism and more as a foundational or service-oriented component of many degree pathways (Guzdial, 2008; Margolis & Fisher, 2003). Yet despite this expanded role, the pedagogy of computing in higher education often remains oriented toward students already aligned with technical language, technical confidence, and technical ways of thinking. This creates a critical mismatch.

The issue is not simply that interdisciplinary students "know less" at the start. More importantly, they often enter computing classrooms with different conceptual anchors, different motivational structures, different professional goals, and different anxieties about what it means to belong in a technical subject (Baxter Magolda, 2009; Carlone & Johnson, 2007). A student from fashion may perceive pattern, repetition, and visual logic differently from a student in electrical engineering. A student in health sciences may be motivated by diagnostic reasoning and patient care, while a student in construction may approach computing through systems coordination, sensing, or monitoring. If computing is taught as though all learners share the same vocabulary, examples, assumptions, and comfort with abstraction, then many learners are disadvantaged before meaningful learning has begun.

This chapter argues that the expansion of computing into interdisciplinary higher education requires not merely wider curriculum distribution but pedagogical translation. Computing must be taught in ways that preserve conceptual rigor while making its ideas intelligible, relevant, and usable across diverse learner backgrounds. Such a shift requires a new pedagogical lens: **translational computing pedagogy**.

1.2 The Pedagogical Gap in Interdisciplinary Classrooms

Interdisciplinary classrooms are often celebrated as dynamic spaces where diverse students engage shared problems, tools, and concepts. In practice, however, such classrooms also expose deep pedagogical gaps. The most immediate concerns alignment. Many computing courses still assume a learner who is already relatively comfortable with formal logic, procedural reasoning, symbolic syntax, and abstract problem decomposition. But interdisciplinary cohorts are not defined by a common technical orientation. They are defined by variation.

This variation appears in at least four ways. First, students differ significantly in prior exposure. Some have coded for years; others are encountering programming for the first time. Second, they differ in confidence. Some approach computing with curiosity and self-efficacy; others approach it with apprehension, seeing it as difficult, alien, or reserved for a particular type of person (Bandura, 1997; Cooper et al., 2019). Third, they differ in disciplinary identity. A student may be deeply invested in design, biology, linguistics, business, or civil engineering, and may initially see computing as peripheral rather than intrinsic to that identity. Fourth, they differ in how they make meaning. The same concept may become understandable through different examples, analogies, or representations depending on what the learner already knows and values (Ambrose et al., 2010; Bransford et al., 2000).

The pedagogical gap emerges when such variation is treated as incidental rather than constitutive. In many introductory settings, computing is presented in a universalized form: a standard sequence of concepts, conventional examples, fixed explanations, polished demonstrations, and assessments that privilege students already fluent in the culture of technical abstraction. This can function reasonably well for more homogeneous technical cohorts, though even there it has limitations. In interdisciplinary settings, however, it often leads to uneven access. Some students quickly orient themselves; others begin imitating code without understanding it, memorizing fragments instead of building reasoning, or disengaging quietly because they do not see how the subject connects to their discipline or future practice (Guzdial, 2015; Lister et al., 2006).

The pedagogical gap is therefore not only an issue of difficulty. It is also a problem of translation failure. Students are asked to cross into computing without enough support in interpreting its language, forms of reasoning, expectations of practice, and relevance to their own disciplinary worlds. When this occurs, the classroom may unintentionally reward those who already operate close to the teacher's assumptions while marginalizing those who require conceptual bridging (Shulman, 1987; Vygotsky, 1978).

This gap becomes more consequential in large-enrollment courses, where individualized explanation is harder to provide and where hesitant students can become invisible. In such settings, the challenge is not merely to cover content, but to create pathways through which learners with different backgrounds can engage productively with shared computing ideas. Translational pedagogy is proposed here as a response to that challenge.

1.3 Why Traditional Computing Pedagogy Fails Diverse Cohorts

Traditional computing pedagogy often rests on assumptions poorly suited to interdisciplinary cohorts. One assumption is that exposure to syntax and sample solutions will naturally lead to understanding. Yet many students can reproduce code patterns without grasping the logic underneath them. Another assumption is that if students do not keep up, the problem lies primarily in their effort or aptitude. This "sink or swim" stance obscures the extent to which teaching design itself may be misaligned with learner needs (Barker et al., 2009; Margolis & Fisher, 2003). A third assumption is that the same explanation is equally usable for all learners so long as it is technically accurate. In reality, technical correctness is not the same as pedagogical accessibility (Shulman, 1986).

Traditional models also frequently privilege finished products over process. Students may see a lecturer present a complete solution but not the reasoning, hesitation, debugging, or conceptual movement that produced it. For novices, especially those from non-technical backgrounds, this can make expertise appear opaque and unattainable. Students are left comparing their own incomplete and error-filled attempts to the polished output of an expert, which can intensify self-doubt (Chi et al., 1989; Collins et al., 1989).

A further limitation is the underestimation of affect. Introductory computing often generates anxiety, particularly for learners who already suspect they may not belong. Technical gatekeeping, rapid pacing, public correction, or heavy reliance on insider terminology can amplify this anxiety. Once fear of failure enters the classroom, students may stop asking questions, stop experimenting, and stop treating confusion as a normal part of learning (Bandura, 1997; Cooper et al., 2019).

Finally, traditional pedagogy frequently underperforms in relation to transfer. Students may complete tasks inside the computing classroom yet fail to see how the concepts apply within their own fields. In interdisciplinary education, this is a serious weakness. If computing is to function as a shared literacy rather than a detached requirement, students must be able to map concepts into domain-relevant purposes. Without that bridge, computing remains externally imposed rather than intellectually integrated (Biggs & Tang, 2011; Bransford et al., 2000).

1.4 Purpose and Contribution of Translational Computing Pedagogy

This chapter introduces **translational computing pedagogy** as a framework for addressing these challenges. The term *translational* is used here to indicate a pedagogical orientation that bridges disciplinary boundaries, learner variability, and forms of meaning without diluting the conceptual integrity of computing. It is not simply a matter of simplifying technical material. It is a matter of redesigning teaching so that computing can be understood, used, and extended by students with diverse academic identities and starting points.

The chapter has four purposes. First, it establishes why interdisciplinary computing classrooms should be treated as a distinct pedagogical context rather than a minor variation on conventional programming instruction. Second, it defines translational computing pedagogy and distinguishes it from traditional content-transmission models. Third, it maps the problem landscape that makes such a pedagogy necessary, including cognitive, linguistic, psychological, disciplinary, and assessment-related barriers. Fourth, it introduces a framework that will organize the rest of this book: cognitive visibility, translational explanation, adaptive support and scaffolded challenge, psychological safety, output conversion, and evidence-informed refinement.

This chapter does not fully develop the theoretical foundations of these ideas; that task belongs to Chapter 2. Nor does it explore in depth components such as cognitive visibility, scaffolding, or adaptive assessment, which are examined later. Instead, the present chapter establishes the scope, need, and organizing logic of the book as a whole. Its central claim is straightforward: **if computing is now a cross-disciplinary academic literacy, then its pedagogy must become cross-disciplinary in design, translational in method, and inclusive in ambition**.

2. INTERDISCIPLINARY CLASSROOMS AS A DISTINCT TEACHING CONTEXT

2.1 Characteristics of Interdisciplinary Cohorts in Higher Education

Interdisciplinary computing classrooms are not simply mixed classrooms; they are structurally different pedagogical environments. Their distinctive character arises from the coexistence of students who bring different forms of prior knowledge, disciplinary languages, habits of problem solving, and relationships to technical identity. In such classrooms, the teacher is not only delivering computing content but teaching across epistemic boundaries (Lattuca et al., 2017; Shulman, 1987).

Students in interdisciplinary cohorts often differ not just in what they know, but in how they know. A student from engineering may have confidence with formal systems and quantitative abstraction, while a student from design may excel in visual iteration and pattern recognition. A student in linguistics may be comfortable with rule systems but unfamiliar with programming syntax. As observed by (Aquil Mirza et al., 2026), a student in applied biology may be highly motivated by data and experimentation but uncertain about computational structure. These students are not empty vessels waiting to receive computing knowledge; they are learners whose existing

This diversity can be a strength. Interdisciplinary classrooms can support richer examples, more flexible applications, and stronger appreciation of computing's broad relevance. They can help students see that computation is not merely a technical skill but a way of thinking that interacts with multiple domains of inquiry and practice. However, diversity becomes pedagogically generative only when the classroom is designed to work with it. If ignored, the same diversity becomes a source of inequity.

Interdisciplinary classrooms are also frequently associated with service teaching and gateway courses. These subjects may be mandatory or semi-mandatory, taken by students who did not choose computing as their primary area of study. This matters because motivation in such contexts cannot be assumed. Students may ask, explicitly or implicitly: *Why do I need this? How does it relate to my discipline? Am I expected to become something I did not choose to be?* Teaching in such environments requires more than procedural instruction. It requires disciplinary mediation and identity-sensitive pedagogy (Baxter Magolda, 2009; Tinto, 2012).

2.2 Variability in Prior Knowledge, Confidence, Identity, and Expectations

One of the defining features of interdisciplinary computing education is extreme learner variability. In a single class, one student may already be familiar with Python, another may know only spreadsheet logic, and another may have never written a line of code. These differences affect how quickly students grasp syntax, how they interpret task demands, how they respond to errors, and whether they experience early success or discouragement (Guzdial, 2015; Lister et al., 2006).

Confidence often varies just as sharply as prior knowledge. Some students have internalized the belief that they are "technical" and therefore capable of learning programming. Others have internalized the opposite. These self-perceptions are shaped by previous educational experiences, peer culture, stereotypes about computing, and disciplinary positioning (Bandura, 1997; Margolis & Fisher, 2003). Students from non-computing fields may assume they are outsiders in the computing classroom even when they are fully capable of success. Such assumptions influence participation, risk-taking, and help-seeking.

Disciplinary identity also matters. A student strongly oriented toward fashion, health sciences, architecture, or linguistics may not wish to become a programmer in the conventional sense. Yet this does not mean the student is uninterested in computing. It may mean that computing needs to be framed as a tool, language, or mode of inquiry that extends rather than replaces the student's existing disciplinary identity. If pedagogy frames computing as a demand to become someone else, resistance is predictable. If it frames computing as a resource for one's own domain, engagement becomes more likely (Carlone & Johnson, 2007; Lattuca et al., 2017).

Students' expectations of the classroom further complicate matters. Some expect lecture-centered delivery. Some expect hands-on practice. Some assume assessment will reward memorization; others anticipate open-ended problem solving. If these expectations are not surfaced and managed, learners may misinterpret what the course values. Students accustomed to polished demonstrations may believe that errors signal incompetence rather than a normal part of reasoning. Students unfamiliar with project-based learning may feel lost if structure is insufficient. Interdisciplinary classrooms therefore require pedagogical clarity as much as content expertise (Biggs & Tang, 2011; Nicol & Macfarlane-Dick, 2006).

2.3 Challenges Faced by Non-Technical and Semi-Technical Students

Students from non-technical or semi-technical programs often enter computing courses carrying a dual challenge: they must learn new content while also learning how to interpret the culture of the subject. For some, the first obstacle is linguistic. Programming languages, technical terms, and symbolic notation can make the subject feel inaccessible before conceptual understanding has begun. For others, the challenge is representational. They may understand an idea when expressed through diagrams, everyday actions, or domain examples, but not when presented abstractly (Bransford et al., 2000; Shulman, 1986).

Another challenge is the hidden expectation of procedural confidence. Computing classrooms often presume that students know how to start solving a problem: break it down, identify variables, choose structures, test assumptions, debug iteratively. But these habits are not universal. Students may not know how to move from a problem statement to a computational strategy. As a result, they may over-rely on copying examples or seeking complete solutions instead of building underlying reasoning (Chi et al., 1989; Collins et al., 1989).

Semi-technical students, such as those in engineering-adjacent or science-based disciplines, face a different but related challenge. They may possess mathematical maturity or analytical discipline, yet still struggle with the specific logic of programming. In such cases, instructors may overestimate readiness because the student appears "technical enough." But procedural logic, debugging practice, and syntax management are learned capacities, not automatic transfers from adjacent disciplines (Guzdial, 2015).

A further challenge concerns social comparison. In mixed cohorts, students who start with less experience may observe peers answering quickly, coding fluently, or using technical language with ease. Unless pedagogy actively normalizes different starting points, such comparisons can become corrosive. Learners may conclude that they are slower, weaker, or unsuited to the subject, even when they are progressing well relative to their own beginnings (Cooper et al., 2019; Tinto, 2012).

2.4 Large-Class Complexity and Diversity of Learner Profiles

The complexity of interdisciplinary teaching intensifies in large-enrollment courses. A class of 250 to 350 students is not simply a bigger version of a small class; it is a different instructional ecology. Diversity becomes harder to see, quieter students are easier to overlook, and the cost of pedagogical misalignment rises because small misunderstandings can affect many learners at once (Gibbs & Jenkins, 2014; Tinto, 2012).

In many large foundational computing subjects, the teacher must respond to diverse disciplines, uneven preparation, varied confidence levels, and often additional support needs such as special educational needs or language-related barriers. This creates a teaching environment in which the average learner does not exist. Any explanation pitched to an imagined middle may miss substantial segments of the cohort. A fast pace may benefit advanced students but lose beginners. A highly simplified pace may frustrate stronger students. The pedagogical challenge is therefore not to find one ideal level, but to design layered access (Ambrose et al., 2010; Biggs & Tang, 2011).

Such large classes also place pressure on feedback systems. Students who are confused may not ask questions publicly. Some may feel embarrassed; others may not know what to ask. Instructors can easily misread silence as understanding. Standard lecture formats magnify this risk. Without mechanisms for visible reasoning, low-stakes checking, or responsive explanation, misconceptions remain hidden until high-stakes assessment reveals them (Hattie & Timperley, 2007; Nicol & Macfarlane-Dick, 2006).

The practical significance of this challenge is visible in many institutions. Large introductory programming and computing fundamentals courses often include the broadest diversity of backgrounds while also carrying the highest stakes for retention and academic confidence. In such contexts, pedagogy materially affects withdrawal, pass rates, confidence trajectories, and whether students see computing as a resource or a barrier. Evidence from large-scale practice suggests that translationally oriented approaches can make substantial differences in retention and attainment when implemented systematically.

3. DEFINING TRANSLATIONAL COMPUTING PEDAGOGY

3.1 Meaning of "Translational" in Educational Contexts

The word *translational* is often associated with moving knowledge from one context into practical use, as in translational medicine or translational research. In education, it can describe pedagogical work that bridges different domains of understanding without collapsing them into sameness. In the present context, translational pedagogy refers to the intentional movement of computing concepts across disciplinary, cognitive, linguistic, and motivational boundaries so that learners with different starting points can engage meaningfully with them.

Translation in this sense does not mean simplification alone. Nor does it mean reducing computing to superficial analogies. Rather, it involves careful re-expression, re-contextualization, and pedagogical mediation so that students can connect concepts to prior knowledge, disciplinary purpose, and usable forms of reasoning. Good translation preserves integrity while increasing access. It does not distort the concept to make it easier; it reconstructs the pathway into the concept so that more learners can reach it (Shulman, 1986; Vygotsky, 1978).

Translational pedagogy therefore includes at least three forms of movement. First, there is movement from expert understanding to novice access. Teachers must render visible what experts often do implicitly. Second, there is movement across disciplines. Concepts such as loops, conditionals, recursion, data structures, or systems interactions may need to be anchored differently depending on students' disciplinary backgrounds. Third, there is movement from classroom learning to practical contribution. Students should be able not only to pass a computing course but also to use what they learn in projects, research, innovation, or professional settings (Kuh, 2008; Wenger, 1998).

3.2 Translational Pedagogy Versus Conventional Pedagogy

Conventional computing pedagogy often assumes a stable content core and treats the teacher's role primarily as one of transmission, explanation, and evaluation. The content is fixed, the examples are generic, and the learner is expected to adapt. Translational pedagogy reverses this logic. The conceptual core remains rigorous, but the pedagogical pathways are adapted so that diverse learners can enter and progress.

This difference can be clarified across several dimensions. In conventional pedagogy, difference among students is often treated as an instructional complication. In translational pedagogy, learner diversity is treated as a design condition. In conventional pedagogy, correctness of explanation may be prioritized over accessibility of meaning. In translational pedagogy, conceptual fidelity and accessibility are co-equal concerns. In conventional pedagogy, failure may be interpreted as evidence of weak student ability or insufficient effort. In translational pedagogy, patterns of confusion are also treated as diagnostic signals about alignment between teaching and learning (Banta & Palomba, 2015; Biggs & Tang, 2011).

A translational classroom does not abandon standards. It does not dilute computing into everyday metaphors with no technical depth. Rather, it insists that rigor is best protected when students genuinely understand the concepts they are asked to apply. This often requires more explicit teaching of reasoning, more careful use of representations, more sensitive support structures, and more opportunities for students to connect learning to their own domain interests (Ambrose et al., 2010; Hattie, 2009). A systematic consolidation of these pedagogical differences across core educational dimensions is detailed in Table 1.

Table 1. Comparison Between Traditional and Translational Computing Pedagogy

Dimension	Traditional Computing Pedagogy	Translational Computing Pedagogy
View of learner diversity	Variation treated as secondary	Variation treated as a design condition
Role of explanation	Technical correctness prioritized	Technical correctness plus accessibility and relevance
Use of examples	Generic or discipline-neutral	Discipline-sensitive and context-bridging
Treatment of mistakes	Often performance-focused	Error treated as part of learning and reasoning
Pace and progression	Uniform pace	Layered access with supported progression
Focus of teaching	Content delivery and task completion	Understanding, transfer, and contribution
Student identity	Student adapts to technical culture	Pedagogy bridges technical culture and learner identity
Improvement process	Instructor-led and fixed	Evidence-informed and iterative

3.3 Core Assumptions of Translational Computing Instruction

Translational computing pedagogy rests on several assumptions.

The first is that students can learn computing effectively from very different starting points, but they may require different forms of access. Prior knowledge matters, but so do explanation, representation, pacing, and emotional climate (Ambrose et al., 2010).

The second is that understanding is not the same as exposure. Seeing code is not the same as grasping logic. Hearing a technical explanation is not the same as being able to apply or transfer the concept. Teaching must therefore make reasoning available, not simply present outcomes (Chi et al., 1989; Collins et al., 1989).

The third is that disciplinary identity influences engagement. Students learn more productively when they can connect computing concepts to purposes and examples that make sense within their own fields or future practice (Carlone & Johnson, 2007; Lattuca et al., 2017).

The fourth is that challenge should be sustained but not destabilizing. Learning computing requires difficulty, iteration, and encounter with error. However, such challenge should occur within structures that support persistence rather than humiliation or withdrawal (Bandura, 1997; Vygotsky, 1978).

The fifth is that student outcomes should extend beyond short-term task completion. While mastery of fundamentals remains essential, higher education increasingly requires that students develop confidence, transfer capacity, collaborative ability, and the possibility of converting coursework into authentic outputs such as prototypes, presentations, publications, or entrepreneurial ideas (Kuh, 2008; Wenger, 1998).

The sixth is that teaching must remain evidence-informed. In diverse classrooms, instructors cannot rely solely on intuition. Patterns in student work, feedback, participation, and outcomes should inform iterative refinement (Banta & Palomba, 2015; Hattie, 2009).

3.4 Key Dimensions: Access, Meaning, Transfer, and Contribution

For the purposes of this book, translational computing pedagogy can be organized through four key dimensions: **access, meaning, transfer, and contribution**.

Access refers to whether students can enter the learning process at all. This includes linguistic accessibility, representational clarity, and suitable entry points for learners with differing backgrounds. A student cannot benefit from rigor that is inaccessible in form.

Meaning refers to whether students can understand the logic and significance of what they are learning. This goes beyond procedural completion. It includes conceptual grasp, the ability to explain ideas, and the ability to connect them to familiar contexts.

Transfer refers to whether students can carry computing learning beyond the immediate example or assessment in which it was first encountered. Can they apply a concept to a new problem? Can they interpret how it might function in their own discipline? Can they shift from imitation to adaptable reasoning? (Bransford et al., 2000).

Contribution refers to whether students can transform learning into output that matters beyond the narrow boundaries of the course. This may include disciplinary application, research engagement, design innovation, community-oriented problem solving, or professional identity development. Not every student will convert coursework into a publication or startup, but all students can be positioned as potential contributors rather than mere recipients of instruction (Kuh, 2008; Wenger, 1998).

Taken together, these dimensions distinguish translational pedagogy from narrower models of skill delivery. The aim is not just to get students through computing, but to help them enter it, understand it, use it across contexts, and potentially create with it. The structural interaction of these four strategic pathways is visually conceptualized in Figure 1.

Figure 1. The Translational Computing Pedagogy Framework

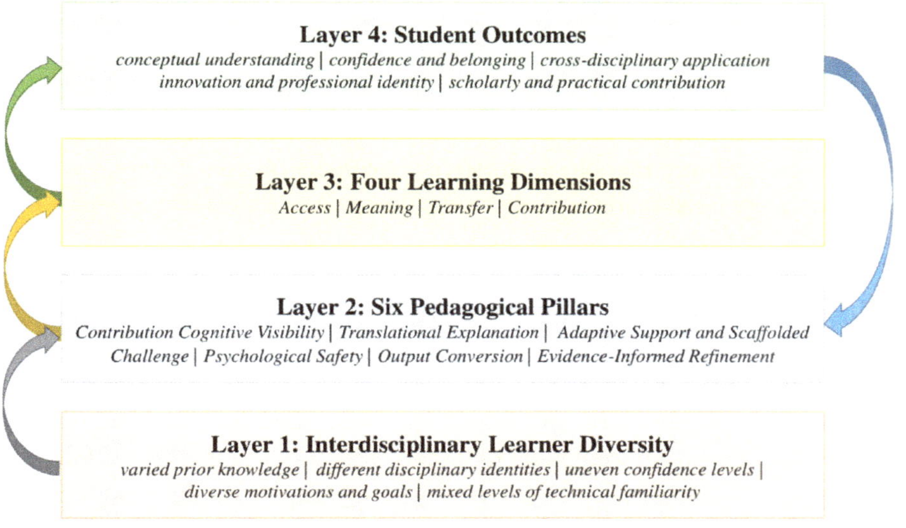

4. PROBLEM LANDSCAPE IN INTERDISCIPLINARY COMPUTING EDUCATION

4.1 Cognitive Barriers

One of the central barriers in interdisciplinary computing education is cognitive. Computing requires learners to coordinate abstraction, sequence, conditionality, state change, decomposition, and procedural logic. For novices, these operations are often unfamiliar not because they are incapable, but because the underlying reasoning remains hidden. They may see the final code but not the mental process through which a problem is transformed into that code (Chi et al., 1989; Lister et al., 2006).

This creates a common novice pattern: students focus on syntax before logic. They ask what to type rather than why a structure is needed. They may copy examples, alter variable names, and hope the pattern transfers. But when the problem changes slightly, they struggle because the conceptual schema has not formed. Cognitive overload further intensifies this issue. Beginners must simultaneously interpret task instructions, recall syntax, anticipate machine behavior, and debug errors. Without pedagogical design that reduces unnecessary load and foregrounds conceptual structure, many students become overwhelmed (Ambrose et al., 2010; Bransford et al., 2000).

Another cognitive barrier is the gap between human intuition and machine exactness. Many learners approach problems with flexible natural-language reasoning, but code requires explicitness. Computers do not infer what the student "meant." This can be frustrating for interdisciplinary learners accustomed to fields where ambiguity, interpretation, or iterative refinement operate differently. Translational pedagogy must therefore help students cross not only a content barrier but a reasoning-style barrier.

4.2 Linguistic and Representational Barriers

Computing is often taught in a language that feels compact, technical, and culturally internal to the field. Terms such as *recursion*, *parameter*, *object*, *iteration*, or *instance* may be introduced as though their meaning is self-evident. For many students, especially those from non-computing backgrounds or multilingual contexts, such terminology becomes a barrier in itself (Shulman, 1986; Vygotsky, 1978).

Language difficulties are often compounded by representational choices. Some students understand a process more easily through diagrams, timelines, visual state changes, or concrete narratives than through abstract code alone. Others need everyday analogies before they can comfortably engage formal notation. When teaching relies too heavily on one representational mode, it privileges learners already aligned with that mode (Bransford et al., 2000).

The issue is not merely simplification. Students eventually need to understand formal computing language. But they may need multiple bridges into it. Translational pedagogy therefore treats representation strategically. It asks not only whether content is accurate, but whether the representational pathway enables understanding.

4.3 Psychological Barriers and Coding Anxiety

Psychological barriers are often underestimated in computing education. Yet many students encounter introductory programming with apprehension, fear of failure, or a pre-existing belief that they are not "the kind of person" who succeeds in technical subjects. Coding anxiety may arise from prior negative experiences, intimidating classroom climates, public comparison with faster peers, unfamiliar terminology, and the sheer frequency of error messages during early learning (Bandura, 1997; Cooper et al., 2019).

Anxiety does not merely affect feelings; it affects cognition and behavior. Students who are anxious are less likely to experiment, less likely to ask questions, and more likely to abandon a task when they encounter difficulty. They may interpret normal struggle as proof of inability. In interdisciplinary classrooms, where many students already identify as outsiders to computing, this problem becomes acute (Margolis & Fisher, 2003; Tinto, 2012).

A pedagogy that ignores affect risks reproducing exclusion even when content is technically sound. Conversely, a pedagogy that normalizes struggle, provides low-stakes opportunities to learn from error, and supports help-seeking can materially improve persistence. Psychological safety does not remove challenge, but it changes how challenge is experienced.

4.4 Disciplinary Relevance Barriers

Students learn more effectively when they can see why the subject matters. In interdisciplinary computing education, relevance cannot be assumed. A generic example may appear meaningful to one student and trivial to another. If students cannot connect computing concepts to their own disciplinary goals, they may remain compliant but uninvested. They may complete tasks without integrating the learning into their broader intellectual framework (Ambrose et al., 2010; Biggs & Tang, 2011).

The relevance barrier is particularly strong in compulsory or gateway courses. Students may perceive the course as an external requirement rather than a disciplinary resource. To address this, teaching must do more than say that computing is "important." It must translate concepts into uses, examples, and problem spaces that students recognize as connected to their domains. This is not motivational decoration; it is part of how meaning and transfer are constructed.

4.5 Assessment and Fairness Barriers

Assessment can either support or distort interdisciplinary computing learning. Fixed-format assessment often privileges students who are already comfortable with technical language, speeded problem solving, or standardized testing conditions. Beginners, multilingual learners, and students who understand concepts better in applied contexts may be disadvantaged by assessment forms that capture only a narrow slice of competence (Biggs & Tang, 2011; Nicol & Macfarlane-Dick, 2006).

Fairness concerns also arise when assessments reward polished final output while ignoring the process through which understanding develops. A student may be capable of reasoning but be penalized heavily for syntax instability early in learning. Conversely, a student may produce correct output through copying without genuine comprehension. In either case, assessment validity becomes questionable.

Interdisciplinary classrooms make fairness especially important because students begin from uneven positions. Assessment should preserve standards, but it should also be designed to measure intended learning rather than prior familiarity with technical conventions. Later chapters address assessment in depth. For now, it is enough to note that assessment barriers are part of the wider problem landscape that translational pedagogy seeks to address as shown in Figure 2.

Figure 2. Barriers Faced by Interdisciplinary Computing Learners

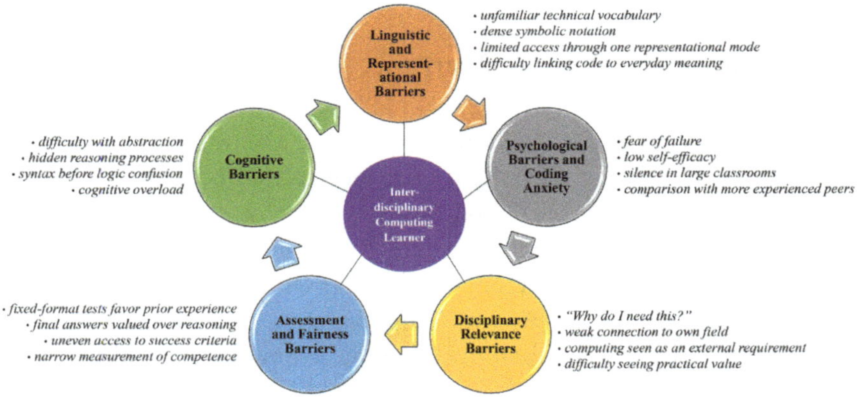

5. A PROPOSED FRAMEWORK FOR TRANSLATIONAL COMPUTING PEDAGOGY

The framework proposed in this book consists of six interconnected pedagogical components. Together, they form a model for teaching computing in ways that are rigorous, inclusive, and transferable across interdisciplinary settings. Each component is developed in depth later; here they are introduced as the core architecture of translational computing pedagogy.

5.1 Cognitive Visibility

Cognitive visibility refers to making the reasoning processes of computing visible to learners. Rather than presenting only finished solutions, translational pedagogy exposes the intermediate thinking through which problems are interpreted, structured, tested, and debugged. It values visible reasoning over hidden fluency (Chi et al., 1989; Collins et al., 1989). This helps students understand not just what works, but how and why it works.

5.2 Translational Explanation

Translational explanation refers to the adaptation of explanations, examples, and conceptual bridges so that computing ideas can be understood across disciplinary backgrounds. It preserves conceptual rigor while altering the entry point. The goal is not to produce a different computing concept for each discipline, but to create multiple pathways into the same core idea (Shulman, 1986, 1987).

5.3 Adaptive Support and Scaffolded Challenge

Adaptive support refers to responsive teaching structures that acknowledge learner variability. Scaffolded challenge means designing progressions that help students move from guided participation toward increasing independence. In translational pedagogy, support is not the opposite of rigor; it is what enables rigorous learning for diverse cohorts (Vygotsky, 1978; Zimmerman, 2002).

5.4 Psychological Safety

Psychological safety in computing education means creating an environment in which students can ask questions, make mistakes, and engage difficulty without fear of humiliation or exclusion. Because introductory computing often involves visible error and uncertainty, psychological safety is essential to persistence and belonging (Bandura, 1997; Tinto, 2012).

5.5 Output Conversion

Output conversion refers to helping students transform coursework into more meaningful forms of contribution. This may include research, competitions, prototypes, publications, patents, community projects, or professional applications. The concept broadens the horizon of learning from course completion to creation (Kuh, 2008; Wenger, 1998).

5.6 Evidence-Informed Refinement

Evidence-informed refinement means using multiple forms of evidence; performance patterns, feedback, participation, and output quality; to improve teaching iteratively. In diverse and large classrooms, teaching quality depends not only on design but on ongoing diagnosis and adjustment (Banta & Palomba, 2015; Hattie, 2009).

These six components should not be seen as isolated techniques. They form a coherent pedagogical orientation. Cognitive visibility supports conceptual access. Translational explanation supports disciplinary relevance and meaning. Adaptive support and psychological safety sustain persistence. Output conversion motivates deeper engagement and professional identity. Evidence-informed refinement keeps the system responsive.

6. RELATIONSHIP OF THE FRAMEWORK TO STUDENT OUTCOMES

6.1 Conceptual Understanding

The most immediate outcome of translational pedagogy is stronger conceptual understanding. When students can see reasoning, connect ideas to prior knowledge, and receive support matched to their stage of learning, they are more likely to grasp underlying logic rather than memorize fragments. Understanding here includes explanation, debugging, and problem interpretation, not merely final correctness (Chi et al., 1989; Hattie, 2009).

6.2 Confidence and Belonging

A second outcome concerns confidence and belonging. Students who are able to understand computing through accessible pathways and safe learning structures begin to see themselves as capable participants. This is particularly important for learners who enter the classroom believing computing is only for naturally technical students. Belonging is not a soft extra; it shapes retention, participation, and willingness to persist through difficulty (Bandura, 1997; Tinto, 2012).

6.3 Transfer Across Contexts

A third outcome is transfer. Translational pedagogy is designed so that computing concepts are not learned as isolated classroom artifacts. By connecting ideas to disciplinary contexts and emphasizing reasoning over imitation, students become better able to apply what they learn in new tasks, later courses, and domain-specific problems (Bransford et al., 2000; Wenger, 1998).

6.4 Innovation, Professional Identity, and Contribution

A fourth outcome concerns contribution. When students experience computing as something they can use to build, investigate, solve, or create, they begin to develop a professional or scholarly identity around it. This may be visible in projects, competitions, research dissemination, entrepreneurial ideas, or a stronger sense that computing is a tool they can deploy meaningfully in their own fields (Baxter Magolda, 2009; Kuh, 2008).

Institutional evidence can support these links. In one teaching context spanning more than 2,091 students from over ten disciplines, translationally aligned practices were associated not only with improved pass and retention outcomes but with broader outputs including conference papers, competition awards, startup finalist teams, and patent-related initiatives. Such outcomes suggest that pedagogy can shape not only immediate learning but also students' sense of future possibility. To align these empirical behavioral signals with demographic and academic baselines, a comprehensive classification of typical learner profiles in interdisciplinary classrooms is compiled in Table 2.

7. SCOPE OF THE BOOK

7.1 How the Chapters Are Organized

This book is organized to move from framing and theory to practice, evidence, scale, and broader institutional implications. Chapter 1 establishes the need for translational computing pedagogy and introduces the framework. Chapter 2 develops the theoretical foundations that support it. Chapters 3 and 4 focus on cognitive visibility and translational explanation as two core practices of making computing accessible across disciplines. Chapter 5 addresses adaptive support, scaffolded challenge, and psychological safety. Chapter 6 turns to assessment and the measurement of translational outcomes. Chapter 7 examines adaptive learning technologies and the pedagogical role of systems such as adaptive testing and personalized support environments. Chapter 8 explores evidence, triangulation, and continuous quality improvement. Chapter 9 presents student transformation through interdisciplinary case studies. Chapter 10 addresses the challenge of teaching at scale in large and diverse settings. Chapter 11 considers how the model generalizes beyond computing into other disciplines. Chapter 12 concludes by examining how higher education institutions can cultivate a creation-oriented culture that sustains translational and interdisciplinary teaching.

Table 2. Typical Learner Profiles in Interdisciplinary Classrooms

Learner Profile	Typical Characteristics	Likely Barrier	Translational Need
Novice anxious non-technical student	Little prior coding, low confidence	Fear of failure, language barriers	Accessible explanation, safe entry, visible reasoning
Quiet capable learner	Understands but rarely speaks	Invisibility in large class	Low-stakes participation routes, concept checks
Semi-technical transfer learner	Strong in adjacent technical field	Overestimated readiness	Explicit logic teaching, representational bridges
High-confidence technical student	Prior coding experience	Risk of disengagement from basics	Extension opportunities, deeper challenge
Discipline-driven applied learner	Wants relevance to own field	Low perceived value of generic tasks	Domain-sensitive examples and output pathways

7.2 Intended Readership

The intended readership includes computing educators, higher education teachers working in interdisciplinary programs, educational developers, curriculum designers, learning scientists, and academic leaders interested in inclusive and scalable pedagogies. It also speaks to researchers in computing education, STEM education, and the scholarship of teaching and learning who are concerned with transfer, learner diversity, and pedagogical design in complex classroom settings.

7.3 Contribution to Higher Education, Computing Education, and Interdisciplinary Pedagogy

This book makes three related contributions. First, it contributes to computing education by addressing a pressing but under-theorized issue: how to teach computing effectively to students whose primary identity is not computing. Second, it contributes to higher education pedagogy by offering a model for teaching foundational yet difficult knowledge in large, diverse classrooms without reducing standards. Third, it contributes to interdisciplinary pedagogy by reframing translation as a central educational practice rather than a secondary accommodation.

The novelty of the book lies in the coherence of its approach. Rather than presenting isolated strategies, it offers a unified pedagogical model linking visibility, explanation, support, safety, contribution, and evidence. It argues that the future of computing education in higher education depends not only on what is taught, but on how effectively it is translated across increasingly diverse learning environments.

8. CONCLUSION

8.1 Key Arguments of the Chapter

This chapter has argued that the expansion of computing across higher education has created a new pedagogical reality. Computing is now a universal academic literacy, but its teaching has not always kept pace with the diversity of learners who encounter it. Interdisciplinary classrooms are not peripheral cases; they are increasingly central to how computing is taught in contemporary universities. These classrooms are marked by variation in prior knowledge, confidence, identity, language, and relevance structures. As a result, pedagogies designed for more homogeneous technical cohorts often fail to serve them well.

The chapter has proposed translational computing pedagogy as a response. Translational pedagogy treats diversity not as an inconvenience but as a design condition. It seeks to preserve rigor while widening access, deepen meaning rather than merely increase exposure, support transfer beyond immediate tasks, and position students as potential contributors rather than passive recipients of instruction. It has identified a problem landscape involving cognitive, linguistic, psychological, disciplinary, and assessment-related barriers, and it has introduced a six-part framework consisting of cognitive visibility, translational explanation, adaptive support and scaffolded challenge, psychological safety, output conversion, and evidence-informed refinement.

8.2 Why Translational Pedagogy Is Timely and Necessary

Translational pedagogy is timely because higher education is changing rapidly. Interdisciplinary programs are expanding, computing is embedded in more fields, student cohorts are increasingly diverse, and digital systems shape nearly every profession. At the same time, universities face pressure to widen access without lowering standards, support large cohorts effectively, and produce graduates who can apply knowledge responsibly and creatively. A pedagogy that merely transmits technical content is insufficient for these demands (Barnett, 2004; NASEM, 2018).

Translational pedagogy is necessary because inclusion in computing cannot be achieved by access to enrollment alone. Students must also have access to meaning, relevance, confidence, and pathways to contribution. If universities are serious about preparing graduates for a computationally mediated world, then teaching must evolve beyond specialist assumptions and become more responsive to how diverse learners actually encounter technical knowledge (Guzdial, 2008; Wing, 2006).

8.3 Transition to Theoretical Foundations

The argument of this chapter has been primarily conceptual and framing-oriented. It has established the scope and need for a translational approach, but it has not yet examined the theoretical foundations that justify and illuminate the model. The next chapter therefore turns to theories of learning, cognition, motivation, identity, and transfer that support translational computing pedagogy. If this chapter has asked *why* a new pedagogical framework is needed, the next chapter asks what bodies of theory help explain *how* such a framework works.

REFERENCES

Ambrose, S. A., Bridges, M. W., DiPietro, M., Lovett, M. C., & Norman, M. K. (2010). *How learning works: Seven research-based principles for smart teaching*. Jossey-Bass.

Aquil Mirza, M., & Cong, W. (Eds.). (2026). *Real-Time Robotics With IoT and Edge AI: Methods, Metrics, and Applications*. IGI Global Scientific Publishing., DOI: 10.4018/979-8-2600-0701-3

Bandura, A. (1997). *Self-efficacy: The exercise of control*. W. H. Freeman.

Banta, T. W., & Palomba, C. A. (2015). *Assessment essentials: Planning, implementing, and improving assessment in higher education* (2nd ed.). Jossey-Bass.

Barker, L. J., Garvin-Doxas, K., & Roberts, E. M. (2009). What can computer science learn from a fine arts approach to teaching? *SIGCSE Bulletin*, *41*(1), 421–425. DOI: 10.1145/1047124.1047482

Barnett, R. (2004). *Learning for an unknown future*. Higher Education Research and Development Society of Australasia. DOI: 10.1080/0729436042000235382

Baxter Magolda, M. B. (2009). Authoring your life: Developing an internal voice to navigate life's challenges. *Stylus (Rio de Janeiro)*.

Bers, M. U. (2020). *Coding as a playground: Programming and computational thinking in the early childhood classroom*. Routledge. DOI: 10.4324/9781003022602

Biggs, J., & Tang, C. (2011). *Teaching for quality learning at university* (4th ed.). Open University Press.

Bransford, J. D., Brown, A. L., & Cocking, R. R. (Eds.). (2000). *How people learn: Brain, mind, experience, and school* (Expanded ed.). National Academy Press.

Carlone, H. B., & Johnson, A. (2007). Understanding the science experiences of successful women of color: Science identity as an analytic lens. *Journal of Research in Science Teaching*, *44*(8), 1187–1218. DOI: 10.1002/tea.20237

Chi, M. T. H., Bassok, M., Lewis, M. W., Reimann, P., & Glaser, R. (1989). Self-explanations: How students study and use examples in learning to solve problems. *Cognitive Science*, *13*(2), 145–182. DOI: 10.1207/s15516709cog1302_1 PMID: 34983624

Collins, A., Brown, J. S., & Newman, S. E. (1989). Cognitive apprenticeship: Teaching the craft of reading, writing, and mathematics. In Resnick, L. B. (Ed.), *Knowing, learning, and instruction: Essays in honor of Robert Glaser* (pp. 453–494). Lawrence Erlbaum.

Cooper, K. M., Gin, L. E., Akeeh, B., Clark, C. E., Hunter, J. S., Roderick, T. B., Elliott, D. B., Gutierrez, L. A., & Brownell, S. E. (2019). Factors that predict life sciences student persistence in undergraduate research experiences. *PLoS One*, *14*(8), e0220186. Advance online publication. DOI: 10.1371/journal.pone.0220186 PMID: 31412071

Denning, P. J. (2017). Remaining trouble spots with computational thinking. *Communications of the ACM*, *60*(6), 33–39. DOI: 10.1145/2998438

Gibbs, G., & Jenkins, A. (Eds.). (2014). *Teaching large classes in higher education: How to maintain quality with reduced resources*. Routledge. DOI: 10.4324/9781315041384

Guzdial, M. (2008). Education: Paving the way for computational thinking. *Communications of the ACM*, *51*(8), 25–27. DOI: 10.1145/1378704.1378713

Guzdial, M. (2015). Learner-centered design of computing education: Research on computing for everyone. *Synthesis Lectures on Human-Centered Informatics*, *8*(6), 1–165. DOI: 10.1007/978-3-031-02216-6

Hattie, J. (2009). *Visible learning: A synthesis of over 800 meta-analyses relating to achievement*. Routledge.

Hattie, J., & Timperley, H. (2007). The power of feedback. *Review of Educational Research*, *77*(1), 81–112. DOI: 10.3102/003465430298487

Jasanoff, S., Hüsing, B., Jochem, E., Lösch, A., Mikhailova, E., & Scheer, D. (2021). *Digital transformations and their social implications*. Springer.

Kuh, G. D. (2008). *High-impact educational practices: What they are, who has access to them, and why they matter*. Association of American Colleges and Universities.

Lattuca, L. R., Knight, D. B., & Bergom, I. (2017). Developing a measure of interdisciplinary competence for engineers. *Proceedings of the ASEE Annual Conference & Exposition*.

Lister, R., Simon, B., Thompson, E., Whalley, J. L., & Prasad, C. (2006). Not seeing the forest for the trees: Novice programmers and the SOLO taxonomy. *SIGCSE Bulletin*, *38*(3), 118–122. DOI: 10.1145/1140123.1140157

Margolis, J., & Fisher, A. (2003). *Unlocking the clubhouse: Women in computing*. MIT Press.

Mohammed, A., & Zangana, H. (Eds.). (2026). *Intelligent Construction Monitoring Systems: Real-Time Safety, Environmental Prediction, and Risk Management*. IGI Global Scientific Publishing., DOI: 10.4018/979-8-3373-9245-5

National Academies of Sciences, Engineering, and Medicine. (2018). *How people learn II: Learners, contexts, and cultures*. National Academies Press. https://doi .org/DOI: 10.17226/24783

Nicol, D. J., & Macfarlane-Dick, D. (2006). Formative assessment and self-regulated learning: A model and seven principles of good feedback practice. *Studies in Higher Education*, *31*(2), 199–218. DOI: 10.1080/03075070600572090

Shulman, L. S. (1986). Those who understand: Knowledge growth in teaching. *Educational Researcher*, *15*(2), 4–14. DOI: 10.3102/0013189X015002004

Shulman, L. S. (1987). Knowledge and teaching: Foundations of the new reform. *Harvard Educational Review*, *57*(1), 1–23. DOI: 10.17763/haer.57.1.j463w79r56455411

Tinto, V. (2012). *Completing college: Rethinking institutional action*. University of Chicago Press. DOI: 10.7208/chicago/9780226804545.001.0001

Vygotsky, L. S. (1978). *Mind in society: The development of higher psychological processes*. Harvard University Press.

Wenger, E. (1998). *Communities of practice: Learning, meaning, and identity*. Cambridge University Press. DOI: 10.1017/CBO9780511803932

Wing, J. M. (2006). Computational thinking. *Communications of the ACM*, *49*(3), 33–35. DOI: 10.1145/1118178.1118215

Zimmerman, B. J. (2002). Becoming a self-regulated learner: An overview. *Theory into Practice*, *41*(2), 64–70. DOI: 10.1207/s15430421tip4102_2

Chapter 2
Theoretical Foundations of Translational Pedagogy in Computing Education

Fuyin Guan
http://orcid.org/0009-0005-7261-6925
Department of Applied Mathematics, The Hong Kong Polytechnic University, Hong Kong

ABSTRACT

This chapter develops a multi-theoretical framework for translational pedagogy in cross-disciplinary computer science education, addressing the limitation that single educational theories fail to support learners from diverse disciplinary backgrounds. The authors integrate learning, cognitive, motivation-identity and cross-disciplinary translation theories to validate six core components of translational pedagogy: cognitive explicitation, translational explanation, adaptive scaffolding, psychological safety, output transformation and evidence-based optimization. By synthesizing constructivism, cognitive load theory and self-efficacy theory, this chapter clarifies mechanisms of knowledge construction, cognitive burden control, learner motivation improvement and cross-domain knowledge transfer. It verifies translational pedagogy as a rigorous and inclusive instructional model, providing solid theoretical support for cross-disciplinary computer education practice and guiding tailored teaching for heterogeneous learners to promote sustainable knowledge transfer.

DOI: 10.4018/979-8-2600-1811-8.ch002

1. INTRODUCTION

1.1 Why Theory Matters in Pedagogical Innovation

Pedagogical innovation in higher education is often judged first by its visible outcomes: stronger student engagement, improved completion rates, better performance, higher confidence, and more meaningful forms of student output. Yet innovation without theoretical grounding risks becoming a collection of attractive practices that lack coherence, explanatory power, and transferability. Theory matters because it helps educators understand not only **what** appears to work, but **why** it works, **for whom**, **under what conditions**, and **with what limitations** (Biggs & Tang, 2011; Shulman, 1986). In the context of computing education; where teaching frequently involves abstraction, symbolic reasoning, rapidly changing tools, uneven learner preparation, and increasingly interdisciplinary cohorts; the need for theory is especially acute.

When computing was taught primarily to students already committed to technical disciplines, many pedagogical assumptions could remain implicit. It was easier to presume a shared vocabulary, relatively aligned aspirations, similar levels of comfort with formal reasoning, and a willingness to tolerate technical challenge. As computing has become a foundational literacy across higher education, however, these assumptions are much less defensible (Denning, 2017; Wing, 2006). Students now enter computing classrooms from design, business, health sciences, architecture, linguistics, biology, media, physics, and the humanities. They arrive with different forms of prior knowledge, different ways of interpreting abstraction, different motivational structures, and different levels of confidence about whether they belong in a technical learning environment (Baxter Magolda, 2009; Carlone & Johnson, 2007; Mohammed at el., 2026). Pedagogy in such settings cannot rely on inherited habits alone. It requires a defensible conceptual basis.

Theory serves several functions in this environment. First, it helps educators interpret learner diversity more accurately. Instead of seeing uneven performance merely as a reflection of ability, theory helps reveal the influence of prior knowledge, cognitive load, representation, motivation, identity, discourse, and classroom climate (Ambrose et al., 2010; Bransford et al., 2000). Second, theory supports design. It provides principles for how to structure learning, sequence challenge, scaffold understanding, reduce unnecessary difficulty, and support transfer. Third, theory strengthens evaluation. It allows educators to ask whether a pedagogical intervention succeeded because it reduced extraneous cognitive burden, activated prior schemas, increased task value, improved self-efficacy, or created better conditions for participation. Fourth, theory supports generalization. A pedagogical model grounded in robust theory is more likely to travel across modules, institutions, and disciplines than a model grounded only in local intuition or personal teaching style (Banta & Palomba, 2015; Hattie, 2009).

This book argues for **translational computing pedagogy** as a distinctive response to the challenges of interdisciplinary computing education. Chapter 1 introduced the need for such a pedagogy and outlined its core components: cognitive visibility, translational explanation, adaptive support and scaffolded challenge, psychological safety, output conversion, and evidence-informed refinement. The purpose of this chapter is to provide the theoretical foundation for that model. Rather than treating translational pedagogy as a practical innovation alone, this chapter situates it within established traditions of educational theory, cognitive psychology, motivation research, interdisciplinary learning, and knowledge transfer.

1.2 Need for a Multi-Theoretical Foundation in Interdisciplinary Teaching

No single theory can adequately explain the complexity of interdisciplinary computing classrooms. These classrooms involve cognition, identity, motivation, language, social participation, disciplinary discourse, and varying forms of transfer. A student learning programming for the first time in a mixed cohort is not simply processing information. That student is also interpreting unfamiliar symbols, comparing themselves with peers, deciding whether the effort is worthwhile, connecting the content to a disciplinary identity, and negotiating uncertainty in a possibly high-stakes environment. A narrow theoretical lens captures only part of this reality.

For this reason, translational pedagogy requires a **multi-theoretical foundation**. Constructivist theories help explain how students build understanding rather than receive it passively. Cognitive theories clarify why abstraction is difficult, how prior knowledge shapes new learning, and why representation matters. Motivation and identity theories explain why some students persist while others disengage even when their apparent cognitive capacity is similar. Interdisciplinary and translational frameworks show how meaning moves across domains and why disciplinary language can either enable or block access. Theories of transfer illuminate how learning in one setting becomes usable in another (Bransford et al., 2000; Perkins & Salomon, 1992; Vygotsky, 1978). Together, these theories form a conceptual ecology rather than a single grand explanation.

A multi-theoretical foundation is also necessary because translational pedagogy is not merely an accommodation strategy for weaker learners. It is a model for rigorous, cross-disciplinary teaching that seeks to preserve conceptual depth while widening access. To justify such a model, one must explain why making reasoning visible enhances understanding, why disciplinary translation supports epistemic access, why scaffolds can enable rather than reduce rigor, why psychological safety matters to persistence, and why contribution-oriented learning shapes identity and transfer. These are different questions, and they require different theoretical resources.

This chapter therefore does not search for one dominant theory. Instead, it assembles a principled foundation from complementary traditions. The aim is not eclecticism for its own sake, but theoretical adequacy for a complex educational problem.

1.3 Chapter Aims and Structure

This chapter has five aims. First, it examines major learning theories that help explain how students learn computing in interdisciplinary settings. Second, it considers cognitive theories that clarify difficulties associated with abstraction, representation, and transfer. Third, it explores theories of motivation, identity, belonging, and affect that are especially relevant to learners who may not initially see themselves as technical insiders. Fourth, it turns to interdisciplinary and translational knowledge frameworks that explain how meaning can move across domains. Fifth, it synthesizes these perspectives into an integrated conceptual model for translational computing pedagogy.

The chapter is organized accordingly. Section 2 discusses learning theories relevant to the pedagogical model, including constructivism, social constructivism, situated learning, cognitive apprenticeship, experiential learning, metacognition, and self-regulated learning. Section 3 turns to cognitive theories supporting visible and transferable learning, including cognitive load theory, schema theory, dual coding, threshold concepts, and transfer theory. Section 4 addresses motivation, identity, and belonging through self-efficacy theory, expectancy-value theory, growth mindset, academic belonging, and psychological safety. Section 5 examines interdisciplinary and translational knowledge frameworks, including boundary crossing, knowledge translation, disciplinary discourse, epistemic access, analogical reasoning, and translational meaning-making. Section 6 synthesizes these traditions in relation to the book's pedagogical model. Section 7 considers implications for curriculum and instruction, while Section 8 concludes and points forward to Chapter 3, where cognitive visibility is explored in depth.

2. LEARNING THEORIES RELEVANT TO TRANSLATIONAL COMPUTING PEDAGOGY

2.1 Constructivism and Social Constructivism

Constructivism remains one of the most influential foundations for contemporary pedagogy because it shifts attention from teaching as transmission to learning as active meaning-making. In constructivist thought, learners do not simply absorb information delivered by an expert. They interpret, organize, test, and reconstruct knowledge through interaction with ideas, tasks, and prior experience (Bransford et al., 2000; Piaget, 1970). This perspective is particularly important for computing education because many learners can appear to understand concepts when they are merely reproducing surface procedures. Constructivism reminds educators that real learning involves internal organization and conceptual restructuring.

In computing, this insight has direct implications. Students do not truly learn loops, variables, conditionals, functions, or data structures simply because these topics are explained clearly or demonstrated correctly. They learn them when they can integrate these concepts into workable mental models. A learner encountering iteration for the first time may initially treat it as a syntactic pattern to imitate. Only through guided engagement does the learner begin to understand repetition as a logical structure involving flow, state change, and condition-based control. Constructivism therefore supports the principle that teaching should focus not only on content coverage, but on how learners actively build computing concepts.

Social constructivism extends this view by emphasizing that meaning is not constructed in isolation. Learning occurs through language, dialogue, shared problem solving, and participation in socially organized practices (Vygotsky, 1978). This is highly relevant to interdisciplinary classrooms because students may lack fluency not only in computing content but also in the discourse of the field. Explanation, questioning, peer talk, tutorial interaction, and collaborative sense-making become crucial sites where understanding is negotiated.

For translational pedagogy, constructivism and social constructivism justify at least three broad commitments. First, students must be given opportunities to actively interpret computing concepts, not merely copy outputs. Second, prior knowledge matters because learners build new understanding through what they already know. Third, explanation and interaction must be designed to support learners whose disciplinary backgrounds create different entry points into the same concept. These ideas form part of the rationale for visible reasoning, translational explanation, and learning environments where students can articulate confusion without stigma.

2.2 Situated Learning

Situated learning theory challenges the idea that knowledge is a purely abstract possession detached from context. It argues that learning is shaped by the settings, tools, practices, and communities in which it occurs. Knowledge is not simply stored; it is enacted through participation in meaningful activity (Lave & Wenger, 1991).

This is highly relevant to computing education. Introductory programming courses often struggle because concepts are taught as isolated technical units rather than as tools for solving meaningful problems. If computing is presented only as syntax and rules, students may fail to understand why those structures matter. Situated learning suggests that concepts become more usable when embedded in recognizable contexts of action.

For interdisciplinary learners, this insight is even more important. A biology student may find conditional logic more meaningful in the context of diagnostic decision pathways or environmental sensing. A design student may understand iteration more deeply when connected to repeated transformation and refinement. A linguistics student may grasp rule-based processing through patterned language systems. In each case, the learning is not less rigorous because it is contextualized; rather, context helps organize meaning (Lave & Wenger, 1991).

Situated learning also highlights participation and identity. Learners move from peripheral participation toward fuller engagement in a community of practice. In interdisciplinary computing classrooms, especially those populated by non-specialists, many students begin at the margins of the disciplinary community. They may feel that computing belongs to others. Translational pedagogy responds by creating legitimate participation pathways for students whose disciplinary identity is not primarily technical. It allows them to engage computing not as outsiders attempting to imitate insiders, but as learners bringing relevant domain knowledge into interaction with computational ideas.

The situated perspective therefore supports the claim that computing should be taught in relation to authentic or recognizable contexts. It also suggests that disciplinary translation is not an optional motivational add-on, but a means of creating more legitimate and meaningful participation in learning.

2.3 Cognitive Apprenticeship

Cognitive apprenticeship extends the apprenticeship model beyond manual or craft-based skills into domains where much of expert practice is hidden. It argues that novices learn most effectively when expert thinking is made visible through modeling, coaching, scaffolding, articulation, reflection, and gradual transfer of responsibility (Collins et al., 1989).

This framework is especially powerful for computing education because programming and systems reasoning often involve invisible mental operations. Experts decompose problems, monitor assumptions, anticipate failure points, and debug strategically, yet much of this expertise remains implicit when teaching focuses only on finished solutions. The central relevance of cognitive apprenticeship to translational pedagogy lies in its insistence that expert reasoning must be externalized. In many technical classrooms, students watch a lecturer produce correct code but do not see the decision-making that generated it. They may therefore misinterpret expertise as effortless fluency. Cognitive apprenticeship reframes teaching as a process of revealing hidden cognition.

The framework also emphasizes the importance of staged support. Novices benefit when task complexity is managed and expert guidance is gradually withdrawn as competence grows. This helps justify scaffolded challenge: support is not a lowering of standards but a condition for developmental progress. Cognitive apprenticeship also highlights reflection and articulation. Students should not merely perform tasks; they should explain their reasoning, compare approaches, and recognize how expert thinking differs from novice trial-and-error.

For interdisciplinary classrooms, cognitive apprenticeship carries an additional implication. Because students begin from different disciplinary resources, the modeling of reasoning must be sensitive to different prior schemas. The expert's task is not simply to demonstrate canonical procedure, but to mediate entry into practice for learners who do not share the same assumptions. Thus, the theory strongly supports both cognitive visibility and adaptive pedagogical framing.

2.4 Experiential Learning

Experiential learning theory emphasizes that learning develops through cycles of concrete experience, reflection, conceptualization, and active experimentation (Kolb, 1984). Although often associated with practical disciplines, it has important implications for computing as well. Students do not fully understand computational ideas through exposition alone. They need to engage with tasks, observe consequences, reflect on outcomes, revise their thinking, and test again.

This cyclical movement is central to programming, where errors, outputs, debugging, and iterative revision form part of the learning process. For translational pedagogy, experiential learning is useful in two ways. First, it reframes error. An error is not merely failure; it is information that can stimulate reflection and restructuring. This matters because many novices interpret errors as proof of inability rather than as normal data in the learning process. Second, experiential learning supports authentic engagement with context. Interdisciplinary students often learn more effectively when computing is attached to tasks that feel purposeful or recognizable. A health sciences learner analyzing decision pathways, a business learner modeling a simple process, or a design learner working through iterative transformation may experience computing concepts through domain-connected activities that feed reflection and conceptualization.

Experience alone is not enough, however. Without guided reflection, students may repeat ineffective patterns. Kolb's model matters because it includes conceptualization and experimentation, not just activity. This aligns well with translational pedagogy: students should engage, reflect, interpret, and reapply, not merely "do" tasks. Experiential learning also helps bridge classroom work and future application. If learning includes cycles of doing, reflecting, and transferring, students are more likely to see computing as a usable intellectual tool rather than a one-time academic hurdle.

2.5 Metacognition and Self-Regulated Learning

Metacognition refers to awareness and regulation of one's own thinking. Self-regulated learning extends this idea to include goal-setting, monitoring, strategy choice, effort management, and reflection on progress (Zimmerman, 2002). These theories are vital in computing education because successful problem solving requires more than knowledge of syntax or structures. Students must monitor whether they understand the problem, decide which strategy to use, evaluate whether code behaves as expected, and revise when it does not.

Many novice difficulties in computing are metacognitive as much as conceptual. Students may not know what they do not understand. They may believe they have learned a concept because they can follow an example, only to discover during independent work that they cannot reconstruct the logic. Others persist with ineffective strategies because they do not know how to step back, trace execution, or analyze the source of an error. Self-regulated learning theory helps explain why students need support not only in content but also in learning processes.

In interdisciplinary classrooms, metacognitive demands may be intensified by uncertainty. Students unfamiliar with the norms of computing may not know what counts as evidence of understanding. They may overestimate the value of memorizing code and underestimate the importance of reasoning. Translational pedagogy benefits from theoretical attention to this because it seeks to build learners who can progressively regulate their own understanding rather than depend entirely on teacher explanation.

Metacognition also matters for transfer. Students are more likely to apply knowledge in new contexts when they can identify what is conceptually general rather than tied only to one example. Thus, theories of self-regulated learning support not only learner independence but the development of flexible computational thinking. The explicit alignment between these primary educational frameworks, their core ideas, and their functional relevance to cross-disciplinary classrooms is detailed in Table 1.

Table 1. Major Learning Theories and Their Relevance to Interdisciplinary Computing

Theory	Core Idea	Relevance to Interdisciplinary Computing
Constructivism	Learners actively construct knowledge	Students must build conceptual understanding rather than imitate code
Social constructivism	Meaning is shaped through interaction and discourse	Dialogue and explanation support learners from diverse backgrounds
Situated learning	Learning is shaped by context and participation	Concepts become meaningful when linked to disciplinary applications
Cognitive apprenticeship	Expert thinking should be made visible to novices	Hidden computational reasoning must be externalized
Experiential learning	Learning develops through action, reflection, and revision	Programming understanding grows through iterative practice and reflection
Metacognition	Learners monitor and regulate their thinking	Students need support in checking, debugging, and reflecting on reasoning
Self-regulated learning	Learning involves strategic goal-setting and monitoring	Interdisciplinary learners need help developing independence in problem-solving

3. COGNITIVE THEORIES SUPPORTING VISIBLE AND TRANSFERABLE LEARNING

3.1 Cognitive Load Theory

Cognitive load theory offers one of the clearest explanations for why novice learners struggle in domains like computing. The theory begins from the premise that working memory has limited capacity. When learners face tasks that impose too many simultaneous demands, learning is hindered because cognitive resources are overwhelmed before stable understanding can form (Sweller, 1988; Sweller et al., 2019).

In computing classrooms, students often experience several layers of demand at once: interpreting the problem statement, recalling syntax, tracking variables, understanding control flow, anticipating machine behavior, and debugging errors. Intrinsic load arises from the inherent complexity of the concept itself. Extraneous load comes from poor design; unclear instructions, dense language, unhelpful examples, or confusing interfaces. Germane load refers to productive effort devoted to building understanding. The pedagogical challenge is not to eliminate difficulty, but to reduce unnecessary burden so students can devote mental resources to meaningful learning.

For interdisciplinary learners, cognitive load theory is especially useful because extraneous load often comes from factors unrelated to the concept itself. Technical vocabulary, unfamiliar disciplinary assumptions, generic examples lacking relevance, or rapid shifts across representations may overload learners before they can focus on the core idea. A student may fail not because loops are intrinsically impossible, but because the explanation demands too many interpretive moves at once. This provides strong theoretical support for pedagogical translation. When explanation aligns with prior knowledge, representation is sequenced carefully, and unnecessary complexity is reduced, conceptual understanding becomes more achievable.

The theory also supports the importance of visible reasoning. When expert thought processes are externalized, learners do not need to infer every hidden step themselves. This can reduce extraneous burden and help direct attention toward conceptual structure.

3.2 Schema Theory

Schema theory explains learning in terms of organized knowledge structures. Learners interpret new information through existing schemas, and expertise develops as those schemas become richer, more interconnected, and more flexible (Anderson, 1984; Rumelhart, 1980). In computing education, schema theory is highly relevant because students must learn to see beyond surface code patterns and recognize deeper structural relationships.

An expert does not encounter each programming problem as wholly new. The expert recognizes familiar structures; repetition, branching, abstraction, decomposition, input-processing-output flow, data organization; and brings existing schemas to bear. Novices, by contrast, often lack these schemas or possess fragmented ones. They may treat each new problem as unique, focusing on superficial features rather than structural similarities. This is why students can complete one example correctly and then fail when the surface features are changed.

Translational pedagogy benefits from schema theory in several ways. First, it foregrounds prior knowledge. Students from different disciplines bring different conceptual resources. A well-designed explanation activates those resources and helps learners anchor new computing ideas to something already meaningful. Second, schema theory supports sequencing from concrete and familiar cases toward more abstract and generalized understanding. Third, it explains transfer: learners can use knowledge in new contexts when they have formed schemas that capture underlying principles rather than isolated examples.

Schema theory also clarifies why translational explanation is not mere simplification. A discipline-sensitive analogy works when it activates an existing schema that can support understanding of the new concept. The quality of the analogy depends on whether it maps a real structural relationship rather than only a superficial resemblance.

3.3 Dual Coding and Multimodal Representation

Dual coding theory proposes that people process information through partly distinct verbal and non-verbal channels, and that learning can be strengthened when concepts are represented through multiple coordinated modes (Paivio, 1986). In computing education, this is particularly important because many concepts are invisible, dynamic, and difficult to infer from code alone.

Multimodal representation may include diagrams, flowcharts, state tables, animations, timelines, verbal reasoning, gesture, and worked traces alongside symbolic code. The theoretical point is not that more representation is always better, but that appropriately aligned representations can support memory, reduce ambiguity, and help learners connect symbolic structures to conceptual meaning.

For interdisciplinary students, multimodal representation can significantly widen access. Some learners understand a process more easily when they see state change visually. Others need narrative explanation to make sense of execution. Others may connect most strongly with spatial or procedural representations drawn from their own disciplines. A single mode of explanation may privilege some students while excluding others. Dual coding therefore supports the translational claim that explanation should not be limited to one representational channel.

At the same time, the theory implies caution. Poorly coordinated multimodal materials can increase rather than reduce confusion. If the diagram, verbal explanation, and code are not aligned, cognitive burden may rise. The value of multimodality depends on coherence, sequencing, and conceptual purpose.

3.4 Threshold Concepts in Computing

Threshold concept theory proposes that certain ideas within a discipline are transformative, integrative, troublesome, and often irreversible once understood (Meyer & Land, 2003). These concepts function like gateways: until students cross them, understanding remains partial and fragile; once crossed, their grasp of the subject changes significantly.

In computing, possible threshold concepts include iteration, recursion, state, abstraction, reference, modularity, and algorithmic thinking. Different researchers identify different candidates, but the central insight is useful: some ideas are difficult not because they involve more information, but because they require a shift in how learners think. This matters greatly for interdisciplinary teaching. Students may appear to understand a concept procedurally while not yet having crossed it conceptually. A learner may write a simple loop by following a pattern yet still not understand repeated state change. Another may use functions without grasping abstraction as a way of organizing thought.

Threshold concept theory helps explain why some aspects of computing produce persistent confusion despite repeated explanation. It also supports pedagogical patience. Troublesome knowledge is not merely a sign of student deficiency; it is often a feature of the conceptual terrain. For interdisciplinary learners, threshold concepts may be even more troublesome because they are entering from different epistemic traditions. Translational pedagogy responds by creating bridges into these concepts, making hidden reasoning more visible and attaching abstract ideas to familiar contexts.

3.5 Transfer of Learning Theory

Transfer of learning theory addresses one of the most important educational questions: how does learning in one context become usable in another? In computing education, this question is fundamental. It is not enough for students to solve a problem exactly as practiced. They should be able to adapt concepts to new tasks, new contexts, and; especially in interdisciplinary education; their own disciplinary problems (Perkins & Salomon, 1992).

A major distinction in transfer research is between **near transfer** and **far transfer**. Near transfer involves applying learning to structurally similar tasks. Far transfer involves application in more distant or transformed contexts. Many students can achieve near transfer by pattern matching, but far transfer requires deeper conceptual understanding and more flexible schema formation. Interdisciplinary computing education depends heavily on far transfer because students must often apply computing ideas outside canonical programming exercises.

Transfer is more likely when learners understand underlying principles, encounter varied examples, reflect on similarities and differences across contexts, and are prompted to abstract generalizable structure (Bransford et al., 2000). This aligns strongly with translational pedagogy. If students are taught through discipline-sensitive examples but never guided back to the general principle, transfer may remain local. Conversely, if they are taught only through abstract generic examples, they may struggle to anchor meaning. Effective teaching must move between context and abstraction.

Transfer theory also has motivational and identity dimensions. Students are more likely to attempt transfer when they perceive a concept as relevant and usable in their own domain. Thus, the theory connects cognitive structure with disciplinary relevance and supports the broader argument that computing education should aim not just for task performance within the course, but for meaningful portability beyond it.

4. MOTIVATION, IDENTITY, AND BELONGING IN INTERDISCIPLINARY LEARNING

4.1 Self-Efficacy Theory

Self-efficacy theory focuses on individuals' beliefs about their capacity to perform specific tasks successfully. These beliefs shape effort, persistence, resilience, and willingness to engage challenging activity (Bandura, 1997). In computing education, self-efficacy is especially consequential because early failure or confusion can quickly be interpreted as evidence of incapacity. Students who believe they cannot succeed are less likely to persist through debugging, less likely to experiment, and less likely to seek help constructively.

For interdisciplinary learners, self-efficacy is often uneven even before instruction begins. Students from non-technical backgrounds may enter the classroom assuming that programming belongs to others. They may compare themselves unfavorably with peers who have prior coding experience. Even when they are capable, low self-efficacy can reduce engagement and increase withdrawal risk.

The theory suggests that pedagogical design can influence efficacy beliefs through mastery experiences, vicarious experience, feedback, and emotional climate. When students experience manageable success, observe reasoning processes rather than polished perfection, receive feedback that emphasizes strategy and growth, and learn in climates where mistakes are normalized, self-efficacy can strengthen. This does not eliminate difficulty, but it changes how difficulty is interpreted. In translational pedagogy, confidence is not treated as a fixed personal trait. It is understood as partly shaped by educational design.

4.2 Expectancy-Value Theory

Expectancy-value theory proposes that motivation depends largely on two judgments: whether the learner expects to succeed and whether the task is valued (Eccles & Wigfield, 2020). Both dimensions are crucial in interdisciplinary computing classrooms. A student may value computing but expect failure, resulting in anxiety or avoidance. Another may feel capable but see little relevance, leading to minimal engagement. Sustainable motivation requires both perceived possibility and perceived worth.

Task value can take several forms: intrinsic value (interest or enjoyment), utility value (usefulness for future goals), attainment value (importance to identity), and cost (what the learner must sacrifice or endure to engage). Interdisciplinary learners often vary sharply across these dimensions. A health sciences student may see utility value in data processing or diagnostic logic. A design student may see value if computing is linked to creative systems. A business student may value automation or analytics. If computing is taught generically without visible connection to these forms of value, motivation may remain weak even when content is well taught.

Expectancy-value theory therefore reinforces the need for translational explanation and disciplinary relevance. Students are more motivated when they can see why the concept matters for their own field and when they believe the classroom gives them a fair chance of success. The theory also highlights the importance of reducing unnecessary cost. If a course imposes high emotional cost through intimidation, shame, or unmanageable pacing, value may not be enough to sustain effort.

4.3 Growth Mindset

Growth mindset theory, in its broad educational interpretation, emphasizes that abilities can develop through effort, strategy, support, and learning rather than being fixed traits (Dweck, 2006). In computing education, this matters because students often interpret early struggle as evidence that they are inherently "not good at coding." Such fixed interpretations are especially damaging in introductory settings, where confusion and error are normal.

For interdisciplinary learners, fixed beliefs about technical aptitude may be reinforced by cultural stereotypes. Some students assume that computing is for naturally logical or mathematically gifted people. Others believe prior exposure determines future success. A growth-oriented stance does not deny the importance of preparation, but it reframes learning as developmental. It encourages students to treat challenge as part of progress and to see mistakes as information.

At the pedagogical level, mindset theory suggests that messages embedded in teaching matter. If classrooms reward only fast correctness, students may infer that speed equals intelligence. If instructors emphasize process, strategy, and revision, students are more likely to interpret effort productively. Growth mindset should be applied carefully, however. It is not a substitute for good design. Telling students to persist is insufficient if pedagogy remains inaccessible. Translational pedagogy therefore uses mindset theory not as a slogan, but as part of a broader environment in which students can realistically experience development.

4.4 Academic Belonging and Identity Formation

Academic belonging refers to the sense that one is accepted, legitimate, and able to participate meaningfully within a learning environment. Identity formation concerns how learners come to see themselves in relation to a field or practice. These constructs are especially important in interdisciplinary computing education because many students begin from uncertainty. They may ask, consciously or not: *Do peo-*

ple like me belong here? Can I participate in this domain without abandoning my original disciplinary identity? (Baxter Magolda, 2009; Carlone & Johnson, 2007).

Belonging is not merely emotional comfort. It influences engagement, risk-taking, help-seeking, and persistence. Students who feel peripheral or illegitimate may withdraw psychologically even if they remain physically present. In large classes, this risk increases because quiet disengagement can go unnoticed. Translational pedagogy treats belonging as an academic issue because learning is inhibited when students perceive the classroom as culturally foreign or socially unwelcoming.

Identity formation in interdisciplinary learning is also complex. The aim is not always for students to become full members of the computing discipline in a traditional sense. Rather, many students need to develop hybrid identities: a designer who can think computationally, a biologist who can use code analytically, a linguist who can apply algorithmic reasoning, a civil engineer who can interpret systems data. This means pedagogy should not force students into an all-or-nothing technical identity. It should help them integrate computing into who they are already becoming.

4.5 Psychological Safety and Affect in Learning

Psychological safety refers to a climate in which individuals feel able to speak, ask, try, err, and learn without fear of humiliation or interpersonal threat. Although often discussed in organizational studies, it has deep relevance to education, especially in subjects like computing where visible failure is common and novices may already feel vulnerable (Edmondson, 1999).

Affective factors such as anxiety, embarrassment, frustration, and fear influence learning profoundly. When students are anxious, working memory can become less available for productive reasoning. When they fear judgment, they may avoid asking questions. When they experience repeated visible failure without supportive framing, they may disengage. This is especially damaging in interdisciplinary settings, where some students already assume they are outsiders.

Psychological safety does not imply comfort without challenge. In effective learning environments, students still encounter difficulty, critique, and revision. The key distinction is whether challenge occurs within an atmosphere of legitimacy and respect. If error is normalized as part of learning rather than shame, students are more likely to persist. If instructors communicate that confusion is diagnosable rather than embarrassing, participation rises.

The affective dimension therefore belongs centrally within the theoretical foundation of translational pedagogy. Learning is not only cognitive and social; it is also emotional.

5. INTERDISCIPLINARY AND TRANSLATIONAL KNOWLEDGE FRAMEWORKS

5.1 Boundary Crossing Theory

Boundary crossing theory examines how individuals learn when moving across domains with different practices, languages, tools, and expectations. Interdisciplinary education is inherently a boundary-crossing endeavor. Students entering computing from other fields are not simply learning new content; they are crossing into a domain with its own discourse, conventions, and epistemic habits (Akkerman & Bakker, 2011).

This perspective is valuable because it reframes learner difficulty. Confusion may arise not only from concept complexity, but from crossing a boundary between knowledge cultures. A design student may think in terms of aesthetics and iteration, while a computing course emphasizes explicit logic and machine execution. A biology student may be comfortable with empirical pattern observation but unfamiliar with procedural abstraction. Boundary crossing theory helps explain why successful pedagogy must provide mediating structures, not just explanations.

Boundary objects, brokers, and translation practices are central concepts here. A well-chosen analogy, problem context, diagram, or project can function as a boundary object linking disciplines. The educator often acts as a broker, helping students move between familiar disciplinary resources and new computational forms. This makes boundary crossing theory highly relevant to translational explanation and interdisciplinary meaning-making.

5.2 Knowledge Translation and Recontextualization

Knowledge translation refers to the movement of knowledge from one context into another in ways that make it actionable, usable, or understandable. Recontextualization involves changing the context in which knowledge is framed, interpreted, or applied. In education, these ideas help explain how disciplinary content can be taught to learners who do not share the native context of the field.

In computing education, knowledge translation is necessary whenever abstract computational concepts must be made accessible to learners from different disciplines. Recontextualization may involve presenting a general idea through examples drawn from health, design, business, science, or civic applications. The challenge is to do this without distorting the concept itself. Good translation preserves conceptual structure while adjusting the pathway of access.

These ideas help clarify why translational pedagogy is not remedial. All teaching involves some degree of translation from expert knowledge to learner understanding.

What changes in interdisciplinary classrooms is the range and importance of such translation. Because students bring diverse disciplinary frames, teaching must more intentionally recontextualize concepts so that they become thinkable and valuable across domains.

5.3 Disciplinary Discourse and Epistemic Access

Disciplinary discourse refers to the ways a field speaks, explains, and legitimizes knowledge. Epistemic access concerns access not only to content, but to the means by which knowledge becomes intelligible within a discipline. In many classrooms, students may be formally admitted yet still denied meaningful epistemic access because the discourse assumes familiarity they do not possess.

Computing discourse can be highly compressed. Technical terms, symbolic shorthand, and procedural forms of explanation often obscure meaning for newcomers. For interdisciplinary learners, the issue is compounded because they may be fluent in another disciplinary discourse and unsure how to interpret the language of computing. Translational pedagogy therefore requires attention to discourse as part of access. Students need help understanding not only the concept, but also how the field talks about the concept (Morrow, 2009; Shulman, 1986).

The notion of epistemic access is particularly important for inclusive higher education. It suggests that educational equity is not achieved merely by opening the classroom door. Students must also be able to enter knowledge practices meaningfully. This lens supports the translational goal of making computing conceptually and linguistically accessible without diluting rigor.

5.4 Analogical Reasoning Across Domains

Analogical reasoning is one of the central cognitive tools for learning unfamiliar material. It allows learners to understand a new concept by mapping its structure onto a more familiar one. In interdisciplinary teaching, analogical reasoning is especially powerful because students often possess rich domain knowledge that can anchor new computational ideas (Gentner, 1983).

A loop may be understood through repetitive sensing, iterative design revision, repeated rule application, or stepwise checking processes depending on the learner's field. A conditional may be understood through diagnostic pathways, policy decisions, or branching procedures. The value of analogy lies in structural correspondence. A weak analogy may motivate briefly but mislead conceptually; a strong analogy helps learners perceive a meaningful transferable relationship.

Analogical reasoning therefore has both cognitive and pedagogical significance. It supports schema activation, reduces abstraction barriers, and helps learners bridge domains. But it also requires care. Students must ultimately be guided back from the analogy to the formal computing concept. Otherwise, the analogy may remain local and fail to support transfer. This tension makes analogical reasoning a central theoretical support for translational explanation.

5.5 Translational Meaning-Making in Computing Instruction

Translational meaning-making refers to the process by which learners construct understanding when concepts are mediated across disciplinary, linguistic, and representational boundaries. It is not a single established theory, but a useful synthesis of the frameworks above. The core insight is that meaning in interdisciplinary computing classrooms is rarely immediate. It is built through mediation: linking prior knowledge to new abstractions, shifting between representations, negotiating disciplinary language, and recognizing relevance across contexts.

This idea is central to the present book. Translational pedagogy is not merely about simplifying technical content. It is about supporting meaning-making across differences without erasing those differences. Learners should come to understand computing both in its own terms and in relation to their own fields. This requires movement between abstraction and context, formalism and familiarity, conceptual integrity and disciplinary relevance.

6. THEORETICAL SYNTHESIS FOR THE BOOK'S PEDAGOGICAL MODEL

6.1 Mapping Theories to Pedagogical Components

The six components introduced in Chapter 1 can now be understood as theoretically grounded rather than intuitively assembled.

Cognitive visibility is supported by constructivism, cognitive apprenticeship, cognitive load theory, and threshold concept theory. These explain why hidden reasoning obstructs learning and why making thought processes visible supports conceptual access.

Translational explanation is supported by schema theory, dual coding, analogical reasoning, disciplinary discourse, epistemic access, and knowledge translation. These clarify why diverse learners need different conceptual entry points into the same idea.

Adaptive support and scaffolded challenge draw support from cognitive apprenticeship, experiential learning, self-regulated learning, and cognitive load theory. These theories show why learners need structured progression and why support can enable rather than weaken rigor.

Psychological safety is underpinned by self-efficacy theory, belonging theory, and affective perspectives on learning.

Output conversion is supported by situated learning, experiential learning, identity formation, and transfer theory, since meaningful contribution often emerges when learners connect classroom concepts to authentic practice.

Evidence-informed refinement is not reducible to one theory, but aligns well with constructivist, metacognitive, and inquiry-oriented approaches that treat teaching as iterative, responsive, and diagnostically informed.

6.2 Why No Single Theory Is Sufficient

The temptation in educational writing is often to privilege one explanatory lens. Yet translational pedagogy requires a plural foundation because the problems it addresses are multi-dimensional. A student who struggles in introductory computing may be carrying excessive cognitive load, lacking prior schemas, feeling low self-efficacy, doubting the task's value, and finding the discourse inaccessible; all at once.

Constructivism explains active meaning-making but not enough about motivation. Cognitive load theory explains mental burden but not identity. Belonging theory explains persistence and participation but not representation and abstraction. Transfer theory explains portability of learning but not disciplinary discourse. Interdisciplinary pedagogy therefore demands theoretical complementarity. The strength of translational pedagogy lies partly in its willingness to work across these traditions rather than reduce the educational challenge to one variable.

This also matters for scholarly legitimacy. A pedagogical model intended for cross-disciplinary application must be justifiable from multiple angles. Theoretical pluralism, when disciplined and coherent, is not a weakness here; it is an appropriate response to an educational reality where cognition, motivation, language, and context are inseparable in practice.

6.3 An Integrated Conceptual Model for Translational Teaching

An integrated conceptual model for translational computing pedagogy can be described as follows. Learners enter with varied prior knowledge, disciplinary identities, confidence levels, and motivational orientations. Learning occurs through active construction, socially mediated interpretation, and context-shaped participation. Because computing involves abstract and often hidden reasoning, pedagogy must reduce unnecessary cognitive burden, activate prior schemas, and employ coherent multimodal representation. Because learners differ in whether they expect success and value the task, pedagogy must support efficacy, relevance, belonging, and safe engagement with challenge. Because the classroom is interdisciplinary, meaning must often be translated across disciplinary boundaries through recontextualization, accessible discourse, and analogical bridging. Because higher education aims at more than short-term task completion, instruction should support transfer, identity development, and meaningful contribution. The visual interaction of these pedagogical tracks and the joint synthesis of these educational principles are represented as a unified framework in Figure 1.

Figure 1. Integrated theoretical model for translational computing pedagogy. The figure illustrates how multiple theoretical traditions jointly support the core pedagogical components of translational computing pedagogy and help explain its intended outcomes in interdisciplinary computing education.

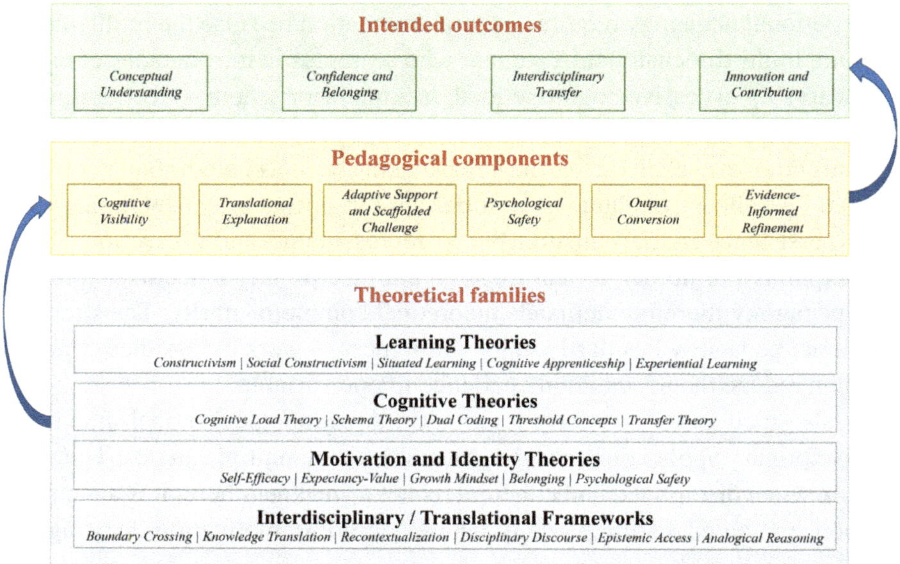

This model does not prescribe a single classroom method. Rather, it provides a conceptual basis for the design principles developed in later chapters. It explains why visible reasoning matters, why explanation must be adaptive across disciplines, why challenge should be scaffolded, why classroom climate affects learning, and why authentic contribution strengthens educational outcomes. A structured translation of these individual theoretical lenses into practical instructional frameworks is organized in Table 2.

7. IMPLICATIONS FOR CURRICULUM AND INSTRUCTION

7.1 Designing for Diverse Prior Knowledge

The theories discussed in this chapter collectively imply that curriculum must be designed with learner variability in mind. Prior knowledge is not a minor background variable; it shapes how new concepts are interpreted, whether examples are meaningful, and how much cognitive load students experience. In interdisciplinary settings, this means curriculum design should anticipate heterogeneous entry points rather than assume a single norm. Sequencing, pacing, explanation, and representation should all be informed by this reality.

7.2 Supporting Reasoning Rather Than Memorization

Constructivist, cognitive apprenticeship, schema, and threshold concept perspectives all support a major pedagogical implication: computing should be taught for reasoning rather than memorization. Students may reproduce code without understanding, but such learning remains fragile. Curriculum should therefore emphasize conceptual structure, articulation of logic, interpretation of process, and strategic reflection. This implication becomes central in the next chapter's treatment of cognitive visibility.

7.3 Promoting Transfer and Interdisciplinary Relevance

Situated learning, transfer theory, knowledge translation, and analogical reasoning all suggest that students learn more powerfully when they can connect computing concepts to meaningful contexts. Curriculum should not isolate abstraction from application. Instead, it should help students move between general principles and domain-relevant cases. This is especially important for non-specialist learners who must apply computing beyond the computing classroom.

7.4 Designing for Confidence and Belonging

Self-efficacy, expectancy-value, belonging, and psychological safety theories imply that curriculum and instruction must be designed with affect and identity in mind. Students should encounter challenge, but not in ways that communicate exclusion or inevitable failure. Learning environments should support persistence, normalize uncertainty, and allow students to imagine themselves as capable users of computing within their own disciplinary pathways. This is not a secondary concern. It is part of how rigorous learning becomes possible.

Table 2. Theory-to-Practice Mapping

Theoretical Lens	What It Explains	Pedagogical Implication
Cognitive load theory	Why students get overwhelmed	Reduce unnecessary complexity and sequence explanation carefully
Schema theory	Why prior knowledge matters	Build explanations from familiar disciplinary anchors
Dual coding	Multiple coordinated representations aid learning	Combine verbal, visual, and symbolic explanation coherently
Threshold concept theory	Why some ideas remain conceptually troublesome	Identify bottlenecks and teach them with focused conceptual support
Transfer theory	Why students fail to generalize learning	Move between abstraction and disciplinary application
Self-efficacy theory	Why confidence shapes persistence	Design early mastery experiences and normalize struggle
Expectancy-value theory	Why students engage when they expect success and see value	Make computing visibly relevant to disciplinary goals
Belonging theory	Why legitimacy influences participation	Create inclusive classroom climates that support help-seeking
Boundary crossing theory	Why interdisciplinary learners struggle at domain boundaries	Use translation, analogy, and recontextualization
Disciplinary discourse / epistemic access	Why technical language can block understanding	Make disciplinary language explicit and accessible

8. CONCLUSION

8.1 Summary of Theoretical Insights

This chapter has argued that translational computing pedagogy requires a broad and integrated theoretical foundation. Constructivist and social constructivist theories emphasize active and socially mediated meaning-making. Situated learning and cognitive apprenticeship explain why context, participation, and visible expert reasoning matter. Experiential learning, metacognition, and self-regulated learning show the importance of reflection, iteration, and learner agency. Cognitive load theory, schema theory, dual coding, threshold concept theory, and transfer theory clarify why novices struggle, how understanding is structured, and how learning becomes portable. Self-efficacy, expectancy-value, growth mindset, belonging, identity, and psychological safety explain why confidence, motivation, and emotional climate are central to success. Boundary crossing, knowledge translation, disciplinary discourse, epistemic access, and analogical reasoning illuminate how meaning moves across interdisciplinary contexts.

Taken together, these theories justify a pedagogical model that is rigorous yet accessible, conceptually grounded yet context-sensitive, supportive yet demanding, and oriented not only toward performance but toward transfer and contribution.

8.2 How Theory Informs the Next Chapters

The remaining chapters of this book build on this theoretical foundation by developing the pedagogical model in more practical and applied terms. Chapter 3 examines cognitive visibility, showing how hidden reasoning in computing can be made pedagogically explicit. Chapter 4 addresses translational explanation across disciplines. Later chapters explore adaptive support, psychological safety, assessment, adaptive technologies, evidence-based refinement, case studies, scale, generalizability, and institutional culture. The value of the present chapter is that it establishes these developments as theoretically coherent rather than merely method-driven.

8.3 Toward Cognitive Visibility

Of all the theoretical strands discussed here, one of the most immediately consequential for computing education is the idea that learners struggle when expert reasoning remains hidden. Constructivism, cognitive apprenticeship, cognitive load theory, schema formation, and threshold concepts all converge on this point. If students are shown only polished solutions, they may never gain access to underlying logic. The next chapter therefore begins where this chapter naturally leads: with the problem of invisibility in computing learning and the pedagogical importance of making thinking visible.

REFERENCES

Akkerman, S. F., & Bakker, A. (2011). Boundary crossing and boundary objects. *Review of Educational Research, 81*(2), 132–169. DOI: 10.3102/0034654311404435

Ambrose, S. A., Bridges, M. W., DiPietro, M., Lovett, M. C., & Norman, M. K. (2010). *How learning works: Seven research-based principles for smart teaching*. Jossey-Bass.

Anderson, J. R. (1984). *The architecture of cognition*. Harvard University Press.

Aquil Mirza, M., & Cong, W. (Eds.). (2026). *Real-Time Robotics With IoT and Edge AI: Methods, Metrics, and Applications*. IGI Global Scientific Publishing., DOI: 10.4018/979-8-2600-0701-3

Bandura, A. (1997). *Self-efficacy: The exercise of control*. W. H. Freeman.

Banta, T. W., & Palomba, C. A. (2015). *Assessment essentials: Planning, implementing, and improving assessment in higher education* (2nd ed.). Jossey-Bass.

Baxter Magolda, M. B. (2009). Authoring your life: Developing an internal voice to navigate life's challenges. *Stylus (Rio de Janeiro).*

Biggs, J., & Tang, C. (2011). *Teaching for quality learning at university* (4th ed.). Open University Press.

Bransford, J. D., Brown, A. L., & Cocking, R. R. (Eds.). (2000). *How people learn: Brain, mind, experience, and school* (Expanded ed.). National Academy Press.

Carlone, H. B., & Johnson, A. (2007). Understanding the science experiences of successful women of color: Science identity as an analytic lens. *Journal of Research in Science Teaching, 44*(8), 1187–1218. DOI: 10.1002/tea.20237

Collins, A., Brown, J. S., & Newman, S. E. (1989). Cognitive apprenticeship: Teaching the craft of reading, writing, and mathematics. In Resnick, L. B. (Ed.), *Knowing, learning, and instruction: Essays in honor of Robert Glaser* (pp. 453–494). Lawrence Erlbaum.

Denning, P. J. (2017). Remaining trouble spots with computational thinking. *Communications of the ACM, 60*(6), 33–39. DOI: 10.1145/2998438

Dweck, C. S. (2006). *Mindset: The new psychology of success*. Random House.

Eccles, J. S., & Wigfield, A. (2020). From expectancy-value theory to situated expectancy-value theory: A developmental, social cognitive, and sociocultural perspective on motivation. *Contemporary Educational Psychology*, *61*, 101859. DOI: 10.1016/j.cedpsych.2020.101859

Edmondson, A. (1999). Psychological safety and learning behavior in work teams. *Administrative Science Quarterly*, *44*(2), 350–383. DOI: 10.2307/2666999

Gentner, D. (1983). Structure-mapping: A theoretical framework for analogy. *Cognitive Science*, *7*(2), 155–170. DOI: 10.1207/s15516709cog0702_3

Hattie, J. (2009). *Visible learning: A synthesis of over 800 meta-analyses relating to achievement*. Routledge.

Kolb, D. A. (1984). *Experiential learning: Experience as the source of learning and development*. Prentice Hall.

Lave, J., & Wenger, E. (1991). *Situated learning: Legitimate peripheral participation*. Cambridge University Press. DOI: 10.1017/CBO9780511815355

Meyer, J. H. F., & Land, R. (2003). Threshold concepts and troublesome knowledge: Linkages to ways of thinking and practising. In Rust, C. (Ed.), *Improving student learning: Theory and practice ten years on* (pp. 412–424). Oxford Centre for Staff and Learning Development.

Mohammed, A. (Ed.). (2026). *Advanced Concurrency, Buffering, and Web-Sync in Sensor Platforms: Zero-Loss Streams*. IGI Global Scientific Publishing., DOI: 10.4018/979-8-2600-1101-0

Mohammed, A., & Zangana, H. (Eds.). (2026). *Intelligent Construction Monitoring Systems: Real-Time Safety, Environmental Prediction, and Risk Management*. IGI Global Scientific Publishing., DOI: 10.4018/979-8-3373-9245-5

Morrow, W. (2009). *Bounds of democracy: Epistemological access in higher education*. HSRC Press.

Paivio, A. (1986). *Mental representations: A dual coding approach*. Oxford University Press.

Perkins, D. N., & Salomon, G. (1992). Transfer of learning. In Postlethwaite, T. N., & Husen, T. (Eds.), *International encyclopedia of education* (2nd ed., pp. 6452–6457). Pergamon Press.

Piaget, J. (1970). *Science of education and the psychology of the child*. Orion Press.

Rumelhart, D. E. (1980). Schemata: The building blocks of cognition. In Spiro, R. J., Bruce, B. C., & Brewer, W. F. (Eds.), *Theoretical issues in reading comprehension* (pp. 33–58). Lawrence Erlbaum.

Shulman, L. S. (1986). Those who understand: Knowledge growth in teaching. *Educational Researcher, 15*(2), 4–14. DOI: 10.3102/0013189X015002004

Sweller, J. (1988). Cognitive load during problem solving: Effects on learning. *Cognitive Science, 12*(2), 257–285. DOI: 10.1207/s15516709cog1202_4

Sweller, J., van Merriënboer, J. J. G., & Paas, F. (2019). Cognitive architecture and instructional design: 20 years later. *Educational Psychology Review, 31*(2), 261–292. DOI: 10.1007/s10648-019-09465-5

Vygotsky, L. S. (1978). *Mind in society: The development of higher psychological processes*. Harvard University Press.

Wing, J. M. (2006). Computational thinking. *Communications of the ACM, 49*(3), 33–35. DOI: 10.1145/1118178.1118215

Zimmerman, B. J. (2002). Becoming a self-regulated learner: An overview. *Theory into Practice, 41*(2), 64–70. DOI: 10.1207/s15430421tip4102_2

Chapter 3
Making Thinking Visible: Cognitive Visibility as a Translational Practice

Chen Tak Hei
http://orcid.org/0009-0008-3136-7581
Department of Applied Physics, Hong Kong Polytechnic University, Hong Kong

ABSTRACT

This chapter, per the authors, addresses the persistent invisibility problem in computing education, where expert reasoning remains hidden behind polished code and correct outputs, leading novices and interdisciplinary learners to guess, imitate, or disengage. The chapter introduces and defines cognitive visibility as a deliberate translational practice that externalizes hidden thinking processes such as logic sequencing, debugging, and state tracking into observable and learnable forms. The chapter distinguishes cognitive visibility from general explanation and positions it within a broader translational pedagogy. Six major forms of visibility are examined, including verbalized reasoning, paper-based tracing, flowcharts, state-change diagrams, debugging narratives, and think-aloud protocols. Pedagogical design strategies such as pre-coding tasks, live coding with intentional errors, slow demonstration, and student explanation routines are presented.

1. INTRODUCTION

1.1 The Invisibility Problem in Computing Education

One of the most persistent problems in computing education is that much of the real learning work remains invisible. Students often encounter polished code, clean diagrams, and correct outputs, but they do not see the thinking that produced them.

DOI: 10.4018/979-8-2600-1811-8.ch003

They see the final answer rather than the chain of reasoning, decision points, failed attempts, debugging moves, or conceptual restructuring that led to that answer. In many classrooms, this invisibility is so normalized that it is rarely recognized as a pedagogical problem. Yet for novice learners, especially those entering computing from non-specialist disciplines, it is often one of the greatest barriers to understanding.

Computing is a field in which the visible artifact can be misleading. A short segment of code may appear simple to an expert but can conceal several layers of reasoning: understanding the problem, selecting appropriate structures, anticipating variable state changes, predicting execution flow, debugging logic errors, and evaluating whether the output actually answers the intended question. When the teaching of computing foregrounds the artifact and conceals the cognitive process, students may mistakenly conclude that mastery consists in reproducing finished forms. They may memorize syntax, imitate patterns, or rely on code fragments from slides, peers, or online tools without developing a genuine mental model of what the program is doing.

This problem is not unique to computing, but it is particularly acute there because the subject combines abstraction, precision, and machine-mediated feedback. Unlike some forms of human communication, code does not tolerate hidden assumptions well. The machine requires explicitness. Students who have not learned to trace logic, track changes in state, or reason through conditions and loops are often left guessing. As a result, introductory programming classrooms can become spaces where students appear active while remaining cognitively passive. They type, run, and revise, but they do not fully understand what they are doing.

The invisibility problem also has an emotional dimension. Students compare their own unfinished reasoning to the teacher's polished demonstration and infer that their confusion is a personal deficiency rather than a normal part of learning. This can be especially discouraging for learners from non-technical or mixed disciplinary backgrounds who may already suspect they do not belong in the subject. When expert reasoning is invisible, expertise itself appears magical. When expertise appears magical, beginners are more likely to disengage.

The argument of this chapter is that one of the most powerful responses to this problem is **cognitive visibility**: the deliberate pedagogical externalization of thinking processes that are normally hidden. Cognitive visibility does not merely mean "showing more." It means helping learners see how logic unfolds, where misconceptions arise, how decisions are made, and why errors are informative. It is a translational practice because it translates expert cognition into forms that novices can access, interpret, and gradually internalize.

1.2 Why Visible Thinking Matters for Novices and Interdisciplinary Learners

Visible thinking matters for all learners, but it matters especially for novices and interdisciplinary learners. Novices often lack the schemas that allow experts to compress many small decisions into a single rapid act of recognition. A lecturer may instantly know why a loop fails, why a conditional is misplaced, or why a variable has the wrong scope. A beginner often cannot even identify where the logic should be examined. Without pedagogical support, the student sees only the surface difficulty, not the structure underneath it.

Interdisciplinary learners face an additional challenge: they are not only new to computing concepts but often new to the modes of reasoning and representation through which computing is taught. A student from civil engineering may be comfortable with systems and quantitative reasoning but not with procedural code tracing. A student from fashion or design may think strongly in visual and iterative terms but find the symbolic compactness of code unfamiliar. A student from linguistics may understand formal rules but not yet connect them to program execution. In each case, the learner's background contains real intellectual resources, but these resources do not automatically align with standard classroom practices. Cognitive visibility helps create that alignment by slowing down expert reasoning and rendering it pedagogically accessible.

Visible thinking also matters because it shifts the center of learning from answer production to reasoning quality. In an era where students can easily access code generators, repositories, or pattern-based solutions, the educational value of computing instruction increasingly depends on whether students can explain, adapt, critique, and debug what they produce. If the classroom rewards only final output, then students may bypass the very thinking that education is meant to develop. Cognitive visibility restores process as an object of learning.

Research in computing education has repeatedly shown that novices struggle with program comprehension, variable state, control flow, tracing, debugging, and transfer from examples to new problems (Lister et al., 2004; Robins et al., 2003; Sorva, 2013). Studies on worked examples, self-explanation, and tracing also suggest that students learn more robustly when the hidden structure of problem solving is made explicit (Atkinson et al., 2000; Chi et al., 1989; Renkl, 2014). More broadly, theories of cognitive apprenticeship, constructivism, and metacognition support the claim that learners benefit when expert thought processes are modeled, articulated, and progressively internalized (Collins et al., 1989; Schraw, 1998; Vygotsky, 1978).

For interdisciplinary classrooms, visible thinking has yet another value: it can reduce the false binary between "technical" and "non-technical" students. When reasoning is made explicit, students discover that computing is not simply a talent one either possesses or lacks. It is a way of thinking that can be learned, practiced, and improved. This realization is often transformative.

1.3 Position of Cognitive Visibility Within Translational Pedagogy

Within the broader framework of translational pedagogy introduced in earlier chapters, cognitive visibility functions as a foundational principle. Before concepts can be translated across disciplines, before support can be optimized, before assessment can capture transfer, learners must first be able to see what thinking in computing looks like. Cognitive visibility is therefore not a minor technique but a pedagogical stance. It assumes that if expert cognition remains hidden, many students will be excluded from meaningful access.

At the same time, cognitive visibility should be understood carefully. It is not identical to explanation in general, and it is not reducible to simply talking through code. Translational explanation, treated in Chapter 4, concerns how concepts are explained across disciplinary backgrounds. Cognitive visibility, by contrast, concerns the externalization of mental process itself; how students and teachers make logic, decision-making, uncertainty, and debugging visible.

This distinction matters. A teacher may provide a clear analogy for a loop without helping students see how to reason through one line by line. Likewise, a teacher may ask students to code actively without first making the relevant cognitive structure visible. Cognitive visibility focuses on the internal mechanics of understanding: tracing, predicting, articulating, mapping, tracking, and diagnosing. It makes thought available for inspection.

The rest of this chapter develops this idea in depth. Section 2 defines cognitive visibility and its conceptual boundaries. Section 3 examines major forms of cognitive visibility in computing classrooms. Section 4 explores pedagogical design strategies. Section 5 considers how cognitive visibility functions differently for diverse disciplines and learner profiles. Section 6 discusses evidence of impact, including student reflections. Section 7 addresses risks and misapplications. Section 8 offers practical design principles. The chapter concludes by positioning cognitive visibility as a gateway to deeper conceptual understanding and as a bridge to the next chapter on translational explanation.

2. UNDERSTANDING COGNITIVE VISIBILITY

2.1 Definition and Conceptual Boundaries

Cognitive visibility refers to the deliberate pedagogical practice of making otherwise hidden thinking processes observable, discussable, and examinable in the learning environment. In computing education, this includes making visible how a problem is interpreted, how program logic is sequenced, how variable states change over time, how a bug is diagnosed, how alternative approaches are compared, and how an expert or novice reasons through uncertainty.

Three aspects of the definition are important. First, cognitive visibility concerns **thinking processes**, not just outputs. A visible program is not the same as visible reasoning. Second, it concerns **pedagogical externalization**. Thought must be represented in some form; verbally, visually, symbolically, procedurally, or dialogically; so that learners can engage with it. Third, cognitive visibility is not only something teachers do for students; it is also something students do for themselves and others. Students reveal their thinking when they trace code, explain decisions, diagram logic, or articulate why an error occurred.

The concept overlaps with but is distinct from several related ideas. It is related to metacognition because students become more aware of their own reasoning when they externalize it. It is related to cognitive apprenticeship because expert thinking is modeled explicitly. It is related to visible thinking traditions in education, which emphasize making reasoning public as part of understanding (Ritchhart et al., 2011). However, in computing education, cognitive visibility has a more domain-specific function: it reveals dynamic logic that is otherwise concealed behind code syntax and finished outputs.

It is equally important to define what cognitive visibility is **not**. It is not mere verbosity. Long explanations can still leave reasoning invisible if they remain abstract or skip key inferential steps. It is not decorative visualization. A colorful flowchart is only useful if it genuinely externalizes the logic students need to understand. It is not full dependence on teacher narration. If only the teacher's thinking is ever visible, students may remain passive observers. Cognitive visibility becomes educationally powerful when learners themselves participate in externalizing thought.

2.2 Expert Blind Spots in Computing Instruction

A major reason cognitive visibility is needed is that experts often underestimate how much of their own reasoning has become automatic. Expertise compresses cognition. What once required conscious effort becomes rapid pattern recognition, tacit sequencing, or unspoken intuition. This compression is beneficial for performance but problematic for teaching. Experts may skip steps without noticing, assume conceptual links are obvious, or present elegant finished solutions that conceal the struggle and experimentation that produced them.

In computing instruction, expert blind spots often appear in the way teachers present code. A teacher may write a loop and explain that it iterates through values, but omit the line-by-line reasoning through which each variable changes. A teacher may discuss debugging as though the source of an error should be apparent. A teacher may assume that students understand why a function is needed, when in fact the students are only following a pattern. Because the expert can "see" the structure mentally, the novice is expected to see it too.

Research on novice programming repeatedly indicates that experts and novices do not experience code in the same way (Pea, 1986; Robins et al., 2003; Sorva, 2013). Experts perceive meaningful chunks and anticipate execution behavior. Novices often focus on isolated lines, syntax fragments, or superficial resemblance to prior examples. If teachers are unaware of this gap, they may mistake student compliance for comprehension. They may think they have explained a concept because they have named it, when in fact the underlying cognitive operation remains hidden.

Expert blind spots also affect pacing. What seems like a reasonable tempo to an experienced instructor may be too fast for learners who are still building schemas. When steps are skipped, students often compensate by memorizing. They copy without conceptual ownership, hoping practice alone will eventually produce clarity. Sometimes it does; often it does not.

Cognitive visibility is partly a response to expert blindness. It forces the teacher to slow down, articulate tacit moves, and model what usually remains internal. In doing so, it not only supports students; it also deepens the teacher's awareness of what understanding actually requires.

2.3 Novice Misconceptions and Hidden Mental Models

Learners do not come to computing as blank slates. They come with intuitions, assumptions, and partial mental models that shape how they interpret code. Some of these intuitions are productive; others are misleading. In novice programming research, common misconceptions include treating variables as labels rather than changing states, misunderstanding assignment as mathematical equality, assuming loops "know" when to stop without explicit logic, or believing that code executes in ways closer to natural language than machine precision (Pea, 1986; du Boulay, 1986; Sorva, 2013).

These misconceptions persist partly because they remain hidden. Students may produce incorrect answers, but the underlying mental model causing the error is often invisible unless the teacher asks the student to trace, explain, or represent their reasoning. Two students may produce the same wrong answer for entirely different reasons. One may misunderstand control flow; another may misunderstand variable initialization. If cognition is not externalized, the teacher can only respond to the artifact of error, not the reasoning behind it.

Interdisciplinary learners may bring additional hidden models based on their own fields. A student from mathematics may expect concise symbolic manipulation and underappreciate execution order. A student from design may think strongly in final form rather than procedural state changes. A student from biology may recognize repeated processes but not yet formalize them computationally. None of these prior orientations are deficiencies. However, they do shape where learners are likely to misread computing processes.

Cognitive visibility helps surface these hidden models. When students draw flowcharts, trace values line by line, or explain the behavior of a program aloud, their reasoning becomes inspectable. This is pedagogically valuable because misconceptions are easier to address when they are visible in their own terms. The goal is not to expose students for judgment, but to make their thinking available for correction and growth.

2.4 Why Finished Solutions Can Hinder Learning

Finished solutions are pedagogically seductive. They are efficient, elegant, and reassuring to instructors because they show what correctness looks like. However, when overused or insufficiently unpacked, they can hinder learning. The polished solution fallacy occurs when the final, correct artifact is mistaken for the learning process itself.

For novices, a finished script often hides too much. It conceals why a structure was chosen, what alternatives were rejected, how variables were tracked mentally, what bugs arose during development, and how the solution was tested. Students may copy the final form but fail to understand how to generate or adapt it independently. Research on worked examples suggests that examples are powerful when learners are guided to self-explain and inspect underlying structure; they are less effective when learners engage only in superficial mimicry (Atkinson et al., 2000; Renkl, 2014).

Finished solutions also distort emotional perception. When learners see only fluent performance, they may conclude that competent programmers rarely struggle. Their own confusion then appears abnormal. This can intensify anxiety and decrease willingness to persist. By contrast, when reasoning, hesitation, and debugging are visible, students learn that difficulty is part of the process.

This does not mean that finished solutions should be abandoned. They have a legitimate role as models of quality and correctness. The issue is sequencing and framing. A finished solution is most pedagogically useful after the reasoning process has been made visible, or when the example itself is annotated, traced, questioned, and unpacked. In other words, solutions should be used as windows into thinking, not substitutes for it. he iterative movement from these static, hidden expert processes toward an explicit, active instructional loop is visually modeled in Figure 1.

Figure 1. From hidden reasoning to visible learning cycle.

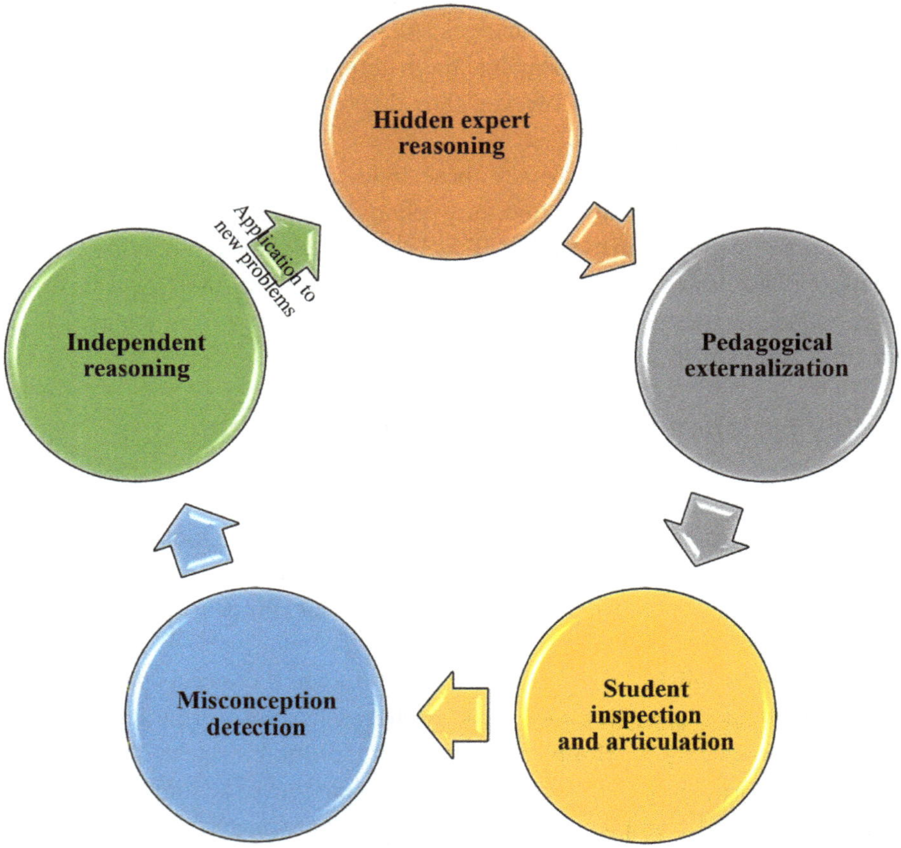

3. FORMS OF COGNITIVE VISIBILITY IN COMPUTING CLASSROOMS

Cognitive visibility can take many forms. The most effective classrooms do not rely on only one; they combine multiple modes so that students can see logic from different angles. This section outlines six major forms of cognitive visibility relevant to computing education.

3.1 Verbalizing Reasoning

One of the simplest and most powerful ways to externalize thinking is through verbalization. Teachers can narrate their reasoning as they solve a problem: why they choose a loop instead of repeated statements, how they identify a condition, how they decide where to initialize a variable, or what clues lead them to a particular bug. Students can also verbalize their reasoning, either individually, in pairs, or in small groups.

Verbalization matters because many students can mimic a structure without being able to explain it. Asking a student to say what a line of code does in ordinary language often reveals whether the concept is actually understood. If a student can describe the role of a loop, the meaning of a condition, or the reason a variable change, conceptual ownership is more likely. If the student can only restate syntax, understanding may still be shallow.

Verbal reasoning is especially useful because it slows cognition down. It forces choices and assumptions into language. It also allows instructors to hear where conceptual gaps lie. A student who says, "This loop prints until it finishes the list," may not yet understand what controls iteration. A student who says, "This variable remembers the total so far," is showing a more developed mental model.

Importantly, verbalization should not be restricted to high-performing students. If only confident students speak, cognitive visibility becomes socially uneven. Structured routines; such as pair explanation, short oral check-ins, or guided talk prompts; allow more learners to externalize thought without excessive performance pressure.

3.2 Tracing Logic on Paper

Paper-based tracing remains one of the most effective forms of cognitive visibility in introductory computing. It requires students to predict and record how a program behaves line by line, often by tracking variable values across iterations. While digital tools can support tracing, paper tracing has a distinctive pedagogical advantage: it slows students down and prevents premature dependence on "run and see" as the only strategy.

Tracing helps students move from vague intuition to explicit execution logic. Instead of guessing what the code does, they must examine each line, update variables, test conditions, and observe output formation. This practice is especially helpful for loops, conditionals, nested structures, and function calls, where learners often lose track of state and control flow.

A student from Civil and Environmental Engineering reflected on this effect succinctly: *"Tracing Python loops line-by-line on paper before typing forced me to see where variables actually change, not just guess."* This testimonial captures a central pedagogical truth: tracing transforms hidden state change into visible sequence. It converts a moving conceptual process into an inspectable record.

Paper tracing also supports assessment of understanding. When students annotate their trace, instructors can identify whether errors come from misreading syntax, misunderstanding repetition, or failing to update variables correctly. This makes misconceptions diagnosable in ways that final code alone may not. A typical layout demonstrating how students systematically log state transformations and variable adjustments during an execution cycle is illustrated in Figure 2.

Figure 2. Example of paper-based loop tracing.

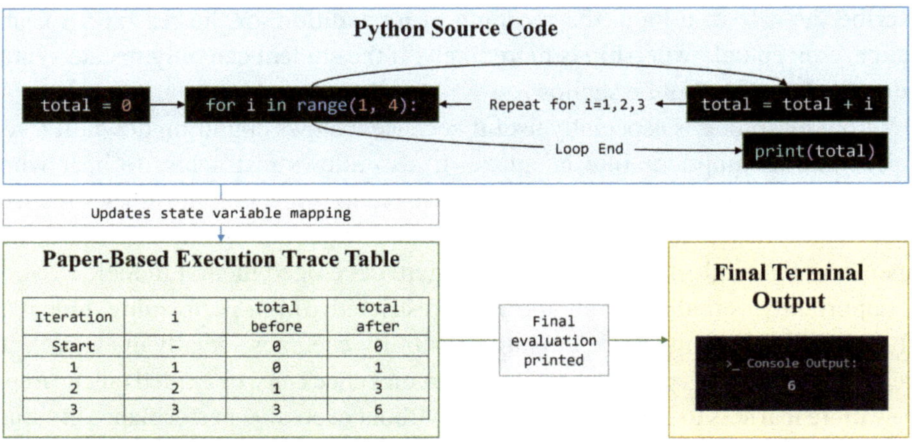

3.3 Flowcharts and Visual Logic Maps

Flowcharts and logic maps externalize program structure visually. They can be especially valuable for students who struggle to infer control flow directly from code. A flowchart makes sequence, branching, repetition, and termination conditions explicit in spatial form. It can help learners see the "shape" of logic before confronting syntax.

Visual logic mapping is not limited to formal flowcharts. It can include hand-drawn arrows, decision trees, modular blocks, input-processing-output diagrams, or problem decomposition maps. The pedagogical goal is to represent the structure of reasoning in a way that reduces cognitive ambiguity.

Visual representations are particularly helpful when students are struggling with compound conditions or branching logic. For example, a student who repeatedly misplaces if and elif logic may understand the problem much better when the conditional branches are drawn with the student's own variable names. One learner described a moment like this: when struggling with if statements in a grading project, the instructor drew a literal flowchart using the learner's variable names, and *"suddenly I saw where my logic broke."* The importance of this moment lies not in the flowchart as a generic tool, but in its use as a personalized visibility mechanism.

Flowcharts also serve a pre-coding function. They encourage students to think about the logic of a solution before becoming entangled in syntax. This is important in foundational courses where learners often try to code immediately without first clarifying the program's structure.

3.4 State-Change Diagrams and Variable Tracking

One of the hardest ideas for novices in programming is that variables are not static labels but dynamic states that change during execution. Students often read variable names semantically but fail to track their evolving values. State-change diagrams make this dynamic explicit. They may show a table of variables across iterations, memory-like boxes whose values update, or diagrams of references and assignments.

Research has shown that program visualization tools and variable-tracking aids can help learners build stronger mental models of execution, especially when used with explanation rather than as passive animations (Hundhausen et al., 2002; Sorva, 2013). State-change representation is valuable because it attacks a common source of novice error: not seeing that the meaning of a variable lies in its role over time, not merely in its name.

In introductory teaching, even simple tracking tables as shown in Table 1 can have powerful effects. For a loop such as:

```
total = 0
for i in range(3):
total = total + i
```

Table 1: Loop tracking tables

Iteration	i	total before	total after
Start	–	0	0
1	1	0	1
2	2	1	3
3	3	3	6

a student who writes the evolving values of i and total after each pass is much more likely to understand the loop than a student who merely sees the code. The visible record supports prediction, debugging, and transfer to similar patterns.

3.5 Debugging Narratives and Error Analysis

Debugging is one of the richest opportunities for cognitive visibility because it forces reasoning about failure. Yet in many classrooms, debugging remains hidden. Teachers present corrected code without showing how the error was found, or students silently change lines until the program runs without understanding what was wrong.

A debugging narrative externalizes the steps of diagnosis. It may include questions such as: What is the program supposed to do? What is it doing instead? Where does the first mismatch appear? Is the issue syntactic, semantic, or logical? What evidence supports that interpretation? What should be tested next? Such narratives transform debugging from blind trial-and-error into a structured form of reasoning.

Error analysis is pedagogically powerful because mistakes expose mental models. If a student places an update statement outside a loop, misunderstands indexing, or writes mutually inconsistent conditions, the error can become a site of conceptual clarification. This is consistent with research emphasizing the learning value of negative knowledge and productive failure when errors are used analytically rather than punitively (Kapur, 2008; Ohlsson, 1996).

Students also benefit from seeing the instructor debug imperfect code live. One beginner from English described live coding sessions in which the teacher intentionally introduced bugs and walked through the debugging thought process. For the student, this was transformative because it taught not just code form but *"how to think like a programmer, not just memorize the structure of the code."* The comment is significant because it captures the essence of cognitive visibility: making process, not just product, the focus of learning.

3.6 Think-Aloud and Worked-Example Variations

Think-aloud protocols involve speaking one's reasoning while solving a problem. In teaching, they can be used by the instructor to model expert thinking or by students to reveal their own logic. Worked examples, meanwhile, provide a structured solution path that students can inspect and explain. Research suggests that worked examples are especially effective for novices when they reduce unnecessary search and direct attention to structure, particularly if paired with self-explanation prompts (Atkinson et al., 2000; Chi et al., 1989).

In computing education, think-alouds are useful because they expose the sequencing of thought. Instead of seeing only the final line of code, students hear the questions that guide its construction: What do I know? What repeats? What changes? What stays fixed? What condition should stop the process? Where should I store the result? These questions teach a method of reasoning.

Worked-example variations can increase cognitive visibility further. For example, a partially completed example can ask students to fill in missing reasoning steps, predict outputs before running code, compare two alternative solutions, or diagnose why one version fails. Such designs encourage active inspection rather than passive imitation.

Together, think-alouds and worked examples show that visibility is not limited to one medium. It can be spoken, written, diagrammed, traced, or analytically reconstructed. The key is that students can see the hidden cognitive structure that underlies programming performance.

4. PEDAGOGICAL DESIGN STRATEGIES

4.1 Designing Visible Reasoning Tasks Before Coding

One of the most effective design principles in introductory computing is to require reasoning before implementation. Many students try to write code immediately, using syntax as a substitute for thought. Visible reasoning tasks interrupt this pattern. They ask students to predict, outline, trace, or map the logic of a problem before they touch the keyboard.

This sequencing matters because novice learners often become overwhelmed when problem interpretation and code production occur simultaneously. By separating conceptual planning from syntax execution, the teacher allows students to focus on the structure of the problem first. Pre-coding tasks may include identifying inputs and outputs, describing repeated patterns, predicting what each row of a pattern should contain, sketching a flow of decisions, or filling a variable-tracking table based on pseudocode.

Such tasks are not busywork. They make hidden reasoning available and create evidence of understanding that can be discussed. They also reduce premature guessing. A student who traces a loop on paper before coding is less likely to write the loop mechanically and more likely to understand its control logic.

4.2 Live Coding with Intentional Errors

Live coding has become a common practice in computing education because it allows students to see code being developed in real time. However, live coding becomes far more powerful when it includes intentional errors and explicit debugging. Rather than presenting perfect fluency, the teacher demonstrates how mistakes arise and how they are examined.

The value of intentional error lies in demystification. Students see that competent programmers do not simply "know" the answer instantly. They test ideas, misplace conditions, forget syntax, inspect outputs, and revise. This helps normalize struggle and reveals debugging as a central intellectual practice rather than a sign of failure.

A Year 2 beginner learner reflected that the most helpful aspect of the course was precisely this style of live coding: the instructor would introduce bugs and *"walk us through his debugging thought process."* For that learner, the lesson was not only how to repair code, but how to reason under uncertainty. This is a critical form of cognitive visibility because it exposes the diagnostic logic hidden in expert performance. The systematic progression of this adaptive diagnostic logic, from error identification to resolution strategy, is visually mapped in Figure 3.

4.3 Slow Demonstration as Instructional Practice

In many technical classrooms, the pace of demonstration is tuned to expert fluency rather than novice comprehension. Slow demonstration counters this tendency. It involves deliberately reducing speed, pausing at decision points, and revisiting lines or structures that might seem obvious to the instructor but not to the learners.

Slow demonstration is not merely a matter of speaking slowly. It is a matter of pacing cognition. The teacher pauses to ask what changes next, what a condition means, or what will happen after the next iteration. Students are invited to predict rather than merely observe. This transforms demonstration into interactive reasoning.

Such pacing is especially useful in large and diverse classes because it creates more entry points for learners who process the material at different speeds. It also allows time for students to notice hidden steps. In visible-thinking pedagogy, speed is not neutral; it can either reveal structure or conceal it.

4.4 Student Explanation Routines During Labs

Cognitive visibility becomes much stronger when it is not confined to teacher demonstration. Students themselves need routines that require explanation. During labs, this can include asking students to explain their code in everyday language, justify why they chose a particular structure, predict the next output before execution, or describe what a variable is doing at a particular point.

One student described this initially unfamiliar but ultimately powerful experience: being required to explain code aloud during labs *"felt weird at first but helped independent thinking a ton."* This comment is pedagogically important. Explanation routines may feel uncomfortable because they interrupt passive completion. Yet that discomfort is often the threshold between imitation and reasoning.

These routines can be structured in manageable ways: short paired explanation, tutor check-ins, mini whiteboard tracing, or quick verbal checkpoints before submission. The aim is not performance for its own sake but the normalization of reasoning as a visible part of practice.

Figure 3. Sample debugging process map.

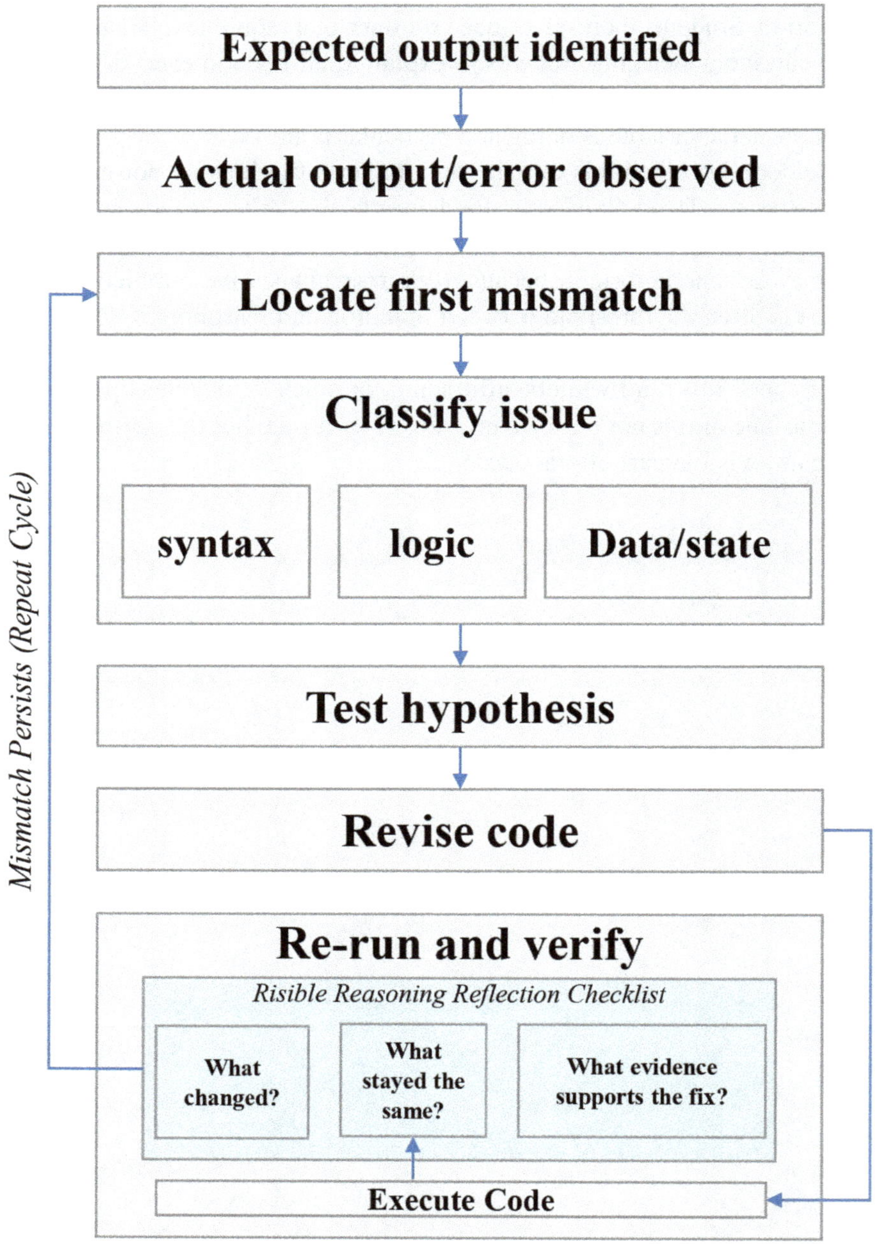

4.5 Reflection Prompts and Metacognitive Checkpoints

Visible thinking is strengthened when students reflect on how they arrived at an answer, not just whether it worked. Metacognitive checkpoints can ask: What part of this problem was hardest? What did you first misunderstand? How did you know where the bug was? What would you check first if the program failed again? Which idea in this task is generalizable to other problems?

Such reflection supports transfer because it encourages students to extract principles from experience. It also helps them develop internal monitoring habits. Over time, what is first externalized through prompts can become internalized as self-questioning during independent work.

Metacognitive reflection is particularly useful after debugging or tracing tasks. Students are not only learning the solution; they are learning how to learn in computing. This is essential in interdisciplinary settings, where students often need support in becoming autonomous computational thinkers rather than one-course survivors.

5. COGNITIVE VISIBILITY FOR DIVERSE DISCIPLINES

5.1 Why Non-Computing Learners Benefit Differently

Cognitive visibility benefits all students, but it is especially important for students whose primary identity is outside computing. Such learners may not have previous exposure to program tracing, debugging habits, or technical discourse. They often need help not only with the concept itself but with the form of reasoning the subject demands.

For non-computing learners, visible reasoning reduces the sense that programming is an opaque technical ritual. It shows that the subject consists of understandable decisions and processes. It also helps prevent a common novice pattern: treating code as something to be copied rather than interpreted. When learners can see how logic unfolds, they are more likely to believe that they can participate meaningfully.

This matters for access and belonging. Students from fields such as fashion, design, applied biology, linguistics, or building sciences may not initially expect to succeed in programming. Cognitive visibility can reshape that expectation by making expertise look learnable rather than mysterious.

5.2 Using Disciplinary Representations to Reveal Logic

While Chapter 4 will discuss cross-disciplinary analogy more fully, it is worth noting here that cognitive visibility can be strengthened by using representational forms that resonate with different disciplinary habits of thought. A design student may understand logic more clearly through visual sequencing and pattern decomposition. A biology student may benefit from process flow and repeated state transitions. An engineering student may respond well to system diagrams or tabular tracking.

The key point is not to change the computing concept itself, but to make its internal logic visible through representational choices that students can process more readily. This is still cognitive visibility because the emphasis remains on exposing reasoning, not merely contextualizing it.

5.3 Supporting Learners with Anxiety or Low Confidence

Visible thinking also has an affective function. Students with anxiety often fear hidden judgment. If they do not understand a concept, they may assume everyone else does. When reasoning is made public; especially when errors and uncertainty are normalized; students can see that confusion is common, diagnosable, and improvable.

One transformative testimonial illustrates this clearly. A student who had considered dropping the course was encouraged to remain, eventually earning an A+, and later described the experience as a shift in identity. Cognitive visibility contributes to such transformations because it gives learners a way to understand their confusion rather than interpret it as permanent incapacity.

5.4 Accessibility Considerations and SEN-Responsive Approaches

Cognitive visibility can also support accessibility when designed thoughtfully. Students with special educational needs, attention difficulties, language-processing challenges, or anxiety may benefit from external representations that reduce memory load and clarify structure. Tracing sheets, annotated flowcharts, stepwise demonstrations, and visible state changes can reduce ambiguity and support processing.

However, accessibility requires flexibility. Not all students benefit from the same visible forms. Some may prefer visual mappings; others may need verbal explanation or structured written steps. The principle should therefore be multimodal visibility rather than one mandated form. The goal is to make thought available, not to enforce a single way of displaying it.

6. EVIDENCE OF IMPACT

6.1 Conceptual Understanding and Debugging Ability

Evidence from computing education literature and from classroom practice suggests that visible reasoning improves conceptual understanding, especially in core areas such as loops, conditions, tracing, and debugging (Lister et al., 2004; Sorva, 2013). When students are required to trace values, explain logic, or diagnose errors explicitly, they are more likely to build functional mental models of execution.

In large foundational classes, the difference often appears in debugging behavior. Students who have practiced visible reasoning are less likely to change code randomly and more likely to test hypotheses. They know to ask what the variable value is at each stage, whether the condition is being reached, or where control flow diverges from expectation.

6.2 Reduction in Guessing and Imitation

One of the clearest effects of cognitive visibility is a reduction in guessing. Students move from hoping the code works to examining why it should work. This shift can be observed in classroom dialogue. Instead of asking only, "Is this right?" students begin asking, "Does this variable update before the condition?" or "Why does the loop stop here?" Such questions indicate that the learner is operating at the level of logic rather than surface form.

A Civil Engineering student described exactly this shift, noting that tracing on paper helped him see variable change "not just guess." That distinction; between seeing and guessing; is the heart of cognitive visibility.

6.3 Confidence Gains and Participation Shifts

Visible reasoning practices also influence confidence. When students understand how to inspect their own code, they feel less dependent on the teacher for immediate rescue. They gain a sense of procedural control. This does not mean they stop needing help, but it changes the nature of their help-seeking. They can identify where they are confused.

Course feedback can reflect this shift. In one foundational computing context, strong majorities of students agreed that the course improved their understanding of programming concepts and increased their confidence in computing. Such perceptions cannot be attributed to one factor alone, but visible thinking practices were a significant part of the instructional design.

6.4 Sample Student Reflections and Testimonial-Based Evidence

Selective student reflections help illustrate how cognitive visibility is experienced by learners:

- A student from **Civil and Environmental Engineering** wrote that tracing loops line by line and explaining code aloud helped him move from guessing to real understanding and eventually debug independently.
- A student from **English** reported that live coding with intentional errors made complex concepts surprisingly accessible and taught the student how to think through bugs rather than fear them.
- A student from **Applied Biology with Biotechnology** described how patient one-to-one explanation of syntax, logic, and debugging helped build stronger logical thinking and programming confidence.
- A student from **Fashion** noted that visual explanations, well-structured slides, and teacher insistence on clarity helped transform a course first approached as a passing requirement into a meaningful learning experience.
- A student who had nearly withdrawn later reported that the course changed not only performance but confidence and professional orientation, suggesting that visible reasoning can have longer-term identity effects.

Compactly interpreted, these testimonials point to recurring outcomes: clearer logic, reduced fear, improved debugging, stronger self-explanation, and the movement from passive completion toward independent reasoning. The explicit alignment between these individual student experiences, the underlying instructional methods, and their targeted learning objectives is systematically mapped in Table 2.

Table 2. Cognitive Visibility Strategies and Intended Learning Outcomes

Cognitive Visibility Strategy	What It Makes Visible	Intended Learning Outcome
Verbalizing reasoning	Decision process and conceptual language	Deeper explanation ability
Paper tracing	Control flow and variable state	Stronger program comprehension
Flowcharts / logic maps	Structure of conditions and loops	Better problem decomposition
State-change diagrams	Dynamic behavior of variables	Reduced misconceptions about assignment and iteration
Debugging narratives	Diagnostic reasoning	Improved independent debugging
Think-aloud / worked examples	Expert problem-solving process	Better transfer from examples to new problems

7. RISKS, CONSTRAINTS, AND MISAPPLICATIONS

7.1 Over-Scaffolding vs Genuine Reasoning

Cognitive visibility can be misapplied if it becomes excessive spoon-feeding. If every step is always provided, students may become dependent on external representations without learning to internalize them. The goal is not permanent transparency of all teacher thinking, but progressive transfer of cognitive responsibility.

A useful principle is staged visibility: externalize heavily when concepts are new, then gradually require students to produce the visibility themselves. For example, early lessons may provide full trace tables; later tasks may ask students to construct them independently.

7.2 Time Constraints in Large Classes

One practical objection is that visible reasoning takes time. Tracing, verbal explanation, and careful debugging discussion can seem difficult in large-enrollment subjects. This concern is valid. However, hidden misunderstanding also consumes time later through repeated confusion, poor assessment performance, and remedial support. The issue is not whether cognitive visibility costs time, but whether it saves time by improving understanding earlier.

Efficient routines can help. Short paper tracing tasks, one-minute prediction prompts, paired explanation, and selective live debugging can be integrated without overwhelming the timetable.

7.3 Performance Pressure During Public Explanation

Asking students to explain their reasoning publicly can create pressure, especially for shy learners or those already anxious. Cognitive visibility should not become public exposure. Teachers need multiple formats: pair discussion, anonymous polling, written reasoning, and optional oral explanation. Psychological safety, treated more fully in Chapter 5, is essential here.

7.4 Balancing Visibility with Autonomy

The final challenge is balancing visibility with independence. Students must eventually be able to reason internally and work autonomously. If visibility practices remain too externally controlled, learners may not make that transition. Good design therefore uses visible thinking as a bridge: first model it, then share it, then require students to generate it, and finally help them internalize it.

8. Practical Design Principles

8.1 Minimum Viable Cognitive Visibility in Foundational Courses

For foundational computing courses, a minimum viable model of cognitive visibility should include four elements:

1. **Pre-coding reasoning tasks** for major concepts like loops and conditionals.
2. **Teacher modeling of thought process**, not only finished code.
3. **Student explanation opportunities**, verbal or written.
4. **Explicit debugging analysis**, including why an error occurred.

These elements can be implemented even in large classes and create a baseline of visible reasoning.

8.2 Classroom Protocols for Tutorials and Labs

Tutorials and labs can use simple protocols:

- Predict before run.
- Trace before type.
- Explain before submit.
- Identify the first point of mismatch when debugging.
- Use one visual representation for each new logic structure.

Such routines gradually build a culture where reasoning is expected, not optional.

8.3 Assessment Alignment for Visible Thinking

If visible reasoning matters pedagogically, assessment should recognize it. This does not require abandoning code-based tasks. Rather, it means including items that ask students to trace outputs, explain logic, annotate steps, or diagnose faulty code. When assessment values reasoning, students are more likely to treat cognitive visibility seriously.

8.4 Recommendations for Instructors

Instructors seeking to adopt cognitive visibility should begin modestly but intentionally:

- choose one difficult concept and add a tracing routine;
- model one live debugging narrative each week;
- ask students to explain code in everyday language;
- use simple visual state representations;
- collect evidence of misconceptions and revise explanations accordingly.

The aim is not theatrical performance but systematic externalization of thought.

9. CONCLUSION

9.1 Cognitive Visibility as a Gateway to Understanding

This chapter has argued that one of the deepest obstacles in computing education is that the reasoning required for understanding often remains hidden. Students see syntax and outputs but not the thought processes that make those outputs meaningful. For novices and interdisciplinary learners, this invisibility can lead to guessing, imitation, anxiety, and disengagement. Cognitive visibility addresses this problem by making reasoning public, inspectable, and learnable.

Through verbalization, tracing, flowcharts, state tracking, debugging narratives, and think-aloud methods, computing concepts become more than patterns to copy. They become processes that students can follow, question, and eventually own. When designed carefully, cognitive visibility strengthens conceptual understanding, improves debugging, reduces blind imitation, and supports learner confidence.

9.2 Transition to Translational Explanation Across Disciplines

However, making thinking visible is only one part of the pedagogical challenge. Even when reasoning is externalized, students still need explanations that connect computing concepts to the forms of meaning available within their own disciplinary backgrounds. Cognitive visibility reveals process; translational explanation helps students enter that process from where they are. The next chapter therefore turns to the question of explanation itself: how computing concepts can be taught across disciplines without losing rigor.

REFERENCES

Aquil Mirza, M., & Cong, W. (Eds.). (2026). *Real-Time Robotics With IoT and Edge AI: Methods, Metrics, and Applications*. IGI Global Scientific Publishing., DOI: 10.4018/979-8-2600-0701-3

Atkinson, R. K., Derry, S. J., Renkl, A., & Wortham, D. (2000). Learning from examples: Instructional principles from the worked examples research. *Review of Educational Research*, *70*(2), 181–214. DOI: 10.3102/00346543070002181

Chi, M. T. H., Bassok, M., Lewis, M. W., Reimann, P., & Glaser, R. (1989). Self-explanations: How students study and use examples in learning to solve problems. *Cognitive Science*, *13*(2), 145–182. DOI: 10.1207/s15516709cog1302_1 PMID: 34983624

Collins, A., Brown, J. S., & Newman, S. E. (1989). Cognitive apprenticeship: Teaching the crafts of reading, writing, and mathematics. In Resnick, L. B. (Ed.), *Knowing, learning, and instruction: Essays in honor of Robert Glaser* (pp. 453–494).

Hundhausen, C. D., Douglas, S. A., & Stasko, J. T. (2002). A meta-study of algorithm visualization effectiveness. *Journal of Visual Languages and Computing*, *13*(3), 259–290. DOI: 10.1006/jvlc.2002.0237

Kapur, M. (2008). Productive failure. *Cognition and Instruction*, *26*(3), 379–424. DOI: 10.1080/07370000802212669

Lawrence Erlbaum. du Boulay, B. (1986). Some difficulties of learning to program. *Journal of Educational Computing Research*, *2*(1), 57–73. DOI: 10.2190/3LFX-9RRF-67T8-UVK9

Lister, R., Adams, E. S., Fitzgerald, S., Fone, W., Hamer, J., Lindholm, M., McCartney, R., Moström, J. E., Sanders, K., Seppälä, O., Simon, B., & Thomas, L. (2004). A multi-national study of reading and tracing skills in novice programmers. *SIGCSE Bulletin*, *36*(4), 119–150. DOI: 10.1145/1041624.1041673

Ohlsson, S. (1996). Learning from performance errors. *Psychological Review*, *103*(2), 241–262. DOI: 10.1037/0033-295X.103.2.241

Pea, R. D. (1986). Language-independent conceptual "bugs" in novice programming. *Journal of Educational Computing Research*, *2*(1), 25–36. DOI: 10.2190/689T-1R2A-X4W4-29J2

Renkl, A. (2014). Toward an instructionally oriented theory of example-based learning. *Cognitive Science*, *38*(1), 1–37. DOI: 10.1111/cogs.12086 PMID: 24070563

Ritchhart, R., Church, M., & Morrison, K. (2011). *Making thinking visible: How to promote engagement, understanding, and independence for all learners*. Jossey-Bass.

Robins, A., Rountree, J., & Rountree, N. (2003). Learning and teaching programming: A review and discussion. *Computer Science Education*, *13*(2), 137–172. DOI: 10.1076/csed.13.2.137.14200

Schraw, G. (1998). Promoting general metacognitive awareness. *Instructional Science*, *26*(1–2), 113–125. DOI: 10.1023/A:1003044231033

Sorva, J. (2013). Notional machines and introductory programming education. *ACM Transactions on Computing Education*, *13*(2), 8. Advance online publication. DOI: 10.1145/2483710.2483713

Vygotsky, L. S. (1978). *Mind in society: The development of higher psychological processes*. Harvard University Press.

Winslow, L. E. (1996). Programming pedagogy; A psychological overview. *SIGCSE Bulletin*, *28*(3), 17–22. DOI: 10.1145/234867.234872

Chapter 4
Translational Explanation:
Explaining Computing Concepts Across Disciplines

Huahua Chen
http://orcid.org/0009-0008-3804-4734
Department of English and Applied Linguistics, Hong Kong Polytechnic University, Hong Kong

ABSTRACT

Effective teaching in interdisciplinary computing classrooms requires more than technical accuracy; it requires translational explanation, a pedagogical process that renders computational concepts intelligible across disciplinary boundaries while preserving rigor. This chapter argues that explanation must bridge the formal structures of computing and the diverse disciplinary worlds students inhabit. A five-step framework is proposed for constructing translational explanations, and discipline-specific models are provided for engineering, health sciences, design, business, linguistics, and biology students. Attention is given to language, multimodal representation, and visual design, alongside guidelines for evaluating explanation quality and building institutional capacity for translational teaching. The chapter concludes by positioning translational explanation as a foundational form of interdisciplinary bridgework.

DOI: 10.4018/979-8-2600-1811-8.ch004

1. INTRODUCTION

1.1 Explanation as a Pedagogical Bridge

Explanation lies at the heart of teaching. In every discipline, students rely on explanations to move from unfamiliarity to understanding, from confusion to structure, and from passive exposure to active interpretation. In computing education, however, explanation performs an especially consequential role because the subject is often experienced by learners as abstract, compressed, and linguistically dense. Concepts such as recursion, iteration, state, abstraction, data structures, and algorithmic logic are not always intuitively accessible, particularly to learners whose prior disciplinary training lies elsewhere. In such contexts, explanation is not merely a verbal supplement to content delivery; it is the bridge through which students cross into computational understanding.

This chapter argues that explanation in interdisciplinary computing classrooms must be more than technically correct. It must be **translational**. That is, explanation must preserve the conceptual integrity of computing while enabling learners from different disciplinary backgrounds to connect new ideas to familiar ways of thinking, seeing, and reasoning. A technically precise explanation can still fail pedagogically if students cannot enter it. Conversely, an accessible explanation can become misleading if it simplifies away the conceptual core. Translational explanation is therefore an art of pedagogical mediation: it does not dilute computing, but redesigns the path by which learners reach it.

Explanation has often been treated as a generic teaching skill; something any knowledgeable teacher naturally does. Yet research in teaching and learning suggests otherwise. Effective explanation depends on understanding learners' prior knowledge, likely misconceptions, cognitive load, language demands, and conceptual bottlenecks (Chi et al., 1994; Mayer, 2004; Shulman, 1986). In interdisciplinary settings, it also depends on recognizing that a concept "sounds different" depending on the learner's disciplinary orientation. A loop, for instance, may feel like repetitive sensing to an engineering student, iterative pattern-making to a design student, repeated rule application to a linguistics student, or an ongoing measurement routine to a biology student. The underlying computational principle does not change, but the explanatory pathway should.

Seen in this way, explanation becomes not only a communication act but a form of educational design. It links theory to learner experience, formal abstraction to recognizable purpose, and computing language to discipline-specific meaning. This chapter explores that work in depth.

1.2 Why Disciplinary Translation Matters in Computing Education

The expansion of computing across higher education has dramatically widened the range of students who encounter programming and computational thinking. Computing is now relevant not only to computer science majors, but also to students in health, biology, engineering, business, architecture, design, humanities, social sciences, and emerging interdisciplinary programs. This shift has transformed the classroom. Many computing courses now enroll learners who do not initially identify as "technical," who possess highly varied prior knowledge, and who judge the value of the subject in relation to very different disciplinary futures.

In such classrooms, explanation must do more than define terms and demonstrate syntax. It must connect computational concepts to students' existing intellectual resources. Without such translation, computing risks being experienced as an externally imposed technical language rather than a meaningful tool for thought and action. Students may ask, implicitly or explicitly: Why does this matter for what I study? How should I understand this if I do not already think like a computer scientist? What in my existing knowledge can help me make sense of this new abstraction?

Disciplinary translation matters because prior knowledge is not uniform. Research on learning consistently shows that new knowledge is interpreted through what learners already know (Bransford et al., 2000; Ausubel, 1968). In interdisciplinary classrooms, prior knowledge differs not only in amount but in structure. Students bring different schemas, examples, problem framings, and professional imaginaries. A concept explained in ways natural to one disciplinary culture may feel obscure in another. If instruction assumes a single universal explanatory pathway, it privileges learners already closest to the teacher's own disciplinary perspective.

Disciplinary translation also matters because relevance influences motivation. Expectancy-value theory suggests that learners engage more deeply when they see both the possibility of success and the value of the task (Eccles & Wigfield, 2002). A computing explanation that connects to a student's disciplinary interests does not merely decorate the content; it signals utility, legitimacy, and purpose. It tells learners that computing is not alien to their field, but available for use within it.

Student reflections frequently illustrate this effect. One data science student noted that slides containing "graphs for visualisation, analogies, and examples for illustration" made learning more accessible and engaging, while a design-oriented learner described how classroom explanation made computing feel like "a natural next step" toward research and innovation rather than a disconnected requirement. These responses suggest that translation is not incidental. It shapes how learners interpret the subject's accessibility and significance.

1.3 From Technical Correctness to Conceptual Accessibility

A central challenge in computing education is that technical correctness is often mistaken for explanatory adequacy. An instructor may define a loop accurately, describe a function precisely, or explain recursion formally, yet students may still fail to understand. This happens because conceptual accessibility is not guaranteed by correctness alone. Technical explanations can remain inaccessible when they rely on dense terminology, skip tacit inferential steps, overload working memory, or fail to connect with learners' prior knowledge (Mayer, 2004; Sweller, 1988).

This distinction between correctness and accessibility is especially important in interdisciplinary classrooms. The issue is not whether computing should remain rigorous; it must. The issue is whether rigor is being confused with opacity. Explanations that are too compressed, too insider-oriented, or too abstract too early can create the impression that complexity itself is the mark of academic seriousness. But in practice, such explanations often widen inequity by rewarding only students who already possess suitable interpretive resources.

Translational explanation seeks a more productive balance. It begins by identifying the underlying computational principle, then frames that principle through language, contexts, and representations that learners can enter, and finally returns learners to the formal structure of the concept. In this sense, translational explanation is neither simplification nor mere analogy. It is a structured pedagogical movement from accessibility toward rigor.

This systemic barrier is heavily compounded by what educational psychologists term the *expert blind spot* (Nathan & Petrosino, 2003). As instructors achieve advanced expertise in computer science, their pedagogical content knowledge frequently undergoes a process of encapsulation. Complex operations, multi-layered syntax abstractions, and structural dependencies that once required deliberate, slow cognitive processing become compressed into monolithic mental chunks. Consequently, when an expert views a block of code, they do not consciously experience the operational steps required to interpret it; they perceive its holistic function instantly.

When translating this code for interdisciplinary novices, the expert instructor frequently omits the fundamental, intermediate sub-steps of execution, assuming them to be universally intuitive. For a non-technical student, however, every token, punctuation mark, and implicit state change demands a discrete application of attention. When the instructor skips these tacit steps in favor of a clean, high-level technical summary, an instructional void opens. The student is left trying to mimic the expert's holistic conclusions without possessing the structural roadmap required to generate those conclusions independently. Mitigating this blind spot requires instructors to intentionally de-encapsulate their own knowledge structures, methodically unpacking the micro-steps of program execution that technical correctness takes for granted but conceptual accessibility fundamentally requires.

This chapter develops that movement. Section 2 defines translational explanation and distinguishes it from simplification. Section 3 identifies barriers to cross-disciplinary explanation. Section 4 proposes a framework for constructing translational explanations. Section 5 provides discipline-specific explanation models. Section 6 examines language, representation, and multimodal explanation. Section 7 explores how explanation quality can be evaluated, and Section 8 offers design guidelines for instructors. The chapter concludes by positioning translational explanation as a core form of interdisciplinary bridgework and a foundation for later discussions of support, scaffolding, and psychological safety.

2. WHAT MAKES AN EXPLANATION TRANSLATIONAL?

2.1 Defining Translational Explanation

Translational explanation may be defined as the pedagogical process of rendering a concept intelligible across disciplinary, linguistic, and experiential differences while preserving its essential structure and rigor. In computing education, translational explanation helps learners from varied fields understand computational ideas by linking those ideas to familiar conceptual anchors, recognizable practices, or learner-accessible representations.

Three elements are central to this definition. First, translational explanation is **relational**: it depends on who the learners are, what they already know, and what disciplinary assumptions they bring. Second, it is **concept-preserving**: it does not change the computational principle itself, only the explanatory route into it. Third, it is **bridging**: it moves between the formal language of computing and other domains of meaning rather than remaining confined to either one.

This concept builds on longstanding work in pedagogy, especially Shulman's (1986, 1987) notion of pedagogical content knowledge, which emphasizes that expert teaching involves not only knowing a subject but knowing how to represent it in ways comprehensible to learners. It also aligns with work on analogical reasoning, prior knowledge activation, and knowledge recontextualization (Gentner, 1983; Glynn, 2008; Vosniadou, 1994). In interdisciplinary classrooms, however, translational explanation acquires added importance because the range of learner backgrounds is larger and more consequential.

A translational explanation therefore does not merely "make things easier." It makes them *approachable without being distorted*. A design student and a biology student may require different conceptual entry points into the idea of iteration, but both must eventually understand the same computational logic of repeated execution governed by explicit conditions or ranges. Translation occurs in the route, not in the truth of the concept.

2.2 Translation Versus Simplification

A common misunderstanding is to equate translation with simplification. While simplification may sometimes be part of explanation, the two are not synonymous. Simplification reduces complexity, often by omitting detail. Translation, by contrast, re-expresses complexity in a form that is more accessible to a particular audience while maintaining conceptual fidelity.

This difference is crucial in computing education. If a recursive function is explained simply as "a function that repeats itself," the explanation may be easy to hear but conceptually weak. It misses the role of self-reference, base cases, and problem reduction. By contrast, a translational explanation might begin with a familiar recursive pattern, such as nested design motifs or self-similar branching structures, then connect that pattern back to the formal logic of self-calling functions with termination conditions. Here the concept is not trivialized; it is entered from a more accessible point.

Research on conceptual change and analogical instruction suggests that oversimplified explanations can create robust misconceptions if learners form the wrong mental model early (Chi, 2008; Duit & Treagust, 2003). Thus, explanation must be accessible without becoming conceptually careless. Translation is not the removal of difficulty; it is the redesign of the learner's pathway through difficulty.

To formalize this distinction between translation and simplification, educators can look to the concept of *semantic waves* derived from Legitimation Code Theory (Maton, 2013). This framework tracks two distinct dimensions of knowledge: semantic gravity (the degree to which meaning is tied to its concrete, empirical context) and semantic density (the condensation of meaning within symbols, terms, or concepts). Superficial simplification merely lowers semantic density by stripping away technical complexity and anchoring the discussion permanently in a high semantic gravity environment; meaning the lesson stays trapped within an everyday story or a casual analogy.

True translational explanation, by contrast, executes a deliberate semantic wave. It begins at the peak of high abstraction and low semantic gravity (the formal computing principle). It then downshifts systematically, increasing semantic gravity by translating that abstract concept into a contextualized, discipline-specific anchor that students can readily grasp. Crucially, the explanation does not terminate at the bottom of the wave. A weak pedagogy leaves students stranded in the analogy; translational pedagogy completes the wave by riding it back upward. It uses the concrete anchor as momentum to return to high semantic density, systematically reintroducing the technical vocabulary, syntax rules, and formal architectures of the computing domain. By intentionally constructing these complete semantic waves, the instructor ensures that the discipline-specific context serves as an escalator to rigorous, abstract computational literacy rather than a permanent substitute for it.

2.3 Preserving Rigor While Increasing Accessibility

The greatest strength of translational explanation lies in its refusal to frame rigor and accessibility as opposites. In many technical subjects, there is an implicit assumption that if an explanation is easily understood, it must have become less rigorous. This assumption is pedagogically damaging. In reality, inaccessible explanations often produce superficial imitation rather than deep understanding. Accessibility, when well designed, is what allows rigor to be meaningfully encountered.

Preserving rigor requires that the explanatory process return learners to the formal structure of the concept. If explanation remains only at the level of familiar context, students may enjoy the example but fail to acquire computational understanding. Effective translation therefore involves movement: from familiar anchor to underlying principle, from principle to formal representation, and from representation back to application. The explanation must be transparent about where the analogy holds, where it does not, and what the technical language ultimately means.

For instance, when explaining a conditional structure to a health sciences student through the logic of diagnostic decision pathways, the teacher should eventually state clearly that in code, the program does not "reason clinically." It evaluates Boolean expressions in a formal sequence. The analogy supports entry; the formalism secures rigor.

2.4 Risks of Weak Analogy and Oversimplification

Not all explanation that sounds accessible is pedagogically sound. Weak analogies can obscure more than they clarify. If the mapped example and the computational concept do not share meaningful structural similarity, learners may transfer the wrong features and build fragile understanding (Gentner, 1983). A loop compared only to "doing something again and again" may be too vague to help students understand control flow, indexing, or termination. Likewise, a stack explained only as "a pile of things" may fail to capture the critical LIFO property.

Oversimplification can also hide the very aspects students need to learn. If explanations avoid technical language entirely, students may feel temporarily comfortable but remain excluded from the discourse of the field. Epistemic access requires that learners eventually engage formal terminology and structure, not be permanently shielded from them (Morrow, 2009).

A further risk is false familiarity. Students may believe they understand because the example feels familiar, while not actually grasping the computational principle. This creates an illusion of comprehension. Teachers must therefore check whether learners can move from the familiar context back into formal reasoning.

3. BARRIERS TO CROSS-DISCIPLINARY EXPLANATION

3.1 Vocabulary Mismatch

Computing is full of terms that are ordinary in one context and technical in another: function, object, class, argument, exception, recursion, state, stack, queue, and model, to name only a few. For students outside computing, such terms can be misleading, especially when every day and technical meanings diverge. Vocabulary mismatch becomes a barrier when students think they understand a term because they know it colloquially, while missing its disciplinary meaning.

This issue is intensified in interdisciplinary classrooms because students may bring strong disciplinary uses of related terms. For example, a "model" means something rather different in fashion, biology, economics, and machine learning. A "function" carries different connotations in mathematics, linguistics, and programming. Good translational explanation anticipates such collisions. It does not assume that a technical definition automatically displaces prior meanings.

Research on disciplinary literacy and academic language emphasizes that learners need explicit support in entering specialized vocabulary systems (Shanahan & Shanahan, 2008). In computing education, this means carefully distinguishing technical usage, explaining terms through examples, and checking whether students have mapped the meaning correctly.

3.2 Disciplinary Assumptions and Prior Schemas

Explanations fail when they assume a schema the learner does not possess. A teacher might explain arrays through mathematical vectors, expecting the learner to find the comparison illuminating. For some students that works; for others, especially those from non-quantitative backgrounds, it simply relocates confusion. Likewise, a teacher may explain recursion through mathematical induction, which is efficient for some learners but inaccessible to many others.

Prior schema shape how explanations are interpreted (Ausubel, 1968; Bransford et al., 2000). In interdisciplinary classrooms, the challenge is not that learners lack schemas, but that their schemas differ. A design student may think visually and iteratively, a health student procedurally and diagnostically, a linguistics student rule-wise, and a business student structurally and organizationally. Similarly, a civil engineering or construction management student may look at software architecture purely as an anchor for environmental analytics and site risk mitigation (Mohammed et al., 2026). If explanation fails to connect with these schemas, students may experience the concept as excessively abstract even when they are fully capable of understanding it.

3.3 Symbolic Density and Abstraction Overload

Computing explanations often compress large amounts of information into symbolic form. A few lines of code may encode multiple conditions, transformations, and assumptions. To experts, this density is efficient; to novices, it can be overwhelming. Symbolic density becomes especially problematic when introduced before conceptual grounding. Learners are asked to decode syntax and meaning simultaneously, often while also interpreting unfamiliar task contexts.

Cognitive load theory helps explain why this becomes a barrier (Sweller, 1988; van Merriënboer & Sweller, 2005). If learners must process too many novel elements at once, explanation becomes ineffective not because the concept is impossible, but because working memory is overloaded. Translational explanation therefore often requires staged entry: beginning with accessible language or representation, then progressively introducing formal notation once conceptual structure is clearer.

This structural overload is further aggravated because novices must simultaneously process two distinct categories of cognitive demands: *syntactic cognitive load* and *conceptual logic load*. For an experienced computer scientist, the syntax of a language; such as matching brackets, terminal semicolons, or indentation constraints; is completely automated and places negligible demands on working memory. The expert's cognitive capacity is preserved entirely for solving the core logical or algorithmic problem.

For the interdisciplinary novice, however, these two distinct tasks compete aggressively for identical, highly limited working memory resources (Sweller, 1988). While the student is actively trying to reason through the conditional flow or structural transformation of a dataset, they are simultaneously forced to expend significant mental energy tracking commas, casing rules, and structural punctuation. If an instructor presents a highly dense, symbolic code block prematurely, the extraneous cognitive load imposed by decoding unfamiliar syntax completely eclipses the germane cognitive load required to comprehend the underlying computational logic. The student's working memory experiences an immediate bottleneck, resulting in cognitive paralysis. To mitigate this barrier, translational explanation must partition these loads, exposing the conceptual logic through pseudocode, natural language, or visual maps before forcing the learner to negotiate the unforgiving syntax constraints of a production programming language.

3.4 Relevance Perception and Motivation Barriers

Even a technically and cognitively well-designed explanation can fail if students do not perceive the concept as relevant. In interdisciplinary classrooms, relevance cannot be assumed. A student from spatial data science, fashion, architecture, or applied biology may not initially see why learning about functions, loops, or data structures matters for their field. If explanation remains detached from disciplinary purpose, motivation may weaken and attention may fragment.

Expectancy-value theory suggests that students are more likely to invest effort when they see utility and attainment value in what they are learning (Eccles & Wigfield, 2002). Translational explanation addresses this by linking concepts to domain-recognizable forms of action and reasoning. Such relevance is not motivational sugar. It is part of how learners decide that understanding is worth the cognitive effort.

4. FRAMEWORK FOR TRANSLATIONAL EXPLANATION

This section proposes a five-step framework for constructing translational explanations in interdisciplinary computing classrooms. The framework is not a rigid formula but a design heuristic that helps instructors move from concept to learner-accessible explanation without losing rigor.

4.1 Identifying the Underlying Computational Principle

The first step is to identify the irreducible computational principle behind the topic. Before designing examples or analogies, the teacher must ask: What is the core idea here? What must remain intact no matter how the concept is explained?

For a loop, the principle might be repeated execution under defined conditions or across a sequence. For a conditional, it might be branch selection based on Boolean evaluation. For recursion, self-reference plus problem reduction plus a base case. For a data structure, organized storage enabling particular operations and trade-offs. Without this clarity, explanatory translation risks wandering into context-rich but conceptually thin territory.

This step is essential because translational teaching is not simply learner-centered improvisation. It begins with disciplined conceptual analysis. The teacher must know what cannot be lost.

4.2 Mapping to Disciplinary Analogies

The second step is to identify one or more disciplinary anchors that share a meaningful structural resemblance to the computational principle. These anchors should not merely be familiar; they should map in a way that supports understanding of the target concept.

For example:

- Iteration may map to repeated sensor sampling in engineering.
- Conditional branching may map to diagnostic pathways in health.
- Recursive patterning may map to self-similar design generation.
- Rule-based logic may map to grammar constraints in linguistics.
- Data organization may map to inventory or customer record systems in business.

The point is not to create separate truths for separate disciplines, but to help learners access the same principle through different conceptual doors.

4.3 Reframing Through Learner-Familiar Contexts

Once an appropriate anchor is identified, the explanation should be reframed in language and context the learner finds familiar. This may involve everyday wording, contextual examples, visual scenarios, or narrativized task framings. The goal is to lower the entry barrier, not by reducing the concept's depth, but by reducing unnecessary interpretive distance.

For instance, a conditional can be introduced as "a system deciding what to do next based on what it detects," before formal if-elif-else syntax is shown. A stack can be described in terms of access order before formal implementation details are introduced. Reframing is especially important when students are early in the learning process and still building confidence.

4.4 Returning from Analogy to Technical Formalism

The fourth step is perhaps the most important: return explicitly from the analogy or familiar context to the technical structure of computing. This is where rigor is secured. The teacher should state what the analogy has helped illuminate and what the formal concept actually requires.

For example, after using diagnostic pathways to explain conditionals, the instructor should clarify that the computer evaluates expressions using explicit Boolean logic and follows code order. After using a design motif to explain recursion, the instructor should specify how recursive calls reduce the problem and why a base case prevents infinite recursion. Students must not be left inside the analogy.

This return movement is what distinguishes translational explanation from mere contextualization. It ensures that accessibility leads into disciplinary competence.

4.5 Checking Understanding and Misconceptions

The final step is to verify whether the explanation worked as intended. This requires concept checks that probe more than surface agreement. Can the student restate the concept in technical terms? Can they identify where the analogy breaks down? Can they apply the concept in a new context? Can they distinguish the computational principle from the contextual wrapper?

Explanation is successful only when learners can move beyond the original example. Therefore, feedback loops are essential. Misconceptions should be treated as evidence that the mapping was incomplete, overloaded, or misleading, rather than simply as student failure. The Figure 1 shows effective translational explanation begins with the core computational principle, connects it to learner-accessible disciplinary anchors, returns explicitly to formal computing language, and is refined through checking for understanding and misconception.

Figure 1. Translational Explanation Cycle

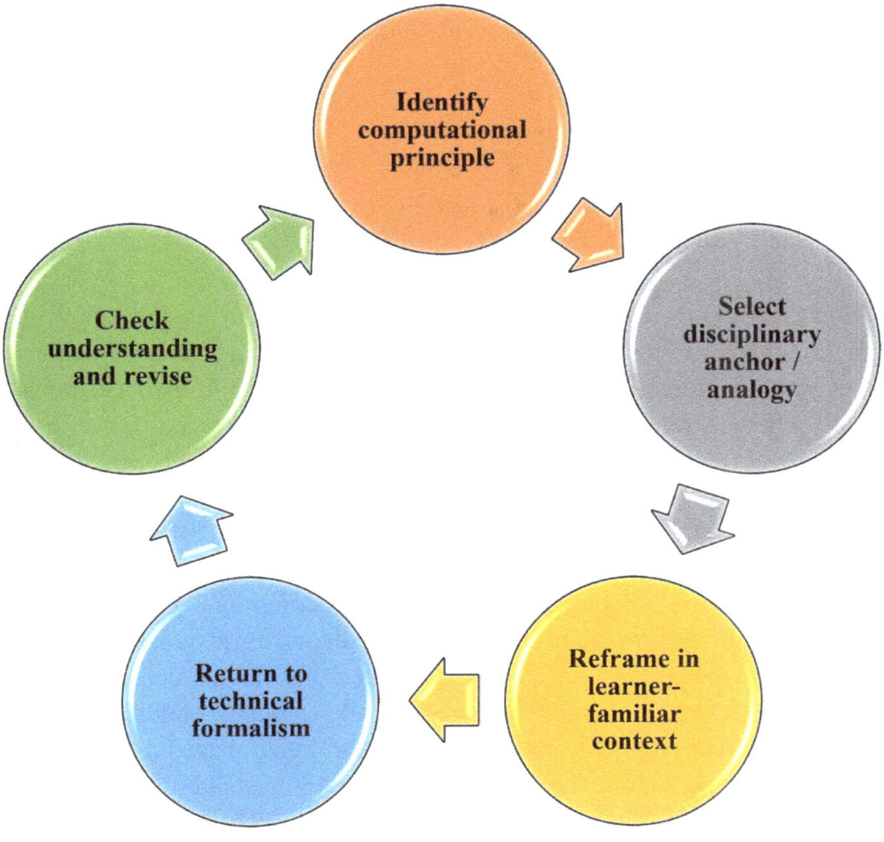

5. DISCIPLINE-SPECIFIC EXPLANATION MODELS

This section offers illustrative models, not exhaustive prescriptions. The goal is to show how computing concepts may be explained translationally to learners from different disciplines while preserving conceptual rigor.

5.1 Explaining Loops to Engineering Students

Engineering students often respond well to systems-based explanation. A loop can be introduced as a process that repeats an operation across time, components, or measurement cycles until a predefined condition is met. For example, an instructor might explain a for loop through the repeated collection of sensor values at regular intervals. Each iteration corresponds to one reading, and the loop structure governs repetition and data handling.

What matters pedagogically is not just the example but the mapping:

- repeated action = iteration
- current measurement count = loop variable
- stop after n samples = range or termination condition
- storing results = accumulation or list updating

After this framing, the teacher should return to formal syntax and show how the engineering scenario corresponds to program execution. Such an explanation works not because it is "practical" in a vague sense, but because it activates a systems-oriented schema already available to many engineering learners.

5.2 Explaining Conditionals to Health Sciences Students

Health sciences students frequently think in terms of observations, thresholds, branching decisions, and intervention pathways. A conditional can therefore be introduced through decision points in screening or diagnosis: if symptom A is present, follow one route; if not, check symptom B; otherwise take a default action. This makes visible the logic of branching and mutually exclusive conditions.

However, it is essential to move beyond the clinical narrative and emphasize formal Boolean evaluation. The computer is not "understanding" symptoms; it is checking whether specific conditions evaluate as true or false. The instructor should also clarify code order, overlap of conditions, and the role of else as a fallback. The health context opens the concept; formal clarification secures it.

5.3 Explaining Recursion to Design and Arts Students

Recursion is often difficult because it requires learners to accept self-reference and repeated reduction without becoming lost. For design and arts students, self-similar patterns, nested motifs, or iterative transformations can provide an accessible starting point. One might explain recursion through a pattern that contains a smaller version of itself, such as repeated branching, nested frames, or generative design forms.

The explanation should then identify the essential recursive components:

- the design contains a smaller instance of the same structure,
- each step reduces scale or complexity,
- the process must stop at a defined smallest unit,

- in code, this is represented by a function calling itself with a smaller input and a base case.

For students who think visually, this explanation can be especially powerful if supported by sketches or diagrams.

5.4 Explaining Data Structures to Business and Management Students

Business and management students often understand organization, categorization, prioritization, and retrieval processes through institutional or operational examples. Lists, queues, stacks, dictionaries, and trees can be explained through workflows such as customer records, service lines, inventory categories, or task priorities.

For example, a queue may be explained through customer service systems in which first-in first-out order matters. A dictionary can be framed as a key-value system like employee ID to employee record. A tree can be linked to organizational hierarchies or category structures. But as always, translation must return to computational trade-offs: why one structure is chosen over another, what operations it supports efficiently, and how access patterns differ.

5.5 Explaining Rule-Based Logic to Linguistics Students

Linguistics students often possess strong intuitions about rule systems, grammatical constraints, pattern application, and symbolic transformation. This makes them well positioned to understand computational logic if explanation draws on familiar linguistic structures. Conditionals can be linked to rule application; pattern matching can be linked to morphological or syntactic structures; finite-state logic can be linked to language-processing sequences.

A linguistics-oriented explanation of rule-based logic might show how a computational rule applies when a certain condition is met, much like a grammatical rule applies in a given environment. The teacher should then clarify that computational rules are explicit, formal, and unambiguous in execution. The learner's disciplinary strength becomes a bridge into coding logic rather than a separate intellectual territory.

5.6 Explaining Sensing and Automation to Biology and Environmental Students

Biology and environmental students often think in terms of monitoring, response, systems interaction, and data interpretation. Concepts such as sensing, automation, loops, and event-driven logic can be explained through ecological monitoring, lab instrumentation, or environmental threshold systems. A sensor repeatedly collecting data can illustrate iteration; threshold-triggered action can illustrate conditionals; automation can illustrate the relationship between input, logic, and output. While these concepts are framed here for environmental contexts, they belong to a broader framework of cross-disciplinary mappings, as detailed in Table 1.

These students may also benefit from explanation that foreground's purpose: why computational logic matters for analyzing change, monitoring conditions, and responding to dynamic systems. Again, the explanation should move from context to formal structure rather than stopping at application alone.

Table 1. Computing Concept to Discipline-Specific Analogy Map

Computing Concept	Underlying Principle	Discipline-Specific Entry Example
Loop	Repeated execution under a rule	Sensor sampling in engineering
Conditional	Branching based on evaluated condition	Diagnostic pathway in health sciences
Recursion	Self-reference with reduction and base case	Nested pattern generation in design
Data structure	Organized storage for operations	Customer record systems in business
Rule-based logic	Formal rule application	Grammar constraints in linguistics
Sensing/automation	Input-logic-output interaction	Environmental monitoring in biology

6. LANGUAGE, REPRESENTATION, AND MULTIMODAL EXPLANATION

6.1 Everyday Language and Formal Language

One of the most delicate tasks in translational explanation is balancing everyday language with formal language. Everyday language supports accessibility. It gives students a foothold in meaning before technical precision is required. Formal language supports disciplinary rigor. It enables students to participate in the discourse of computing and communicate accurately.

These two forms of language should not be treated as enemies. Effective teaching moves between them. An instructor may first explain iteration as "doing the same step repeatedly under a rule," then connect that to the formal definition of a loop. Or explain a variable as "a named place that stores a changing value," then show how assignment updates state in code. This movement is crucial because if teaching stays only in everyday language, students may never gain technical fluency; if it stays only in formal language, many learners may never gain initial understanding.

6.2 Visual, Narrative, and Procedural Explanation Forms

Explanations in computing need not be purely verbal. Visual explanation can reveal structure through diagrams, annotated code, flow pathways, and state change illustrations. Narrative explanation can contextualize a concept through a meaningful scenario or sequence of events. Procedural explanation can break a process into steps that learners can follow and internalize.

Research on multimedia learning suggests that appropriately coordinated verbal and visual representations improve understanding, especially when they reduce extraneous load and support coherent integration (Mayer, 2021). For interdisciplinary learners, multimodal explanation can widen access because different students may enter meaning through different channels. A design student may respond strongly to visual structure, a business student to procedural organization, a biology student to process narrative, and a linguistics student to rule description.

This multimodal approach finds its theoretical foundation in Paivio's (1986) *dual-coding theory*, which demonstrates that working memory processes visual and verbal information through separate, parallel channels. When a translational explanation utilizes synchronized visual diagrams alongside verbal narratives, it expands the student's total cognitive processing capacity, facilitating deeper mental integration. Within computing education, this visualization is most effective when it takes the form of a *notional machine* (Sorva, 2013); an idealized, schematic depiction of the computer's internal behavior that explains the execution of code artifacts.

Novices frequently struggle because code is textually static, whereas program execution is dynamically fluid; the text remains unchanged on the screen while variables, call stacks, and pointers shift invisibly in memory. A well-designed notional machine serves as a visual translational interface. By explicitly drawing out a variable as an annotated container, the stack as a physical chamber where frames drop down, or a pointer as a physical arrow linking two memory locations, the instructor materializes these invisible operations. This visual framework prevents students from constructing highly erratic, fragmented mental models of execution. When a design student sees execution memory represented as spatial arrangements, or a business student views data flows mapped out like operational supply chains, the textual code ceases to be a mysterious incantation and becomes a predictable sequence of structural transformations.

6.3 Gesture, Boardwork, and Slide Design

Explanation is also embodied and material. Gesture, pacing, whiteboard organization, and slide design shape comprehension. An instructor pointing to branches while describing a conditional, spacing code to reveal structure, or using the board to map input–process–output relationships can materially improve understanding. Conversely, overcrowded slides, poor visual hierarchy, or inconsistent notation can undermine even a verbally strong explanation.

Students frequently notice these details. One learner reported that clear slides containing graphs, examples, and visual elements improved the learning experience significantly. This suggests that translational explanation is not confined to spoken words; it is also built into representational design.

6.4 AI-Supported Personalized Explanation

Although adaptive systems will be discussed more fully in Chapter 7, it is worth noting here that AI-supported explanation raises new possibilities for translational pedagogy. Personalized systems may eventually provide alternative examples, layered explanation levels, or discipline-sensitive prompts based on learner profile and previous responses. However, the pedagogical principle remains the same: explanation must preserve conceptual accuracy while adapting entry points. Technology can scale translation, but it cannot replace the conceptual care required to design it well.

7. EVALUATING EXPLANATION QUALITY

7.1 Indicators of Successful Translational Explanation

A translational explanation can be considered successful when students can do more than restate the analogy that introduced it. Several indicators are especially useful:

1. **Conceptual restatement**: students can explain the computational principle in their own words.
2. **Formal re-entry**: students can connect the familiar example back to code or technical terminology.
3. **Transfer**: students can apply the concept in a new but related task.
4. **Misconception resistance**: students do not overgeneralize the analogy in misleading ways.
5. **Increased participation**: more students ask meaningful questions or offer explanations.

These indicators align with broader research on meaningful learning and self-explanation (Chi et al., 1994; Renkl, 2014).

7.2 Student Response Patterns and Concept Checks

Concept checks are essential because students often appear to understand an explanation when they have only recognized the familiar example. Useful checks include asking students to predict behavior, choose between similar code patterns, identify where an analogy stops applying, or explain the concept to a peer from another discipline.

Student response patterns can also reveal explanation quality. If students can answer routine examples but fail when the context changes, the explanation may have remained too local. If they remember the story but not the logic, the explanation may have been engaging but insufficiently formalized.

7.3 Explanation Failures and How to Detect Them

Explanation failures are common and should be treated diagnostically. Signs of failure include:

- students repeating vocabulary without being able to explain it,
- consistent confusion around the same concept across multiple cohorts,
- learners relying on memorized phrases rather than reasoning,
- transfer failure to slightly changed tasks,
- students asking questions that reveal the analogy has replaced rather than supported the concept.

These failures often indicate one of several problems: the analogy was too weak, the explanation skipped inferential steps, symbolic load was too high, or the return to formalism was insufficient.

7.4 Reflective Revision of Explanations

Good explanations are revised explanations. Instructors should treat student misunderstanding as evidence about the explanation itself. If many students misread a concept, the issue may not be only their effort but the explanatory route provided. Evidence from quizzes, tutorials, lab questions, and student comments can help identify which concepts require redesigned explanations.

This reflective stance aligns with the broader evidence-informed pedagogy discussed later in the book. Explanations should be tested, refined, and diversified over time, especially in large interdisciplinary courses where one cohort's needs may differ from another's. To assist in this diagnostic process, Table 2 categorizes common explanation pitfalls alongside targeted corrective strategies.

Table 2. Common Explanation Pitfalls and Corrective Strategies

Pitfall	Likely Consequence	Corrective Strategy
Overly abstract explanation	Student disengagement or confusion	Start with accessible context, then formalize
Weak analogy	Misconception or false mapping	Use structurally aligned analogies only
Staying only in everyday language	Lack of technical fluency	Reintroduce formal terminology explicitly
Too much symbolic density too early	Cognitive overload	Stage representation and reduce extraneous load
No concept check	Illusion of understanding	Use transfer-oriented follow-up questions

8. DESIGN GUIDELINES FOR INSTRUCTORS

8.1 Building an Explanation Bank by Discipline

One practical strategy is to create an explanation bank organized by concept and discipline. For each major computing idea, instructors can maintain:

- the underlying computational principle,
- common novice misconceptions,
- one or more discipline-sensitive entry examples,
- the formal terminology to be introduced,
- a quick concept check,
- known limitations of the analogy.

Over time, such a bank becomes a valuable teaching resource, especially in courses with recurring interdisciplinary diversity.

8.2 Using Student Background Data Ethically

To explain translationally, instructors need some sense of who their learners are. Background information on discipline, prior exposure, and goals can help tailor examples. However, this should be done ethically. Instructors should avoid stereotyping students or assuming that all students from one discipline think identically. Background data should inform flexible explanation options, not rigid categorization.

8.3 Explanation Design for Large and Mixed Classes

In large classes, it is often impossible to produce a unique explanation for every learner in real time. Instead, instructors can design layered explanation:

- start with a universally accessible everyday explanation,
- add one or two discipline-sensitive examples,
- return to formal language,
- provide optional supplementary examples in notes or slides.

This "mass personalization through layered explanation" can help diverse learners find an entry point without fragmenting the whole class.

8.4 Training Faculty in Translational Explanation

Translational explanation should be treated as a professional teaching capability, not a natural talent some instructors simply possess. Faculty development can include:

- identifying threshold concepts and common misconceptions,
- practicing analogy design,
- learning how to move from context back to formalism,
- reviewing student misunderstandings as evidence,
- building shared explanation banks across departments.

As computing becomes more interdisciplinary, this capacity will only grow in importance.

9. CONCLUSION

9.1 Translational Explanation as Interdisciplinary Bridgework

This chapter has argued that explanation in interdisciplinary computing education is both an art and a science. It is an art because it requires pedagogical judgment, sensitivity to learner background, representational creativity, and careful linguistic design. It is a science because it can be grounded in research on prior knowledge, conceptual change, cognitive load, analogy, and pedagogy. In such settings, explanation must do more than define. It must translate.

Translational explanation is best understood as bridgework. It connects the formal structure of computing to the varied disciplinary worlds students inhabit. It preserves rigor while widening access. It uses familiar contexts without becoming trapped inside them. It helps students move from "I do not understand this field" to "I can see how this idea works and why it matters."

This bridgework is especially important in higher education environments where computing is increasingly encountered by students whose futures lie in diverse professions and intellectual communities. To teach computing well in such contexts is not to water it down. It is to teach it so that more students can genuinely enter it.

9.2 Transition to Support, Scaffolding, and Psychological Safety

Yet explanation alone is not enough. Even strong translational explanations do not automatically ensure persistence, confidence, or sustained progress. Students also require environments that support challenge without intimidation, feedback without shame, and structured progression without dependence. The next chapter therefore turns from explanation to the broader ecology of learning support: adaptive assistance, scaffolded challenge, and psychological safety in multidisciplinary computing classrooms.

REFERENCES

Ausubel, D. P. (1968). *Educational psychology: A cognitive view*. Holt, Rinehart and Winston.

Bransford, J. D., Brown, A. L., & Cocking, R. R. (Eds.). (2000). *How people learn: Brain, mind, experience, and school* (Expanded ed.). National Academy Press.

Chi, M. T. H. (2008). Three types of conceptual change: Belief revision, mental model transformation, and categorical shift. In Vosniadou, S. (Ed.), *International handbook of research on conceptual change* (pp. 61–82). Routledge.

Chi, M. T. H., de Leeuw, N., Chiu, M.-H., & LaVancher, C. (1994). Eliciting self-explanations improves understanding. *Cognitive Science*, *18*(3), 439–477. DOI: 10.1207/s15516709cog1803_3

Duit, R., & Treagust, D. F. (2003). Conceptual change: A powerful framework for improving science teaching and learning. *International Journal of Science Education*, *25*(6), 671–688. DOI: 10.1080/09500690305016

Eccles, J. S., & Wigfield, A. (2002). Motivational beliefs, values, and goals. *Annual Review of Psychology*, *53*(1), 109–132. DOI: 10.1146/annurev.psych.53.100901.135153 PMID: 11752481

Gentner, D. (1983). Structure-mapping: A theoretical framework for analogy. *Cognitive Science*, *7*(2), 155–170. DOI: 10.1207/s15516709cog0702_3

Glynn, S. M. (2008). Making science concepts meaningful to students: Teaching with analogies. In Mikelskis-Seifert, S., Ringelband, U., & Brückmann, M. (Eds.), *Four decades of research in science education; From curriculum development to quality improvement* (pp. 113–125). Waxmann.

Maton, K. (2013). Making semantic waves: A key to cumulative knowledge-building. *Linguistics and Education*, *24*(1), 8–22. DOI: 10.1016/j.linged.2012.11.005

Mayer, R. E. (2004). Should there be a three-strikes rule against pure discovery learning? *The American Psychologist*, *59*(1), 14–19. DOI: 10.1037/0003-066X.59.1.14 PMID: 14736316

Mayer, R. E. (2021). *Multimedia learning* (3rd ed.). Cambridge University Press.

Mohammed, A., & Zangana, H. (Eds.). (2026). *Intelligent Construction Monitoring Systems: Real-Time Safety, Environmental Prediction, and Risk Management*. IGI Global Scientific Publishing., DOI: 10.4018/979-8-3373-9245-5

Morrow, W. (2009). *Bounds of democracy: Epistemological access in higher education.* Human Sciences Research Council Press.

Nathan, M. J., & Petrosino, A. J. (2003). Expert blind spots in the education of preservice teachers. *American Educational Research Journal, 40*(4), 905–928. DOI: 10.3102/00028312040004905

Paivio, A. (1986). *Mental representations: A dual coding approach.* Oxford University Press.

Renkl, A. (2014). Toward an instructionally oriented theory of example-based learning. *Cognitive Science, 38*(1), 1–37. DOI: 10.1111/cogs.12086 PMID: 24070563

Shanahan, T., & Shanahan, C. (2008). Teaching disciplinary literacy to adolescents: Rethinking content-area literacy. *Harvard Educational Review, 78*(1), 40–59. DOI: 10.17763/haer.78.1.v62444321p602101

Shulman, L. S. (1986). Those who understand: Knowledge growth in teaching. *Educational Researcher, 15*(2), 4–14. DOI: 10.3102/0013189X015002004

Shulman, L. S. (1987). Knowledge and teaching: Foundations of the new reform. *Harvard Educational Review, 57*(1), 1–23. DOI: 10.17763/haer.57.1.j463w79r56455411

Sorva, J. (2013). Notional machines and learner misconceptions in introductory programming. [TOCE]. *ACM Transactions on Computing Education, 13*(2), 1–25. DOI: 10.1145/2483710.2483713

Sweller, J. (1988). Cognitive load during problem solving: Effects on learning. *Cognitive Science, 12*(2), 257–285. DOI: 10.1207/s15516709cog1202_4

Van Merriënboer, J. J. G., & Sweller, J. (2005). Cognitive load theory and complex learning: Recent developments and future directions. *Educational Psychology Review, 17*(2), 147–177. DOI: 10.1007/s10648-005-3951-0

Vosniadou, S. (1994). Capturing and modeling the process of conceptual change. *Learning and Instruction, 4*(1), 45–69. https://doi.org/Vygotsky, L. S. (1978). *Mind in society: The development of higher psychological processes.* Harvard University Press.DOI: 10.1016/0959-4752(94)90018-3

Chapter 5
Adaptive Support, Scaffolded Challenge, and Psychological Safety in Multidisciplinary Computing Classrooms

Kam Yung Yang
http://orcid.org/0009-0006-2455-4085
School of Fashion and Textiles, The Hong Kong Polytechnic University, Hong Kong

ABSTRACT

This chapter per the authors argues for deliberate, design-driven support in multidisciplinary computing classrooms, articulating how scaffolded challenge and psychologically safe environments enable rigorous learning for diverse student cohorts. It outlines how support structures; low-stakes checks, guided examples, visible reasoning, progressive tasks, and flexible consultation; can reduce cognitive load while maintaining high standards, thereby promoting belonging and persistence. The chapter integrates theory from motivation and social-cognitive perspectives with practical guidance on assessment, feedback, governance, and ethical considerations, and offers design principles and evaluative prompts to inform researchers and practitioners aiming to foster equitable, high-quality learning across disciplines.

DOI: 10.4018/979-8-2600-1811-8.ch005

1. INTRODUCTION

1.1 Why Support Systems Matter in Interdisciplinary Classrooms

As computing expands beyond computer science into engineering, health, design, business, humanities, architecture, biology, and other fields, the introductory computing classroom has changed in both composition and purpose. It is no longer a space populated only by learners who have already chosen technical identity as a central part of their academic path. Increasingly, it is a mixed classroom in which students arrive with varied prior exposure to programming, sharply different levels of confidence, uneven disciplinary relevance, and highly diverse expectations of what learning computing should feel like. In such settings, support is not a peripheral kindness. It is part of the instructional architecture.

The need for support becomes especially visible in foundational programming courses, where many learners are encountering syntax, debugging, abstraction, and algorithmic thinking for the first time. Some students may have coded before and seek challenge; others may have no prior exposure and feel intimidated before the first class begins. Some may come from technical disciplines but still struggle with program logic. Others may possess strong analytical abilities but interpret computing as culturally alien. In a single classroom, then, difficulty does not stem from one source. It emerges from the interaction of cognitive demands, identity, prior knowledge, language, affect, and disciplinary distance.

In these contexts, support must be understood carefully. It does not mean reducing expectations, simplifying all tasks, or protecting students from rigor. Rather, it means constructing conditions under which rigorous learning becomes possible for a more diverse range of students. Support is educationally necessary because without it, many learners are not being challenged fairly; they are simply being filtered by prior familiarity, confidence, or willingness to tolerate uncertainty. A pedagogy that appears rigorous on the surface may in fact be poorly designed if it rewards only those students who already know how to navigate the hidden rules of the subject.

Research across higher education, STEM education, and computing education shows that retention, persistence, and academic confidence are shaped not only by ability but also by learner support, self-efficacy, belonging, and opportunities for early success (Bandura, 1997; Freeman et al., 2014; Margolis & Fisher, 2002; Tinto, 2012). In computing specifically, students often leave or disengage not because they are incapable of learning, but because they interpret normal struggle as personal inadequacy, do not see pathways through difficulty, or experience the classroom as an environment in which confusion is costly to reveal (Barker et al., 2009; Lewis, 2011).

Interdisciplinary classrooms intensify these issues. Learners who are already uncertain about belonging in computing are particularly sensitive to pedagogical design. If the course structure assumes technical fluency, if assessments arrive before understanding stabilizes, if feedback is delayed or opaque, or if students feel that only fast responders are legitimate participants, then many will retreat into silence or imitation. Conversely, when support systems are intentionally designed; through low-stakes checks, guided examples, visible reasoning, progressive tasks, flexible consultation, and psychologically safe participation; students often develop confidence and independence more rapidly than expected.

The role of support is therefore both pedagogical and ethical. It allows the instructor to maintain standards while widening access to those standards. It recognizes that equal treatment is not always equitable treatment, particularly in classrooms where students begin from unequal positions.

1.2 Challenge Without Intimidation

A recurring tension in technical education concerns the relationship between challenge and support. Many educators worry, sometimes understandably, that increased support may reduce rigor. Others respond to learner struggle by lowering expectations in ways that unintentionally deprive students of meaningful growth. Both responses are problematic. The more productive aim is not support *instead of* challenge, but **challenge without intimidation**.

Challenge is essential to computing education. Students must learn to reason through unfamiliar problems, tolerate partial understanding, debug imperfect code, and engage with concepts that are genuinely difficult. Without challenge, there is no substantial learning. Yet challenge becomes educationally destructive when it is poorly staged, unmediated, or paired with environments that communicate exclusion. A blank page can be a meaningful challenge for an advanced learner and a paralyzing one for a novice. A large open-ended project can foster creativity for some students while leaving others unable to identify a starting point. The issue is not the existence of challenge, but its structure.

Scaffolded challenge offers a more balanced model. Here, tasks are demanding but sequenced. Complexity grows progressively. Learners are expected to do increasingly independent work, but support is present at critical transition points. This approach aligns with long-standing research on scaffolding, guided participation, and cognitive apprenticeship (Collins et al., 1989; Wood et al., 1976). It also reflects contemporary evidence from active learning and inclusive STEM pedagogy showing that student learning improves when challenge is accompanied by opportunities for feedback, revision, and sense-making rather than abrupt performance exposure (Freeman et al., 2014; Theobald et al., 2020).

In multidisciplinary computing classrooms, challenge without intimidation is especially important because many students are negotiating more than the task itself. They are also negotiating identity: Am I the kind of student who can do this? Do I belong here if I ask a "basic" question? Does struggle mean I am behind everyone else? These hidden questions can either amplify or suppress challenge. Well-designed support helps students interpret challenge as developmental rather than threatening.

1.3 The Human Dimension of Computing Education

Computing education is sometimes discussed primarily in technical or cognitive terms: problem-solving, abstraction, algorithmic logic, debugging competence, transfer of learning. These dimensions are indispensable, but they do not exhaust the educational experience. Students are also emotional, social, and identity-bearing learners. They experience confidence, fear, comparison, shame, aspiration, frustration, and belonging. In many introductory classrooms, these human dimensions are not peripheral to success; they are constitutive of it.

The human dimension becomes especially visible when learners are newcomers to computing. They may hesitate to ask questions because they do not wish to appear unintelligent. They may remain silent when confused, compare themselves unfavorably with more experienced peers, or overinterpret one failure as evidence that they do not belong in a technical field. This is particularly true for students from non-traditional backgrounds in computing, including those from non-computing disciplines, those with little prior exposure, multilingual learners, and students with special educational needs.

A humane pedagogy does not remove standards. It removes unnecessary humiliation. It recognizes that students learn more effectively when they can engage challenge without fearing that misunderstanding will expose them as outsiders. The human dimension also includes attention to relational trust. Students are more likely to persist when they believe that the instructor cares about their progress, that feedback is intended to help them improve, and that errors are data for learning rather than grounds for embarrassment (Cohen & Steele, 2002; Edmondson, 1999).

In one large foundational computing context serving interdisciplinary cohorts, this human-centered approach was associated with notable improvements in student outcomes: withdrawal fell from 5% to 0%, pass rates improved from 90% to 100%, and A-range attainment increased from 20% to 25%, alongside teaching effectiveness scores between 4.6 and 4.9 on a 5-point scale. These figures should not be interpreted as simple causal proof, but they strongly suggest that support, scaffolding, and psychological safety are not merely pleasant additions to technical teaching. They are part of what enables durable student success.

This chapter explores those themes in depth. It examines learner diversity in support design, defines adaptive support as a pedagogical principle, develops the idea of scaffolded challenge, analyzes psychological safety in technical learning environments, and identifies classroom practices that combine rigor with support. It then considers evidence of impact and offers a design framework for educators seeking to build more inclusive and demanding computing classrooms.

2. UNDERSTANDING LEARNER DIVERSITY IN SUPPORT DESIGN

2.1 Variations in Prior Knowledge

No interdisciplinary computing classroom begins from a level starting point. Students arrive with sharply different forms of preparation. Some have years of informal coding experience through school, hobbies, robotics clubs, or online learning platforms. Others may have encountered spreadsheet logic or block-based programming but never written formal code. Others encounter programming for the first time at university. These differences influence how students interpret instructions, how quickly they can recognize patterns, how much cognitive load they experience, and whether they interpret early difficulty as ordinary or catastrophic.

Prior knowledge also differs qualitatively, not just quantitatively. A student from physics may be strong in mathematical reasoning but uncertain about syntax and debugging. A student from design may think iteratively and visually but not yet procedurally. A student from biology may understand repeated processes and conditional responses conceptually but not in formal code structure. Similarly, a student from an architectural or building sciences background may view algorithmic thinking exclusively through its utility for real-time site analytics and systemic risk forecasting (Mohammed & Zangana, 2026). Thus, "preparedness" cannot be reduced to a simple technical/non-technical distinction. Learners often possess useful conceptual resources, but these resources may not align automatically with the forms in which computing is taught.

Support design must therefore begin with the recognition that the same task can represent very different levels of difficulty for different students. Asking all students to start from an empty file and build a complete program may be an appropriate challenge for some and a demoralizing barrier for others. Conversely, highly constrained tasks may bore stronger students unless extension pathways exist. Effective support does not erase these differences; it responds to them by designing multiple routes into the same learning outcomes.

This aligns with broader educational research on prior knowledge as one of the strongest predictors of learning success and as a crucial determinant of how new information is interpreted (Ausubel, 1968; Bransford et al., 2000). It also supports the pedagogical argument that support should not be viewed as compensation for weakness alone. It is a structural response to heterogeneity.

2.2 Confidence, Identity, and Fear of Failure

Students do not enter computing classrooms with neutral self-perceptions. Many carry strong beliefs about whether they are "technical," whether programming is "for people like them," and whether making mistakes in front of others is tolerable. These beliefs matter because confidence shapes persistence, willingness to seek help, and interpretation of struggle. Self-efficacy theory has shown repeatedly that learners' beliefs in their capability to perform specific tasks influence the effort they invest, the challenges they take on, and the resilience they display when confronted with setbacks (Bandura, 1997).

In computing education, confidence and fear of failure are deeply intertwined. Beginners often encounter error messages, unexpected outputs, and failed attempts from the earliest stages of learning. For a student with strong confidence, these are informative signals. For a student with low confidence, they can feel like confirmation of inability. The same debugging experience is therefore not psychologically neutral; it is filtered through identity.

Identity matters particularly in multidisciplinary classes because some students are disciplinary insiders to computing while others are not. A student in data science or electronic engineering may assume that computing is naturally part of their field, even if they still struggle. A student in fashion, building sciences, English, or applied biology may not have the same assumption. Without support, such students may quietly decide that difficulty means they do not belong. This can produce withdrawal not only from the course but from future engagement with computational tools.

Fear of failure also interacts with peer comparison. In large classes, students often overestimate others' competence and underestimate the extent to which struggle is shared. If the classroom culture celebrates only fast correctness, many learners will hide confusion rather than reveal it. Support design must therefore account for confidence as a pedagogical variable, not a private trait. This includes early mastery experiences, low-stakes practice, clear feedback, visible normalization of error, and opportunities to ask for help without stigma.

2.3 Non-Traditional Learners and Disciplinary Outsiders

The term "non-traditional learner" can refer to many forms of difference: mature-age learners, students from historically underrepresented backgrounds, those returning to study, those studying outside conventional disciplinary pipelines, or students whose prior educational experiences did not prepare them for technical confidence. In multidisciplinary computing education, disciplinary outsiders deserve particular attention. These are learners whose home discipline does not position computing as central, and who may therefore experience programming as both cognitively new and culturally foreign.

Disciplinary outsiders are often highly capable students. Their challenge lies not in a lack of intelligence, but in the hidden assumptions of the classroom. They may not know what kinds of questions are expected, how to read code strategically, or how much uncertainty is normal. They may interpret technical shorthand as evidence that the subject has rules everyone else somehow already knows. This is especially common in first-year or gateway courses.

Supportive design for such learners does not require lowering intellectual expectations. It requires making participation more legitimate. That may mean explicitly naming those diverse starting points are normal, linking computing to different disciplinary futures, giving students structured ways to begin, and ensuring that help-seeking is framed as part of competence rather than evidence of deficiency. In translational pedagogy, these students are not peripheral exceptions. They are central to why the pedagogy exists.

2.4 Students with SEN and Additional Support Needs

Inclusive support design must also account for students with special educational needs (SEN) and other learning-related support needs. In computing classrooms, this may include students with attention-related differences, dyslexia, language-processing challenges, anxiety disorders, autism spectrum conditions, depression, or other circumstances that affect pacing, concentration, sensory tolerance, task initiation, or classroom participation. It may also include temporary vulnerabilities related to health, family circumstances, or emotional stress.

The presence of such learners is not unusual, especially in large foundational subjects. Yet support often remains reactive rather than integrated into pedagogy. A better approach is to treat accessibility and flexibility as part of general course design. Clear structure, consistent routines, multimodal explanation, chunked tasks, visual organization, option-rich help systems, low-stakes formative activities, and explicit transition points can all support students with additional needs while also benefiting the wider class. This is consistent with universal design for learning principles, which emphasize flexible pathways of engagement, representation, and action (CAST, 2018).

Students with anxiety or depression may particularly benefit from psychologically safe structures: private consultation, anonymous question channels, visible normalization of difficulty, and reduced public exposure when possible. The aim is not to create a separate pedagogy for a small group, but a learning environment broad enough to support variation without stigma.

3. ADAPTIVE SUPPORT AS A PEDAGOGICAL PRINCIPLE

3.1 What Adaptive Support Means Beyond Technology

The term "adaptive" is often associated with digital systems that personalize learning pathways algorithmically. While such systems are important and will be discussed later in the book, adaptive support in pedagogy has a broader and more immediate meaning. It refers to the instructor's capacity to respond to learner variation in real classrooms by adjusting explanation, pacing, task structure, examples, feedback, and opportunities for practice. In this sense, adaptive support is not primarily a software feature; it is a pedagogical stance.

Adaptive support begins from the premise that one form of help is rarely sufficient for all learners. A student confused about syntax may need something different from a student confused about logic. A student with high motivation but low confidence may need something different from a student with high confidence but shallow conceptual understanding. A student in engineering may require a different conceptual bridge than a student in health sciences. Adaptivity therefore depends on diagnosis. The teacher must gather cues; from questions, errors, concept checks, body language, participation patterns, and assessment data; to determine what kind of support is needed and when.

This broader view of adaptivity aligns with responsive teaching traditions in education, where instruction is shaped by close attention to student thinking rather than fixed delivery alone (Hammer et al., 2012). In multidisciplinary computing classrooms, such responsiveness is especially important because misunderstandings can emerge for very different reasons. Two students may get the same wrong answer while needing different forms of support.

Adaptive support also implies variation in timing. Some support is anticipatory, such as structuring tasks in stages or clarifying common misconceptions before they occur. Some support is just-in-time, such as intervening when a misconception becomes visible. Some support is retrospective, such as revisiting a concept after noticing recurring errors. All three forms matter.

3.2 Responsive Teaching in Real Classrooms

Responsive teaching involves a shift from seeing student error as failure to seeing it as evidence. In computing classrooms, this means asking not only *what* is wrong in a student's output, but *what kind of understanding is currently operating*. Is the learner guessing? Misreading the task? Treating code as text rather than execution? Overgeneralizing a prior pattern? Failing to distinguish syntax from logic? Each diagnosis points toward a different support response.

In real classrooms, responsiveness often appears in modest but powerful adjustments. An instructor notices that many students misunderstand function parameters and revisits the concept using a clearer sequence of examples. A tutorial reveals recurring confusion about loop variables, so the teacher introduces a tracing routine before the next lab. Students indicate that a project feels too distant from their current knowledge, so the instructor adds milestone prompts and partial code frameworks. These are not departures from rigor. They are refinements that make rigor more reachable.

Responsive teaching also includes emotional responsiveness. Instructors who notice signs of discouragement, silence, or avoidance can intervene in ways that preserve dignity. For example, a student who appears close to withdrawing may need encouragement, reassurance, and a clearer pathway forward rather than simply more content. Student reflections in large foundational classes have shown that such moments can be transformative. One student who had considered dropping the course later reported that encouragement to stay, paired with structured support, led not only to success but to a complete change in confidence about computing.

3.3 Matching Support to Learner Stage

Support should not be static. Beginners need different structures than intermediate learners, and learners' needs change as competence develops. Early in a course, support may need to be highly explicit: guided examples, visible reasoning, low-stakes quizzes, structured labs, and clear syntax support. As learners gain confidence and schema, support can shift toward strategic feedback, broader problem framing, and opportunities for independent extension.

This developmental matching is consistent with Vygotskian perspectives on the zone of proximal development and with the original notion of scaffolding as contingent support that responds to the learner's current capacity (Vygotsky, 1978; Wood et al., 1976). The challenge in computing classrooms is to avoid two opposite errors: giving too little support too early, or continuing to over-structure tasks after learners are ready for greater independence.

Support matched to stage also helps with motivation. Early success matters because it shapes efficacy beliefs. If initial tasks are so difficult that many learners fail before understanding begins, confidence may be damaged unnecessarily. Conversely, if learners are never stretched beyond guided modification, independence may not develop.

3.4 Fading Support Over Time

A defining feature of genuine scaffolding is that support fades. The purpose of adaptive support is not long-term dependency but increasing autonomy. Fading support means that as learners internalize reasoning processes, the instructor gradually withdraws prompts, structures, and direct assistance, allowing students to assume greater responsibility.

In computing education, fading might involve moving from fully worked examples to partially completed examples, from detailed lab instructions to open-ended tasks, from supplied frameworks to self-generated code structures, or from instructor-led debugging to student-led diagnosis. This progression is pedagogically important because it helps students experience growth. They can recognize that what once required heavy support can now be done more independently.

The timing of fading, however, must be handled carefully. If support is removed too early, students may feel abandoned rather than empowered. If removed too late, they may become dependent on templates and struggle to transfer learning. Effective fading depends on observation, concept checking, and attention to class patterns.

4. SCAFFOLDED CHALLENGE IN COMPUTING EDUCATION

4.1 Concept of Scaffolded Challenge

Scaffolded challenge refers to the design of learning experiences that remain intellectually demanding while being structured in ways that make progression possible. The term combines two commitments: challenge, because meaningful learning requires effort and complexity; and scaffolding, because learners often need temporary supports to engage that complexity productively.

In computing, scaffolded challenge is particularly important because novices are asked to work across multiple layers simultaneously: syntax, semantics, algorithmic logic, debugging, interpretation of instructions, and often team-based project work. This cognitive strain is compounded when students encounter specialized, advanced environments that require managing data buffering, web synchronization, and concurrent sensor platforms (Mohammed, 2026). If all of these demands are activated at once without support, learners can become cognitively and emotionally overloaded. Conversely, if challenge is oversimplified, students may complete tasks without developing genuine computational reasoning.

The aim, then, is not to make computing easy, but to make difficult learning *possible*. This echoes the distinction between "productive struggle" and destructive struggle. Productive struggle occurs when students can engage challenge with enough structure to continue reasoning. Destructive struggle occurs when the learner has too little orientation to begin or persist (Hiebert & Grouws, 2007; Kapur, 2008).

4.2 Structured Progression From Guided to Independent Work

A core feature of scaffolded challenge is progression. Students should not be asked to perform highly independent tasks before they have encountered the relevant conceptual structures in manageable form. Instead, courses can move through stages such as:

1. concept introduction and guided demonstration,
2. tightly structured practice,
3. partially completed tasks,
4. guided application in new contexts,
5. more independent problem-solving,
6. open or semi-open project work.

This progression is consistent with gradual release of responsibility models and cognitive apprenticeship frameworks (Collins et al., 1989; Fisher & Frey, 2014). In computing classrooms, it allows students to build confidence while still moving toward autonomy. It also creates fairness. Students are not judged simply on whether they can produce expert-like output immediately; they are supported in becoming capable of it over time.

4.3 Milestone-Based Project Design

Projects can be powerful sites of interdisciplinary computing learning, but they can also overwhelm novices if poorly staged. Milestone-based project design addresses this by breaking a larger task into developmentally sensible phases. Early milestones may focus on understanding the problem, reading and modifying given code, tracing logic, or implementing one limited feature. Later milestones can involve extension, debugging, interpretation, reflection, or adaptation to student-specific interests.

This kind of design is especially beneficial in large classes because it creates multiple points of feedback and reduces the risk that students disappear into confusion until the final deadline. It also supports both weaker and stronger learners. Beginners gain structure; more advanced students gain opportunities to extend beyond the basic milestones.

A student who learned Python from scratch reflected positively on a project design where the main code framework was provided in advance and the task centered on understanding, analyzing, and modifying key sections rather than writing a complete program from nothing. The student noted that this matched the actual learning stage of beginners. This reflection demonstrates a crucial principle: scaffolding can preserve rigor by aligning challenge with developmental readiness.

4.4 Guided Labs, Starter Code, and Progressive Release

In foundational computing courses, guided labs and starter code are sometimes criticized for reducing authenticity. Used poorly, they can indeed promote dependence. Used well, they function as temporary bridges. Starter code can focus student attention on the conceptual target of the task rather than burdening them with all aspects of program construction at once. Guided labs can provide structure in the moment of learning, when misconceptions are still fragile and correctable.

The key lies in progressive release. Early labs may provide substantial support, while later labs ask students to supply more of the structure themselves. Starter code should be designed to illuminate, not obscure. Students should understand what is given, why it is given, and what they are expected to modify or create. In this way, support helps learners cross into more complex work rather than replacing that work.

4.5 Designing Challenge for Mixed-Ability Cohorts

A recurrent difficulty in large interdisciplinary classes is that learners vary widely in experience. A single task may be too easy for some and too difficult for others. Scaffolded challenge can address this through layered task design: core tasks required for all learners, optional extension tasks for advanced students, and support prompts for those who need more structure.

Such differentiation does not require separate courses. It requires thoughtful design. For example, a programming assignment might include two core questions and one optional extension, with grading structured to reward mastery while not excessively penalizing beginners for failing advanced extensions. This kind of approach can maintain ambition while reducing unnecessary discouragement.

5. PSYCHOLOGICAL SAFETY IN TECHNICAL LEARNING ENVIRONMENTS

5.1 Defining Psychological Safety in Classrooms

Psychological safety refers to a learning climate in which students feel able to ask questions, reveal confusion, make mistakes, and participate without fear of humiliation or interpersonal threat (Edmondson, 1999). In technical classrooms, this is especially significant because visible error is built into the learning process. Programs fail, outputs are wrong, logic breaks, and students often need help publicly or semi-publicly.

Psychological safety in education does not mean comfort without standards. Rather, it means that standards are encountered in an environment where the learner's dignity is protected. Students can be wrong without being shamed. They can try without being ridiculed. They can struggle without being silently classified as incapable.

In multidisciplinary computing classrooms, this matters deeply because many learners already feel uncertain about belonging. If the classroom magnifies that uncertainty through dismissive responses, public comparison, or narrow participation norms, psychological withdrawal can happen quickly. Students may remain enrolled but stop engaging meaningfully.

5.2 Safe-to-Fail Learning and Error Normalization

A safe-to-fail classroom is one in which error is expected as part of learning and treated as diagnostically useful. This is particularly important in programming, where failure messages and incorrect outputs are routine. If students interpret every failure as proof of incapacity, then learning becomes emotionally expensive. If they interpret failure as data, they are more likely to persist.

Error normalization can occur through several means: instructors openly debugging imperfect code, discussing common misconceptions without ridicule, framing mistakes as checkpoints in reasoning, and designing low-stakes opportunities to test ideas. These practices align with research on productive failure and the educational value of error when learners are supported in analyzing it (Kapur, 2008; Ohlsson, 1996).

Student reflections often indicate how meaningful this can be. One learner described a course in which mistakes became "learning opportunities" because the instructor consistently explained logic patiently rather than simply marking responses wrong. Another described live coding with intentional bugs as the moment programming stopped feeling like memorization and began to feel like reasoning.

These experiences suggest that safe-to-fail environments are not merely emotionally supportive; they are cognitively generative.

5.3 Reducing Shame, Comparison, and Silence

Shame is one of the most corrosive emotions in technical learning. It often appears when students believe that misunderstanding will expose them as less capable than others. In large classes, shame can lead to silence. Students stop asking questions, copy from peers, or rely on AI-generated output without understanding because revealing confusion feels too risky.

Reducing shame requires active design. Teachers can explicitly state that varied starting points are normal, praise thoughtful questions, respond to error without sarcasm, and avoid pedagogies that celebrate speed as the primary marker of competence. Group work should also be designed carefully; if one experienced student simply dominates while others remain silent, comparison is intensified rather than reduced.

Silence should not automatically be interpreted as comprehension. In many computing classrooms, silence is a protective strategy. Psychological safety therefore requires channels through which students can reveal confusion without excessive exposure.

5.4 Anonymous Channels, Low-Stakes Checks, and Instructor Stance

Anonymous question forms, polling tools, digital message boards, and written minute papers can help students reveal uncertainty safely. Low-stakes quizzes and concept checks also support psychological safety because they allow students to test understanding without catastrophic penalty. Such practices lower the social and evaluative cost of being imperfect while still holding students accountable for engagement.

Instructor stance matters as much as structures. Students are highly sensitive to whether the teacher appears approachable, patient, and genuinely interested in their learning. A student in Operating Systems described appreciating optional quizzes, clear slides, and an instructor who was "always patient and open to questions." Such descriptions indicate that psychological safety is conveyed through tone, consistency, and response style as much as through formal policy. The dynamic relationship between these supportive behaviors, the classroom climate, and student outcomes is illustrated in the Psychological Safety and Learning Persistence Model in Figure 1.

Figure 1. Psychological Safety and Learning Persistence Model

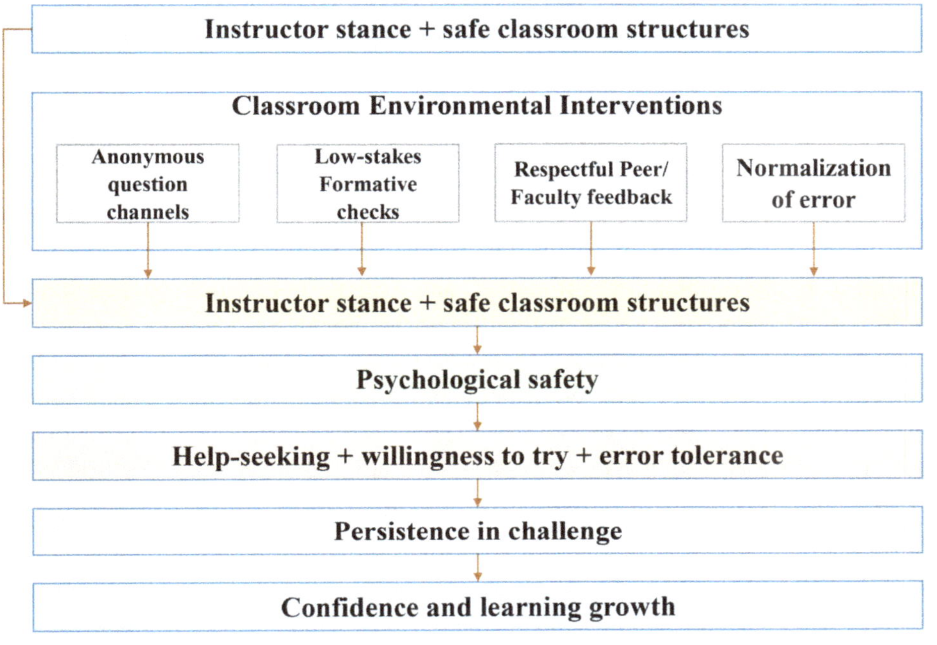

6. CLASSROOM PRACTICES FOR SUPPORTIVE RIGOR

6.1 Low-Stakes Quizzes

Low-stakes quizzes are one of the most effective tools for combining support with rigor. They encourage continuous engagement, provide frequent feedback, reveal misconceptions early, and reduce dependence on high-stakes cramming. For beginners, they help structure study habits and create manageable opportunities for success.

Students often value such quizzes not because they are easy, but because they make learning cumulative. One learner from Applied Physics reflected those frequent quizzes forced regular review and reinforced concepts progressively, increasing both confidence and preparedness. Another student from Applied Biology emphasized that low-stakes, segmented quizzes helped identify learning gaps early and supported steady improvement.

The educational value of low-stakes quizzes is well supported by retrieval practice research, which shows that regular testing can enhance retention and transfer when aligned with meaningful feedback (Agarwal & Bain, 2019; Roediger & Karpicke, 2006). In supportive pedagogy, quizzes function not only as checks but as learning devices.

6.2 Feedback Routines

Feedback is supportive when it is timely, specific, and oriented toward improvement rather than merely judgment. In computing education, effective feedback often identifies not only that an answer is wrong, but what kind of reasoning error may underlie it. Is the problem one of syntax, sequencing, condition logic, misunderstanding of iteration, or poor interpretation of the question?

Feedback routines can include annotated code comments, lab checkpoints, common-error reviews in class, verbal feedback during consultation, and short written prompts that ask students to revise rather than only receive. The tone of feedback also matters. Harsh feedback can discourage vulnerable learners; vague praise can mislead. Productive feedback combines clarity with respect.

6.3 Consultation Systems

Consultation opportunities are particularly important in diverse computing classrooms because students often need individualized explanation at moments where confusion is specific. Office hours, booked consultations, after-class questions, and short online response channels can all serve this function. Students repeatedly report that one-to-one explanation of syntax, logic, and debugging is especially valuable when they are beginners.

However, consultation systems must be manageable and equitable. If only highly confident students use them, existing gaps may widen. Instructors can normalize consultation by mentioning it explicitly, integrating reminders into the course, and making it clear that seeking help is part of learning rather than a sign of weakness.

6.4 Peer Interaction and Belonging Structures

Peer interaction can either increase safety or increase comparison. Its educational value depends on design. Well-structured pair work, peer explanation, small-group tracing, and near-peer mentoring can support belonging and make help-seeking feel more normal. Poorly structured group work can leave weaker students silent while stronger students carry the task.

Belonging structures might include mixed-ability pairings with rotating roles, peer explanation protocols, project groups with defined contributions, or near-peer mentoring systems where more experienced undergraduates help newer students.

Such arrangements can reduce isolation and allow students to see that learning is collaborative rather than purely individual competition.

6.5 Support Strategies in Large Classes

Large classes present logistical challenges, but supportive rigor can still be implemented through layered systems:

- frequent low-stakes checks,
- visible reasoning in lectures,
- structured tutorials and labs,
- anonymous question channels,
- clear slide design and recap materials,
- discussion forums,
- consultation slots,
- peer support systems,
- milestone-based tasks,
- extension opportunities for advanced learners.

The principle is not one-to-one customization for every student, but the creation of enough pathways that learners are less likely to fall invisibly behind. In a large foundational computing setting, such an approach coincided with strong outcomes: teaching effectiveness scores of 4.6–4.9, no student withdrawals, full pass rates, and improved A-range performance. These outcomes suggest that support can scale when designed systemically, balancing structured guidance with academic rigor as conceptualized in the Scaffolded Challenge Model in Figure 2.

Figure 2. Scaffolded Challenge Model

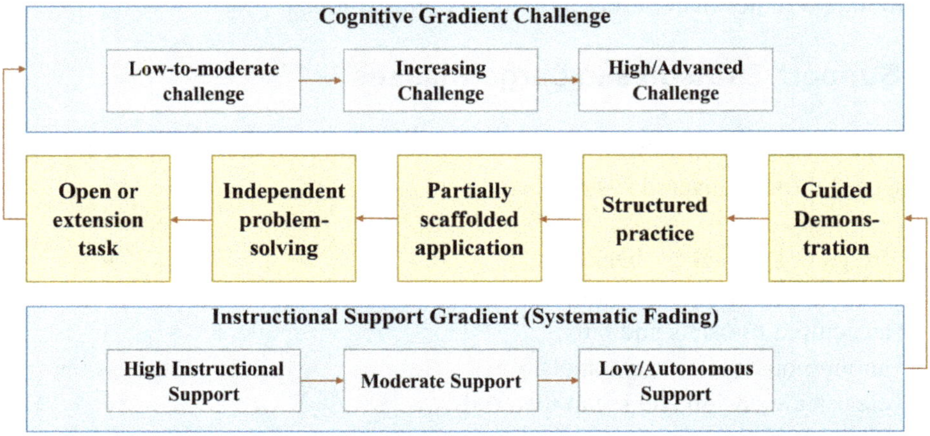

7. EVIDENCE OF STUDENT IMPACT

7.1 Confidence and Retention Outcomes

One of the clearest indicators of effective support is student confidence. In interdisciplinary computing classrooms, confidence does not simply affect emotion; it shapes behavior. Students with greater confidence are more likely to attempt problems independently, ask questions, persist through bugs, and interpret challenge productively. Student feedback data from foundational programming courses have shown strong agreement that structured support improved both conceptual understanding and confidence in computing.

Retention is another important indicator. In one large teaching context, the withdrawal rate fell from 5% to 0% after the adoption of a more supportive and scaffolded model. While multiple factors influence retention, such a reduction strongly suggests that learners felt more able to remain engaged rather than self-selecting out.

7.2 Help-Seeking Behavior

Supportive environments often change not only whether students ask for help, but how they ask. Instead of vague panic or silent avoidance, students begin to identify more precisely where they are confused. This is a sign of growing metacognition and self-efficacy. Students who use consultations, low-stakes quizzes, and guided labs productively often become more independent over time because support has helped them learn how to diagnose their own learning.

7.3 Reduced Withdrawal and Increased Persistence

Persistence in technical learning often depends on whether students interpret temporary failure as recoverable. When challenge is scaffolded and mistakes are normalized, learners are more likely to stay in the course long enough to improve. In the UGC evidence base informing this book, pass rates improved from 90% to 100%, and A-range attainment rose from 20% to 25% under a pedagogy emphasizing support, challenge, and psychological safety. These improvements suggest that supportive rigor does not merely help weaker students survive; it can also raise overall performance.

7.4 Student Voice as Evidence of Safety and Support

Student testimonials provide qualitative confirmation of these trends. A beginner learner described entering the course with anxiety and little coding background but gradually gaining confidence because the instructor explained patiently, welcomed questions, and used live coding and real-world analogies. Another student highlighted how frequent quizzes, flexible assignments, and patient one-to-one consultation built "solid practical skills, clear logical thinking, and strong confidence." A transformative case involved a student who had nearly dropped the course but, after encouragement and structured support, stayed and earned an A+, reporting a fundamental shift in confidence and professional identity.

Such voices matter because they reveal dimensions of support not fully captured by scores alone: felt legitimacy, reduced intimidation, increased courage to ask questions, and the movement from fear to participation. The specific learner profiles behind these voices, along with the targeted strategies that foster this participation, are summarized in Table 1.

Table 1. Support Strategies by Learner Profile

Learner Profile	Common Need	Effective Support Strategy
Beginner with no coding background	Clear entry and reduced intimidation	Guided labs, low-stakes quizzes, starter code
Quiet but capable learner	Safe participation pathway	Anonymous question channels, pair explanation
Anxious learner	Reduced fear of failure	Safe-to-fail environment, patient feedback, consultation

continued on following page

Table 1. Continued

Learner Profile	Common Need	Effective Support Strategy
Advanced learner	Higher ceiling	Optional extensions, open-ended challenge
SEN / additional support need	Structured clarity and flexibility	Chunked tasks, multimodal explanation, consistent routines

8. DESIGN FRAMEWORK FOR EDUCATORS

8.1 Support Architecture for Foundational Courses

A practical support architecture for a foundational interdisciplinary computing course should include five layers:

1. **Accessible entry**: clear expectations, beginner-aware framing, visible normalization of varied starting points.
2. **Regular formative structure**: low-stakes quizzes, guided labs, trace tasks, concept checks.
3. **Scaffolded challenge**: milestone-based assignments, starter frameworks, progressive release.
4. **Relational support**: approachable instructor stance, consultation systems, respectful feedback.
5. **Psychological safety structures**: anonymous question channels, normalization of error, non-shaming participation norms.

These layers work best as a system rather than isolated interventions. To help identify when these safety structures are missing or breaking down, Table 2 details the warning signs of an unsafe classroom climate along with practical, immediate remedies.

Table 2. Signs of Unsafe Classroom Climates and Remedies

Sign of Unsafe Climate	Likely Effect on Students	Possible Remedy
Students rarely ask questions	Silent confusion, disengagement	Anonymous question options, normalize uncertainty
Public correction feels harsh	Shame, avoidance	Use respectful error analysis
Fast students dominate discussion	Comparison, reduced belonging	Structured turn-taking, pair-share
Many students submit copied or AI-generated work without understanding	Fear-driven shortcut behavior	Increase low-stakes reasoning tasks and support
Students disappear before deadlines	Hidden overload	Add milestones and earlier check-ins

8.2 Balancing Autonomy and Assistance

The central design challenge is balance. Too little support can turn rigor into exclusion. Too much support can turn learning into dependency. A useful guiding question is: *What support is necessary now to make independent reasoning possible later?* Support should point toward autonomy, not replace it.

This means instructors should regularly ask whether learners are doing meaningful thinking or simply following structures. If support has become overly directive, it should be adjusted. If confusion remains paralyzing, more structure may be temporarily needed.

8.3 Avoiding Overdependence

Overdependence can emerge when students rely excessively on templates, step-by-step instructions, or constant instructor rescue. To avoid this, support should increasingly require decision-making from students: predicting before running, choosing between strategies, explaining why a line is needed, debugging with hints rather than direct correction, and extending examples into new contexts.

Fading, as discussed earlier, is crucial. Students should feel supported, but they should also feel increasingly responsible for their own problem-solving. The best support architecture ends with greater learner agency.

8.4 Recommendations for Interdisciplinary Instructors

For instructors teaching large and diverse computing classes, several recommendations follow:

- Diagnose learner diversity early rather than assuming a common starting point.
- Design challenge progressively; do not equate abrupt independence with rigor.
- Use low-stakes formative structures to build confidence and reveal misconceptions.
- Normalize help-seeking and mistakes explicitly.
- Protect dignity when students are wrong.
- Provide multiple support channels, including private and anonymous ones.
- Build extension routes so stronger students remain challenged.
- Treat support as a system, not an occasional intervention.
- Use student feedback and performance evidence to refine support design continuously.

9. CONCLUSION

9.1 Supportive Rigor as a Principle of Translational Pedagogy

This chapter has argued that adaptive support, scaffolded challenge, and psychological safety are not secondary features of good teaching. They are central to how rigorous learning becomes possible in multidisciplinary computing classrooms. Support is necessary because learners enter from unequal positions. Scaffolding is necessary because difficulty must be structured if it is to be productive. Psychological safety is necessary because students cannot fully engage challenge if they fear humiliation or exclusion.

Taken together, these ideas form a model of **supportive rigor**. Such a model rejects both the harshness of sink-or-swim pedagogy and the false generosity of lowered expectations. Instead, it aims to create classrooms where learners are stretched, supported, respected, and gradually empowered to reason independently.

The evidence discussed here suggests that supportive rigor can improve not only student feeling but also student outcomes: higher persistence, stronger confidence, lower withdrawal, better achievement, and richer engagement with computing across disciplinary boundaries.

9.2 Transition to Assessment and Outcomes

If supportive rigor helps students reach understanding, the next question is how that understanding should be assessed. Traditional assessment often captures only a narrow slice of learning and may fail to recognize transfer, reasoning, and interdisciplinary application. The next chapter therefore turns to assessment: how translational pedagogy can move from supportive learning processes toward meaningful, fair, and outcome-oriented evaluation.

REFERENCES

Agarwal, P. K., & Bain, P. M. (2019). *Powerful teaching: Unleash the science of learning*. Jossey-Bass. DOI: 10.1002/9781119549031

Ausubel, D. P. (1968). *Educational psychology: A cognitive view*. Holt, Rinehart and Winston.

Bandura, A. (1997). *Self-efficacy: The exercise of control*. W. H. Freeman.

Barker, L. J., McDowell, C., & Kalahar, K. (2009). Exploring factors that influence computer science introductory course students to persist in the major. *SIGCSE Bulletin*, *41*(1), 153–157. DOI: 10.1145/1539024.1508923

Bransford, J. D., Brown, A. L., & Cocking, R. R. (Eds.). (2000). *How people learn: Brain, mind, experience, and school* (Expanded ed.). National Academy Press.

CAST. (2018). *Universal design for learning guidelines version 2.2*. http://udlguidelines.cast.org

Cohen, G. L., & Steele, C. M. (2002). A barrier of mistrust: How negative stereotypes affect cross-race mentoring. In Aronson, J. (Ed.), *Improving academic achievement: Impact of psychological factors on education* (pp. 303–327). Academic Press. DOI: 10.1016/B978-012064455-1/50018-X

Collins, A., Brown, J. S., & Newman, S. E. (1989). Cognitive apprenticeship: Teaching the crafts of reading, writing, and mathematics. In Resnick, L. B. (Ed.), *Knowing, learning, and instruction: Essays in honor of Robert Glaser* (pp. 453–494). Lawrence Erlbaum.

Edmondson, A. (1999). Psychological safety and learning behavior in work teams. *Administrative Science Quarterly*, *44*(2), 350–383. DOI: 10.2307/2666999

Fisher, D., & Frey, N. (2014). *Better learning through structured teaching: A framework for the gradual release of responsibility* (2nd ed.). ASCD.

Freeman, S., Eddy, S. L., McDonough, M., Smith, M. K., Okoroafor, N., Jordt, H., & Wenderoth, M. P. (2014). Active learning increases student performance in science, engineering, and mathematics. *Proceedings of the National Academy of Sciences of the United States of America*, *111*(23), 8410–8415. DOI: 10.1073/pnas.1319030111 PMID: 24821756

Hammer, D., Goldberg, F., & Fargason, S. (2012). Responsive teaching and the beginnings of energy in a third grade classroom. *Review of Science. Mathematics and ICT Education*, *6*(1), 51–72.

Hiebert, J., & Grouws, D. A. (2007). The effects of classroom mathematics teaching on students' learning. In Lester, F. K.Jr., (Ed.), *Second handbook of research on mathematics teaching and learning* (pp. 371–404). Information Age. DOI: 10.1108/978-1-28141-200-320251013

Kapur, M. (2008). Productive failure. *Cognition and Instruction*, *26*(3), 379–424. DOI: 10.1080/07370000802212669

Lewis, C. M. (2011). Is pair programming more effective than other forms of collaboration for young students? *Computer Science Education*, *21*(2), 105–134. DOI: 10.1080/08993408.2011.579805

Margolis, J., & Fisher, A. (2002). *Unlocking the clubhouse: Women in computing*. MIT Press.

Mohammed, A. (Ed.). (2026). *Advanced Concurrency, Buffering, and Web-Sync in Sensor Platforms: Zero-Loss Streams*. IGI Global Scientific Publishing., DOI: 10.4018/979-8-2600-1101-0

Mohammed, A., & Zangana, H. (Eds.). (2026). *Intelligent Construction Monitoring Systems: Real-Time Safety, Environmental Prediction, and Risk Management*. IGI Global Scientific Publishing., DOI: 10.4018/979-8-3373-9245-5

Ohlsson, S. (1996). Learning from performance errors. *Psychological Review*, *103*(2), 241–262. DOI: 10.1037/0033-295X.103.2.241

Roediger, H. L.III, & Karpicke, J. D. (2006). Test-enhanced learning: Taking memory tests improves long-term retention. *Psychological Science*, *17*(3), 249–255. DOI: 10.1111/j.1467-9280.2006.01693.x PMID: 16507066

Theobald, E. J., Hill, M. J., Tran, E., Agrawal, S., Arroyo, E. N., Behling, S., Chambwe, N., Cintrón, D. L., Cooper, J. D., Dunster, G., Grummer, J. A., Hennessey, K., Hsiao, J., Iranon, N., Jones, L.II, Jordt, H., Keller, M., Lacey, M. E., Littlefield, C. E., & Freeman, S. (2020). Active learning narrows achievement gaps for underrepresented students in undergraduate science, technology, engineering, and math. *Proceedings of the National Academy of Sciences of the United States of America*, *117*(12), 6476–6483. DOI: 10.1073/pnas.1916903117 PMID: 32152114

Tinto, V. (2012). *Completing college: Rethinking institutional action*. University of Chicago Press. DOI: 10.7208/chicago/9780226804545.001.0001

van Merriënboer, J. J. G., & Kirschner, P. A. (2018). *Ten steps to complex learning: A systematic approach to four-component instructional design* (3rd ed.). Routledge.

Vygotsky, L. S. (1978). *Mind in society: The development of higher psychological processes*. Harvard University Press.

Wood, D., Bruner, J. S., & Ross, G. (1976). The role of tutoring in problem solving. *Journal of Child Psychology and Psychiatry, and Allied Disciplines*, *17*(2), 89–100. DOI: 10.1111/j.1469-7610.1976.tb00381.x PMID: 932126

Chapter 6
From Assessment to Translational Outcomes:
Measuring Understanding, Transfer, and Contribution

Ka Chung Lai
http://orcid.org/0009-0001-6890-4140
Department of Computing, The Hong Kong Polytechnic University, Hong Kong

ABSTRACT

This chapter examines the limitations of conventional computing assessments that prioritize syntactic correctness over deep comprehension, arguing that such models fail to measure knowledge transfer or cognitive reasoning. To address these gaps within interdisciplinary university cohorts, this chapter per the authors proposes a "translational outcomes" framework. This model expands evaluative scope to capture conceptual portability, metacognitive awareness, and learner self-efficacy across diverse domain applications without sacrificing technical rigor. By unpacking structural methodologies like process-oriented milestones, multi-tiered transfer tasks, and neutral linguistic variations, this text demonstrates how to dismantle construct-irrelevant barriers that isolate non-technical students. Finally, this chapter per the authors explores "output conversion," detailing how scaffolded classroom capstones can be converted into tangible external contributions, including academic publications, industry competitions, and functional startup prototypes.

DOI: 10.4018/979-8-2600-1811-8.ch006

1. INTRODUCTION

1.1 Limits of Conventional Computing Assessment

Assessment has long occupied a central role in computing education, but it has often been narrower than the learning it claims to represent. In many introductory and intermediate computing courses, assessment is dominated by tasks that reward final correctness, syntax accuracy, and procedural completion. Students may be asked to write code under timed conditions, predict outputs, or solve standardized programming questions whose success depends largely on whether they can produce the expected artifact. Such assessment is not without value. Computing does require precision, and the ability to construct functioning programs remains essential. However, when assessment is reduced mainly to final-code correctness, several educational limitations emerge.

First, conventional assessment frequently underrepresents reasoning. A student may arrive at a correct answer by memorization, pattern copying, or tool-assisted assembly without fully understanding why the solution works. Another student may possess strong conceptual understanding and debugging logic, yet lose marks because of minor syntax instability or incomplete polishing under pressure. In both cases, the assessment captures only part of what matters educationally. If the goal of higher education is not merely to produce code but to cultivate computational reasoning, then assessment must be able to see beyond the final script.

To move beyond this final script, assessment frameworks must explicitly isolate what is known as the **hidden cognitive path** of code development. In traditional grading setups, a student who struggles with syntactic mechanics like bracket placement or minor typing errors receives a failing score, even if their underlying algorithmic logic is perfectly sound. Conversely, another student might turn in a flawless, running piece of code that was assembled through unthinking copy-pasting, mindless pattern matching, or uncritical reliance on generative AI tools.

Standard autograders check only the output accuracy, completely missing this deep divergence in understanding. This creates a misleading evaluation loop where surface fluency masks conceptual gaps, and minor implementation struggles obscure genuine computational insight. To break this pattern, assessment design must actively integrate process-oriented milestones. We need grading checkpoints that look at historical compilation sequences, intermediate debugging decisions, and incremental code changes over time. By elevating these hidden phases of problem-solving to visible, graded activities, the evaluation model shifts away from a high-pressure, pass-fail approach. It becomes an instructional mirror that reveals how a student thinks, ensuring that beginners from non-technical backgrounds are graded on their structural logic rather than just their initial typing speed or familiarity with complex syntax conventions.

Second, conventional assessment often struggles to capture transfer. Students may solve a familiar problem in the exact form in which it was taught, yet fail to apply the same principle in a new context, across disciplines, or in an open-ended scenario. This is especially problematic in interdisciplinary classrooms where students are expected to use computing as a tool in fields such as design, health, biology, linguistics, business, architecture, and engineering. If learners pass a programming subject but cannot recognize how the underlying ideas travel into their own domain, the educational value of the course remains only partially realized.

Third, traditional assessment can unintentionally privilege prior exposure. Fixed-format tests, high-pressure coding tasks, and abstract decontextualized problems often reward students already familiar with computing conventions, testing culture, or technical language. In mixed cohorts, this can produce inequity. Students with less prior experience may be judged not only on what they learned in the course, but on what they already knew before it began. Such assessment can preserve standards, but it does not always preserve fairness.

Fourth, conventional approaches often separate assessment too sharply from learning. Students experience assessment as something done *to* them rather than something that helps them understand their own development. In computing, where errors and revisions are central to growth, overly summative models can distort motivation and encourage surface strategies. Learners may optimize for grades rather than insight, memorizing patterns that will pass the test without building durable reasoning capacity.

These limitations do not imply that coding tests, quizzes, or formal examinations should be abandoned. Rather, they suggest that assessment in computing education must be broadened. It should still measure correctness, but it should also measure understanding, transfer, reasoning, explanation, confidence, and where appropriate, contribution beyond the classroom.

1.2 Why Interdisciplinary Classrooms Require Broader Assessment Models

Interdisciplinary classrooms intensify the need for broader assessment because the educational purposes of computing shift when students come from multiple domains. In a relatively homogeneous computer science cohort, assessment may focus more directly on mastery of disciplinary conventions, complexity, and implementation skills. In a multidisciplinary classroom, those goals remain relevant, but they are no longer sufficient. Students are not all preparing for the same professional role, nor do they all encounter computing through the same conceptual pathways.

A student in civil engineering may need to apply computation to sensing, simulation, or systems monitoring. A student in health sciences may need to reason through decision logic, data interpretation, or patient-facing digital tools. A student in design may apply programming to interaction, pattern generation, or media systems. A student in linguistics may use rule-based logic or text processing. If assessment remains tied only to narrow forms of syntax production, it may fail to reveal whether these students can actually use computing meaningfully in their own fields.

Broader assessment models are therefore required for at least three reasons. The first is **validity**: assessments should reflect the full range of intended learning outcomes, not just the most easily testable ones. The second is **fairness**: learners with different backgrounds should have multiple legitimate ways to demonstrate understanding while still meeting rigorous standards. The third is **transferability**: if computing is being taught as a cross-disciplinary literacy, then assessment should examine whether students can carry learning across contexts.

Such models are increasingly supported by research in higher education and authentic assessment, which argues that meaningful assessment should align with real cognitive, disciplinary, and professional practices rather than only with decontextualized test performance (Boud & Falchikov, 2006; Gulikers et al., 2004; Wiggins, 1998). In computing education, this means that assessment should not only ask whether students can write code under idealized conditions, but whether they can explain, adapt, debug, justify, and apply computational thinking across varying settings.

1.3 From Achievement Measurement to Translational Outcomes

This chapter proposes a shift from assessment as narrow achievement measurement to assessment as the evaluation of **translational outcomes**. Translational outcomes include not only technical attainment but also conceptual understanding, cross-context transfer, problem-solving, confidence, self-efficacy, interdisciplinary application, and, in some cases, contribution beyond the classroom. This broader view aligns with the central argument of the book: that computing pedagogy in interdisciplinary classrooms should be designed not only for content coverage, but for access, meaning, transfer, and contribution.

Assessment in this framework remains rigorous. It does not lower standards or avoid evaluating correctness. Instead, it expands the set of outcomes worth measuring. A student who can reason through a program, explain why a solution works, adapt a concept to a new discipline-specific scenario, and develop a project into a conference paper or prototype has demonstrated a range of learning that conventional syntax-based assessment alone may miss. Such outcomes matter not only educationally but institutionally, especially in higher education systems increasingly concerned with impact, employability, innovation, and responsible knowledge use.

This chapter therefore explores how assessment can be reimagined for translational pedagogy. Section 2 defines translational outcomes. Section 3 outlines principles of assessment design for interdisciplinary computing. Section 4 examines assessment formats that measure more than syntax. Section 5 discusses designing for transfer and generalization. Section 6 introduces output conversion as an assessment horizon. Section 7 considers evidence and indicators of effectiveness. Section 8 presents an assessment design blueprint. The chapter concludes by reframing assessment as a pathway from learning evidence to meaningful contribution.

2. WHAT ARE TRANSLATIONAL OUTCOMES?

2.1 Conceptual Understanding

The first translational outcome is conceptual understanding. In computing, conceptual understanding goes beyond being able to recall syntax or imitate a demonstrated example. It includes understanding how control flow works, how variables change over time, how functions organize logic, how data structures support different operations, and why a particular computational approach is appropriate for a given problem. It also includes being able to explain one's reasoning, debug meaningfully, and distinguish superficial code resemblance from deep structural similarity.

This outcome is foundational because all other outcomes depend on it. Transfer cannot occur reliably without conceptual understanding. Interdisciplinary application remains fragile if students only memorize patterns. Confidence built on shallow success may collapse when the problem changes. Thus, assessment must ask not only whether students can produce a correct answer, but whether they understand the computational principle that makes the answer correct.

Research in computing education has repeatedly shown that novice learners can often produce or recognize correct code without robust understanding, especially when relying on memorized patterns or syntactic mimicry (Lister et al., 2004; Robins et al., 2003; Sorva, 2013). Assessment that values conceptual understanding therefore needs tasks that elicit reasoning, prediction, explanation, and interpretation, not only final implementation.

2.2 Transfer Across Contexts

A second translational outcome is transfer: the ability to apply computing knowledge beyond the immediate situation in which it was learned. Transfer may be near, such as recognizing the same loop logic in a differently worded programming problem, or far, such as applying algorithmic thinking to a domain-specific problem in another discipline. In interdisciplinary computing education, transfer is especially important because students are often learning programming not as an end in itself, but as a literacy that should become useful elsewhere.

To successfully measure this flexible recognition, evaluations should use **multi-tiered transfer tasks** that track a student's cognitive journey from near to far transfer applications. In a near-transfer task, the surface context remains very close to the original lecture examples; for instance, changing a student grade analyzer into an employee payroll calculator. This confirms basic procedural mastery. To measure true far-transfer within an interdisciplinary setting, the assessment must completely strip away familiar vocabulary and replace it with domain-specific terms from other fields.

A student who mastered a sorting algorithm using numerical arrays should be asked to apply that exact same logical approach to arrange environmental data points or track customer behavior patterns. This cross-domain shift challenges the student to look past the surface code and find the core computational concept beneath. If the learner can easily find that abstract core and adapt it to a new field, they prove that their understanding has transitioned from simple, rote memorization into a flexible, practical literacy. Testing this boundary prevents the dangerous educational illusion where students look highly capable in a controlled computer lab, but are totally unable to use those exact same technical skills when they return to their primary majors or enter professional interdisciplinary workplaces.

Transfer is difficult to assess when tasks remain too repetitive or too tightly aligned with classroom examples. Students may perform well because they recognize the pattern, not because they can generalize the principle. Assessment for transfer should therefore include novel scenarios, changed contexts, cross-domain applications, or explanation tasks that ask students to identify how a concept travels. If computing is to become meaningful in health sciences, design, business, biology, or linguistics, assessment must ask whether students can use it in those spaces.

Educational research distinguishes near transfer from far transfer and emphasizes that the latter requires abstraction, schema formation, and varied practice rather than one-off repetition (Barnett & Ceci, 2002; Perkins & Salomon, 1992). Assessment designed for translational outcomes should therefore examine not only whether students can reproduce a method, but whether they can recognize when and why that method should be used elsewhere.

2.3 Problem-Solving and Reasoning

A third translational outcome is problem-solving and reasoning. Computing is not only about code production; it is about interpreting a problem, selecting or constructing an appropriate approach, testing assumptions, and revising strategy when needed. These forms of reasoning are central to professional and academic practice. Yet they are often only partly visible in conventional grading systems.

Assessment for reasoning includes tasks that require students to choose between approaches, explain decisions, trace logic, diagnose faults, or compare solutions. It also includes open-ended problems where the path is not fully prescribed. Such tasks can reveal whether students are becoming strategic thinkers rather than procedural imitators.

Reasoning-oriented assessment is strongly supported by work on metacognition, self-explanation, and authentic learning, all of which suggest that deep learning involves monitoring one's thinking and being able to justify choices rather than merely execute routines (Chi et al., 1994; Schraw, 1998; Wiggins, 1998).

2.4 Confidence and Self-Efficacy

A fourth translational outcome concerns confidence and self-efficacy. At first glance, these may seem too affective to belong within assessment. Yet in interdisciplinary computing classrooms, confidence is not incidental. Students' beliefs about whether they can think computationally influence persistence, help-seeking, willingness to engage difficult tasks, and openness to future learning (Bandura, 1997). A learner who completes a course but leaves convinced that success was accidental or unrepeatable has not developed the same educational outcome as one who leaves with grounded confidence.

This does not mean that confidence should be graded in simplistic ways. Rather, it should be monitored and understood as part of the broader outcome profile. Reflection tasks, self-assessment prompts, project commentary, and course feedback can all provide insight into whether students are developing efficacy as computational learners. This is particularly important for students from non-technical backgrounds who may enter with low confidence and strong anxiety.

2.5 Professional Identity and Output Conversion

A fifth translational outcome is the development of professional or scholarly identity, often expressed through output conversion. Some students move beyond completing assignments to seeing themselves as contributors: researchers, developers, designers, innovators, or interdisciplinary problem-solvers. In such cases, coursework becomes a starting point for conference papers, competition entries, prototypes, startup ideas, or community-facing applications.

Not every course can or should require such outcomes from every student. However, assessment design can create conditions in which stronger or more motivated students may extend work into authentic outputs. This matters because higher education increasingly values student agency, impact, and contribution. It also matters because these extended outputs often represent a high form of transfer: students use classroom learning in public, disciplinary, or entrepreneurial contexts.

Evidence from interdisciplinary computing contexts suggests that when assessment is designed with this horizon in view, student outcomes can extend substantially. Since 2025, students mentored through course and follow-on supervision have produced more than 40 conference papers, won more than 10 external awards, reached more than 10 startup finalist teams, and generated more than 5 patent or startup initiatives. These outputs should not be romanticized or made compulsory for all learners, but they indicate what is possible when assessment is linked to creation as well as measurement. The integrated structure of these achievements within a broader evaluation framework is captured in the Translational Outcomes Assessment Model in Figure 1.

Figure 1. Translational Outcomes Assessment Model

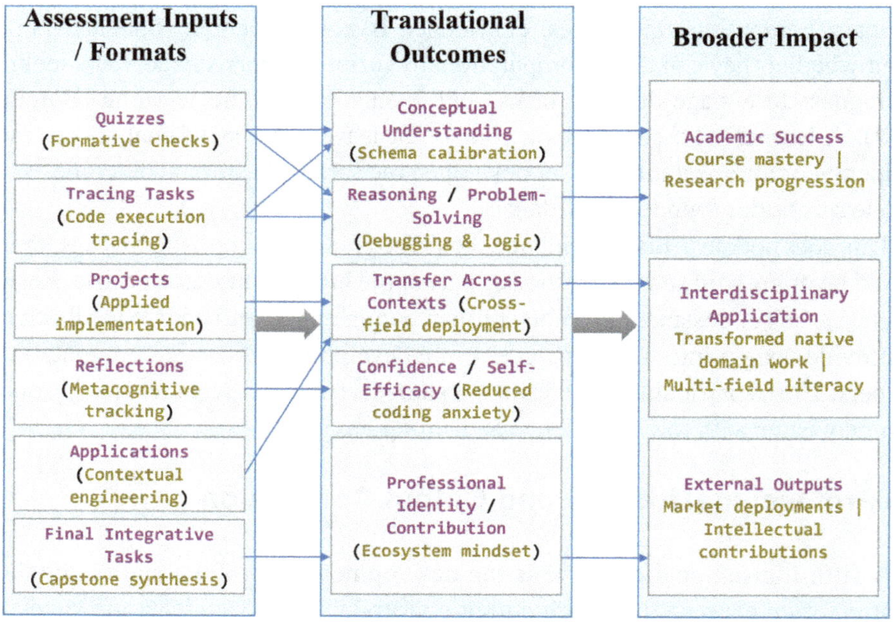

3. PRINCIPLES OF ASSESSMENT DESIGN FOR TRANSLATIONAL PEDAGOGY

3.1 Validity Across Diverse Learners

Assessment validity concerns whether a task actually measures what it claims to measure. In interdisciplinary computing classrooms, validity becomes especially important because students bring diverse prior knowledge, disciplinary language, and modes of reasoning. A task may appear valid on paper while in practice measuring technical fluency, test-taking speed, or familiarity with computing culture more than conceptual understanding itself.

Valid assessment for translational pedagogy should therefore ask: Does this task measure the intended computational principle? Does it allow learners to demonstrate understanding in a form appropriate to the learning goal? Is it evaluating reasoning, transfer, or application where these are intended outcomes, or only surface production? Constructive alignment theory is useful here: assessment should align with the learning activities and intended outcomes of the course rather than defaulting to inherited formats (Biggs & Tang, 2011).

For example, if a course explicitly values debugging, explanation, and interdisciplinary application, but the final assessment measures only unseen code writing under time pressure, validity is weakened. This does not make the exam useless; it means the assessment system is incomplete. Validity in interdisciplinary teaching requires plural evidence of learning.

Creating this plural evidence requires instructors to dismantle **construct-irrelevant variances** that compromise assessment validity in mixed-major classrooms. In computing, construct-irrelevant variance often manifests as dense, domain-specific vocabulary or overly complex cover stories that have nothing to do with the programming logic being tested. For example, a programming question wrapped in a complex financial trading scenario or an abstract mathematical matrix can easily confuse a design or linguistics student. In this case, the student fails the item not because they lack programming skills, but because they struggled to understand the background setting of the question.

To fix this validity gap, assignments must use **neutral linguistic structures** or offer multiple, parallel domain variations for the same core problem. A question about loop control flow can be offered in three distinct versions: an eco-system model for biology students, an interaction loop for design students, and a text parser for humanities students. Every version tests the exact same algorithmic complexity and shares an identical grading rubric. This strategy ensures that students from fields such as civil engineering or construction management are evaluated on core programmatic logic rather than their familiarity with niche structural infrastructure contexts (Mohammed & Zangana, 2026). By taking this approach, the assessment stops favoring students who happen to be familiar with standard tech jargon or engineering concepts. It ensures that the final grade accurately reflects the student's true computational reasoning and mastery of the course material, creating a fair and valid measurement for every student in the cohort.

3.2 Fairness and Accessibility

Fairness does not mean making assessment easier. It means ensuring that tasks do not unnecessarily advantage students who already possess background knowledge or familiarity unrelated to the intended learning outcome. In computing, this includes attention to language load, representational clarity, time pressure, task framing, and accessibility for students with different needs.

Students from non-computing backgrounds should not be assessed only on how quickly they internalize disciplinary shorthand. Similarly, students with special educational needs may require clarity, chunking, or alternative modes of response to demonstrate the same outcome fairly. Universal design for learning provides useful principles here, emphasizing multiple means of engagement, representation, and expression where appropriate (CAST, 2018).

Fairness also includes transparency. Students should know what good performance looks like, what is being valued, and how the task connects to course learning. Rubrics, exemplars, and clearly communicated criteria help reduce hidden expectations that disproportionately disadvantage beginners or disciplinary outsiders.

3.3 Alignment with Learning Design

Assessment should grow naturally from the pedagogy that precedes it. If teaching emphasizes visible reasoning, translational explanation, and scaffolded challenge, then assessment should capture those qualities rather than abruptly rewarding only polished end products. When assessment is misaligned with pedagogy, students often abandon productive learning strategies and revert to grade-oriented survival behavior.

Alignment matters not only cognitively but motivationally. Students take cues from assessment about what the course truly values. If explanation, reflection, and interdisciplinary application are discussed in class but never meaningfully assessed, students may infer that these are secondary. Conversely, when assessment includes tracing tasks, debugging analysis, reasoning-based project milestones, or domain-application components, it signals that such learning matters.

3.4 Formative-to-Summative Progression

Effective assessment in translational pedagogy should not begin with high-stakes judgment. It should move from formative to summative through a progression that supports learning. Formative assessment helps students understand where they stand, identify misconceptions, and improve before major evaluation points. Low-stakes quizzes, concept checks, annotated drafts, mini-labs, and milestone reviews all play this role.

This progression is pedagogically important because interdisciplinary learners often need time to stabilize understanding before being judged at scale. It is also ethically important because students should not be penalized heavily for misunderstandings that formative design could have revealed earlier. Black and Wiliam's (1998) work on formative assessment remains highly influential here, emphasizing that assessment for learning can significantly improve educational outcomes when used responsively.

3.5 Balancing Standardization and Personalization

A further principle concerns balance. In large university courses, some standardization is necessary for fairness, comparability, and efficient administration. At the same time, interdisciplinary computing education benefits from some personalization—especially in project topics, applied scenarios, and forms of transfer. The challenge is to design an assessment system that preserves common standards while allowing students to demonstrate learning through domain-relevant pathways.

One solution is layered assessment. Core tasks may be standardized to assess shared fundamentals, while applied or project-based components allow disciplinary personalization. For example, all students might complete common reasoning and coding tasks, but project applications can be chosen from different domain contexts. This approach maintains comparability without erasing interdisciplinary relevance.

4. ASSESSMENT FORMATS FOR INTERDISCIPLINARY COMPUTING

4.1 Low-Stakes Quizzes and Concept Checks

Low-stakes quizzes are among the most practical and powerful assessment tools in interdisciplinary computing classrooms. Their value lies not only in checking whether students have studied, but in supporting retrieval, revealing misconceptions, and reducing the psychological burden of assessment by distributing it over time.

Because they are low stakes, they can be used to reinforce learning rather than to punish incomplete understanding.

Students frequently report that regular quizzes help them stay engaged with the material and build confidence gradually. One Applied Physics student observed that quizzes every one or two weeks required regular study, reinforced concepts repeatedly, and made later examinations less stressful. A student from Applied Biology similarly noted that frequent quizzes helped identify gaps early and supported steady progress. Such reflections align with evidence from retrieval practice research, which shows that repeated low-stakes testing can improve retention and transfer when coupled with meaningful feedback (Agarwal & Bain, 2019; Roediger & Karpicke, 2006).

For translational pedagogy, quizzes should include more than syntax recall. They can ask for output prediction, small conceptual explanations, error spotting, matching of logic structures to contexts, or brief scenario interpretation. This makes them not only efficient, but aligned with broader learning goals.

4.2 Tracing and Reasoning-Based Tasks

Tracing and reasoning-based tasks are especially valuable because they assess understanding of process rather than only final output. Students may be asked to trace variable values through a loop, explain what a program does line by line, identify the first point at which logic diverges, or compare two code fragments. Such tasks align strongly with the book's emphasis on cognitive visibility and reasoning, but here their importance is specifically assessment-oriented.

These formats are useful because they reduce the risk that students pass through imitation. A learner who can explain or trace logic has likely developed a more robust mental model than one who can only reproduce a final answer. This method is especially critical when tracking complex architectural issues like buffer allocations, synchronization rules, and network stream management, where visual trace execution isolates deep logic gaps (Mohammed, 2026). They also help instructors distinguish syntax weakness from conceptual misunderstanding. A student may write slightly imperfect code but display strong reasoning in tracing tasks; assessment can then capture learning more accurately.

4.3 Project-Based Assessments

Project-based assessment allows learners to integrate concepts over time, apply computing to meaningful problems, and demonstrate growth through creation. In interdisciplinary settings, projects are particularly valuable because they can invite domain-relevant applications. Students may explore environmental sensing, health monitoring, design pattern recognition, smart construction, language analysis, or financial modeling, depending on the course and cohort.

Well-designed projects, however, should not assume immediate independent mastery. For beginners, project-based assessment is most effective when structured through milestones, partial frameworks, staged feedback, and transparent criteria. This allows the project to assess understanding, adaptation, and problem-solving rather than mere endurance.

Projects also create space for translational outcomes beyond the classroom. Stronger project work may be developed into research posters, conference papers, prototypes, competitions, or startup ideas. A student from Applied Physics described how an early programming project led to exploration of the mathematical foundations of machine learning and influenced later coursework. Another student from Electrical Engineering noted that research-level project assignments provided a first glimpse of what research could be and later supported conference publication. These reflections suggest that project assessment can function not only as evaluation, but as developmental launching ground.

4.4 Reflection and Explanation Tasks

Reflection and explanation tasks assess whether students can make sense of their own learning, justify their code or design choices, and identify what they have understood or misunderstood. These tasks may include short reflective commentaries, explanations of why a solution works, notes on debugging decisions, or accounts of how a concept connects to the student's disciplinary interests.

Such tasks are especially useful for assessing confidence, transfer, and metacognitive growth. They also humanize assessment by allowing the learner's reasoning process to become visible. Reflection tasks should not replace technical assessment, but they can supplement it by revealing dimensions of understanding that final code alone cannot show.

4.5 Interdisciplinary Application Assignments

Assignments that explicitly require disciplinary application are central to translational outcomes. These tasks ask students to apply computing concepts in scenarios related to their own or neighboring disciplines. For example, a health student might use conditional logic in a triage simulation, a design student might explore pattern generation, a biology student might analyze sensor thresholds, or a business student might structure a small data workflow.

The aim is not to turn every computing course into a domain project, but to test whether students can recognize and enact the relevance of computational thinking outside the canonical programming exercise. Such assignments can be highly motivating because they make the subject feel intellectually connected to students' futures.

4.6 Rubric-Based Authentic Assessment

Authentic assessment attempts to evaluate student learning through tasks that resemble real use, real decision-making, or real communicative purposes (Gulikers et al., 2004; Wiggins, 1998). In interdisciplinary computing, rubric-based authentic assessment is especially useful because it can combine technical correctness with criteria such as conceptual understanding, appropriateness of application, explanation quality, debugging rationale, teamwork, and clarity of communication.

Rubrics make expectations explicit and help preserve fairness across more open-ended tasks. They also allow instructors to reward more than polished output. For example, a student may be assessed on whether the chosen computational method fits the problem, whether reasoning is explained clearly, whether the application reflects disciplinary relevance, and whether the work shows thoughtful revision. To see how these authentic project tasks fit into a broader evaluation strategy, Table 1 maps the full spectrum of interdisciplinary computing assessment types against their primary purposes and measured outcomes.

Table 1. Assessment Types and Outcomes Measured

Assessment Type	Primary Purpose	Outcomes Measured
Low-stakes quizzes	Frequent formative checking	Understanding, retention, confidence
Tracing tasks	Reveal execution logic	Reasoning, conceptual understanding
Programming assignments	Apply concepts in code	Implementation, debugging, adaptation
Reflection/explanation tasks	Make thinking explicit	Metacognition, explanation, confidence
Interdisciplinary applications	Connect computing to domain use	Transfer, relevance, conceptual adaptability
Project-based assessment	Integrate and create	Problem-solving, collaboration, contribution
Final integrative assessment	Summative synthesis	Core knowledge, reasoning, independent application

5. DESIGNING FOR TRANSFER AND GENERALIZATION

5.1 Near Transfer and Far Transfer

Assessment for transfer should distinguish between near and far transfer. Near transfer occurs when students apply a concept in a closely related task with similar structure. Far transfer occurs when they apply that concept in a more distant or transformed context. Both matters. Near transfer helps verify whether learners can generalize within the immediate domain; far transfer reveals whether the concept has become portable across contexts.

In computing education, many assessments unintentionally stop at near transfer. Students see one type of loop problem in class and another very similar one in assessment. This tests whether they recognized the pattern, but not necessarily whether they understood its broader applicability. To assess translational learning, some tasks should move further. They should alter context, wording, representation, or disciplinary frame while preserving the underlying computational principle.

5.2 Cross-Domain Problem Scenarios

Cross-domain scenarios are useful because they show whether learners can identify computational logic beneath different surface forms. A sorting concept might appear in inventory management, lab sample arrangement, or playlist organization. A conditional structure might appear in health screening, access control, or environmental alerts. If students can move across such scenarios, then explanation and assessment are beginning to work together translationally.

These tasks should be designed carefully. The goal is not to introduce irrelevant novelty, but to test whether students can abstract the principle and reapply it appropriately. Too much novelty may create construct-irrelevant difficulty; too little may fail to assess transfer at all.

5.3 Assessing Whether Students Can Apply Computing in Their Own Discipline

One of the strongest tests of translational pedagogy is whether students can apply computing in their own field. Assessment can address this by inviting project choices, short applied tasks, contextualized reflections, or mini-case analyses tied to disciplinary interests. For example:

- a biology student may automate repeated threshold analysis,
- a linguistics student may structure a rule-checking problem,

- a design student may generate iterative patterns,
- a business student may build a simple customer data classifier.

The assessment challenge is to preserve a common standard while allowing different contexts. Rubrics should therefore focus on shared principles—correct computational logic, clear explanation, fit between problem and method, and quality of implementation—rather than requiring the same surface topic from everyone.

5.4 Measuring Explanation Quality and Conceptual Adaptability

Because translational pedagogy values explanation, assessment should also capture whether students can explain a concept flexibly. One useful approach is to ask students to explain a computational idea to a specified audience, such as a peer from another discipline. This tests conceptual adaptability: can the student preserve the idea while changing the explanatory register?

Such tasks are valuable because they measure both understanding and communicative transfer. A student who can explain recursion to a design peer or conditionals to a health peer likely possesses a more robust grasp than one who can only restate textbook language. Explanation quality can be assessed through criteria such as accuracy, accessibility, appropriate analogy use, and successful return to formal meaning.

6. OUTPUT CONVERSION AS AN ASSESSMENT HORIZON

6.1 From Coursework to Publication

One of the most distinctive possibilities in translational computing pedagogy is the idea that coursework can, in selected cases, become scholarly output. A strong project may be revised into a conference paper, poster, workshop submission, or student publication. This should not be treated as a universal expectation for every learner, but as an assessment horizon: an indication that some assessed work has the potential to cross the boundary from course product to public contribution.

This shift changes how students interpret assessment. Instead of seeing assignments as disposable exercises that end with grading, they may begin to see them as the early stages of real intellectual work. One student described this as a distinctive element of teaching: the course did not stop at passing assessments but opened opportunities for publication, conference participation, mentoring, and professional growth. Such outcomes reflect high-level transfer, ownership, and identity development.

6.2 From Project to Competition

Competitions offer another form of output conversion. When students refine assessed work into a submission for an external challenge, hackathon, innovation award, or domain-specific contest, assessment becomes linked to authentic external criteria. Competitions can motivate refinement, communication skills, teamwork, and cross-disciplinary framing.

Evidence from interdisciplinary computing teaching contexts suggests that this pathway can be substantial. Student projects have gone on to win major competition recognition, including first-place distinctions in large external events. Such success should not be romanticized as the main goal of teaching, but it provides strong evidence that learning has become transferable and publicly legible.

6.3 From Assignment to Startup/Patent/Prototype

Some assessed work may also develop into prototypes, startup ideas, or patent-related initiatives. In this model, assessment does not directly grade entrepreneurship, but creates the conditions for technically sound, contextually meaningful work that could later move into innovation pathways. The educational value lies in helping students see that computing is generative. They are not only learning to answer teacher-set questions; they are learning to build things that might matter.

This outcome horizon aligns with contemporary higher education emphases on innovation, impact, and student agency. It is particularly relevant in interdisciplinary settings, where students may combine computational learning with domain-specific problem awareness to generate novel solutions.

6.4 Ethical Issues in High-Performance Output Cultures

While output conversion can be inspiring, it also raises ethical concerns. Not all students should be pushed into publication or competition cultures. Such cultures can produce pressure, inequity, and performative productivity if handled poorly. Students vary in interest, capacity, time, and personal circumstances. Assessment should not make high-visibility outputs the hidden measure of worth.

There are also concerns around authorship, intellectual ownership, mentoring burden, and the possibility that students pursue impressive outputs without sufficient conceptual depth. Educators must therefore frame output conversion carefully: as an opportunity for some, not a coercive expectation for all; as developmentally supportive, not exploitative; and as grounded in learning, not mere credential accumulation. To design this progression safely and equitably, instructors can look to the structured milestones outlined in the Pathway from Coursework to External Outputs in Figure 2.

Figure 2. Pathway from Coursework to External Outputs

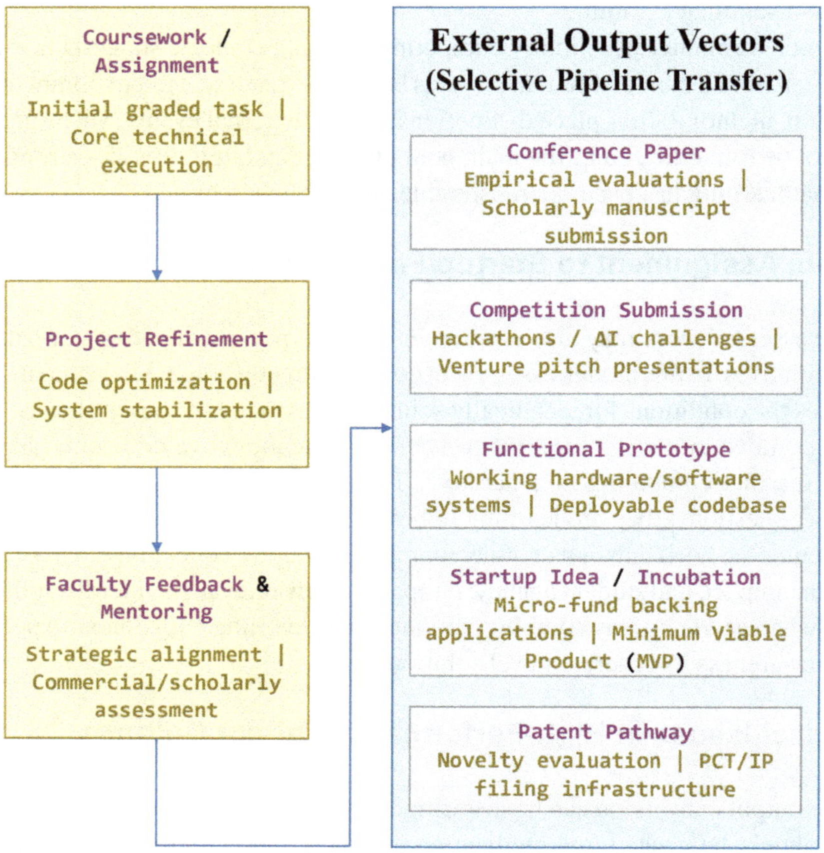

The institutionalization of high-performance output horizons introduces a critical pedagogical paradox that educators must navigate with immense care. When coursework is positioned as an incubator for public scholarship or commercial enterprise, the traditional boundaries of the classroom expand, occasionally exposing novice learners to systemic vulnerabilities. Chief among these is the risk of academic stratification within mixed-major cohorts. If the pedagogical framework implicitly celebrates external validation; such as conference acceptances or startup funding; as the ultimate indicator of educational success, it inadvertently marginalizes students whose immediate goals are rooted simply in foundational digital literacy or cross-disciplinary competency. For a design or humanities student working to stabilize rudimentary programmatic loops, the sudden structural pressure to scale an assignment into a patentable prototype can induce acute cognitive overload and debilitating evaluation anxiety.

Furthermore, an uncritical embrace of output cultures can skew student motivations away from authentic, self-regulated learning and toward performative productivity. Students may begin optimizing their technical projects exclusively for external metrics; tailoring their code to appease specific hackathon rubrics or conference trends; rather than investigating the underlying structural logic of the computational principles themselves. This shift risks resurrecting the "polished solution fallacy" under a different guise, where a visually striking user interface or a highly marketable venture pitch masks significant architectural instability or unaddressed conceptual misconceptions in the codebase.

7. EVIDENCE AND INDICATORS OF ASSESSMENT EFFECTIVENESS

7.1 Performance Trends

Assessment effectiveness can be examined through performance patterns over time. In one interdisciplinary computing teaching context, pass rates improved from 90% to 100%, withdrawal fell from 5% to 0%, and A-range attainment rose from 20% to 25% under a pedagogy that aligned assessment more closely with support, reasoning, and translational goals. Such figures suggest that broader assessment design can coexist with strong or improved academic performance.

These outcomes are important because critics sometimes assume that broader or more authentic assessment necessarily lowers standards. The data suggest otherwise. When assessment is aligned with how students actually learn, achievement can rise without sacrificing rigor.

7.2 Grade Distributions and Mastery Patterns

Beyond aggregate pass rates, instructors should examine mastery patterns. Are students performing better on reasoning tasks over time? Do project and application components reveal growth not visible in early quizzes? Are grade distributions showing healthier differentiation between surface completion and deeper conceptual command? Such patterns help determine whether assessment is measuring the intended learning.

7.3 Student Perception of Fairness and Challenge

Student perception is not the sole measure of assessment quality, but it matters. Learners often know when assessment feels arbitrary, disconnected, or misaligned with what they were taught. They also recognize when it is demanding but fair. Student testimonials in interdisciplinary computing courses frequently praise assessments that are challenging, customized, and strongly aligned with course learning rather than repetitive recycling of past papers.

One student from Applied Biology emphasized that quizzes and exams were "well-customized, reasonable, and closely aligned with what we have learned," fairly testing true understanding rather than rote memorization. Another beginner learner appreciated assignment policies that created room for practice and tolerated minor mistakes without making the entire course punitive. These responses suggest that fairness and challenge need not be opposites.

7.4 External Validation Through Scholarly and Entrepreneurial Outcomes

External outputs provide another indicator of assessment effectiveness, especially when course-designed projects translate into visible achievement beyond the classroom. More than 40 conference papers, over 10 external awards, over 10 startup finalist teams, and over 5 patent or startup initiatives represent not only student ambition but evidence that assessment has been able to seed transferable and authentic work.

Of course, external recognition should not be the only indicator, nor should it overshadow quieter forms of student development. But when students are able to carry assessed work into conferences, competitions, and innovation pathways, this strongly suggests that learning was substantive, applicable, and publicly meaningful.

8. ASSESSMENT DESIGN BLUEPRINT

8.1 Sample Assessment Architecture for Introductory Programming

A translational assessment architecture for an introductory interdisciplinary programming course might include the following components:

1. **Low-stakes quizzes (15–20%)**

Frequent concept checks on recent material, emphasizing reasoning, output prediction, and small applied interpretations.

2. **Tracing and explanation tasks (10–15%)**

Short tasks requiring students to trace variable states, explain control flow, or diagnose small code fragments.

3. **Programming assignments (20–25%)**

Guided but progressively less scaffolded tasks that assess implementation, debugging, and concept application.

4. **Interdisciplinary mini-application or reflection (10–15%)**

A small task connecting computing to the student's own or chosen disciplinary context, with explanation of fit.

5. **Project-based assessment (25–30%)**

Milestone-driven, rubric-based, possibly team-oriented, with room for domain relevance and extension.

6. **Final integrative assessment (15–20%)**

A summative component testing core conceptual understanding, reasoning, and moderate implementation ability.

This architecture preserves multiple forms of rigor while distributing risk and making room for translational outcomes.

8.2 Sample Rubric for Interdisciplinary Computing Projects

A useful project rubric might include:

- **Computational correctness**
- **Conceptual understanding**
- **Appropriateness of domain application**
- **Quality of reasoning and explanation**

- **Debugging and revision evidence**
- **Clarity of communication / presentation**
- **Creativity or originality where relevant**

Such a rubric allows interdisciplinary variation without sacrificing technical expectations. A complete breakdown of these criteria across various performance levels is provided in Table 2.

Table 2. Sample Rubric for Interdisciplinary Project Work

Criterion	Excellent	Good	Developing	Limited
Computational correctness	Solution functions reliably and efficiently	Mostly correct with minor issues	Partial correctness; important flaws remain	Major technical failure
Conceptual understanding	Strong evidence of clear underlying understanding	Good understanding with minor gaps	Surface understanding evident	Weak or unclear understanding
Domain relevance	Computing method is well matched to disciplinary problem	Generally relevant and appropriate	Relevance present but weakly justified	Little meaningful connection to context
Reasoning and explanation	Choices are justified clearly and coherently	Explanations mostly clear	Limited explanation of decisions	Minimal or inaccurate explanation
Debugging/ revision	Strong evidence of testing and thoughtful revision	Some evidence of revision	Limited revision process	Little evidence of debugging or refinement
Communication/ presentation	Clear, organized, professional presentation	Mostly clear and organized	Uneven clarity	Poorly communicated

8.3 Sample Rubric for Translational Explanation Tasks

For tasks where students explain a computing concept to a specified audience, rubric criteria may include:

- accuracy of the computational principle,
- suitability of explanation for the target audience,
- effective use of example or analogy,
- ability to return to formal computing meaning,
- clarity and coherence of communication.

This kind of rubric helps assess whether students can not only understand concepts but communicate them across contexts.

8.4 Recommendations for Institutions and Instructors

Several recommendations follow from this chapter:

- Broaden computing assessment beyond syntax and final-code correctness.
- Preserve technical rigor while including reasoning, transfer, and application.
- Use formative assessment to support development before high-stakes judgment.
- Design for both standardized fundamentals and personalized application.
- Treat student outputs beyond the classroom as possible extensions, not compulsory expectations.
- Build rubrics that make hidden criteria visible.
- Monitor fairness, especially for interdisciplinary and beginner learners.
- Use assessment to support identity development and confidence, not only classification.

Assessment in interdisciplinary computing should not simply sort students. It should help them see what they know, what they can do, what they can transfer, and what they might contribute.

9. CONCLUSION

9.1 Rethinking Assessment as Outcome Conversion

This chapter has argued that computing assessment in interdisciplinary classrooms must move beyond narrow achievement measurement. While syntax accuracy and implementation remain important, they do not capture the full range of educational outcomes now expected in translational pedagogy. Assessment should also measure conceptual understanding, reasoning, transfer, interdisciplinary application, confidence, and, where appropriate, contribution beyond the course.

Seen in this way, assessment becomes more than a grading mechanism. It becomes a system for outcome conversion: a way of recognizing how learning moves from comprehension to transfer, from transfer to application, and from application to contribution. When designed well, assessment helps students become not only successful course completers but emerging computational thinkers capable of working meaningfully across domains.

9.2 Transition to Adaptive Learning Technologies

Yet broader assessment also raises a practical challenge: how can such nuanced, personalized, and evidence-rich evaluation be supported at scale, especially in large classes? The next chapter addresses that question by turning to adaptive learning technologies and pedagogy. There, the discussion shifts from assessment design principles to the technological systems and teaching architectures that can help personalize support, explanation, and assessment pathways for diverse interdisciplinary learners.

REFERENCES

Agarwal, P. K., & Bain, P. M. (2019). *Powerful teaching: Unleash the science of learning*. Jossey-Bass. DOI: 10.1002/9781119549031

Bandura, A. (1997). *Self-efficacy: The exercise of control*. W. H. Freeman.

Barnett, S. M., & Ceci, S. J. (2002). When and where do we apply what we learn? A taxonomy for far transfer. *Psychological Bulletin*, *128*(4), 612–637. DOI: 10.1037/0033-2909.128.4.612 PMID: 12081085

Biggs, J., & Tang, C. (2011). *Teaching for quality learning at university* (4th ed.). Open University Press.

Black, P., & Wiliam, D. (1998). Assessment and classroom learning. *Assessment in Education: Principles, Policy & Practice*, *5*(1), 7–74. DOI: 10.1080/0969595980050102

Boud, D., & Falchikov, N. (2006). Aligning assessment with long-term learning. *Assessment & Evaluation in Higher Education*, *31*(4), 399–413. DOI: 10.1080/02602930600679050

CAST. (2018). *Universal design for learning guidelines version 2.2*. http://udlguidelines.cast.org

Chi, M. T. H., de Leeuw, N., Chiu, M.-H., & LaVancher, C. (1994). Eliciting self-explanations improves understanding. *Cognitive Science*, *18*(3), 439–477. DOI: 10.1207/s15516709cog1803_3

Gulikers, J. T. M., Bastiaens, T. J., & Kirschner, P. A. (2004). A five-dimensional framework for authentic assessment. *Educational Technology Research and Development*, *52*(3), 67–86. DOI: 10.1007/BF02504676

Lister, R., Adams, E. S., Fitzgerald, S., Fone, W., Hamer, J., Lindholm, M., McCartney, R., Moström, J. E., Sanders, K., Seppälä, O., Simon, B., & Thomas, L. (2004). A multi-national study of reading and tracing skills in novice programmers. *SIGCSE Bulletin*, *36*(4), 119–150. DOI: 10.1145/1041624.1041673

Mohammed, A. (Ed.). (2026). *Advanced Concurrency, Buffering, and Web-Sync in Sensor Platforms: Zero-Loss Streams*. IGI Global Scientific Publishing., DOI: 10.4018/979-8-2600-1101-0

Mohammed, A., & Zangana, H. (Eds.). (2026). *Intelligent Construction Monitoring Systems: Real-Time Safety, Environmental Prediction, and Risk Management*. IGI Global Scientific Publishing., DOI: 10.4018/979-8-3373-9245-5

Perkins, D. N., & Salomon, G. (1992). Transfer of learning. In Postlethwaite, T. N., & Husen, T. (Eds.), *The international encyclopedia of education* (2nd ed., pp. 6452–6457). Pergamon Press.

Robins, A., Rountree, J., & Rountree, N. (2003). Learning and teaching programming: A review and discussion. *Computer Science Education, 13*(2), 137–172. DOI: 10.1076/csed.13.2.137.14200

Roediger, H. L.III, & Karpicke, J. D. (2006). Test-enhanced learning: Taking memory tests improves long-term retention. *Psychological Science, 17*(3), 249–255. DOI: 10.1111/j.1467-9280.2006.01693.x PMID: 16507066

Schraw, G. (1998). Promoting general metacognitive awareness. *Instructional Science, 26*(1–2), 113–125. DOI: 10.1023/A:1003044231033

Sorva, J. (2013). Notional machines and introductory programming education. *ACM Transactions on Computing Education, 13*(2), 8. Advance online publication. DOI: 10.1145/2483710.2483713

Wiggins, G. (1998). *Educative assessment: Designing assessments to inform and improve student performance*. Jossey-Bass.

Chapter 7
Adaptive Learning Technologies and Pedagogy:
Personalization for Interdisciplinary Computing Education

Zeyuan Ren
http://orcid.org/0009-0006-0202-4331
Department of Industrial and Systems Engineering, The Hong Kong Polytechnic University, Hong Kong

ABSTRACT

This chapter investigates how adaptive learning technologies can advance translational and interdisciplinary computing education in diverse, large-scale classrooms. It presents a framework in which adaptive systems tailor access, explanation, progression, and support while preserving shared learning outcomes. The discussion covers ALTS (Adaptive Learning and Teaching Systems), CAT (Computerized Adaptive Testing), instructor dashboards, background-aware question banks, and personalized learning pathways, illustrating how mass personalization can occur without fragmenting the curriculum. It also addresses ethical considerations, data privacy, and bias, and outlines scalable design principles, including governance, staffing, assessment, and sustainability. By linking pedagogy to infrastructure, the chapter outlines concrete pathways for institutions to deploy adaptive technologies to improve engagement, equity, and transfer, with examples and guiding questions to aid researchers and practitioners in evaluation and implementation of adaptive learning strategies.

DOI: 10.4018/979-8-2600-1811-8.ch007

1. INTRODUCTION

1.1 Why Adaptive Learning Matters in Diverse Computing Classrooms

As computing becomes a foundational literacy across higher education, the diversity of students entering computing classrooms has increased substantially. Introductory and intermediate computing subjects now often include learners from engineering, design, health sciences, applied biology, business, linguistics, architecture, and data-related programs, alongside students from core computing disciplines. This expansion has produced not only larger classes, but also more heterogeneous ones. Students differ in prior programming exposure, technical vocabulary, disciplinary identity, confidence, expectations, and preferred modes of understanding. In such settings, fixed instructional pathways and one-size-fits-all assessments often fail to serve learners equitably or efficiently.

Adaptive learning matters because diversity in the classroom is no longer an exception to be managed occasionally; it is a structural condition of contemporary higher education. When all students receive the same examples, the same pace, the same assessment sequence, and the same form of explanation, many are underserved. Stronger students may become under-challenged, while beginners may become overwhelmed. Students from non-computing disciplines may understand the same underlying concept more easily when it is framed through different disciplinary contexts. Students with low confidence may need more graduated support before they can benefit from the same high-level challenges given to others.

Adaptive learning offers a way to respond to this variation without abandoning common academic standards. At its best, it does not fragment the curriculum into unrelated personalized tracks. Rather, it preserves shared learning outcomes while adjusting the route through which students reach them. This can include adapting difficulty, pacing, sequencing, feedback, examples, and explanatory contexts. For interdisciplinary computing education, one particularly important extension is the ability to adapt not only to performance level, but also to disciplinary background. A student in Electronic Engineering, Mechanical Engineering, and Computing may all need to understand network latency, but they may grasp it more readily through different contextual framings.

The relevance of adaptive learning has grown further in an era shaped by data-rich learning environments, AI-mediated instruction, and increasing pressure on institutions to support large classes without sacrificing quality. Adaptive learning systems promise "mass personalization" in settings where human instructors alone may struggle to individualize learning for hundreds of students. Yet the educational value of such systems depends on more than technological sophistication. It depends on whether they are grounded in sound pedagogy, aligned with learning goals, and implemented ethically.

This chapter argues that adaptive learning technologies can strengthen translational computing pedagogy when they are used to personalize access, explanation, progression, and support for diverse interdisciplinary learners. It focuses especially on the pedagogical role of Adaptive Learning and Teaching Systems (ALTS), Computerized Adaptive Testing (CAT), instructor dashboards, background-aware question banks, and personalized learning pathways.

1.2 Personalization Challenges in Large-Scale Higher Education

The idea of personalized learning is appealing, but its implementation in higher education is difficult. In large classes, instructors must often teach 200 to 350 students simultaneously, many of whom vary substantially in preparation and confidence. Institutional systems tend to support scale through standardization: fixed assessments, common lecture materials, uniform assignment structures, and centralized learning management systems. While standardization can improve consistency, it often reduces flexibility. The consequence is a tension between fairness through sameness and fairness through responsiveness.

Large-scale computing education highlights this tension vividly. An instructor may know that some students need simpler explanations, additional practice, or slower conceptual progression, while others are ready for extension. The instructor may also know that some concepts are best introduced differently to students from different disciplines. Yet in a traditional large-class format, time and infrastructure often prevent meaningful personalization. The result is a common pedagogical compromise: teach to an imagined middle, support the most vocal students directly, and hope that others can self-correct through practice or external resources. This is rarely sufficient.

The challenge is not only one of numbers, but of complexity. Personalization in interdisciplinary computing may need to occur across multiple dimensions:

- difficulty level: easier or harder questions depending on current mastery;
- explanatory framing: different contextual examples based on disciplinary background such as mapping environmental data inputs to risk management structures in built-environment contexts (Mohammed & Zangana, 2026);
- feedback timing: immediate versus delayed, automated versus human;
- pathway selection: remediation for struggling students, extension for stronger students;

- evidence interpretation: identifying whether difficulty reflects conceptual misunderstanding, language barriers, or lack of prior experience.

Without systematic support, teachers may personalize only informally and inconsistently. Some students benefit from office-hour conversations or tutorial intervention; others remain invisible.

Adaptive technologies offer a possible response. By using learner data to guide question selection, explanation pathways, and follow-up support, they can reduce some of the burden of real-time differentiation. Research on adaptive educational systems suggests that such systems can improve efficiency, support more precise diagnosis, and increase engagement when designed well (Brusilovsky & Millán, 2007; Corbett & Anderson, 1994). However, such benefits are not automatic. Poorly designed adaptive systems can become opaque, biased, mechanistic, or pedagogically shallow. Thus, the key issue is not whether adaptive technology should be used, but how it should be designed as part of pedagogy.

1.3 Positioning ALTS Within Translational Pedagogy

Within the broader framework of translational computing pedagogy developed in this book, adaptive systems should be understood as pedagogical enablers, not replacements for teaching. They do not replace the need for cognitive visibility, translational explanation, scaffolded challenge, psychological safety, or evidence-informed refinement. Instead, they help scale and coordinate those pedagogical commitments in contexts where class size and diversity would otherwise make them difficult to sustain consistently.

Adaptive Learning and Teaching Systems (ALTS) are especially relevant because they can personalize in two ways simultaneously: by level and by context. Many conventional adaptive systems focus only on performance; making a question harder when a student answers correctly and easier when a student struggles. This is useful, but in interdisciplinary classrooms it is not sufficient. Students may also benefit when the same learning goal is framed differently based on disciplinary background. A networking concept such as congestion, latency, routing, or transmission delay may be understood differently by a Computing student, an Electrical and Electronic Engineering student, or a Mechanical Engineering student. The concept remains the same, but the representational pathway changes.

ALTS therefore extends the pedagogical logic of translational explanation into digital learning design. It can choose not only the next difficulty level, but also the next explanatory form or contextual example most suitable for a learner's background. In this sense, ALTS operationalizes a key principle of the book: rigor is preserved, but entry points become more responsive.

This chapter proceeds as follows. Section 2 discusses the conceptual foundations of adaptive learning. Section 3 introduces ALTS as a pedagogical system, including its rationale, architecture, and background-aware personalization. Section 4 examines CAT in teaching practice. Section 5 discusses pedagogical uses of adaptive technologies. Section 6 explores design and implementation considerations. Section 7 analyzes benefits, risks, and limitations. Section 8 looks ahead to future directions such as generative AI and translational AI tutors. Section 9 concludes by situating adaptive systems within the broader ecology of evidence-informed teaching.

2. CONCEPTUAL FOUNDATIONS OF ADAPTIVE LEARNING

2.1 What Makes a Learning System Adaptive

A learning system is adaptive when it changes its behavior in response to evidence about the learner. This evidence may include prior knowledge, recent responses, pace of progress, error patterns, disciplinary background, preferences, or engagement signals. Adaptation may occur at the level of task difficulty, content sequencing, explanatory style, recommended resources, or feedback timing.

Not all digital learning environments are adaptive. Many are interactive, automated, or data-collecting, but still static in the path they offer to all students. A system becomes genuinely adaptive when learner input influences what happens next. In classic intelligent tutoring systems, for example, adaptation may take the form of step-by-step hints tailored to the learner's current state of understanding (Anderson et al., 1995; Corbett & Anderson, 1994). In adaptive testing, it may involve selecting the next question based on estimated ability. In more recent learning systems, it may include recommending personalized resources, adjusting conceptual examples, or sequencing tasks dynamically.

For interdisciplinary computing education, a useful working definition is this: an adaptive system is one that uses learner data to provide more appropriate next-step learning experiences than a fixed system would provide. "More appropriate" may mean more accurate in difficulty, more accessible in representation, more timely in feedback, or more relevant in context.

This definition highlights that adaptation is meaningful only relative to pedagogy. A system that adapts quickly but toward the wrong educational target is not educationally useful. Similarly, a system that personalizes surface features while ignoring conceptual structure may create the appearance of sophistication without improving learning. What matters is whether adaptation helps learners progress toward shared outcomes more effectively.

2.2 Personalization Versus Individualization

The terms personalization and individualization are often used interchangeably, but the distinction is helpful. Individualization usually refers to allowing different learners to move at different speeds through the same curriculum or task sequence. Personalization, in contrast, often implies greater responsiveness to learner differences in pathway, context, explanation, or support. Individualization changes timing; personalization may change form, route, or representation.

In large-scale higher education, full individualization is rarely feasible if it means creating completely separate courses for each learner. Nor is it always educationally desirable. Students in a shared class still need common reference points, shared standards, and collective discussion. Adaptive pedagogy therefore aims less at radical individualization than at structured personalization. This means preserving common outcomes while adapting difficulty, explanation, and support in ways that help different learners access those outcomes.

For example, in a Computer Networking course, all students may need to understand latency. A fixed system gives everyone the same question, phrased in one disciplinary language. A personalized adaptive system may present the same learning goal through server response time for Computing students, signal propagation for Electrical and Electronic Engineering students, and control system response delay for Mechanical Engineering students. The concept is common, but the explanatory path is personalized.

This form of personalization is especially relevant to translational pedagogy because it respects both rigor and diversity. It does not fragment learning goals, but it acknowledges that different learners may reach the same conceptual destination through different starting points.

2.3 Data-Informed Pedagogy and Learner Modeling

Adaptive learning depends on some form of learner modeling. A learner model is a representation; explicit or implicit; of what the system currently believes about the learner. This may include ability estimates, concept mastery levels, error patterns, background information, pace, or prior interactions. The model is updated as the learner engages with the system, and the system uses that evolving representation to guide decisions.

In CAT, the learner model is often psychometric, expressed as an estimate of ability on a latent scale. In broader adaptive learning, the model may also include conceptual mastery maps, misconceptions, preferences, or demographic and disciplinary information. For translational computing pedagogy, one especially useful extension is background-aware learner modeling, where the system incorporates not only performance history but also disciplinary background or prior preparation. This allows it to choose examples and question framings more strategically.

Data-informed pedagogy does not mean surrendering pedagogy to data. Rather, it means using data as one source of insight to support teaching decisions. Adaptive systems can reveal patterns instructors may not easily detect in large classes: which background groups struggle with which topics, where concept progression stalls, which learners need easier follow-up questions, and which may be ready for extension. Such information can support more precise intervention.

However, learner modeling also raises important concerns. Models are always simplifications. They may misrepresent students, over-interpret limited evidence, or reinforce prior assumptions. Therefore, adaptive systems should be designed with transparency and humility. They should support instructor judgment, not replace it.

To accurately capture a learner's evolving understanding, contemporary adaptive architectures rely on sophisticated modeling frameworks, primarily bifurcated into Bayesian Knowledge Tracing (BKT) and Deep Knowledge Tracing (DKT). The traditional BKT approach treats a student's mastery of a specific computational concept as a hidden state within a latent Markov model (Corbett & Anderson, 1994). It constantly computes four distinct probabilities: the probability that a student has mastered the skill (L0), the probability of a transition from the unmastered to mastered state (T), the probability that a student makes a mistake despite knowing the concept (G or *slip*), and the probability that a student accidentally answers correctly despite lacking true understanding (S or *guess*).

While BKT operates efficiently within narrow, highly structured programming domains, it struggles to adapt to the fluid cognitive environments of interdisciplinary cohorts. When an applied biology student switches contexts from a raw mathematical array to an environmental sensor data log, BKT often misinterprets their syntax confusion as a total collapse of conceptual logic. To resolve this limitation, modern ALTS implementations increasingly adopt Deep Knowledge Tracing (DKT), which uses recurrent neural networks; specifically Long Short-Term Memory (LSTM) networks—to model student performance. DKT integrates broad temporal sequences of interactions across multiple disparate skills simultaneously, mapping how a student's performance on a design analogy in week two mathematically predicts their troubleshooting efficacy during a control-system simulation in week six. This modeling approach is particularly powerful when tracking how a learner handles complex IoT telemetry strings or automated kinematics errors within distributed edge AI configurations (Aquil Mirza & Cong, 2026). By capturing these non-linear, cross-domain cognitive dependencies, the data-informed system can construct a multidimensional learner profile that anticipates errors before they manifest.

2.4 Ethical Considerations in Adaptive Systems

Adaptive systems operate through data, prediction, and algorithmic decision-making, which means they inevitably raise ethical questions. These include privacy, consent, fairness, transparency, accessibility, and the risk of over-automation. In higher education, where assessment and progression carry significant consequences, these concerns are especially serious.

One major issue is algorithmic opacity. If students do not know why they received certain questions, explanations, or recommendations, trust may erode. Instructors too may struggle to interpret system outputs if the adaptation logic is hidden. A pedagogically responsible adaptive system should therefore be explainable enough that both teachers and students can understand, at least in broad terms, how decisions are made.

A second issue is fairness. If background-aware personalization is used, care must be taken that students are not stereotyped, pigeonholed, or permanently tracked into lower-expectation pathways. The purpose of background information should be to support access, not to constrain aspiration. Systems should be able to adapt dynamically as students progress, rather than assume that disciplinary background rigidly determines understanding.

A third issue concerns data governance. Systems that collect learner responses, progression data, and profile information must protect privacy and comply with institutional policy. Students should know what data are being collected and for what purpose. Sensitive interpretation of data is essential, especially if background or accessibility information is involved.

Finally, adaptive systems must avoid becoming substitutes for human care. Personalization through technology can improve efficiency, but it cannot replace the relational and interpretive dimensions of teaching. This chapter returns repeatedly to this principle: adaptive systems should enable pedagogy, not automate it away.

3. ADAPTIVE LEARNING AND TEACHING SYSTEM (ALTS)

3.1 Rationale and Design Goals

The Adaptive Learning and Teaching System (ALTS) is conceived as a pedagogical response to a common problem in interdisciplinary computing education: how to provide meaningful personalization in large, diverse classes without fragmenting the curriculum or overburdening the instructor. ALTS is grounded in the belief that students in the same course can pursue the same learning goals while benefiting from different difficulty levels, explanatory pathways, and contextual framings.

Its rationale arises from three converging educational realities. First, learners in large computing classes vary significantly in prior knowledge and confidence. Second, interdisciplinary students often understand the same concept better when it is framed through discipline-relevant examples. Third, instructors in large classes have limited capacity to manually personalize at scale. ALTS addresses these issues by combining performance-aware adaptation with background-aware translation.

The design goals of ALTS can therefore be summarized as follows:

1. Preserve common learning goals while varying pathways.
2. Adapt by difficulty to estimate and support learner level efficiently.
3. Adapt by context to provide discipline-sensitive examples and explanations.
4. Provide actionable feedback to both students and instructors.
5. Support large-class teaching through structured but flexible personalization.
6. Remain pedagogy-led, with technology serving instructional aims rather than driving them.

In this sense, ALTS is not merely a testing engine or a recommendation system. It is a broader learning-and-teaching environment that helps coordinate explanation, practice, progression, and evidence.

3.2 System Architecture Overview

At a high level, ALTS can be understood as comprising five interacting components:

1. Learner profile layer

Stores relevant information such as course, disciplinary background, prior responses, and current estimated understanding.

2. Question and explanation bank

Contains calibrated items linked not only to difficulty and topic, but also to contextual framing or disciplinary variants.

3. Adaptive engine

Uses learner data to select the next appropriate question, explanation, hint, or follow-up task.

4. Student-facing interface

Delivers questions, feedback, explanations, and progression pathways in an accessible form.

5. Instructor dashboard

Visualizes class patterns, subgroup performance, item behavior, and possible intervention points.

The key innovation in ALTS is the integration of background-aware question generation or selection with traditional adaptive difficulty logic. Rather than asking only, "How hard should the next question be?" the system also asks, "In what contextual language is this concept most accessible to this learner right now?" This multi-layered interaction between learner profiles, the adaptive engine, and contextualized content delivery is illustrated in the ALTS Conceptual Architecture as shown in Figure 1.

For example, in a Computer Networking course, the system can present the topic of congestion through server requests and packet queues for Computing students, through bandwidth and transmission channels for EEE students, and through traffic flow or pipe-flow analogy for Mechanical Engineering students. The learning goal remains constant; the explanatory surface changes.

Figure 1. ALTS Conceptual Architecture

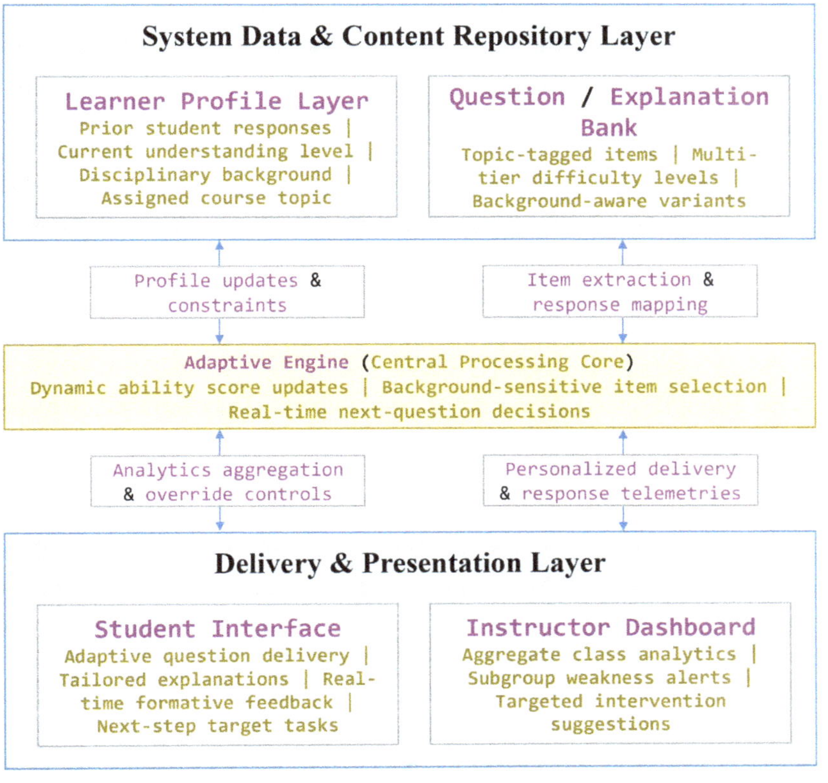

Mechanistically, the Adaptive Engine serves as the core computational nervous system of ALTS, executing a continuous three-phase loop: telemetry ingestion, state recalibration, and item optimization. When a student submits a response within the presentation layer, the engine captures a high-density string of interaction telemetry. This telemetry includes not only binary correctness, but also keystroke latency, chronological sequence of compilation attempts, and total dwell time on provided hints. Managing this real-time data pipeline effectively mirrors the data synchronization frameworks required to maintain zero-loss streams across concurrent sensor networks (Mohammed, 2026).

Once ingested, this data is routed directly to the Central Processing Core. Here, optimization algorithms compare the incoming telemetry stream against the learner's existing historical vector stored in the Learner Profile Layer. If the core detects an elevated response latency paired with a baseline conceptual error, it momentarily overrides standard difficulty scaling. Instead of pulling a mathematically harder question from the repository, the engine executes a contextual pivot. It queries the Question/Explanation Bank using metadata filters designed around the student's declared major. The metadata matching process uses a structural distance algorithm to pull an item that shares the exact same logical abstraction level as the failed question but is wrapped inside an alternate, high-familiarity disciplinary schema. This real-time programmatic routing ensures that the presentation layer remains dynamically responsive, continuously balancing cognitive load without dropping the underlying academic standard or requiring manual intervention from the teaching team.

3.3 Personalization Based on Responses, Background, and Progression

A central strength of ALTS is that it personalizes along multiple dimensions. The most immediate dimension is response history: whether the learner answered previous items correctly, incorrectly, or inconsistently. This allows the system to infer probable understanding level and adjust difficulty.

The second dimension is background. If the system knows that a learner belongs, for example, to Computing, Mechanical Engineering, Electrical and Electronic Engineering, or a non-technical track, it can draw from question variants and explanation forms that align more closely with that background. This is particularly useful in courses where the same abstract idea can be interpreted through multiple domain lenses.

The third dimension is progression. Personalization should not be static. A student who initially needs simpler context-rich explanations may later be ready for more formal or abstract treatment. Similarly, a learner who struggles at one stage may need easier follow-up questions and clearer explanation before moving on. Progression data allow the system to support such movement.

Taken together, these dimensions enable a more nuanced form of adaptation than simple "right/wrong therefore harder/easier" logic. They embody the pedagogical idea that personalization in interdisciplinary classrooms involves both level and context.

3.4 Support for Discipline-Sensitive Explanations

One of the distinctive educational features of ALTS is its ability to support discipline-sensitive explanations. This makes it particularly relevant to translational pedagogy. In many courses, students from different majors are expected to learn the same underlying computing concepts, but the explanatory entry point may differ.

The Computer Networking example illustrates this clearly. Consider latency. For a Computing student, latency may be explained as the time a server takes to respond to a request, including processing and transmission delay. For an EEE student, latency may be framed as the time required for a signal to travel through a medium, depending on propagation and system response. For a Mechanical Engineering student, it may be framed as the delay between an input and visible control-system output. For a general learner, it may simply be described as the waiting time before a system responds. The underlying learning goal; understanding that higher latency means more delay; remains constant. What changes is the language of access.

This kind of translation is pedagogically important because it activates prior schemas rather than forcing all students through the same disciplinary doorway. It also helps reduce the alienation some students experience when computing examples feel culturally or conceptually remote from their own field.

3.5 Feedback Loops Between Student and Instructor

ALTS is not only adaptive for the student; it is also informative for the instructor. The system can generate feedback loops that help teachers understand how different learners and learner groups are progressing. For instance, after students complete a set of exercises, the instructor can analyze which background groups; such as Computing, EEE, or Mechanical Engineering; are weaker on specific networking topics. This allows more targeted revision of explanation, examples, or classroom emphasis.

Students, meanwhile, can receive immediate feedback on their current level, which topics need reinforcement, and which follow-up tasks may be appropriate. In this sense, ALTS supports two-way adaptation:

- the system adapts to the learner,
- and the teacher adapts to patterns the system reveals.

This dual feedback loop is crucial. Without it, adaptive systems risk becoming isolated student tools rather than integrated pedagogical instruments.

4. COMPUTERIZED ADAPTIVE TESTING (CAT) IN TEACHING PRACTICE

4.1 Principles of CAT

Computerized Adaptive Testing (CAT) is a form of assessment in which the next question is selected based on the student's responses to previous ones. Unlike fixed tests, where every student receives the same items in the same order, CAT seeks to estimate ability more efficiently by tailoring item difficulty dynamically.

The basic intuition is straightforward. If a student answers correctly, the system presents a more difficult item; if the student struggles, the system presents an easier one. Over time, the test converges toward a more accurate estimate of the student's ability level. This makes CAT potentially more efficient and less frustrating than fixed testing, because students are not repeatedly given items that are far below or far above their current level.

Research has shown that adaptive testing can often measure ability with comparable precision using fewer questions than traditional fixed tests, sometimes reducing test length by around one-third under appropriate conditions (Weiss & Kingsbury, 1984; Wainer, 2000). This efficiency matters in higher education because it reduces assessment burden while potentially generating richer diagnostic information.

4.2 Item Response Theory Basics

Most CAT systems rely on Item Response Theory (IRT), which models both student ability and item characteristics on a shared scale. Without going deeply into psychometric technicalities, the core idea is that each item has properties such as difficulty, and the learner has an estimated ability level. Based on the learner's responses, the system updates that estimate and chooses subsequent items that are likely to be most informative.

IRT is useful because it allows adaptive testing to go beyond crude right/wrong branching. Instead of simply escalating or lowering difficulty arbitrarily, the system selects items that maximize information about the learner's current estimated position. In educational practice, this leads to more efficient testing and potentially more stable estimates of understanding.

For teaching purposes, the psychometric machinery does not need to dominate the pedagogical conversation. What matters educationally is that CAT can use statistically grounded item selection to support better diagnosis and more tailored follow-up.

4.3 Adaptive Question Selection

In CAT, item selection is central. After each student response, the system updates its estimate of the learner and selects the next question accordingly. In a traditional CAT, this selection is driven mainly by ability estimation and item information. In a translationally extended CAT, however, question selection can also account for background-aware contextualization.

This means that the system may choose not only an item of appropriate difficulty, but one framed in a context more suitable to the learner's disciplinary background.

For example, in a networking module, the same concept may be tested through a server-response scenario, a signal-transmission scenario, or a control-system-delay scenario depending on the learner profile. In all cases the intended learning goal is identical.

This two-dimensional adaptation; difficulty plus contextual framing; moves CAT closer to a teaching tool rather than a mere measurement device. It becomes part of pedagogy.

4.4 Precision, Efficiency, and Student Experience

A major pedagogical advantage of CAT is efficiency. Students do not spend large amounts of time answering questions that are too easy or too difficult. Stronger learners are challenged earlier; weaker learners are not immediately discouraged by an overly hard fixed paper. This can improve student experience, particularly in formative contexts where the purpose is diagnosis and learning rather than only grading.

Efficiency also supports instructional design. If a shorter adaptive assessment can produce a reliable estimate of understanding, more time remains for teaching, feedback, and follow-up practice. In large classes, this efficiency can be significant.

However, student experience depends on transparency. If learners do not understand why the test behaves differently for different people, they may perceive unfairness. Clear communication is therefore essential: students should know that adaptation is designed to identify understanding more accurately and support appropriate next steps.

4.5 Integration of CAT Into Course Teaching

CAT is most educationally powerful when integrated into course teaching rather than used only as an isolated high-stakes testing tool. It can serve several roles:

- entry diagnostics at the beginning of a course,
- formative checks during the semester,
- targeted revision before a major assessment,
- adaptive practice sessions linked to support resources.

In such roles, CAT becomes part of the learning cycle. It reveals level, triggers explanation, and guides progression. This fits well with translational pedagogy, which treats assessment not only as classification but as support for learning movement. The continuous looping mechanism of this integrated learning cycle is mapped out in the CAT Workflow as shown in Figure 2.

Figure 2. CAT Workflow

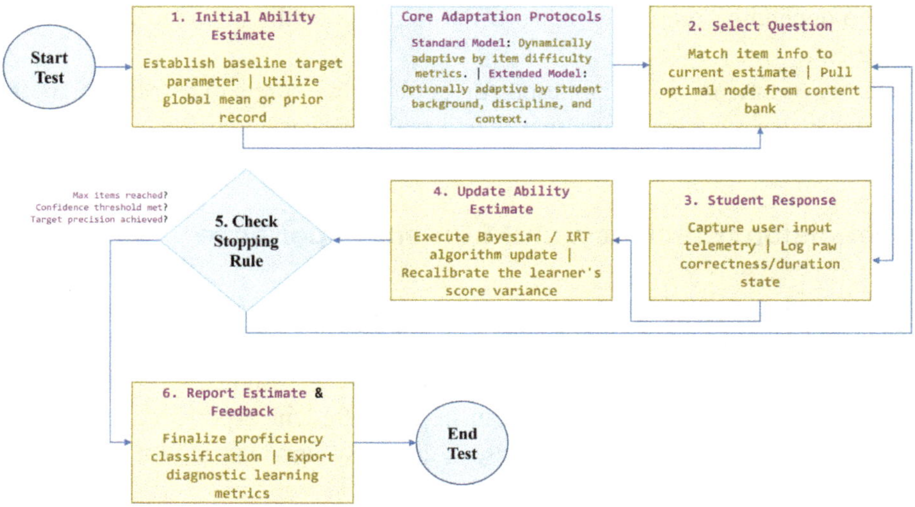

5. PEDAGOGICAL USES OF ADAPTIVE TECHNOLOGIES

To effectively implement adaptive systems in the classroom, educators must understand how specific system tools translate into teaching methods. Table 1 outlines these core adaptive features alongside their primary pedagogical functions, providing a structural map for the application strategies discussed throughout this section.

Table 1. Adaptive Features and Pedagogical Functions

Adaptive Feature	Pedagogical Function
Difficulty adjustment	Matches challenge to current learner level
Background-aware examples	Improves conceptual accessibility across disciplines
Immediate tailored feedback	Supports correction and confidence
Diagnostic entry testing	Identifies starting points and support needs
Adaptive remediation	Provides easier follow-up tasks for struggling learners
Adaptive extension	Provides higher-level challenge for advanced learners
Instructor dashboard analytics	Supports targeted teaching intervention
Progress tracking	Helps monitor growth over time

5.1 Diagnostic Use at Course Entry

Adaptive technologies are particularly valuable at the beginning of a course, when instructors need to understand learner diversity quickly. Entry diagnostics can reveal who has prior exposure, who needs foundational reinforcement, which topics are likely to require extra support, and whether different background groups show different strengths or vulnerabilities.

In interdisciplinary computing courses, such diagnostics can also inform translational explanation. If a class contains clusters from Computing, EEE, Mechanical Engineering, Design, or other fields, the instructor can anticipate which concept framings may be needed and where explanatory differentiation might matter most.

5.2 Formative Adaptation During the Semester

During the semester, adaptive systems can support formative learning by selecting follow-up questions, remediation sequences, or concept review tasks based on student performance. This allows support to be more targeted and timely than fixed worksheets or generic review material.

For example, a student struggling with routing concepts in networking may receive easier intermediate questions and clearer explanations before moving on, while another student already demonstrating mastery can receive more challenging or integrative items. This supports progression without requiring the teacher to manually sort every learner.

5.3 Personalized Explanation Pathways

One of the most pedagogically rich uses of adaptive technology is the personalization of explanation pathways. This goes beyond testing. It means that after a response; particularly an incorrect one; the system can deliver an explanation tailored not only to the error pattern but also to the learner's background.

This is where ALTS becomes especially valuable for interdisciplinary classrooms. The same misconception can be addressed through different context-sensitive explanations. Such personalization extends the pedagogical logic of Chapter 4 into technology-supported practice.

To observe how personalized explanation pathways function within a live translational framework, consider a real-world remediation scenario involving a Business Analytics student encountering iterative structures. The student is presented with a standard code assignment tracking customer transaction histories, but they inadvertently author an infinite loop because they failed to properly update the counter variable inside the loop body. The presentation layer records an execution timeout error.

Rather than displaying a generic technical notification like "Error: Execution Timeout. Check Loop Termination Conditions," the ALTS engine triggers a multi-stage translational remediation pipeline. First, the engine reads the student's profile to confirm their business background. Second, it suppresses the broken source code layout and presents a localized visual narrative model. The system displays a clear inventory pipeline analogy: *"Imagine an automated supply chain conveyor belt. The sensor is instructed to count exactly 50 incoming boxes before stopping. However, the mechanism tracking the box count is stuck at zero. What happens to the conveyor belt?"*

The student interacts with this spatial model, recognizing that the conveyor belt will run endlessly because the tracking signal never advances. Once this conceptual breakthrough is logged via a quick confirmation prompt, the ALTS interface immediately executes the upward semantic wave described in Ch4.docx. It shifts the interface view back to the text editor, highlighting the un-incremented loop index pointer, and prompts the learner: *"Now, look back at your script. Which specific line of code is failing to update our digital box counter?"* This structured technological pipeline moves the student seamlessly from an abstract operational crisis to a concrete domain-specific anchor, and then directly into precise, syntax-level correction.

5.4 Adaptive Remediation and Extension

Adaptive systems can also support both remediation and extension. Struggling students can receive more foundational practice and simpler concept entry before moving forward. Stronger students can receive extension tasks that deepen or broaden their understanding. This helps maintain a high ceiling without abandoning those who need more time.

Importantly, remediation should not become hidden tracking. Students should be able to move out of support pathways as understanding improves. Likewise, extension should not be available only to those already advantaged by prior experience; students who progress rapidly during the course should also gain access to deeper challenge.

5.5 Large-Class Mass Personalization

Perhaps the strongest practical argument for adaptive technologies is their role in mass personalization. In classes of 200–350 students, instructors cannot manually deliver individualized next-step tasks and discipline-specific explanation to everyone. Adaptive systems can make a meaningful difference by automating part of that personalization while preserving pedagogical intent.

This does not eliminate the need for teaching teams, tutorials, or office-hour support. But it can make large classes more responsive than fixed models allow. In this sense, adaptive systems are not only about learning efficiency; they are about educational justice in scale.

6. DESIGN AND IMPLEMENTATION CONSIDERATIONS

6.1 Building Question Banks

A good adaptive system depends on a strong question bank. Items should be aligned to learning goals, calibrated for difficulty, and where relevant, developed in multiple contextual variants. In interdisciplinary computing, this means that the bank may include several versions of the same learning goal framed for different backgrounds.

Item writing is therefore both a psychometric and pedagogical task. Poorly written items can undermine the entire system by confusing students, misrepresenting difficulty, or introducing irrelevant background load. Banks must be reviewed, refined, and expanded over time.

6.2 Calibration and Quality Control

Adaptive systems require some form of item calibration or validation. Even when formal psychometric calibration is still developing, items should be tested through pilots, reviewed for discrimination and difficulty, and checked for misleading bias. If one "background-aware" version of a question is accidentally easier for reasons unrelated to the concept, fairness is compromised.

Quality control also involves monitoring item performance across groups, ensuring that adaptive decisions remain defensible, and revising items that generate systematic confusion for the wrong reasons.

6.3 Instructor Dashboards and Intervention Design

Instructor dashboards are essential because adaptive systems should generate insights, not just student-level pathways. Good dashboards can show:

- class distribution of understanding,
- subgroup performance by background,

- topic-specific weakness patterns,
- students at risk of falling behind,
- questions that are malfunctioning.

The pedagogical value of the dashboard lies in helping teachers decide where to intervene. For example, if Mechanical Engineering students are consistently weaker on a networking concept, the instructor may revise explanation or add targeted examples. Dashboards therefore connect adaptive technology to human teaching judgment.

6.4 Interoperability With LMS and Classroom Workflows

For adaptive systems to be sustainable, they must fit existing workflows. If ALTS or CAT requires instructors to operate entirely outside the LMS, manually move data, or use highly specialized infrastructure, adoption may remain limited. Interoperability matters: secure login, data export, assignment integration, and compatibility with class scheduling and grading systems all influence usability.

Practical sustainability is an educational issue. Even a pedagogically strong system will not scale if it is too cumbersome for teaching teams to use.

6.5 Accessibility and Usability

Adaptive systems must also be accessible. Interfaces should be readable, navigable, and usable across devices. Students with disabilities or additional support needs should not be disadvantaged by the platform. Explanations should be presented clearly, and interaction design should minimize unnecessary cognitive load. Accessibility is not an extra requirement; it is part of pedagogical fairness.

7. BENEFITS, RISKS, AND LIMITATIONS

7.1 Benefits for Students

For students, adaptive technologies can provide:

- more appropriately leveled questions,
- faster identification of learning gaps,
- less discouragement from overly difficult tests,
- more challenging pathways for stronger learners,
- more relevant explanations through background-aware framing,

- increased sense that the system responds to their learning rather than treating them as anonymous.

These benefits are especially important in interdisciplinary classrooms where students often begin from unequal positions.

7.2 Benefits for Instructors

For instructors, adaptive systems can:

- reveal hidden patterns in large classes,
- reduce time spent on low-value repetitive assessment,
- support earlier intervention,
- provide more fine-grained evidence of understanding,
- help scale translational explanation more systematically,
- support course redesign through analytics.

In other words, adaptive systems can enhance pedagogical precision.

7.3 Risks of Algorithmic Opacity

A major risk is opacity. If the adaptation logic is too hidden, students may not trust the system, and instructors may not know how to interpret outputs. Opaque systems can also make it difficult to identify bias or error. Therefore, adaptive learning environments should provide some explainability at the level of policy and design, even if students do not need the psychometric details.

7.4 Data Privacy and Fairness

Data privacy is another major concern. Adaptive systems necessarily collect student response data and sometimes background data. Such information must be stored securely, used transparently, and governed ethically. Fairness concerns also arise if background-aware personalization inadvertently stereotypes students or creates persistent lower-expectation tracks.

7.5 Avoiding Over-Automation of Pedagogy

The final risk is over-automation. Not everything valuable in teaching can or should be automated. Adaptive systems cannot fully replace human encouragement, interpretive judgment, or the relational trust that supports psychological safety. If institutions treat adaptive systems as substitutes for teaching rather than supports for it, the result may be efficient but impoverished learning. To navigate these challenges responsibly, Table 2 outlines the primary risks associated with adaptive learning systems alongside essential pedagogical safeguards.

Table 2. Risks and Safeguards in Adaptive Learning Systems

Risk	Why It Matters	Safeguard
Algorithmic opacity	Students/instructors may not trust decisions	Provide clear explanation of adaptation logic
Biased background use	May stereotype or limit learners	Use background as flexible support cue, not fixed track
Data privacy concerns	Sensitive learner data may be misused	Strong governance, consent, secure storage
Over-automation	Human teaching may be displaced	Keep instructor oversight central
Poor item calibration	Wrong difficulty decisions distort learning	Pilot, calibrate, and review items regularly
Accessibility failures	Some students may be disadvantaged by interface	Design for usability and inclusive access

8. FUTURE DIRECTIONS

8.1 Generative AI and Adaptive Explanation

As adaptive learning technologies continue to evolve, future systems will build upon established system capabilities. Table 2 provides a baseline mapping of current adaptive features and their intended pedagogical functions, serving as the foundation for the emerging directions discussed below. Generative AI opens new possibilities for adaptive explanation. Systems may increasingly be able to generate multiple context-sensitive explanations of the same concept on demand, tuned to disciplinary background, current misconception, or reading level. This could significantly enrich translational pedagogy if carefully controlled for accuracy and pedagogical quality.

However, generative explanation also introduces risks of inconsistency, hallucination, and over-personalization without conceptual discipline. Human oversight will remain essential.

8.2 Multimodal Learner Modeling

Future adaptive systems may move beyond response correctness to incorporate multimodal evidence such as interaction time, revision patterns, hint use, eye-tracking in research settings, or other learning signals. Such multimodal learner modeling could improve diagnosis, especially for distinguishing confusion, disengagement, and strategic experimentation.

8.3 Translational AI Tutors Across Disciplines

A promising long-term direction is the development of translational AI tutors capable of explaining the same computing concept differently to students from different disciplines while preserving formal rigor. Such tutors could act as always-available explanatory companions, particularly useful in large classes and self-study environments.

8.4 Research Agenda for ALTS

Future research on ALTS should address:

- whether background-aware explanation improves understanding more than difficulty-only adaptation,
- how students perceive fairness and transparency in such systems,
- what balance of automation and human intervention yields the best outcomes,
- how adaptive systems perform across different disciplines and courses,
- how to evaluate long-term transfer and identity effects, not just short-term efficiency.

9. CONCLUSION

9.1 Adaptive Systems as Pedagogical Enablers, Not Replacements

This chapter has argued that adaptive learning technologies can play a significant role in interdisciplinary computing education when they are understood as pedagogical enablers rather than replacements for teaching. In diverse and large-scale classrooms, adaptive systems can personalize learning by level and by context, helping students receive questions, explanations, and pathways that better match their current understanding and disciplinary background.

ALTS extends this potential by integrating background-aware translation into adaptive learning design. CAT contributes precision and efficiency in diagnosis. Instructor dashboards create new opportunities for targeted intervention. Together, these tools support a model of mass personalization that aligns well with translational pedagogy.

At the same time, the chapter has emphasized limits and responsibilities. Adaptive systems must be transparent, fair, accessible, and ethically governed. They should support human judgment, not displace it. They should widen access to rigor, not create hidden tracking or mechanized instruction detached from care.

9.2 Transition to Evidence and Continuous Quality Improvement

Adaptive technologies generate rich data, but data alone do not improve teaching. They must be interpreted, triangulated, and used for pedagogical refinement. The next chapter therefore turns to evidence, triangulation, and continuous quality improvement in cross-disciplinary teaching. If this chapter has focused on how adaptive systems personalize learning, the next explores how evidence from such systems and from broader classroom practice can be used to improve teaching over time.

REFERENCES

Anderson, J. R., Corbett, A. T., Koedinger, K. R., & Pelletier, R. (1995). Cognitive tutors: Lessons learned. *Journal of the Learning Sciences*, *4*(2), 167–207. DOI: 10.1207/s15327809jls0402_2

Aquil Mirza, M., & Cong, W. (Eds.). (2026). *Real-Time Robotics With IoT and Edge AI: Methods, Metrics, and Applications*. IGI Global Scientific Publishing., DOI: 10.4018/979-8-2600-0701-3

Brusilovsky, P., & Millán, E. (2007). User models for adaptive hypermedia and adaptive educational systems. In P. Brusilovsky, A. Kobsa, & W. Nejdl (Eds.), *The adaptive web* (pp. 3–53). Springer. https://doi.org/DOI: 10.1007/978-3-540-72079-9_1

Corbett, A. T., & Anderson, J. R. (1994). Knowledge tracing: Modeling the acquisition of procedural knowledge. *User Modeling and User-Adapted Interaction*, *4*(4), 253–278. DOI: 10.1007/BF01099821

Mohammed, A. (Ed.). (2026). *Advanced Concurrency, Buffering, and Web-Sync in Sensor Platforms: Zero-Loss Streams*. IGI Global Scientific Publishing., DOI: 10.4018/979-8-2600-1101-0

Mohammed, A., & Zangana, H. (Eds.). (2026). *Intelligent Construction Monitoring Systems: Real-Time Safety, Environmental Prediction, and Risk Management*. IGI Global Scientific Publishing., DOI: 10.4018/979-8-3373-9245-5

Wainer, H. (2000). *Computerized adaptive testing: A primer* (2nd ed.). Lawrence Erlbaum. DOI: 10.4324/9781410605931

Wainer, H. (2000). *Computerized adaptive testing: A primer* (2nd ed.). Lawrence Erlbaum. [cite: 4] DOI: 10.4324/9781410605931

Weiss, D. J., & Kingsbury, G. G. (1984). Application of computerized adaptive testing to educational problems. *Journal of Educational Measurement*, *21*(4), 361–375. DOI: 10.1111/j.1745-3984.1984.tb01040.x

Chapter 8
Evidence, Triangulation, and Continuous Quality Improvement in Cross-Disciplinary Computing Teaching

Wan'xu Sun
http://orcid.org/0009-0003-2418-2611
Department of Applied Mathematics, The Hong Kong Polytechnic University, Hong Kong

Jiaming Zhang
Department of Applied Mathematics, The Hong Kong Polytechnic University, Hong Kong

ABSTRACT

This chapter introduces systematic approaches to improve cross-disciplinary computing teaching using multi-source evidence collection, triangulation verification and continuous quality improvement. Per the authors, teaching evidence falls into five categories: quantitative statistics, qualitative feedback, student coursework, in-class performance data and long-term follow-up records, preventing biased evaluation from sole test scores or surveys. A four-dimensional triangulation model verifies teaching results via varied data sources, research methods, stakeholder opinions and different teaching periods to avoid one-sided assessment. Combined with iterative CQI, the chapter demonstrates how teachers adjust curricula, class-

DOI: 10.4018/979-8-2600-1811-8.ch008

room arrangements and grading standards based on verified empirical evidence. It also summarizes practical teaching difficulties and optimization advice to support instructional reform and quality control for interdisciplinary computing education.

1. INTRODUCTION

Teaching in cross-disciplinary computing environments is rarely improved by intuition alone. Instructors may sense that a class "went well," that students appeared engaged, or that an assignment produced interesting work, yet such impressions are only partial windows into actual learning. In translational and interdisciplinary computing education; where learners often come from different disciplinary cultures, possess uneven prior knowledge, and pursue different professional goals; the need for systematic evidence is even greater. A student in biology may struggle with abstraction in programming but excel in data interpretation; a design student may produce elegant interfaces yet avoid algorithmic reasoning; an engineering student may achieve high task completion while still misunderstanding the conceptual rationale for a method. These asymmetries mean that pedagogical decisions must be informed by evidence that is broad enough to capture variation, sensitive enough to detect hidden gaps, and structured enough to support continuous improvement.

Figure 1. Continuous Quality Improvement Cycle

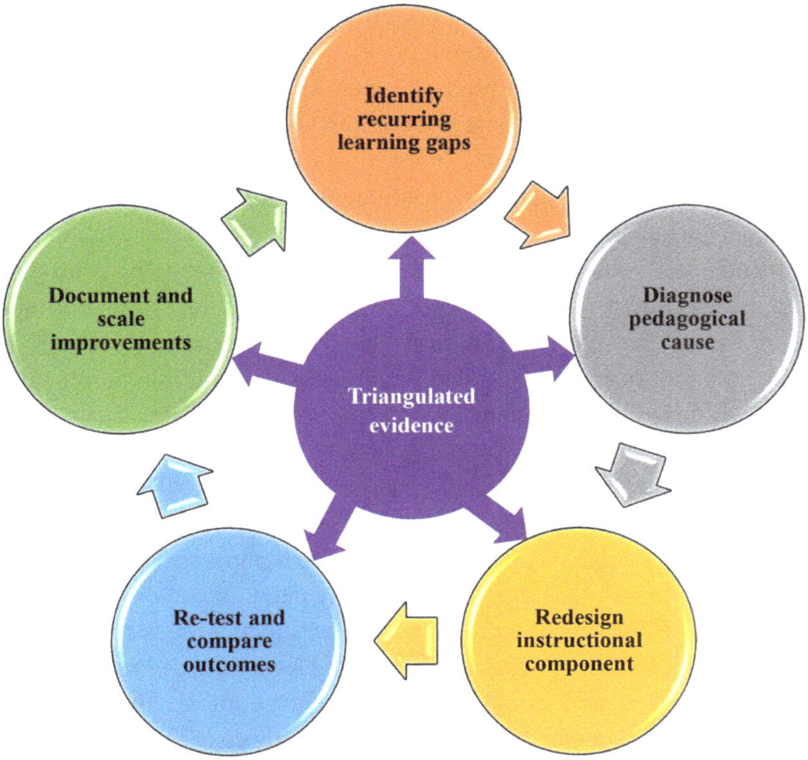

Evidence matters because teaching is a design activity. It involves selecting goals, sequencing tasks, framing concepts, timing feedback, calibrating difficulty, and aligning assessment with desired learning outcomes. Like any design activity, teaching improves through cycles of observation, testing, revision, and re-evaluation. Without evidence, pedagogical refinement is vulnerable to anecdote, habit, and bias. Instructors may overestimate the effectiveness of clear-sounding explanations, mistake participation for comprehension, or infer deep understanding from a small number of highly visible students. Conversely, they may undervalue a successful intervention simply because its effects are gradual or distributed across less vocal learners. Evidence provides a basis for moving from impressionistic teaching to evidence-informed teaching (Biggs & Tang, 2011; Hattie, 2009). This systematic progression of diagnostic refinement is modeled structurally in the Continuous Quality Improvement Cycle as shown in Figure 1.

The challenge is that no single indicator can adequately represent teaching quality. Course evaluation scores may be helpful, but student satisfaction does not map neatly onto learning gains. Assessment results may reveal achievement patterns, but they are shaped by task design, grading criteria, and prior experience. Attendance or online engagement data may suggest commitment, yet frequent participation can coexist with conceptual confusion. Student projects may demonstrate capability, but output quality may reflect team composition, topic familiarity, or external support. Even teacher reflection; essential for professional growth; can remain selective if not confronted with other forms of evidence. For this reason, the central argument of this chapter is that pedagogical quality in cross-disciplinary computing teaching is best improved through triangulation: the deliberate use of multiple forms of evidence, gathered from multiple stakeholders, across multiple points in time, and interpreted as part of a continuous quality improvement cycle.

Triangulation is especially valuable in interdisciplinary teaching because the meaning of "success" is inherently plural. Students do not all arrive with the same vocabulary, confidence, or identity as computing learners. Nor do they all need the same outcomes. A public health student may need computational literacy sufficient to critically use data tools; a media student may need practical scripting capability to automate workflows; an environmental science student may need modeling skills integrated with domain-specific interpretation. Because learning is situated differently for different learners, quality teaching in such contexts should be judged not by a single benchmark alone, but by converging patterns of evidence: what students say, what they do, what they produce, how they progress, where they struggle, and how these patterns change after instructional redesign.

This chapter explains how systematic evidence gathering and triangulation can be used to improve teaching quality in cross-disciplinary computing education. It clarifies what counts as evidence, outlines a triangulation framework, identifies relevant evidence sources in translational computing pedagogy, and presents a continuous quality improvement cycle that links evidence to redesign. It also examines ethical cautions in interpretation, particularly around student evaluation bias, mixed-cohort data, and responsible data use. The chapter concludes by showing how evidence-informed teaching can be institutionalized through dashboards, peer review, scholarship of teaching and learning, and program-level quality assurance. While detailed student transformation narratives are reserved for the next chapter, selected short student voice excerpts are included here where they help illustrate how evidence can reveal improvement opportunities.

2. WHAT COUNTS AS EVIDENCE IN TEACHING?

A common obstacle in pedagogical improvement is the narrow definition of evidence. In many settings, "evidence" is reduced to end-of-semester student evaluations or final grades. Both are useful, but neither is sufficient. Teaching evidence should be understood more broadly as any systematically gathered information that can reasonably inform judgments about learning, engagement, inclusion, instructional effectiveness, and the alignment between intended and achieved outcomes (Banta & Palomba, 2015; Biggs & Tang, 2011).

2.1 Quantitative indicators

Quantitative indicators are often the most visible because institutions routinely collect them. These include satisfaction scores, pass rates, withdrawal rates, grade distributions, attendance figures, online learning management system activity, response rates to practice tasks, and counts of support requests. In cross-disciplinary computing teaching, quantitative indicators are valuable because they can reveal macro-patterns that may be hard to detect through casual observation. For example, an instructor may notice that a few students are struggling with debugging, but grade distributions across cohorts may show that algorithmic reasoning has been a recurring bottleneck for three consecutive years. Similarly, a withdrawal pattern concentrated among learners from one disciplinary background may indicate that the entry assumptions of the course require reconsideration.

A useful quantitative profile often includes both central tendency and distribution. Average scores can conceal substantial subgroup variation. A course with a strong mean evaluation score may nonetheless have a cluster of students reporting very low confidence or very low relevance. In interdisciplinary classrooms, this matters because one subgroup's positive experience may mask another subgroup's exclusion. Therefore, where ethically and practically appropriate, quantitative indicators should be disaggregated by prior discipline, level of prior programming experience, study mode, or other relevant variables. Such disaggregation must be handled carefully, especially in small cohorts, but it can illuminate whether a course is equitable in effect rather than only effective on average (Kuh, 2008).

Illustrative institutional data can make this concrete. Suppose a computing-for-non-specialists module consistently receives overall student feedback scores in the range of 4.6 to 4.9 on a 5-point scale, while the departmental average remains around 4.2. This is encouraging, but the teaching team should not stop there. They should also ask: Are these scores stable across majors? Do students who report high satisfaction also demonstrate conceptual understanding? Have improved satisfaction scores coincided with reduced withdrawals, stronger pass rates, and more high-quality project outputs? If, for example, withdrawals decrease from 12% to 6%, pass rates increase from 82% to 91%, and the proportion of A-range work rises from 18% to 31% after specific pedagogical redesigns, then the numerical pattern is much more compelling than evaluation scores alone. The convergence of multiple quantitative indicators better supports a claim of improvement.

2.2 Qualitative indicators

Qualitative evidence captures what numbers alone cannot. It includes open-ended student feedback, reflective writing, focus group discussions, tutor observations, classroom field notes, instructor journals, peer observation comments, and consultation records. Qualitative evidence is particularly important in cross-disciplinary settings because the "why" behind performance or satisfaction often lies in disciplinary identity, confidence, and perceived relevance. A score may tell us that students found an assignment difficult; a written comment may reveal that they did not understand why the task mattered for their own field. A low participation rate in coding labs may suggest disengagement; interview data may show that students were avoiding embarrassment because they believed everyone else was more experienced.

Open-ended student comments are often especially useful when they are analyzed thematically rather than anecdotally. It is easy to overreact to one strong opinion, whether positive or negative. More rigorous use of qualitative evidence involves coding recurring themes: pace, clarity, workload, anxiety, relevance, support, collaboration, feedback timeliness, or confidence growth (Braun & Clarke, 2006). Such analysis helps distinguish isolated dissatisfaction from systematic patterns that warrant action.

A short student comment can sometimes identify a precise redesign need. Consider the following illustrative feedback:

"The examples were clear once explained, but I needed more time seeing the code change line by line before trying it myself."

This comment points not to wholesale failure, but to a specific instructional pacing issue. Another student might write:

"I finally understood loops when the example used ecological data instead of abstract numbers."

Here the issue is not simply cognitive difficulty but contextual relevance. Such comments are highly actionable when read alongside quantitative performance data and classroom observations.

2.3 Output-based indicators

Student outputs provide direct evidence of what learners can do with the knowledge and skills a course intends to develop. These outputs include code submissions, data analyses, visualizations, reports, capstone projects, interdisciplinary prototypes, poster presentations, and externally assessed work. Output-based evidence is often stronger than satisfaction measures because it reflects performance in relation to explicit tasks. In cross-disciplinary computing teaching, outputs can show whether students are not only learning syntax or tools but also transferring computing methods into domain-specific problem solving.

However, outputs must be interpreted carefully. Strong final products do not always indicate evenly distributed learning. Some students may rely heavily on templates, peers, or prior experience. Group projects can conceal uneven participation. Conversely, modest outputs from novice students may represent substantial learning gains if baseline knowledge was very low. The value of output-based evidence therefore depends on assessment design, rubric transparency, scaffolding, and opportunities to compare performance over time.

Useful output-based evidence may include rubric-level trends rather than only overall marks. For instance, students might score well on implementation but poorly on interpretation of computational outputs in disciplinary terms. Or they may produce visually polished dashboards but weak documentation and poor reproducibility. Such patterns help identify which dimensions of interdisciplinary computing competence need reinforcement. External recognition; such as student work accepted for showcase events, competitions, or partner use; can also serve as a meaningful indicator, though it should not be overgeneralized as proof of broad cohort success.

2.4 Process indicators and participation data

Process indicators focus on how students engage during learning rather than only what they produce at the end. These include class attendance, lab attendance, completion of formative quizzes, frequency of code execution attempts, forum participation, help-seeking behavior, office-hour usage, peer discussion patterns, and revision submissions. Process data are especially valuable in computing because struggle is often distributed across the learning journey. Students may disengage quietly long before their final grades reveal trouble.

Help-seeking patterns deserve particular attention. Frequent consultation requests may initially seem like a sign of weakness, but in many contexts they are a healthy indicator of engagement and self-regulation. Students who ask early questions often recover from confusion more effectively than those who remain silent until assessment deadlines. Thus, an increase in consultation uptake after introducing low-stigma support structures may signal instructional success rather than deficiency. In the same way, repeated attempts on low-stakes coding tasks can suggest productive persistence.

Participation data can also reveal equity issues. For example, students from non-computing backgrounds may attend lectures regularly but avoid practical labs where they fear public failure. Others may watch recordings repeatedly but rarely post questions. These patterns should not be pathologized automatically, but they should prompt inquiry into whether the learning environment is psychologically safe, whether expectations are clear, and whether support pathways are visible (Brookfield, 2017; Tinto, 2012).

2.5 Longitudinal indicators

Longitudinal evidence tracks change over time across a semester, across cohorts, or across students' broader educational pathways. It is among the most powerful forms of evidence because teaching improvements often produce effects that are cumulative rather than immediate. A redesigned introduction to computational thinking may not transform one assignment dramatically, but it may reduce later attrition, improve project quality in advanced modules, or increase students' willingness to take optional computing electives.

Longitudinal indicators include pre/post confidence surveys, repeated concept inventories, year-on-year grade trends, retention into subsequent modules, delayed student reflections, alumni reports of transfer into professional practice, and curriculum-level tracking of progression. For interdisciplinary teaching, longitudinal evidence can show whether an introductory course merely helps students survive one module or actually changes their relationship to computing as a disciplinary tool.

For example, if a computing-for-life-sciences course introduces domain-relevant datasets and scaffolded labs, and three years later the program observes higher enrollment in advanced data analysis electives, stronger final-year research methods projects, and more students independently using code in dissertations, then the pedagogical effects exceed immediate module metrics. Such evidence supports a broader claim: that good teaching can alter trajectories, identities, and capabilities over time (Henderson et al., 2011; Kuh, 2008).

3. TRIANGULATION AS A QUALITY FRAMEWORK

3.1 Definition and purpose of triangulation

Triangulation refers to the use of multiple data sources, methods, perspectives, or time points to strengthen understanding of a phenomenon. Originally associated with social research methodology, triangulation is now widely recognized as a robust strategy for educational inquiry because it reduces the risk of drawing conclusions from partial or biased evidence (Denzin, 1978; Patton, 1999). In the context of teaching quality, triangulation does not imply that all evidence must perfectly agree. Rather, it aims to produce a richer and more credible interpretation by examining where evidence converges, diverges, or complicates one another. To assist educators in selecting and balancing these diverse metrics, Table 1 outlines the primary teaching evidence sources alongside their core strengths, structural limitations, and optimal analytical cross-references.

Table 1. Evidence Sources, Strengths, and Limitations

Evidence Source	**What it Reveals**	**Strengths**	**Limitations**	**Best Used With**
Student Evaluations (e.g., eSFQ)	• Student perception of teaching clarity, engagement, and course organization. • Subjective learner satisfaction.	• Quantifiable and easy to track across semesters. • High response rates when institutionalized. • Direct measure of the student experience.	• Vulnerable to popularity biases, grading expectations, and timing. • Does not directly measure actual cognitive learning or skill acquisition.	**Peer Observations & Assessment Trends** (to cross-verify student perception against actual performance and teaching practice).
Assessment Trends	• Distribution of student performance over time. • Mastery of specific learning outcomes across cohorts.	• Objective, quantifiable data directly tied to grading benchmarks. • Highlights systemic grading anomalies or shifting cohort standards.	• Grade inflation or changes in assessment difficulty can distort long-term comparison. • Does not capture why a cohort struggled.	**Learning Analytics** (to see behavioral patterns leading to specific grade outcomes) and **Student Outputs**.
Consultation Logs	• Granular, qualitative student misconceptions. • Individual learning barriers and common roadblocks outside of class.	• Unfiltered, qualitative insight into specific areas where students struggle most. • Shows student help-seeking behavior.	• Small, self-selecting sample size (typically captures struggling or highly motivated students only). • Time-consuming to document systematically.	**Student Evaluations** (to check if individual consultation complaints align with macro-level course feedback).

continued on following page

Table 1. Continued

Evidence Source	What it Reveals	Strengths	Limitations	Best Used With
Peer / Expert Observations	• Alignment of pedagogy with curriculum standards. • Real-time classroom management, delivery rhythm, and student interaction.	• High professional validity and constructive feedback from disciplinary peers. • Evaluates actual teaching mechanics rather than perceptions.	• Can cause a "Hawthorne effect" (altered teaching behavior due to being observed). • Represents a snapshot/single point in time.	**Student Evaluations** (to balance professional pedagogical critique with consumer-end student experience).
Student Outputs & Portfolios	• Direct evidence of student work quality, authentic problem-solving, and synthesis of concepts.	• Authentic proof of achieved learning outcomes. • Highlights the tangible application of knowledge (e.g., code, prototypes, designs).	• Subjective and highly variable across different project scopes. • Time-intensive to evaluate systematically across large classes.	**Assessment Trends & Learning Analytics** (to evaluate the final mastery alongside the digital engagement process).
Learning Analytics	• Digital engagement behaviors (LMS page views, video watch times, quiz attempts, submission timing).	• Objective, continuous, and non-intrusive digital tracking. • Early detection of disengaged students before final assessments.	• High engagement metrics do not automatically equal deep cognitive processing or understanding. • Relies entirely on LMS-based activity.	**Assessment Trends** (to correlate digital study habits directly with actual academic performance).
Progression Data	• Long-term retention, prerequisite readiness, and student success rates in subsequent advanced courses.	• Reveals the long-term impact and foundational durability of your teaching. • Highly valued by institutional curriculum boards.	• Confounded by many external factors (subsequent teachers, student life changes). • Delayed feedback loop (takes semesters or years to collect).	**Assessment Trends** (to compare immediate course performance with long-term downstream academic success).

The purpose of triangulation in pedagogy is not bureaucratic accumulation of data. It is disciplined sense-making. A triangulated approach asks questions such as: Do student perceptions of clarity align with actual performance on conceptually related tasks? Do consultation records support the themes emerging in survey comments? Does the same issue appear in teacher observations, assessment outcomes, and project quality? Did an intervention improve one indicator while worsening another? Such questions move teaching evaluation beyond simplistic judgments and toward more actionable diagnosis.

In cross-disciplinary computing teaching, triangulation is especially important because learner heterogeneity increases the likelihood of misleading signals. A lecture may receive high satisfaction because it was accessible to novices, while advanced learners feel underchallenged. A practical assignment may produce strong grades because students followed templates effectively, while transfer of learning remains weak. A group project may look successful in external presentation but conceal widespread anxiety or unequal participation. Triangulation helps uncover these layered realities. The structural overlap of these diverse evaluative modes is illustrated in the Triangulation Model for Teaching Evidence in Figure 2.

Figure 2. Triangulation Model for Teaching Evidence

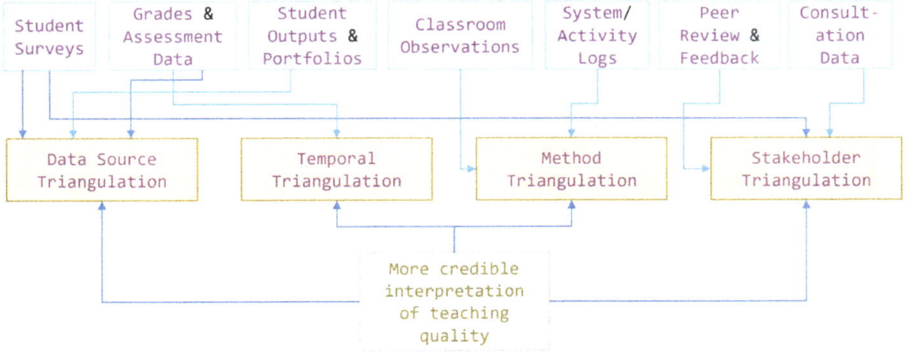

3.2 Data source triangulation

Data source triangulation involves comparing evidence from different sources. In teaching, this might include student surveys, student work, teacher logs, peer observations, learning analytics, tutor reports, and external examiner comments. The central principle is that each source captures only one angle. Student comments provide lived experience; assessment data reflect task performance; observations illuminate enacted pedagogy; analytics show patterns of behavior; external reviewers bring comparative perspective.

Consider a recurring concern about students' understanding of debugging. A single data source might be ambiguous. End-of-semester evaluations may not mention debugging at all. Yet weekly lab notes may show repeated requests for help with tracing errors, formative quiz data may reveal low performance on code interpretation items, and project submissions may exhibit copy-and-paste fixes without explanation. Together, these sources suggest that debugging is not a minor inconvenience but a structural learning gap requiring redesign.

Data source triangulation is particularly helpful when sources disagree. Suppose students rate a course highly for support, but attendance in support sessions remains low. This discrepancy could suggest that support exists but is not needed; or, alternatively, that students value the idea of support without feeling comfortable using it. Additional sources, such as interviews or consultation records, may clarify whether low uptake results from confidence, scheduling barriers, or stigma.

3.3 Method triangulation

Method triangulation refers to using different ways of collecting evidence on the same issue; for example, surveys, interviews, observations, artifact analysis, and statistical trend analysis. Different methods generate different forms of knowledge. Surveys can capture breadth; interviews can reveal nuance; observations can document actual behavior; artifact analysis can demonstrate quality of learning products. Using only one method risks distortion. Student surveys may capture perceptions but not performance. Observations may capture visible dynamics but not private confusion. Grades may capture outcomes without showing process.

Method triangulation supports stronger pedagogical decisions because it allows instructors to test whether an apparent problem is robust across modes of inquiry. If students report that weekly practicals feel rushed, and observational notes confirm that many are still completing guided steps when discussion moves on, and consultation records show a spike in "I fell behind in class" messages, then the diagnosis is much stronger than if based on survey sentiment alone.

3.4 Stakeholder triangulation

Stakeholder triangulation incorporates perspectives from different groups affected by the teaching process: students, instructors, tutors, peer reviewers, course leaders, support staff, industry partners, or external examiners. This matters because each stakeholder experiences the course differently. Students experience cognitive load, relevance, confidence, and usability. Instructors understand intended outcomes and design rationale. Tutors often detect recurring micro-level misunderstandings. External reviewers may notice alignment issues or benchmark concerns invisible to those close to the course.

In interdisciplinary computing education, stakeholder triangulation is particularly valuable because the stakes of learning differ by context. A domain specialist co-teaching with a computing educator may observe that students can execute code but cannot interpret results meaningfully in domain terms. A placement supervisor may later report that students are technically capable but hesitant to use their skills independently. These perspectives extend the frame of evidence beyond the classroom itself.

3.5 Temporal triangulation

Temporal triangulation compares evidence across different moments: before, during, and after an intervention; early and late semester; one cohort and the next; or immediate and delayed outcomes. Time matters because many pedagogical interventions have nonlinear effects. An instructional redesign may initially lower satisfaction if students encounter greater productive struggle, yet improve long-term retention or transfer. Conversely, a highly guided experience may produce short-term comfort but weak later independence.

For example, introducing more hands-on coding in the first half of a semester may initially generate comments such as "the class is more demanding now," but mid-semester confidence surveys, reduced final withdrawal rates, and stronger project autonomy may demonstrate that the redesign was beneficial overall. Temporal triangulation protects instructors from overreacting to early discomfort and from declaring success based on short-term positive affect alone (Deslauriers et al., 2019).

4. EVIDENCE SOURCES IN TRANSLATIONAL COMPUTING PEDAGOGY

4.1 Student feedback instruments

Student feedback instruments remain one of the most common sources of teaching evidence, and they can be useful when interpreted carefully. Standard end-of-course surveys often include items on organization, clarity, support, fairness, and overall satisfaction. In some contexts, modules may receive consistently high feedback scores, such as 4.6 to 4.9 out of 5 against a department average of 4.2. Such results can indicate that students perceive the teaching as accessible, responsive, and well-structured. Yet their value increases significantly when complemented by item-level analysis and qualitative comments.

For cross-disciplinary computing teaching, generic teaching evaluation items may miss key dimensions such as perceived relevance to students' home disciplines, confidence in applying computing methods, inclusivity for novices, or availability of low-stakes practice. Therefore, bespoke short pulse surveys can be useful additions. These might ask students, at several points in the semester, whether they understand why current computing topics matter for their field, whether they know where to get help, whether the pace is manageable, and whether practical tasks feel too guided or too open.

A particularly useful strategy is combining Likert-scale agreement items with one open question such as: "What helped your learning most this week, and what made learning harder?" This produces near-real-time evidence for refinement rather than waiting until the course has ended. Where response rates are strong, such instruments can reveal actionable patterns. For example, if 86% of respondents agree that examples are relevant, but only 61% agree that they feel confident working independently after class, then relevance is not the main issue; transfer and autonomy are.

4.2 Assessment performance trends

Assessment trends are among the most important evidence sources because they connect teaching directly to demonstrated achievement. Useful analysis includes pass rates, fail rates, distinction or A-range proportions, criterion-level performance, progression between formative and summative tasks, and comparative trends across cohorts. The goal is not merely to report whether grades went up or down, but to interpret what changed and why.

Suppose a module redesign replaced one large final coding task with staged assignments, including low-stakes formative checkpoints and a reflective interpretation component. If, over two years, pass rates rise from 82% to 91%, withdrawals fall from 12% to 6%, and A-range outcomes increase from 18% to 31%, the data suggest more than random fluctuation. If rubric analysis further shows gains specifically in documentation, code interpretation, and domain-specific framing, then the redesign likely improved alignment between teaching activities and intended interdisciplinary outcomes.

However, grade inflation and cohort differences must always be considered. A stronger performance profile does not automatically prove better teaching. Assessment difficulty may have changed, or one cohort may have entered with more prior experience. Therefore, performance data should be read alongside evidence about entry-level skill, task comparability, moderation processes, and other indicators of learning.

4.3 Consultation and help-seeking patterns

Help-seeking is a rich but often underused evidence source. Office-hour attendance, email themes, forum posts, booking patterns for tutorials, and informal support requests can all reveal where students are encountering friction. In computing teaching, the timing of help-seeking is especially informative. Questions that arise before students begin practical work often indicate uncertainty about instructions or confidence. Questions that cluster after an initial attempt may indicate productive challenge. Questions appearing only near deadlines may signal avoidance, hidden struggle, or poor workload management.

An evidence-informed teaching team might log consultation themes systematically. For example, over one semester, support requests might cluster into categories such as "setting up software," "understanding loops," "debugging errors," "interpreting outputs," and "project topic fit." If 40% of consultations are about software setup in the first two weeks, this suggests a front-loaded barrier that may be reduced through onboarding redesign. If anxiety-laden messages increase before assessments, additional structured drop-ins or peer-led revision sessions may be needed.

Help-seeking data also reveal whether students perceive support as psychologically accessible. After introducing anonymous question boards, peer learning clinics, or explicitly normalizing help-seeking in class, a course may see more support uptake alongside improved completion rates. Rather than interpreting increased support usage as failure, it may be more accurate to see it as evidence that hidden confusion is becoming visible early enough to address (Nicol & Macfarlane-Dick, 2006).

4.4 Classroom observation and teaching logs

Classroom observation adds direct evidence about enacted pedagogy. Peer observation, tutor observation, or structured self-observation can document pacing, interaction quality, question distribution, student participation, transitions between explanation and practice, and responsiveness to confusion. Teaching logs or reflective memos extend this by preserving instructor observations immediately after sessions: what worked, where students hesitated, which examples landed, what instructions proved ambiguous, and what unexpected misconceptions emerged.

Observation evidence is useful because it often captures issues before they appear in assessments. For instance, a peer observer may note that students remain passive during live coding demonstrations and only become active when given explicit pause points to predict outputs. An instructor log may record that students asked very few questions during class but queued afterward with similar uncertainties, indicating that public questioning feels risky. These observations can lead to concrete changes such as built-in think-pair-share moments, anonymous polling, or slower segmenting of demonstrations.

Where possible, observation should be guided by clear prompts rather than general impressions. Example prompts include: Which students participated and which did not? At what points did confusion become visible? Were examples disciplinary-neutral or clearly contextualized? Did students have enough time to attempt tasks before solutions were shown? Such structure makes observation more useful for quality improvement rather than generic affirmation.

4.5 Student outputs and external recognition

Student outputs represent a particularly compelling evidence source in translational computing pedagogy because they embody the integration of technical and disciplinary learning. Good evidence may come from project portfolios, datasets students cleaned and analyzed, code notebooks, interdisciplinary prototypes, reflective commentaries, and final presentations. When these outputs show authentic application of computing to real or realistic domain problems, they provide strong support for claims about relevance and transfer.

External recognition can strengthen this evidence. Examples include projects selected for university showcases, awards in hackathons, adoption by community or industry partners, positive feedback from placement supervisors, or use of student-developed tools in departmental research. Such indicators should be treated as supplementary, not definitive, because they often involve only a subset of students. Still, they can signal that a curriculum is enabling high-value applied work.

A brief student testimony can also illuminate the significance of output-based evidence:

"I never thought I would use coding in my psychology project, but building my own data-cleaning workflow made my dissertation feel more like research and less like just following software menus."

Comments like this are not substitutes for systematic data, but they help interpret what high-quality outputs mean: not simply better grades, but increased ownership, confidence, and disciplinary integration.

5. CONTINUOUS QUALITY IMPROVEMENT CYCLE

Continuous quality improvement (CQI) treats teaching not as a fixed performance but as an iterative process of evidence-informed refinement. CQI is widely used in organizational improvement and increasingly applied to curriculum and pedagogy because it emphasizes disciplined cycles of identifying problems, testing changes, and evaluating effects (Deming, 1986; Banta & Palomba, 2015). In cross-disciplinary computing education, CQI is particularly appropriate because learner needs evolve, technologies change, and disciplinary applications shift over time.

5.1 Identify recurring learning gaps

The first step is identifying recurring learning gaps rather than isolated incidents. A learning gap may be conceptual, procedural, motivational, affective, or contextual. Examples include persistent misunderstanding of variables and iteration, inability to connect computing methods to disciplinary questions, low confidence among novices, poor debugging resilience, or uneven engagement across subgroups.

The key word is recurring. One difficult class session does not necessarily justify redesign. Instructors should look for repeated patterns across evidence sources and time points. If students in multiple cohorts struggle to move from guided exercises to independent tasks, that is a recurrent gap. If the same rubric criteria show weakness each semester, that is a recurrent gap. If support requests repeatedly spike around the same concept, that is a recurrent gap. The aim is to distinguish structural teaching challenges from random noise. This pattern matching becomes highly specialized when students are trying to build software for technical domains; such as processing spatial risk vectors in heavy industrial management (Mohammed & Zangana, 2026) or orchestrating real-time streaming pipelines across physical robotic configurations (Aquil Mirza & Cong, 2026). To clarify how these actionable signals translate into systemic curriculum updates, Table 2 provides a matrix of common evidence patterns linked directly to targeted instructional improvements.

Table 2. Example Improvement Actions Linked to Evidence

Evidence Pattern	Interpretation (The Gap)	Improvement Action (Intervention)	Follow-up Measure (Evaluation)
Pattern 1: Low quiz scores on loops + repeated "I get lost alone" comments + many help requests.	**Explanation-to-application gap:** Students understand syntax passively but lack code-tracing and construction skills when working independently.	Add peer-instruction prediction pauses during lectures and scaffolded, partial-code (Parsons) exercises in labs.	Compare next cohort quiz performance on loop-specific questions and analyze patterns in help-desk tickets.
Pattern 2: Learning Analytics Sudden drop-off in LMS video watch-times and repository commits exactly two weeks before the major project milestone.	**Procrastination or cognitive overload:** The project instructions or environment setup are overwhelming, stalling student momentum early.	Introduce a mandatory, low-stakes "Milestone 0" (e.g., repository initialization and environment handshake setup verification) in Week 4.	Track the percentage of on-time repository initializations and compare final project completion rates against prior terms.
Pattern 3: Mid-Term Evaluations High scores for instructor enthusiasm, but multiple written complaints stating, "The lab tasks don't match what is tested in exams."	**Constructive alignment gap:** The assessments demand higher-order cognitive skills (synthesis/ evaluation) than the procedural practice provided in labs.	Redesign laboratory worksheets to include "Challenge Sections" that mirror the deep troubleshooting and problem-solving required in exams.	Conduct a item-analysis correlation check between lab performance metrics and corresponding exam questions.

continued on following page

Table 2. Continued

Evidence Pattern	Interpretation (The Gap)	Improvement Action (Intervention)	Follow-up Measure (Evaluation)
Pattern 4: Peer Observation Observer notes that student engagement drops significantly during the middle 20 minutes of class, with active participation limited to the front rows.	**Passive delivery vulnerability:** The lecture relies too heavily on one-way transmission, failing to sustain active retrieval or wide participation.	Implement anonymous, interactive polling (e.g., live clicker questions or Think-Pair-Share cycles) every 15–20 minutes.	Review subsequent peer observation field logs focusing on wide-row classroom engagement metrics and track response rates.
Pattern 5: Progression Data Students pass the prerequisite class with high marks, but subsequent instructors report they struggle heavily with basic memory management/ pointers.	**Surface-level retention or artificial inflation:** Assessment setups allowed students to pass via template-matching without building durable mental models.	Revise the foundational course curriculum to incorporate low-level debugging tasks using tools like GDB or Valgrind.	Query instructors of the downstream advanced classes to evaluate student baseline readiness scores at the start of the next term.
Pattern 6: Student Outputs Final project deliverables look polished visually, but code reviews reveal poor architectural structure and a total lack of documentation.	**Assessment criteria misalignment:** The grading rubric inadvertently over-weighted functional outcomes while ignoring code quality and engineering discipline.	Update the assessment rubric to explicitly dedicate 30% of the total grade to software design patterns, commenting standards, and architecture.	Evaluate random code quality samples across cohorts using a standardized code-health matrix.

5.2 Diagnose pedagogical cause

Once a gap is identified, the next step is diagnosis. CQI fails when instructors jump too quickly from symptoms to solutions. Low project quality may result from many causes: unclear task framing, weak feedback timing, insufficient practice, poor prerequisite knowledge, cognitive overload, low perceived relevance, or assessment misalignment. Diagnosis requires triangulating evidence to determine the most plausible pedagogical cause.

Suppose many students misunderstand conditional logic. The cause may not simply be "students are weak." Observations might show that examples were too abstract, feedback comments might indicate that misconceptions were not addressed early, and support logs might reveal that students were confused by syntax as well as logic. Alternatively, if students perform well on isolated exercises but poorly in projects, the issue may be transfer rather than understanding. Good diagnosis resists simplistic deficit explanations and instead examines the teaching ecology.

5.3 Redesign instructional component

The third step is redesign. Redesign should be specific, proportionate, and theory-informed. It may involve changing examples, pacing, sequence, task scaffolding, feedback mechanisms, assessment structure, support channels, or disciplinary framing. In cross-disciplinary computing, redesign often works best when it addresses both cognition and context. Students may need not only clearer explanations but also examples that resonate with their disciplinary motivations.

Examples of redesign include:

- replacing abstract demonstration datasets with field-specific ones;
- inserting prediction pauses into live coding;
- breaking a large project into staged milestones;
- adding low-stakes formative debugging tasks;
- offering multiple project pathways aligned with different disciplinary interests;
- creating short pre-lab onboarding resources for software setup;
- using peer discussion to normalize error-making;
- integrating reflective prompts asking students to interpret computational results in domain language.

5.4 Re-test and compare outcomes

No redesign should be assumed effective simply because it appears sensible. CQI requires re-testing. After implementing a change, instructors gather comparable forms of evidence and examine whether outcomes improved, worsened, or shifted in unexpected ways. Improvement may appear in several forms: better conceptual performance, higher support usage earlier in the semester, stronger confidence reports, lower withdrawal, stronger output quality, or better subgroup equity.

Re-testing should attend not only to whether average outcomes improved, but also to distribution and trade-offs. A redesign that boosts novice success but leaves advanced learners disengaged may require further differentiation. A change that improves satisfaction but not assessment performance may have reduced challenge without improving learning. A modification that produces stronger final outcomes at the cost of unsustainable staff workload may need adaptation before scaling.

5.5 Document and scale improvements

The final step is documentation and scaling. Good teaching often remains private, residing in individual memory rather than institutional practice. CQI becomes sustainable only when improvement actions and their evidential basis are documented. This may take the form of teaching enhancement reports, annual review summaries, shared redesign templates, assessment review notes, or scholarship outputs.

Documentation serves at least three purposes. First, it prevents repeated reinvention and preserves institutional learning. Second, it enables peer scrutiny and collaborative refinement. Third, it supports scaling: if one intervention improved learning in a mixed-discipline coding module, analogous principles may be adapted to related courses. Scaling should still be context-sensitive; an intervention effective for first-year biology students may require modification for postgraduate public policy students. Even so, codifying what was changed, why it was changed, and what evidence supported improvement is essential for quality culture.

6. SAMPLE EVIDENCE-TO-IMPROVEMENT CASES

This section presents concise examples of how triangulated evidence can lead to targeted pedagogical refinement. These are not extended narrative case studies, but structured illustrations of the CQI logic.

6.1 Revising explanations after widespread misunderstanding

A recurring issue in introductory computing is that students appear to follow explanations in class but later cannot apply the concept independently. In one illustrative scenario, students performed reasonably on guided in-class tasks involving loops, yet formative quiz scores on loop construction remained low. Open-ended comments repeatedly mentioned "understanding in class but getting lost alone." Consultation records showed frequent requests for help phrased as "I don't know where to start." Peer observation of live coding sessions noted that students were copying code but not predicting what each section would do.

Triangulation pointed to a pedagogical problem: explanations were too fluent from the instructor's perspective and did not slow down the transition from seeing code to reasoning through it. The redesign involved shorter code segments, explicit verbalization of decision points, prediction pauses, and partially completed exercises requiring students to explain outputs before writing new code. A one-page debugging heuristic sheet was also introduced.

The following semester, quiz performance on loops improved, support requests shifted from "I don't understand loops" to more specific debugging questions, and rubric scores for control-flow logic in project work increased. Student comments reflected the change:

"The stop-and-predict moments were frustrating at first, but they made me realize what I was assuming rather than actually understanding."

This example illustrates how misunderstanding may not be solved by repeating explanations louder or longer. The issue was not exposure, but the cognitive structure of explanation.

6.2 Increasing hands-on work in response to feedback

Cross-disciplinary learners often report that computing makes sense only when they manipulate data or code themselves. In an illustrative module, end-of-term surveys were positive overall, but open comments repeatedly asked for "more time to try things in class." Teaching logs noted that practical tasks were frequently compressed after extended explanations. Attendance remained high, yet office-hour demand surged before assignments, suggesting that students needed more supported practice earlier.

The redesign shifted the session balance from explanation-heavy lectures toward workshop-style classes. Mini-explanations were capped at shorter intervals, followed by immediate hands-on tasks. Students worked first on tightly scaffolded exercises, then on small extensions using disciplinary datasets. Tutors were briefed to capture recurring questions in a shared log.

The results were encouraging. Mid-semester pulse surveys showed stronger agreement with the statement "I feel able to attempt tasks independently after class." Consultation patterns became more evenly distributed rather than deadline-peaked. Final project submissions demonstrated greater variation and originality, indicating that students were less dependent on reproducing examples. This aligns with broader evidence that active learning tends to improve student performance in STEM contexts (Freeman et al., 2014; Prince, 2004).

6.3 Redesigning project pathways for better relevance

One common challenge in interdisciplinary computing courses is that a single project brief may not feel equally meaningful to all students. In one illustrative case, a generic final project required students to analyze a common dataset using prescribed techniques. Grades were acceptable, but qualitative feedback repeatedly described the project as "technically fine but not connected to my field." Some students completed the task competently while expressing little sense of ownership.

The teaching team reviewed student comments, output quality, and consultation themes. They found that students asked many questions not about technical difficulty, but about whether they could adapt the project toward their disciplinary interests. The redesign introduced multiple project pathways: health data, environmental monitoring, business analytics, social science survey analysis, and self-proposed pathways with approval. Common computational learning outcomes were retained, but the application domain became more flexible.

After implementation, student engagement improved noticeably. Project proposals were submitted earlier, consultation questions became more substantive, and final presentations showed stronger disciplinary interpretation. The quality of reflective commentary also improved, suggesting that relevance supported deeper integration rather than merely higher motivation. One student wrote:

"Choosing a dataset related to urban mobility made the coding worth the effort. I was not just learning Python; I was answering a question I actually care about."

This kind of redesign is especially important in translational computing pedagogy because relevance is not decorative; it is often a precondition for sustained effort and transfer (Mishra & Koehler, 2006; Kuh, 2008).

6.4 Enhancing support for anxious or struggling learners

Not all learning barriers are conceptual. Anxiety, impostor feelings, and fear of public failure can significantly shape participation in computing classrooms, especially among students entering from disciplines where coding is perceived as alien or highly technical. In one illustrative setting, attendance remained respectable, but many students reported low confidence in optional surveys. Support uptake was paradoxically low despite repeated encouragement. Open comments included phrases such as "I didn't want to ask a basic question" and "I thought everyone else was coping."

Triangulated evidence suggested that support existed but was not fully accessible. The teaching team introduced several changes: anonymous question submission during class, a weekly "common confusions" summary, peer-assisted drop-in labs, explicit normalization of struggle in teaching scripts, and early-semester messaging that seeking help is a sign of effective learning rather than weakness. Tutors were also trained to use non-judgmental response language and to surface common errors without identifying individuals.

Subsequent evidence showed a rise in early-semester support usage, reduced last-minute panic messages, improved self-reported confidence, and modest but meaningful gains in completion rates. Importantly, comments indicated a shift in classroom climate:

"Once I saw that other people were confused about the same things, I stopped assuming I was the problem."

This case underscores that quality improvement in computing teaching is not only about content delivery. It is also about the social architecture of learning.

7. DATA INTERPRETATION AND ETHICAL CAUTION

Evidence-informed teaching is only as strong as the interpretations made from the evidence. Poor interpretation can lead to inappropriate interventions, overconfident conclusions, and harmful simplifications. In cross-disciplinary computing education, where cohorts are diverse and data may be messy, caution is essential.

7.1 Misreading satisfaction as learning

One of the most common errors in higher education is equating student satisfaction with student learning. Satisfaction matters; students are more likely to engage in environments they experience as respectful, organized, and supportive. Yet a satisfying course may not produce strong learning, and a demanding course that yields significant learning may not always feel comfortable in the moment. Research on active learning and desirable difficulties suggests that students may underestimate learning in more effortful instructional designs even when performance improves (Deslauriers et al., 2019; Hattie, 2009).

In computing education, this tension often appears when instructors reduce challenge to avoid complaints or when students prefer highly guided examples that feel clear but do not promote independent problem solving. Therefore, positive evaluation scores should be interpreted as one component of teaching quality, not its sole or ultimate indicator. The key question is whether satisfaction aligns with evidence of learning, confidence growth, transfer, and persistence.

7.2 Biases in student evaluations

Student evaluations can be influenced by factors unrelated to instructional quality, including gender bias, racial bias, charisma effects, disciplinary expectations, perceived course easiness, and grading expectations (Marsh, 1987; Uttl et al., 2017). These biases do not make evaluations useless, but they require cautious interpretation and should never be the only basis for high-stakes judgments about teaching quality.

In interdisciplinary computing teaching, additional distortions may arise because students evaluate from different epistemic cultures. A student accustomed to open-ended critique may find structured coding exercises restrictive; a student accustomed to right-answer assessment may find exploratory tasks vague. Their evaluations reflect real experience, but not always a common frame of reference. This makes item-level analysis and qualitative contextualization especially important.

Institutions should therefore interpret evaluations alongside other evidence: assessment trends, observation, peer review, support patterns, and output quality. They should also prefer aggregated patterns over isolated comments, and they should avoid incentivizing pedagogical conservatism through overreliance on popularity metrics.

7.3 Small-signal interpretation in mixed cohorts

Cross-disciplinary computing classes are often modest in size and internally diverse. This creates a methodological challenge: small numbers can generate unstable signals, and subgroup analysis may be both informative and risky. A small drop in one year's grades may reflect cohort variation rather than design failure. A cluster of negative comments from one subgroup may indicate a real inclusion issue; or may reflect a temporary mismatch between the course and a particular intake profile.

The solution is not to ignore small signals, but to interpret them proportionately and in context. Mixed-method evidence is especially important here. If a small subgroup appears to underperform, do qualitative comments, attendance patterns, and support requests point in the same direction? Is the issue recurring over multiple cohorts? Are there plausible curricular or entry-level explanations? Do external examiners or peer reviewers see the same concern? Instructors should treat small signals as prompts for inquiry, not immediate proof.

7.4 Ethical use of student data

As evidence gathering becomes more systematic, ethical responsibility increases. Student data should be collected transparently, used proportionately, and protected carefully. Learners should understand what kinds of data are being gathered, why they are being used, and how confidentiality will be maintained. Data use should serve educational improvement rather than surveillance. Particular caution is needed with learning analytics, attendance monitoring, and help-seeking records, which can easily drift from support-oriented use into deficit labeling if poorly governed.

Ethical use also means avoiding stigmatizing interpretations. Students from non-computing backgrounds should not be framed as problems to be fixed; rather, their experiences should inform more inclusive design. Likewise, students who use support frequently should not be pathologized if support use is part of successful learning. Where testimonials or quotations are shared, they should be anonymized or used with explicit permission.

Finally, ethical evidence use requires reflexivity about power. Instructors decide what counts as evidence, which patterns matter, and what interventions follow. This interpretive authority should be exercised with humility, particularly when evidence touches on inclusion, confidence, and student identity.

8. INSTITUTIONALIZING EVIDENCE-INFORMED TEACHING

For evidence-informed teaching to move beyond isolated good practice, it must become part of institutional culture. This means creating structures that support collection, interpretation, sharing, and use of teaching evidence at multiple levels.

8.1 Department-level dashboards

Department-level dashboards can help instructors and leaders monitor broad trends in student experience and performance without reducing teaching to simplistic rankings. A well-designed dashboard might include module feedback trends, pass and withdrawal rates, subgroup summaries where ethically viable, support uptake, progression to subsequent modules, and selected rubric-level indicators. The purpose should be developmental rather than punitive.

In interdisciplinary computing programs, dashboards are especially helpful when they integrate data across modules. A single course may look successful in isolation, but curriculum-level data may reveal bottlenecks at transition points; for example, students passing introductory coding but struggling in later data analysis because interpretation skills were underdeveloped. Dashboards can surface such patterns and support coordinated responses.

However, dashboard design matters. Overly crude metrics encourage gaming and defensive teaching. A better dashboard supports inquiry: Where are students thriving? Where are gaps recurring? Which redesigns appear to have helped? What additional evidence is needed? Used well, dashboards can focus departmental attention on educational quality rather than anecdotal reputation.

8.2 Peer review and teaching communities

Peer review of teaching and communities of practice are essential for interpreting evidence well. Teaching quality is difficult to improve in isolation because instructors are often too close to their own courses to see recurring design assumptions clearly. Peer observation, assessment review meetings, and interdisciplinary teaching circles create spaces where evidence can be discussed, challenged, and translated into action (Brookfield, 2017; Felten, 2013).

In cross-disciplinary computing education, peer communities are particularly valuable because they bring together different forms of expertise. A computing lecturer may identify technical misconceptions; a domain academic may identify relevance problems; a learning developer may recognize issues of academic confidence or assessment literacy. When such perspectives are pooled around actual evidence; student comments, assignment samples, support logs, observation notes; the quality of diagnosis improves substantially.

8.3 Scholarship of teaching and learning

The scholarship of teaching and learning (SoTL) extends evidence-informed practice by treating pedagogical questions as legitimate objects of systematic inquiry. Rather than simply making local improvements, instructors investigate their teaching in ways that are methodologically transparent, theoretically informed, and shareable with wider communities (Felten, 2013). This is especially valuable in emerging cross-disciplinary computing contexts where effective pedagogical models are still evolving.

SoTL encourages educators to articulate questions such as: Which forms of contextualization help novices transfer computing concepts into disciplinary problem-solving? How does low-stakes debugging practice affect student confidence and performance? What support structures reduce attrition among non-specialist learners? By studying such questions systematically and disseminating findings, institutions contribute not only to local quality assurance but also to broader pedagogical knowledge.

8.4 Quality assurance in interdisciplinary programs

Quality assurance in interdisciplinary programs requires more than checking compliance with standard metrics. Because interdisciplinary courses often combine distinct epistemologies, pedagogical traditions, and outcome expectations, quality assurance should explicitly consider integration. Are assessments aligned with both technical and disciplinary aims? Are students supported in bridging vocabularies across fields? Are learning outcomes realistic for learners with varied prior experience? Are support systems visible and non-stigmatizing? Is evidence reviewed in ways that detect subgroup inequities?

Program-level review processes should therefore include triangulated evidence portfolios rather than single-number summaries. A robust review might consider student feedback, assessment trends, project samples, peer observation, progression data, and examples of redesign based on prior evidence. This shifts quality assurance from static compliance toward a developmental model of continuous improvement.

9. CONCLUSION

9.1 Evidence as a design resource

The central claim of this chapter is that evidence should be understood not as a retrospective judgment alone, but as a design resource. In cross-disciplinary computing teaching, quality improves when instructors and programs gather evidence systematically, interpret it triangulatively, and use it to refine pedagogical choices. No single measure can adequately represent teaching quality. Student satisfaction, grades, engagement analytics, support usage, project outputs, and reflective testimony each illuminate different dimensions of the learning experience. Their value lies in combination.

Triangulation helps educators avoid overconfidence in narrow indicators, especially in heterogeneous classrooms where students' prior knowledge, goals, and identities vary significantly. Continuous quality improvement then translates evidence into action: identify recurring gaps, diagnose their causes, redesign instruction, test effects, and document what works. When done carefully, this process supports better conceptual understanding, stronger relevance, more inclusive participation, and more durable learning trajectories.

Importantly, evidence-informed teaching is not mechanistic. It does not eliminate professional judgment; it disciplines it. It invites instructors to remain curious, reflective, and responsive. It also requires ethical caution: student data must be used transparently, evaluation bias must be recognized, and small signals in mixed cohorts must be interpreted with humility.

9.2 Transition to student transformation cases

If this chapter has focused on systems, evidence, and pedagogical refinement, the next chapter turns to a complementary perspective: student transformation. The data and frameworks discussed here explain how teaching quality can be improved; the student cases that follow show what such improvement can mean in lived educational terms. They reveal how learners who initially doubted their place in computing can become confident participants, how relevance can shift identity, and how carefully designed pedagogy can alter not only outcomes but trajectories. In that sense, evidence is not the end of the story. It is the bridge between teaching intention and student transformation.

REFERENCES

Aquil Mirza, M., & Cong, W. (Eds.). (2026). *Real-Time Robotics With IoT and Edge AI: Methods, Metrics, and Applications*. IGI Global Scientific Publishing., DOI: 10.4018/979-8-2600-0701-3

Banta, T. W., & Palomba, C. A. (2015). *Assessment essentials: Planning, implementing, and improving assessment in higher education* (2nd ed.). Jossey-Bass.

Biggs, J., & Tang, C. (2011). *Teaching for quality learning at university* (4th ed.). Open University Press.

Braun, V., & Clarke, V. (2006). Using thematic analysis in psychology. *Qualitative Research in Psychology*, *3*(2), 77–101. DOI: 10.1191/1478088706qp063oa

Brookfield, S. D. (2017). *Becoming a critically reflective teacher* (2nd ed.). Jossey-Bass.

Deming, W. E. (1986). *Out of the crisis*. MIT Press.

Denzin, N. K. (1978). *The research act: A theoretical introduction to sociological methods* (2nd ed.). McGraw-Hill.

Deslauriers, L., McCarty, L. S., Miller, K., Callaghan, K., & Kestin, G. (2019). Measuring actual learning versus feeling of learning in response to being actively engaged in the classroom. *Proceedings of the National Academy of Sciences of the United States of America*, *116*(39), 19251–19257. DOI: 10.1073/pnas.1821936116 PMID: 31484770

Felten, P. (2013). Principles of good practice in SoTL. *Teaching & Learning Inquiry*, *1*(1), 121–125. DOI: 10.20343/teachlearninqu.1.1.121

Freeman, S., Eddy, S. L., McDonough, M., Smith, M. K., Okoroafor, N., Jordt, H., & Wenderoth, M. P. (2014). Active learning increases student performance in science, engineering, and mathematics. *Proceedings of the National Academy of Sciences of the United States of America*, *111*(23), 8410–8415. DOI: 10.1073/pnas.1319030111 PMID: 24821756

Hattie, J. (2009). *Visible learning: A synthesis of over 800 meta-analyses relating to achievement*. Routledge.

Henderson, C., Beach, A., & Finkelstein, N. (2011). Facilitating change in undergraduate STEM instructional practices: An analytic review of the literature. *Journal of Research in Science Teaching*, *48*(8), 952–984. DOI: 10.1002/tea.20439

Kuh, G. D. (2008). *High-impact educational practices: What they are, who has access to them, and why they matter*. Association of American Colleges and Universities.

Marsh, H. W. (1987). Students' evaluations of university teaching: Research findings, methodological issues, and directions for future research. *International Journal of Educational Research, 11*(3), 253–388. DOI: 10.1016/0883-0355(87)90001-2

Mishra, P., & Koehler, M. J. (2006). Technological pedagogical content knowledge: A framework for teacher knowledge. *Teachers College Record, 108*(6), 1017–1054. DOI: 10.1111/j.1467-9620.2006.00684.x

Mohammed, A., & Zangana, H. (Eds.). (2026). *Intelligent Construction Monitoring Systems: Real-Time Safety, Environmental Prediction, and Risk Management*. IGI Global Scientific Publishing., DOI: 10.4018/979-8-3373-9245-5

Nicol, D. J., & Macfarlane-Dick, D. (2006). Formative assessment and self-regulated learning: A model and seven principles of good feedback practice. *Studies in Higher Education, 31*(2), 199–218. DOI: 10.1080/03075070600572090

Patton, M. Q. (1999). Enhancing the quality and credibility of qualitative analysis. *Health Services Research, 34*(5 Pt 2), 1189–1208. PMID: 10591279

Prince, M. (2004). Does active learning work? A review of the research. *Journal of Engineering Education, 93*(3), 223–231. DOI: 10.1002/j.2168-9830.2004.tb00809.x

Tinto, V. (2012). *Completing college: Rethinking institutional action*. University of Chicago Press. DOI: 10.7208/chicago/9780226804545.001.0001

Uttl, B., White, C. A., & Gonzalez, D. W. (2017). Meta-analysis of faculty's teaching effectiveness: Student evaluation of teaching ratings and student learning are not related. *Studies in Educational Evaluation, 54*, 22–42. DOI: 10.1016/j.stueduc.2016.08.007

Chapter 9
Student Transformation Across Disciplines:
Case Studies of Learning, Identity, and Transfer

Jiayan Sun
http://orcid.org/0009-0000-5158-0584
Department of Applied Biology and Chemical Technology, The Hong Kong Polytechnic University, Hong Kong

ABSTRACT

This chapter examines student transformation in cross-disciplinary computing education through a series of case studies that highlight changes in learning, identity, transfer, and contribution. The purpose of this chapter by the authors is to move beyond traditional performance metrics and provide a richer understanding of how students from diverse disciplinary backgrounds evolve when exposed to translational pedagogy. This chapter presents cases of beginners from non-technical fields, students in technical disciplines, and those who extend coursework into research, competitions, or innovation pathways, by using evidence from reflections, assessments, mentoring records, and project outputs. The findings emphasize the importance of cognitive visibility, translational explanation, structured support, and authentic output opportunities in enabling transformation.

DOI: 10.4018/979-8-2600-1811-8.ch009

1. INTRODUCTION

1.1 Why case studies matter in pedagogy research

Metrics can show that teaching works, but they often cannot show how it works or what it means for students' lives, identities, and trajectories. In interdisciplinary computing education, this limitation is especially important. A pass rate may improve, withdrawals may fall, and student evaluations may rise, yet such indicators do not fully reveal how a hesitant learner becomes confident, how a non-technical student begins to see computing as relevant, or how an assignment evolves into a conference paper, prototype, or startup idea. For those questions, narrative and case-based inquiry are indispensable.

Case studies matter because educational transformation is rarely linear. Students do not arrive as blank slates, nor do they leave as identical products of instruction. They bring prior disciplinary habits, anxieties, ambitions, misconceptions, and latent strengths. Their development often unfolds through small turning points: a class explanation that suddenly makes sense, a low-stakes success that reduces fear, a project that connects computing to a domain they care about, or a mentor who insists they are capable when they are ready to quit. These moments are easy to miss in aggregated data but central to understanding pedagogy in action (Merriam & Tisdell, 2016; Yin, 2018).

Case studies are particularly valuable in cross-disciplinary computing education because transformation is not only cognitive. It also involves belonging, self-efficacy, professional imagination, and transfer of learning into new contexts. A fashion student who once saw programming as alien may begin to view it as a tool for pattern logic, automation, or digital creativity. A civil engineering student may move from completing coding exercises to reasoning algorithmically about systems and data. A linguistics student may stop seeing computing as a gatekeeping subject and start seeing themselves as someone who can think computationally. A physics or electrical engineering student may use coursework as a springboard into research dissemination or innovation. These are not marginal stories. They are central evidence that pedagogy can widen access to excellence without lowering standards.

This chapter uses case-based narrative inquiry to show how students from different disciplines transformed through translational computing pedagogy. Unlike earlier chapters, which focused on pedagogical principles, evidence, and quality improvement systems, this chapter foregrounds lived student trajectories. It is intentionally human-centered. Its interest lies not only in what students achieved, but in what changed in the way they understood themselves as learners, thinkers, and contributors.

1.2 Student transformation as a multidimensional outcome

Transformation in higher education should not be reduced to grade improvement alone. Grades matter, but they do not fully capture what it means for a learner to cross from anxiety to agency, from imitation to explanation, or from disciplinary distance to interdisciplinary ownership. In computing education, especially among mixed cohorts, meaningful transformation often occurs across at least four dimensions.

First, there is learning transformation: students move from fragmented or superficial understanding toward conceptual clarity and problem-solving ability. They learn not only how to complete tasks, but how to reason through them, explain them, debug them, and adapt them.

Second, there is identity transformation: students who once saw computing as "not for people like me" begin to recognize themselves as legitimate participants. This shift in identity is especially important for students from non-technical disciplines and for students whose prior educational experiences have not prepared them to see themselves as coders, analysts, or builders (Baxter Magolda, 2009; Carlone & Johnson, 2007).

Third, there is transfer transformation: students begin applying computational ideas beyond the immediate course. They connect computing to disciplinary inquiry, later modules, research tasks, competitions, or workplace contexts. They stop treating programming as a contained academic hurdle and begin using it instrumentally and creatively.

Fourth, there is contribution transformation: some students progress from learner to contributor. Coursework becomes publishable research, a competition entry, an entrepreneurial prototype, or a tool with real-world relevance. Such transformations are not expected for every student, but they matter because they illustrate the upper range of what inclusive pedagogy can unlock when support, relevance, and ambition are aligned.

This chapter treats student transformation as multidimensional in precisely this sense. It examines not only what students learned, but how they changed in confidence, belonging, transfer, and contribution. These dimensions are analytically distinct but practically intertwined. Students often need confidence before they risk transfer; they often need relevance before they invest effort; they often need visible support before they imagine contribution. The progression and interconnected nature of these four developmental domains are illustrated in the Student Transformation Pathway Model in Figure 1.

1.3 Scope and selection of cases

The chapter presents three clusters of cases. The first cluster focuses on beginners from non-technical backgrounds; students in fashion and textiles, linguistics, and applied biology. These cases illuminate entry barriers, confidence formation, and the role of translational explanation in widening access. The second cluster examines students in technical but non-computer-science disciplines; civil engineering, applied physics, and electrical engineering. These cases show how students with some technical orientation can still undergo important shifts in reasoning, transfer, and research identity when computing is taught in a visible and applied way. The third cluster addresses output conversion and professional identity, tracing how coursework and project-based learning can be transformed into conference papers, competitions, startup pathways, or early intellectual property initiatives.

These cases are not intended to be statistically representative of all students taught. Rather, they are analytically chosen to illuminate recurring patterns observed across a large and diverse teaching context involving more than 2,000 students across 10 or more disciplines since 2023, with courses such as Programming Fundamentals and Applications, Operating Systems, Computer Networking, and Artificial Intelligence of Things. They are anchored in available evidence from student reflections, course performance, consultation histories, project artifacts, mentoring records, and externally recognized outputs. To align with ethical practice, students are described using pseudonyms or partial identifiers unless the achievements referenced are already part of public recognition. Testimonials are rendered in anonymized form or lightly edited for readability while preserving meaning.

Figure 1. Student Transformation Pathway Model

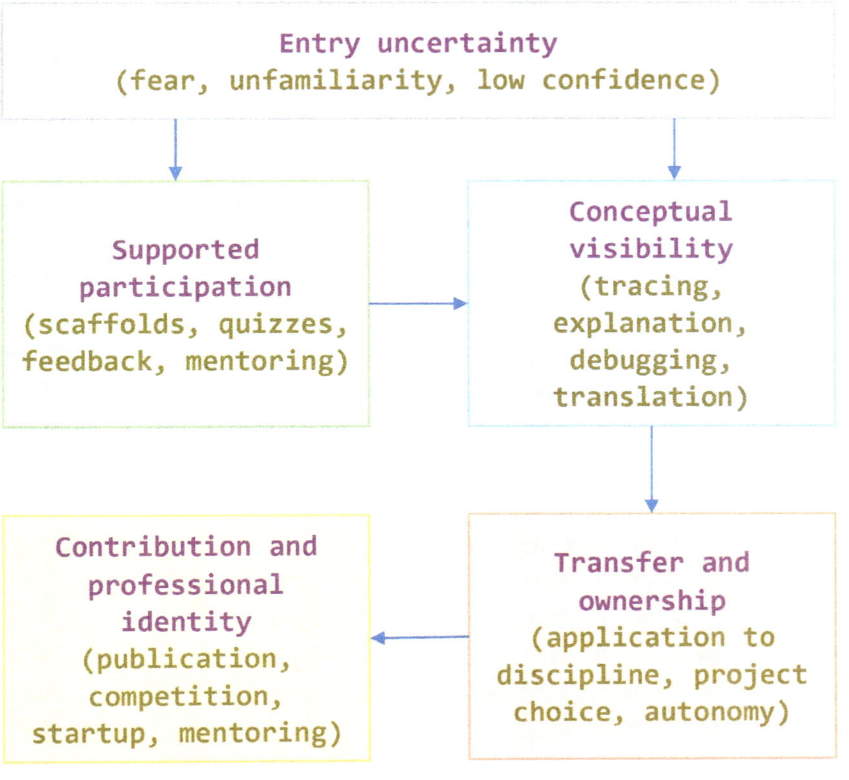

The chapter does not attempt to re-theorize translational pedagogy in detail, since earlier chapters have already addressed conceptual and design frameworks. Instead, it asks a more grounded set of questions: What does student transformation look like in practice? What kinds of barriers do students actually face? What pedagogical moves appear to matter most? And how can educators design environments where students not only survive computing, but begin to own it? To provide an analytical preview of the insights derived from these clusters, Table 1 synthesizes the overarching cross-case themes, their manifestations, and their direct implications for pedagogical design.

Table 1. Cross-Case Themes and Outcomes

Theme	Manifestation in cases	Educational significance	Design implication
Belonging	Non-technical students stopped seeing computing as "not for me"	Supports persistence	Use inclusive examples and safe-to-fail structures
Explanation	Students improved when required to explain code	Deepens understanding	Build oral/written reasoning tasks
Transfer	Students used computing in later courses and projects	Increases long-term value	Connect tasks to disciplinary contexts
Contribution	Projects became papers/competitions/ startups	Strengthens professional identity	Create authentic output pathways

2. CASE STUDY METHODOLOGY

2.1 Rationale for case-based inquiry

Case-based inquiry is well suited to educational settings where context matters, causality is layered, and outcomes are developmental rather than instantaneous. In cross-disciplinary computing education, this is clearly the case. Students do not all begin with the same prior knowledge, and the same pedagogical intervention may be experienced differently depending on discipline, confidence, prior schooling, and career imagination. Case studies enable the researcher-teacher to examine transformation holistically, preserving the interplay of cognition, emotion, environment, and opportunity that broader surveys often flatten (Stake, 1995; Yin, 2018).

The purpose of using case studies in this chapter is not to claim universal causation from isolated stories. Rather, it is to illuminate pedagogical mechanisms through rich examples. A case can show how a student's turning point emerged from the combination of visible reasoning, scaffolded challenge, and timely encouragement. Another case can reveal how a technically capable student needed not more difficulty but more authentic application to shift from course performance to research contribution. Case studies thus provide "explanatory thickness": they help readers see the process by which transformation becomes possible.

They are also appropriate here because the pedagogical model under discussion aims to address hidden barriers—fear of failure, disciplinary alienation, reluctance to seek help, and inability to see relevance. These are difficult to interpret from grades alone. A learner may earn a good result while remaining unconvinced that computing belongs to them. Another may begin with weak performance but undergo a profound shift in self-belief that later shapes future choices. Such developments are best captured through narrative reconstruction grounded in multiple evidence sources.

2.2 Case selection criteria

The cases included in this chapter were selected purposively rather than randomly. Selection was guided by four criteria.

First, each case had to show evidence of meaningful change over time. This change might involve confidence, conceptual understanding, transfer into later learning, or movement from coursework into broader contribution.

Second, each case had to represent a different disciplinary position relative to computing. This was important because the chapter aims to show how transformation operates across disciplinary distance. Students from fashion, linguistics, and applied biology encounter computing differently from students in civil engineering or applied physics.

Third, each case needed to be supported by more than one form of evidence. This could include testimonials, grade progression, project outputs, mentoring records, consultation patterns, or external achievements. Because the chapter is narrative, it is tempting to rely heavily on compelling quotes; however, the cases are stronger when anchored in triangulated evidence.

Fourth, the selected cases needed to have pedagogical interpretive value. In other words, they had to reveal something important about how learning, identity, and transfer developed. Cases were not chosen only because they were successful in a conventional sense, but because they exposed useful mechanisms: the effect of cognitive visibility, the value of translational examples, the role of low-stakes structure, or the significance of authentic output pathways.

This means that the chapter includes both "high-achievement" cases and "threshold-crossing" cases. A student who wins a competition is pedagogically interesting, but so is a student who nearly withdraws and then remains, succeeds, and redefines their own capabilities. In many ways, the latter may be more educationally revealing.

2.3 Data sources: reflections, performance, outputs, interviews

The cases draw on multiple evidence sources. These include:

- student reflective comments from institutional feedback and informal written responses;
- consultation and mentoring records documenting support-seeking and developmental turning points;
- assessment and performance patterns, including progression from early struggle to stronger outcomes;
- project artifacts, such as code, reports, posters, prototypes, and presentations;

- student co-authored outputs including conference papers, competition submissions, startup ideation, or patent-related work;
- short follow-up interviews or testimonial statements in which students described what changed for them.

No single source was treated as definitive. Instead, interpretations were built through triangulation. A student's statement that their confidence increased was considered more meaningful when supported by increased participation, successful project completion, stronger assessment performance, or later use of computing in another context. Likewise, a project receiving external recognition was analyzed not only as an isolated achievement, but in relation to the pedagogical pathway that made it possible.

The cases also rely on the broader teaching context documented in internal records: large enrollment foundational classes of roughly 250–350 students in COMP1012, high student feedback ratings in the range of 4.6–4.9/5 compared to a departmental average of approximately 4.2, and a pattern of reduced withdrawal and improved pass outcomes in redesigned teaching settings. These wider conditions provide context, though the chapter's main focus remains on case-level interpretation.

2.4 Ethical considerations and anonymization

Because this chapter deals with student trajectories, ethics are central. Students occupy a position of relative vulnerability in relation to teacher-authors, and pedagogical scholarship must avoid appropriating student narratives for institutional celebration without adequate care. Accordingly, the cases are presented with attention to anonymization, proportionality, and respect.

Students are identified by pseudonyms, disciplinary background, and broad year level unless public achievements have already rendered parts of the record visible in institutional or competition contexts. Quotations have been lightly edited for grammar and flow, but not in ways that alter meaning. Sensitive details, particularly around anxiety, self-doubt, or moments of possible withdrawal, are presented only insofar as they illuminate pedagogical processes and preserve student dignity.

The goal is not to produce heroic narratives about teaching, but to understand learner development. Accordingly, each case is framed as an interaction between student effort, course design, support structures, and mentoring opportunities. Transformation is not attributed solely to the instructor; it emerges from the student's agency in a pedagogically structured environment.

2.5 Analytical lens: learning, identity, transfer, contribution

To interpret the cases systematically, this chapter uses a four-part analytical lens:

1. Learning: What conceptual or procedural shifts occurred? Did the student move from imitation to explanation, from fragmented understanding to reasoning, or from task completion to independent problem solving?
2. Identity: How did the student's sense of self change? Did they begin to see computing as accessible, useful, or part of who they could become? Did they experience increased belonging or legitimacy?
3. Transfer: Did the student use learning beyond the immediate course? Was computing applied in later modules, research, competitions, or disciplinary inquiry?
4. Contribution: Did the student move from learner to contributor through publication, competition success, mentoring, innovation, or other externally visible outputs?

This analytical lens is intentionally practical. It does not require each case to score equally on all four dimensions. Some novice cases foreground learning and identity; some advanced cases foreground transfer and contribution. Taken together, however, the cases reveal a transformation pathway that extends from access to ownership.

3. CASE CLUSTER I: BEGINNERS FROM NON-TECHNICAL BACKGROUNDS

3.1 Case 1: A fashion and textiles student — from intimidation to computational belonging

"Mei" entered introductory programming with apprehension. As a Year 2 student in fashion and textiles, she did not consider herself technically oriented. Her prior academic identity had been shaped by visual design, materials, aesthetics, and studio-based work. When she first encountered programming, she interpreted it through a deficit lens: coding was for "naturally technical" students, while she belonged to a different intellectual world. This is a common pattern among learners entering computing from creative disciplines, where the cultural coding of programming as mathematical, masculine, abstract, or non-expressive can be especially exclusionary (Margolis & Fisher, 2003; Sax et al., 2018).

In the early weeks of the course, Mei's participation was low. She attended, but she hesitated to answer questions and often delayed beginning practical tasks. Her initial comments suggested not laziness but fear of visible error. She could follow demonstrations when the instructor explained them, but she had difficulty translating that understanding into independent action. The blank code editor represented not possibility but exposure. Consultation patterns showed that she sought clarification only after class, often framing questions apologetically: "This may be very basic, but…" Such phrasing is familiar in novice computing contexts and often signals shame rather than ignorance.

The pedagogical turning point for Mei was not a single assignment but a shift in how computing was presented to her. Two features were especially influential. The first was cognitive visibility. Rather than requiring students to jump directly into syntax, the course often began with line-by-line tracing, paper-based loop reasoning, pattern prediction, and verbal explanation of logic before code entry. This reduced the illusion that competent programmers think in fully formed scripts. Students could see programming as structured reasoning rather than magical fluency. For Mei, who was accustomed to sketching and drafting before producing final work, this mattered. It revealed an unexpected analogy between design process and code construction: both involved iteration, pattern recognition, and refinement.

The second influential feature was translational explanation. Instead of presenting loops and control flow only in abstract terms, examples were reframed through forms of repetition familiar to creative practice. Pattern generation, repeated alteration, conditional variation, and iterative refinement were described in language that connected to design logic. Mei later reflected that this was the first time programming felt "like a way of thinking I already partly knew, even if I did not know the technical words for it." That sentence captures a crucial educational move: translation did not trivialize computing; it gave Mei an entry point into it.

Midway through the semester, Mei's work began to change. Her formative assessments moved from incomplete or hesitant attempts toward more coherent solutions. Importantly, the improvement was not only in correctness but in explanation. In one lab, she was able to describe why a nested loop produced a pattern rather than merely reproducing it. Her comments shifted from "I don't think I can do this" to "I need more practice with this part." This is a subtle but meaningful identity change. The first statement rejects belonging; the second presumes capability and locates difficulty in a manageable task domain.

A student comment from course feedback, adapted here in anonymized form, captures this transition:

"At first I thought programming was completely outside my world. What helped was that we were not expected to just know. Tracing on paper and linking examples to repeated design steps made it less frightening. I started to feel that coding was something I could learn rather than something other people were born able to do."

By the end of the course, Mei's achievement was strong rather than exceptional, but the educational significance lay elsewhere. She had crossed a threshold from avoidance to participation. She no longer saw computing as an externally imposed technical culture from which she was excluded. Instead, she saw it as a tool she could learn and potentially use. In follow-up mentoring discussions, she expressed interest in how simple scripting and automation might support digital workflows in design contexts. This is transfer at an early stage—not yet publication or competition, but conceptual migration from "this is not for me" to "this may have a place in my field."

Pedagogically, Mei's case reveals that belonging in computing is often built before mastery. Students from non-technical and creative backgrounds may not need diluted content; they need pedagogical framing that makes the logic of the field visible, translatable, and survivable. Her case also shows that identity barriers can masquerade as technical weakness. The problem was not merely lack of prior experience. It was a prior self-understanding that had to be gently revised through successful encounters with structured, supported challenge.

3.2 Case 2: A linguistics student — from the brink of withdrawal to A-range confidence

If Mei's case illustrates gradual belonging, "Lina," a Year 2 linguistics student, illustrates a sharper threshold moment. According to mentoring records and student testimony, Lina came close to dropping the course early in the semester. She experienced computing as an alien language layered on top of an already demanding university workload. Her disciplinary background in linguistics had trained her to work with patterns, symbols, and rules, but she did not initially recognize any connection between those capacities and programming. Instead, she interpreted her difficulty through self-doubt: others seemed to move faster, ask more confident questions, and recover from errors more easily.

What pushed Lina toward withdrawal was not simply poor performance. It was the cumulative emotional effect of confusion, silence, and comparative judgment. She worried that every question she might ask was too basic. This is a familiar pattern in introductory computing, where novice learners often overestimate peers' competence and underestimate the normality of struggle (Barker et al., 2009; Cooper et al., 2019). In Lina's case, a timely conversation mattered. During a support interaction, she was encouraged to stay, reassured that difficulty was expected, and shown that the course had been designed around progressive development rather than prior expertise. This moment of encouragement was not miraculous; rather, it was pedagogically effective because it aligned with the actual structure of the course. The message "you can succeed" was credible because scaffolds, low-stakes checks, and support channels were in place.

Several design features then helped Lina re-engage. Frequent low-stakes quizzes allowed her to consolidate material incrementally rather than confronting all uncertainty at assignment deadlines. Because these quizzes were developmental rather than punitive, they gave her repeated opportunities to experience success in small doses. This mattered psychologically as much as cognitively. Success no longer appeared as something reserved for the confident few.

Translational explanation was also important. When programming concepts were connected to repeated rule application, pattern matching, and structured transformation—ideas not foreign to linguistics—Lina began to see analogies between her discipline and computation. What had seemed like a purely technical domain started to look like another way of formalizing patterns. This did not remove difficulty, but it reduced estrangement.

Most significant, perhaps, was the shift from performing code to explaining code. In labs, students were asked to articulate what specific code segments were doing and to trace variable changes. Lina found this unexpectedly helpful. In her own words:

"I had been trying to memorize what to type without understanding the steps. When I started explaining the code line by line, I realized I could actually follow the logic. That was the moment it stopped feeling impossible."

This shift; from memorization to reasoning; is foundational in computing education (Lister et al., 2006). For Lina, it was also identity-changing. If she could follow logic, she could improve. If she could improve, then perhaps she was not inherently unsuited to computing.

Her course outcome was striking: she remained in the class and ultimately achieved an A+ result. Yet the grade alone does not capture the deeper transformation. In later reflections, she described the experience as having "completely changed" her confidence in computing. She also emphasized that the course did not stop at passing. It opened possibilities she had not previously imagined: publication support, conference participation, mentoring, and professional growth. Even if she did not pursue all those avenues immediately, the fact that such possibilities became thinkable indicates a widened identity horizon.

Lina's case is pedagogically important for three reasons. First, it shows how close some capable students can be to exit when confidence collapses. Second, it demonstrates that targeted support can reverse that trajectory when coupled with concrete scaffolded practices. Third, it reveals the role of belief transfer: once students experience themselves as capable in one difficult domain, their willingness to attempt further challenge expands. Educationally, the transformation was not only from near-withdrawal to A+; it was from self-exclusion to self-permission.

3.3 Case 3: An applied biology student — from novice coder to disciplinary integrator

"Arun," a Year 1 applied biology student, entered the course with limited coding experience and little sense that programming would matter in his disciplinary pathway. His academic identity was grounded in biological concepts, laboratory practices, and empirical observation rather than computational abstraction. Unlike Mei, whose barrier was disciplinary distance, or Lina, whose barrier was confidence collapse, Arun's initial challenge was instrumental uncertainty: he did not yet understand why coding should matter for applied biology.

This is a significant pedagogical issue in interdisciplinary teaching. Students are more likely to persist in difficult learning when they can perceive relevance and future use (Eccles & Wigfield, 2020). Without this, effort feels imposed. Arun attended class regularly and completed work conscientiously, but his early engagement was procedural. He was doing what was required, not yet seeing the larger point.

The course structure gradually changed this. Weekly quizzes helped him identify gaps early and avoid cumulative confusion. He later described these quizzes as useful not because they were easy, but because they forced steady review and made progress visible. In other words, the quizzes functioned as both academic scaffolds and metacognitive mirrors. They showed him where he stood and where he needed reinforcement.

Equally important were clear lectures and patient support. Arun's reflections emphasized the value of "carefully designed assessments" and "patient individual support," suggesting that what mattered was not merely exposure to content but the design of a learning sequence in which difficulty was manageable. Over time, he reported building "a solid foundation in coding," alongside clearer logical thinking and greater confidence. This language is notable because it links skill development to cognitive restructuring. Programming was not just another technical task; it sharpened the way he approached problems.

The transfer dimension became more visible later. As examples and projects increasingly used realistic data and applied reasoning, Arun began to understand computing as a means of handling, interpreting, and organizing biological information. Rather than seeing coding as peripheral, he began to recognize its role in modern scientific inquiry. His engagement strengthened when disciplinary connection became explicit.

A representative student testimony captures this development:

"With clear lectures, regular quizzes, and individual support, I slowly built confidence in coding. The biggest change was that I started seeing programming as useful for biological data, not just as something abstract, I had to pass."

This is a concise statement of translational success. The student did not become a computer scientist; instead, he became a biology student with computational agency. That is precisely the aim of cross-disciplinary computing pedagogy.

Arun's assessment profile improved over the semester, but the more interesting outcome was his developing ability to connect code with domain reasoning. In project work, he showed growing competence not only in implementing tasks but in explaining what outputs meant and why a computational approach was useful. Such integrative explanations are especially important in interdisciplinary education, where students must bridge technical procedure and disciplinary interpretation.

Arun's case also demonstrates that transformation does not always require dramatic crisis. Some students begin in a position of uncertainty rather than fear. For them, the central pedagogical challenge is not rescue but activation: helping them see why learning matters, how it connects, and what it enables. His trajectory suggests that relevance and structure together can generate commitment. Students often do not resist computing because they reject effort; they resist when effort appears disconnected from who they are becoming.

3.4 Themes from Cluster I: belonging, confidence, access

Taken together, the three beginner cases reveal several recurring themes.

The first is belonging before fluency. None of these students began with strong computational identity. What changed first was not technical mastery but a growing sense that computing was survivable, interpretable, and not reserved for an innately gifted minority. This aligns with broader research showing that belonging and self-efficacy are central to persistence in challenging domains (Bandura, 1997; Freeman et al., 2007; Tinto, 2012).

The second theme is confidence through structured success. In each case, confidence did not emerge from vague encouragement alone. It was built through concrete pedagogical design: tracing, explanation, low-stakes quizzes, visible debugging, and progressive scaffolding. Students gained confidence because they experienced intelligible progress.

The third theme is access through translation. Disciplinary distance was reduced when concepts were explained through familiar analogies, examples, or problem frames. Translation did not simplify away complexity; it created pathways into complexity. For students from fashion, linguistics, and biology, this was decisive.

The fourth theme is that novice transformation is often relational. Support conversations, patient responses, and the normalization of struggle played important roles. This reminds us that pedagogy is not only cognitive architecture but also emotional climate.

Cluster I therefore suggests that when cross-disciplinary computing is taught with visible reasoning, translational framing, and scaffolded support, students from non-technical backgrounds can move from intimidation to legitimate participation. The educational achievement lies not merely in passing such students through computing, but in enabling them to inhabit it differently. A comprehensive breakdown of how these four themes manifest, along with their educational significance and design implications, is summarized in Table 2. This developmental journey from initial intimidation to self-directed capability is visually mapped in the From Anxiety to Agency Trajectory in Figure 2.

Table 2. Cross-Case Themes and Outcomes

Theme	**Manifestation in cases**	**Educational significance**	**Design implication**
Belonging	Non-technical students stopped seeing computing as "not for me"	Supports persistence	Use inclusive examples and safe-to-fail structures
Explanation	Students improved when required to explain code	Deepens understanding	Build oral/written reasoning tasks
Transfer	Students used computing in later courses and projects	Increases long-term value	Connect tasks to disciplinary contexts
Contribution	Projects became papers/competitions/ startups	Strengthens professional identity	Create authentic output pathways

Figure 2. From Anxiety to Agency Trajectory

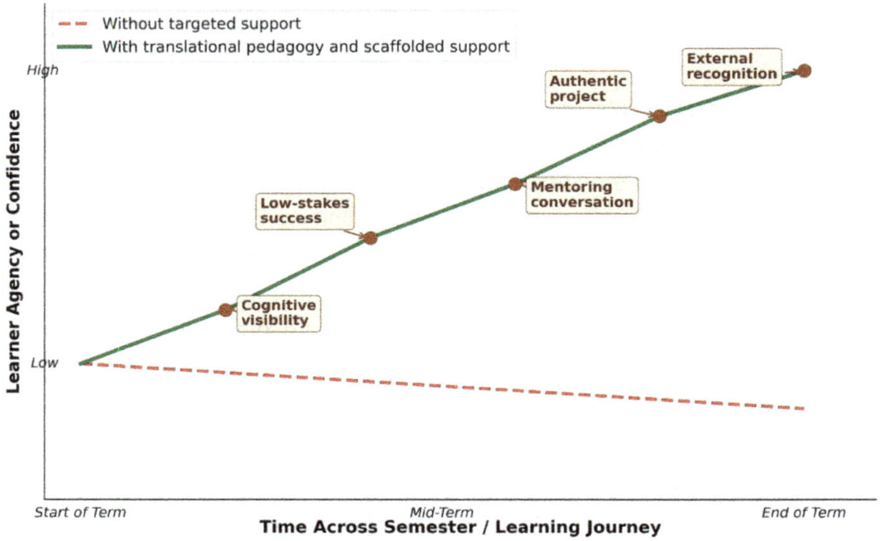

4. CASE CLUSTER II: STUDENTS IN TECHNICAL BUT NON-CS DISCIPLINES

4.1 Case 4: A civil engineering student — from procedural coding to disciplined reasoning

"Victor," a Year 2 civil engineering student, entered computing with a profile quite different from the learners in Cluster I. He was not alienated by technical language in the same way. Engineering had already accustomed him to quantitative reasoning, systems thinking, and structured problem solving. Yet his early approach to programming was largely procedural. He could often imitate methods and produce working code, but his understanding of why the code behaved as it did remained fragile. This distinction matters. Students in technical disciplines may appear comparatively strong in introductory computing, but they too can rely on shallow pattern matching rather than robust conceptual reasoning (Guzdial, 2015).

Victor's own reflection makes this visible. He noted that one of the most effective features of the course was being made to trace Python loops line by line on paper before typing. This "forced" him to see where variables actually changed rather than guessing. That comment reveals a shift from intuitive approximation to disciplined inspection. For many learners, especially those with enough prior confidence to move quickly, the risk is not fear but premature fluency. They can produce surface-correct code without fully understanding internal state changes or logic flow.

The course challenged this through cognitive visibility. Paper tracing, code explanation, and verbal reasoning slowed down performance just enough to expose assumptions. For Victor, who may initially have preferred moving directly to implementation, this was unexpectedly helpful. He later described the teaching style as "low-pressure but firm on fundamentals." That phrase is pedagogically revealing. The course did not equate rigor with intimidation; it combined psychological safety with conceptual insistence.

Victor's lab participation and project performance suggest that this emphasis on fundamentals strengthened his later independence. As his understanding of loops, variables, and program structure deepened, he became more capable of debugging without immediate tutor intervention. More importantly, he could explain his logic. In engineering education, explanation is often undervalued relative to correct output, yet the ability to articulate reasoning is essential for transfer, collaboration, and safe professional practice.

The transfer dimension of Victor's case emerged in how he began to connect computational reasoning to engineering systems. Once variables and iteration were understood more concretely, he found it easier to relate programming to repeated measurement, simulation loops, and structural risk configurations within intelligent construction monitoring systems (Mohammed & Zangana, 2026). Once variables and iteration were understood more concretely, he found it easier to relate programming to repeated measurement, simulation loops, and process monitoring. In other words, the course did not merely add a coding skill; it sharpened a mode of reasoning relevant to his disciplinary field.

A representative anonymized testimonial from this case reads:

"The hands-on coding really clicked when we had to trace loops before typing. It stopped me from guessing. I think that made programming feel more like engineering logic and less like memorizing syntax."

This statement captures the key transformation: computing became aligned with disciplined reasoning rather than opaque syntax reproduction. Victor's case thus shows that technical students may need a different kind of support from non-technical beginners. They often require not simplified access, but pedagogical structures that interrupt superficial competence and develop explanatory depth.

4.2 Case 5: An applied physics student — from course competence to research orientation

"Rayan," a Year 2 applied physics student, approached computing with curiosity and analytical strength. He was less intimidated by abstraction than many beginners and relatively quick to appreciate the mathematical dimensions of programming. Yet what is striking in his case is not simply that he performed well, but that the course appears to have shifted his orientation toward research and future learning.

Rayan later reflected that Python became very useful in subsequent courses such as data analysis and machine learning. He also noted that regular quizzes helped him "constantly study" lecture materials and reinforce concepts. This is a valuable reminder that even analytically strong students benefit from structured retrieval and distributed practice. The quizzes did more than test recall; they sustained engagement and built readiness for later transfer.

More importantly, the course project sparked deeper inquiry. According to his reflection, the project inspired him to explore the mathematical principles behind machine learning. This comment suggests a movement from instrumental use to conceptual curiosity. Programming did not remain merely a utilitarian skill; it became an entry point into research-oriented thinking. For a physics student, such a transition is particularly significant because it links computational competence with theoretical exploration.

What pedagogical conditions enabled this? First, the course appears to have offered scaffolded challenge rather than only beginner-level repetition. Rayan had enough support to develop confidence but enough openness to pursue harder questions. Second, project work was not framed as a dead-end assignment. Students were encouraged to build on interests, extend strong ideas, and see coursework as potentially connected to broader scholarly pathways. This matters greatly for learners capable of deeper engagement. Without such pathways, a foundational course may feel artificially bounded.

Rayan's trajectory also shows how transfer and identity can reinforce one another. As he used programming in later subjects, his sense of competence grew. As his competence grew, he became more willing to explore research-level questions. This recursive relationship between use and identity is common in high-engagement learning environments (Lave & Wenger, 1991). Students begin by participating peripherally, then gradually see themselves as capable of more central forms of contribution, transitioning from basic script writing to designing edge AI pipelines for real-time robotic deployments (Aquil Mirza & Cong, 2026). Students begin by participating peripherally, then gradually see themselves as capable of more central forms of contribution.

An anonymized student statement captures the transformation:

"The course made Python useful later in data analysis and machine learning. At first, I learned it as a requirement, but the project made me curious about the mathematical ideas behind what the code was doing."

This is more than positive feedback. It indicates a pedagogical transition from compliance to inquiry. The student did not simply complete a programming course; he acquired a research orientation.

Rayan's case suggests that translational pedagogy is not only for anxious novices. It can also create upward pathways for technically inclined students by making computing intellectually generative rather than procedurally narrow. In mixed cohorts, this is important. Inclusive teaching should not mean flattening ambition. It should provide multiple zones of entry and extension.

4.3 Case 6: An electrical engineering student — from coursework to scholarly confidence

"Ethan," a Year 1 electrical engineering student, illustrates perhaps the clearest example in this cluster of movement from course participation to scholarly identity. He reported that some assignments in the course targeted research-level projects, giving students "their first glimpse of research." He also emphasized learning LaTeX in class and later finding it useful—an interesting detail because it shows how seemingly peripheral tools can contribute to professional formation. LaTeX here functioned not merely as formatting software but as an introduction to disciplinary communication norms.

Most importantly, Ethan described being helped to publish course papers, present at conferences, and win a best paper award. This does not mean that all students in the course became conference authors. Rather, it shows that strong work was identified, mentored, and extended into authentic output pathways. Such output conversion is pedagogically significant because it changes the meaning of coursework. Assignments cease to be terminal exercises and become developmental platforms.

From an identity perspective, this matters enormously. Many undergraduates, even in technical disciplines, do not initially imagine themselves as capable of scholarly dissemination. Research appears distant, reserved for postgraduate study or elite peers. When a course includes project structures, mentoring, and feedback that allow some students to convert work into external outputs, it expands the horizon of possibility. Students begin to see themselves not only as consumers of knowledge but as potential producers of it.

Ethan's transformation thus operates on several levels. There is learning, in the sense of acquiring technical and communicative tools. There is transfer, in the use of those tools beyond the immediate assignment. There is contribution, in conference presentation and award recognition. And there is identity, in seeing oneself as someone who can participate in research culture.

A concise anonymized testimonial from this case states:

"Some assignments felt like my first real exposure to research, not just coursework. Learning tools like LaTeX and then being supported to present and publish changed how I saw what an undergraduate could do."

This statement points to a larger pedagogical lesson: professional identity can begin earlier than institutions sometimes assume. When students are invited into authentic practices with sufficient guidance, they often rise to levels of contribution that conventional curricula underestimate.

4.4 Themes from Cluster II: deeper reasoning, transfer, research orientation

The cases in Cluster II reveal that students from technical but non-CS disciplines also undergo important forms of transformation, though often along different lines from Cluster I.

The first theme is deeper reasoning over procedural fluency. Students like Victor may appear comfortable with technical work, yet still benefit from slowing down, tracing logic, and making reasoning explicit. This is critical because unexamined fluency can conceal fragile understanding.

The second theme is transfer through disciplined structure. Regular quizzes, visible reasoning, and applied projects helped students carry programming into later modules, especially in data analysis and machine learning contexts. Transfer did not happen automatically; it was scaffolded by pedagogical design and reinforced by disciplinary relevance.

The third theme is research orientation. When assignments are designed with authentic output potential and accompanied by mentoring, students can move quickly from coursework toward scholarly confidence. This is not limited to elite or advanced learners. Well-supported undergraduates can begin to inhabit research practices earlier than expected.

The fourth theme is identity expansion through contribution. Students in engineering and physics may not struggle with belonging in the same way as fashion or linguistics students, but they too can experience significant identity shifts when they see themselves as capable of more than assignment completion. They become analysts, presenters, authors, and emerging innovators.

Cluster II therefore shows that translational computing pedagogy has two obligations: it must reduce barriers for the hesitant and deepen pathways for the technically capable. Good interdisciplinary teaching does both.

5. CASE CLUSTER III: OUTPUT CONVERSION AND PROFESSIONAL IDENTITY

5.1 Case 7: From coursework to conference paper

One of the most distinctive features of translational pedagogy is the idea that coursework need not end at grading. In several documented instances, student projects developed within course or follow-on mentoring contexts were extended into scholarly outputs. This section presents a composite case, "Team Aurora," representing a pattern observed across multiple student teams whose coursework evolved into conference papers and external recognition.

Team Aurora began as a course project group composed of students from mixed disciplinary backgrounds, including engineering and science. Initially, their task was similar to that of many project teams: define a problem, develop a technical approach, implement a solution, and communicate findings clearly. What distinguished this group was not merely technical competence but ownership. Rather than treating the project as an exercise to be completed at minimum threshold, they became increasingly invested in refining the problem and strengthening the contribution.

The pedagogical environment made such development possible in several ways. First, projects were framed as potentially meaningful beyond the classroom. This altered student motivation from compliance to seriousness. Second, the students received iterative mentoring on both the technical and communicative dimensions of their work. They were encouraged to clarify novelty, justify methods, improve writing, and think about audience. Third, the project topic aligned with an authentic interdisciplinary application area, giving the students a reason to care about precision and usefulness.

As the project matured, it was converted into a conference paper. The students learned that publication required not only stronger results but stronger articulation: a title, abstract, literature positioning, methodological explanation, result interpretation, and visual communication. In this sense, the shift from coursework to paper was itself educational. Students were not merely rewarded for what they had already done; they were apprenticed into a more rigorous form of academic practice.

The eventual recognition of such work; including, in some cases, best paper or best student paper awards at international venues; matters not only as achievement but as identity confirmation. Students who once saw themselves as ordinary undergraduates discovered that their work could withstand external scrutiny and even be celebrated. This can have durable effects on ambition and self-concept.

A representative student voice from this pathway reads:

"What changed for me was realizing that a course project could become something other people would actually read. Once we started revising it like a paper,

I felt I was no longer just submitting an assignment; I was contributing to a conversation."

This is the language of scholarly emergence. The student has shifted from private performance to public contribution.

5.2 Case 8: From coursework to competition success

A second pattern in the teaching record is the conversion of coursework and mentored projects into competition success. This pathway differs slightly from publication because competitions often foreground problem-solving speed, practical impact, innovation, or presentation under pressure. Yet they similarly help students move from classroom learning to externally validated performance.

Consider the composite case "Team Nova," based on mentored teams that developed projects into competition entries, including internationally recognized outcomes such as first-place distinction in an AI and big data competition involving approximately 800 teams. Team Nova's initial work emerged from course-related project development. Like many students, they began by implementing a proof-of-concept solution. What transformed the work was the insistence on iterative refinement and real-world framing. Students were asked not only, "Does this work?" but also, "Who is this for? Why does it matter? How can it be demonstrated persuasively?"

Competition preparation developed a different dimension of identity from conference writing. Students had to pitch, defend, and communicate value succinctly. They learned to tell the story of their work, often to mixed audiences. This sharpened not only technical understanding but professional confidence. It also made interdisciplinary collaboration more meaningful, as students recognized that diverse expertise could strengthen a team's problem framing and solution design.

One of the powerful features of competition pathways is that they convert learning into urgency. Students experience deadlines, standards, comparison, and the possibility of public recognition. For some, this is the first time they feel that academic work can directly encounter the world rather than remaining internal to a course. When they succeed, the impact on self-belief can be substantial.

An anonymized testimony representative of this pathway states:

"The competition made us take the project seriously in a different way. We had to explain why it mattered, not just how it worked. Winning was exciting, but the bigger change was that I began to think of myself as someone who could build something valuable."

This illustrates the chapter's central theme well. Recognition matters, but the deeper outcome is professional identity.

5.3 Case 9: From coursework to startup or patent pathway

A third transformation pathway extends from coursework into entrepreneurship or early intellectual property development. Not all student innovations should become startups, and not all ideas are suited to patenting. Even so, the existence of such pathways has pedagogical significance. They signal that student work can have utility, originality, and developmental potential beyond assessment.

The composite case "Project Cobalt" reflects several examples in which course or supervised project work became linked to startup ideation schemes, finalist recognition, or early-stage patent-related activity. In these cases, the pedagogy did not begin by demanding entrepreneurship. Rather, it began with authentic problem identification and interdisciplinary application. Students were encouraged to pursue topics relevant to health monitoring, environmental sensing, robotics, AIoT, or intelligent systems. When a project demonstrated unusual promise, mentoring expanded to include questions of user need, scalability, novelty, and implementation context.

For students, this process can be transformative because it reframes technical work in terms of agency and impact. Instead of asking only whether they can complete a project, they begin asking whether they can create something that others might use, support, or invest in. This often generates a new kind of seriousness about design, reliability, and communication.

A representative student statement for this pathway reads:

"I had never imagined that an undergraduate project could turn into something like a startup idea. The moment we started discussing users, feasibility, and what problem we were actually solving, I stopped thinking like a student doing coursework and started thinking like a builder."

This is a crucial identity shift. "Builder" is not simply a synonym for coder. It implies ownership, initiative, and outward-facing design.

5.4 Themes from Cluster III: contribution, ownership, innovation

The output conversion cases reveal four major themes.

First, they show that authentic output pathways change the meaning of coursework. Assignments become beginnings rather than endings. This can elevate effort and deepen investment.

Second, they highlight the importance of mentored extension. High-potential work rarely converts itself. Students need feedback on technical quality, framing, writing, pitching, and audience awareness. The educator's role here is less about delivering more content and more about curating possibility.

Third, they demonstrate that contribution strengthens identity. Publication, competition, and startup development are not only external achievements. They are identity-forming experiences through which students begin to see themselves as researchers, innovators, and professionals.

Fourth, they suggest that inclusive pedagogy can raise ceilings as well as lower barriers. A teaching model that helps anxious beginners is not incompatible with high-level output. In fact, the same principles—visible reasoning, translational explanation, scaffolded challenge, and supportive mentoring—can serve both functions.

6. CROSS-CASE ANALYSIS

6.1 Common transformation patterns

Across the nine cases and case clusters, several common transformation patterns emerge. The first is that student development often begins with a change in relationship to difficulty. Many learners initially interpreted difficulty as evidence that they did not belong. Over time, through visible reasoning and supportive structure, difficulty was reframed as part of learning rather than proof of inadequacy. This reframing is foundational because students cannot persist in a field if every mistake confirms exclusion.

A second common pattern is the movement from imitation to explanation. In nearly every case, progress accelerated when students stopped relying solely on copying examples and began articulating logic, tracing execution, and reasoning through change. Explanation was not an afterthought; it was the medium through which learning became durable.

A third pattern is identity widening through successful participation. Students did not need complete mastery before identity shifted. Often, one or two intelligible successes—finishing a quiz with understanding, explaining a loop correctly, presenting a project, receiving recognition—were enough to change what they thought was possible.

A fourth pattern is trajectory extension. Once students began seeing computing as relevant and themselves as capable, they were more likely to use it elsewhere: in later subjects, research projects, competitions, or early professional activities. Transformation was thus cumulative. It started in the classroom but did not end there.

6.2 Role of cognitive visibility

The cases repeatedly show the importance of cognitive visibility. Students benefited when expert thinking was externalized through tracing, flowcharts, line-by-line explanation, live coding, and intentional debugging. This aligns with educational work on modeling, worked examples, and the need to make tacit expert processes visible to novices (Chi et al., 1989; Collins et al., 1989).

Cognitive visibility mattered for different reasons across groups. For non-technical students, it reduced intimidation by revealing that programming is a process rather than a performance of innate brilliance. For technical students, it disrupted superficial fluency and built deeper explanatory control. For advanced project teams, it supported the move from implementation to defensible contribution. In all cases, visibility made reasoning available for inspection, correction, and growth.

6.3 Role of translational explanation

Translational explanation was another recurring mechanism. Students learned more effectively when computing concepts were connected to familiar disciplinary logics: patternmaking in design, rule structures in linguistics, repeated measurement in engineering, data interpretation in biology, and mathematical modeling in physics. This did not mean over-customizing every lesson to every discipline. Rather, it meant teaching in a way that respected disciplinary difference and used analogy strategically.

The cases suggest that translation supports both access and transfer. It helps students understand the immediate concept and also imagine where it might matter later. This is especially significant in interdisciplinary curricula, where abstraction without relevance can quickly produce disengagement.

6.4 Role of support and mentoring

Support and mentoring appear across nearly all cases, though in varied forms. Sometimes support was informal reassurance at a critical moment, as in Lina's near-withdrawal case. Sometimes it was embedded structurally through low-stakes quizzes, guided projects, and consultation opportunities. Sometimes it took the form of high-level mentoring for publication, competition, or startup development.

The broader lesson is that support should not be equated with remediation alone. In effective pedagogical environments, support serves multiple functions: reducing fear, clarifying confusion, sustaining effort, extending ambition, and converting potential into output. This reflects socio-constructivist understandings of learning as relational and scaffolded (Vygotsky, 1978).

6.5 Role of authentic output pathways

Finally, the cases show that authentic output pathways have motivational and identity power. Students who can see a route from coursework to publication, presentation, competition, or innovation often engage differently. Their work becomes consequential. The classroom becomes a launch site rather than a containment zone.

Such pathways are not appropriate for every task or every learner, but their existence matters. They challenge the low-ceiling assumption that introductory or mixed-disciplinary students should only be expected to consume existing knowledge. On the contrary, many can produce meaningful work when pedagogy is designed to support ownership.

7. LESSONS FOR EDUCATORS

7.1 Identifying hidden potential in students

One of the strongest lessons from these cases is that hidden potential is often masked by confidence, prior exposure, or disciplinary stereotype. A student who hesitates may be capable but unconvinced. A student who appears competent may still lack deep reasoning. A student who completes work quietly may be on the verge of major growth if given a suitable pathway.

Educators should therefore avoid sorting students too quickly into fixed categories such as "strong," "weak," "technical," or "non-technical." Instead, they should ask what kind of access or extension each learner needs. Some need more visibility. Some need more relevance. Some need lower-stakes opportunities to succeed. Some need encouragement to pursue more ambitious outputs.

7.2 Supporting hesitant learners

Hesitant learners require more than kindness. They need pedagogical conditions that make success possible before confidence fully forms. This includes explicit normalization of struggle, low-stakes retrieval practice, opportunities to explain rather than merely perform, and channels for asking questions without social penalty. It also includes careful language. When students interpret confusion as evidence of unfitness, supportive framing matters.

The cases suggest that timely intervention can be decisive. A student close to dropping a course may remain and thrive if support is concrete, credible, and accompanied by structures that reward persistence.

7.3 Designing pathways from novice to contributor

A key insight from this chapter is that novice-friendly teaching and high-level contribution are not opposites. The same course ecosystem can support beginners and cultivate contributors if it is designed with layered pathways. Foundational tasks should build reasoning and confidence; later opportunities should invite ownership, relevance, and extension. Some students will stop at competence, which is entirely appropriate. Others will use the same ecosystem to move into research, competition, or innovation.

This means curriculum design should include points of upward permeability. Strong student work should have somewhere to go. Courses should not assume that the boundary between "student" and "contributor" is fixed.

7.4 Case-based insights for interdisciplinary curriculum design

For interdisciplinary curriculum design more broadly, the cases suggest five practical principles:

1. Make reasoning visible so students can inspect and build understanding.
2. Translate without diluting by connecting abstract concepts to disciplinary logics.
3. Scaffold challenge through low-stakes practice and progressive project structures.
4. Mentor beyond minimum requirements when student work shows promise.
5. Value identity shifts as real educational outcomes, not soft extras.

These principles are applicable beyond computing. They are relevant wherever students cross disciplinary boundaries and risk misrecognizing difficulty as exclusion.

8. CONCLUSION

8.1 Transformation beyond grades

The cases presented in this chapter show that student transformation in cross-disciplinary computing education extends far beyond grade attainment. Students changed in how they understood code, how they approached error, how they saw themselves, and how they imagined their future participation in knowledge work. A fashion student found computational belonging. A linguistics student moved from near-withdrawal to high achievement. An applied biology student began to see programming as useful to scientific inquiry. Civil engineering and applied physics students deepened reasoning and transferred computational learning into later study.

Electrical engineering students moved into publication and scholarly confidence. Other students converted coursework into conference papers, competition success, startup pathways, and early innovation.

What unites these stories is not a single technique but a pedagogical stance: learning should be made visible, accessible, and generative. Students should not be sorted prematurely by prior confidence. They should be given structured ways to enter, reasons to care, and opportunities to extend. When that happens, transformation becomes possible across disciplinary lines.

8.2 Transition to scale

This chapter has focused on individual and small-group trajectories because transformation is often clearest in stories. The next step, however, is to ask how such transformation can be sustained and scaled: across larger cohorts, across departments, across institutional structures, and across educational systems that increasingly demand both inclusion and excellence. The challenge is not only to produce compelling student cases, but to build environments in which such cases become less exceptional and more expected. The next chapter turns toward that broader question of scale.

REFERENCES

Aquil Mirza, M., & Cong, W. (Eds.). (2026). *Real-Time Robotics With IoT and Edge AI: Methods, Metrics, and Applications*. IGI Global Scientific Publishing., DOI: 10.4018/979-8-2600-0701-3

Bandura, A. (1997). *Self-efficacy: The exercise of control*. W. H. Freeman.

Barker, L. J., Garvin-Doxas, K., & Roberts, E. M. (2009). What can computer science learn from a fine arts approach to teaching? *SIGCSE Bulletin*, *41*(1), 421–425. DOI: 10.1145/1047124.1047482

Baxter Magolda, M. B. (2009). Authoring your life: Developing an internal voice to navigate life's challenges. *Stylus (Rio de Janeiro)*.

Carlone, H. B., & Johnson, A. (2007). Understanding the science experiences of successful women of color: Science identity as an analytic lens. *Journal of Research in Science Teaching*, *44*(8), 1187–1218. DOI: 10.1002/tea.20237

Chi, M. T. H., Bassok, M., Lewis, M. W., Reimann, P., & Glaser, R. (1989). Self-explanations: How students study and use examples in learning to solve problems. *Cognitive Science*, *13*(2), 145–182. DOI: 10.1207/s15516709cog1302_1 PMID: 34983624

Collins, A., Brown, J. S., & Newman, S. E. (1989). Cognitive apprenticeship: Teaching the craft of reading, writing, and mathematics. In Resnick, L. B. (Ed.), *Knowing, learning, and instruction: Essays in honor of Robert Glaser* (pp. 453–494). Lawrence Erlbaum.

Cooper, K. M., Gin, L. E., Akeeh, B., Clark, C. E., Hunter, J. S., Roderick, T. B., Elliott, D. B., Gutierrez, L. A., & Brownell, S. E. (2019). Factors that predict life sciences student persistence in undergraduate research experiences. *PLoS One*, *14*(8), e0220186. DOI: 10.1371/journal.pone.0220186 PMID: 31412071

Eccles, J. S., & Wigfield, A. (2020). From expectancy-value theory to situated expectancy-value theory: A developmental, social cognitive, and sociocultural perspective on motivation. *Contemporary Educational Psychology*, *61*, 101859. Advance online publication. DOI: 10.1016/j.cedpsych.2020.101859

Freeman, T. M., Anderman, L. H., & Jensen, J. M. (2007). Sense of belonging in college freshmen at the classroom and campus levels. *Journal of Experimental Education*, *75*(3), 203–220. DOI: 10.3200/JEXE.75.3.203-220

Guzdial, M. (2015). Learner-centered design of computing education: Research on computing for everyone. *Synthesis Lectures on Human-Centered Informatics*, *8*(6), 1–165. DOI: 10.1007/978-3-031-02216-6

Lave, J., & Wenger, E. (1991). *Situated learning: Legitimate peripheral participation*. Cambridge University Press. DOI: 10.1017/CBO9780511815355

Lister, R., Simon, B., Thompson, E., Whalley, J. L., & Prasad, C. (2006). Not seeing the forest for the trees: Novice programmers and the SOLO taxonomy. *SIGCSE Bulletin*, *38*(3), 118–122. DOI: 10.1145/1140123.1140157

Margolis, J., & Fisher, A. (2003). *Unlocking the clubhouse: Women in computing*. MIT Press.

Merriam, S. B., & Tisdell, E. J. (2016). *Qualitative research: A guide to design and implementation* (4th ed.). Jossey-Bass.

Mohammed, A., & Zangana, H. (Eds.). (2026). *Intelligent Construction Monitoring Systems: Real-Time Safety, Environmental Prediction, and Risk Management*. IGI Global Scientific Publishing., DOI: 10.4018/979-8-3373-9245-5

National Academies of Sciences, Engineering, and Medicine. (2018). *How people learn II: Learners, contexts, and cultures*. National Academies Press. DOI: 10.17226/24783

Sax, L. J., Lehman, K. J., Jacobs, J. A., Kanny, M. A., Lim, G., Monje-Paulson, L., & Zimmerman, H. B. (2018). Anatomy of an enduring gender gap: The evolution of women's participation in computer science. *The Journal of Higher Education*, *88*(2), 258–293. DOI: 10.1080/00221546.2016.1257306

Stake, R. E. (1995). The art of case study research. *Sage (Atlanta, Ga.)*.

Tinto, V. (2012). *Completing college: Rethinking institutional action*. University of Chicago Press. DOI: 10.7208/chicago/9780226804545.001.0001

Vygotsky, L. S. (1978). *Mind in society: The development of higher psychological processes*. Harvard University Press.

Yin, R. K. (2018). *Case study research and applications: Design and methods* (6th ed.). Sage.

Chapter 10
Teaching Computing at Scale in Interdisciplinary Settings:
Design, Delivery, and Sustainability

Kun Hon Lio
http://orcid.org/0009-0001-1725-3480
Department of Civil and Environmental Engineering, The Hong Kong Polytechnic University, Hong Kong

ABSTRACT

This chapter examines how computing education can be designed, delivered, and sustained in large interdisciplinary classes. It treats scale not only as a logistical problem, but as a pedagogical condition that affects visibility, feedback, assessment, motivation, and student belonging. Drawing on implementation contexts involving cohorts of 200 to 350 students, this chapter outlines a model of scalable translational pedagogy built around strategic standardization, selective personalization, layered support, visible reasoning, aligned lectures, tutorials and labs, coordinated teaching teams, and sustainable workload practices. It argues that large computing classes need not become impersonal if course structures deliberately surface confusion, support diverse learner backgrounds, and preserve meaningful feedback. The chapter also discusses evidence of impact, including strong student feedback, improved pass outcomes, reduced withdrawal, and learning extension beyond the classroom, while acknowledging the limits of scaling individual mentoring and intensive feedback.

DOI: 10.4018/979-8-2600-1811-8.ch010

1. INTRODUCTION

1.1 The challenge of scale in interdisciplinary computing education

Teaching computing well is difficult. Teaching computing well to large, diverse cohorts is significantly harder. Teaching computing well to large, diverse cohorts composed of students from multiple disciplines; some technical, some non-technical, some anxious, some advanced, some convinced of relevance, some unconvinced; is harder still. This is the reality increasingly faced in contemporary higher education. Computing is no longer confined to computer science majors. It has become a foundational literacy for students in engineering, design, business, linguistics, health, biology, architecture, and many other fields. As a result, computing classrooms now often combine students with different prior knowledge, professional aspirations, disciplinary vocabularies, and emotional relationships to technical learning.

Scale intensifies every one of these challenges. A class of 25 allows the instructor to notice hesitation, respond to confusion, vary examples in real time, and track who is drifting toward disengagement. A class of 250 or 350 does not permit such responsiveness through intuition alone. In large classes, students can become administratively visible but pedagogically invisible. Their attendance may be recorded, their grades entered, their quiz attempts logged, yet their uncertainty, confusion, and unrealized potential may remain hidden unless the course is designed deliberately to surface and address them. This is especially true in interdisciplinary settings where students may struggle silently because they believe their confusion reflects personal deficiency rather than a mismatch between teaching assumptions and learner background, a divergence visually conceptualized in the visibility paradox shown in Figure 1.

The challenge of scale is not simply one of logistics. It is a pedagogical problem. Large classes create pressures toward uniformity, efficiency, and standardization. Those pressures are understandable, and in some respects necessary. Yet if pursued without care, they can produce teaching that is administratively manageable but educationally impoverished. Instructors may default to one-way lectures, generic examples, blunt assessments, and reactive support. Such approaches may deliver content to many students, but they rarely ensure that many students genuinely learn, transfer, and belong.

This chapter argues that translational computing pedagogy can scale; but not by pretending that scale does not matter. It scales only when scale is treated as a design condition rather than an unfortunate background fact. To teach large interdisciplinary computing classes effectively, educators need a deliberate architecture for standardization, personalization, support, feedback, assessment, team coordination, and sustainability. The question is not whether all aspects of small-class teaching can be replicated at scale. They cannot. The more productive question is: What must be redesigned so that large classes remain rigorous, humane, and educationally meaningful?

The discussion that follows focuses on the design, delivery, and sustainability of teaching computing at scale in large interdisciplinary settings, particularly classes in the range of 200 to 350 students. It examines scale as a multidimensional pedagogical issue, outlines principles for scaling translational pedagogy, discusses course design and delivery structures, analyzes scalable feedback and assessment systems, and considers workload and sustainability. It draws on implementation contexts that include classes of 229, 291, 331, and 349 students, alongside teaching impact data indicating strong student feedback (eSFQ scores approximately 4.6–4.9 out of 5 compared with a departmental average of 4.2), reduced withdrawal, improved pass outcomes, and evidence of learning extension into projects, competitions, and scholarly outputs.

Figure 1. Scalable Translational Pedagogy Model

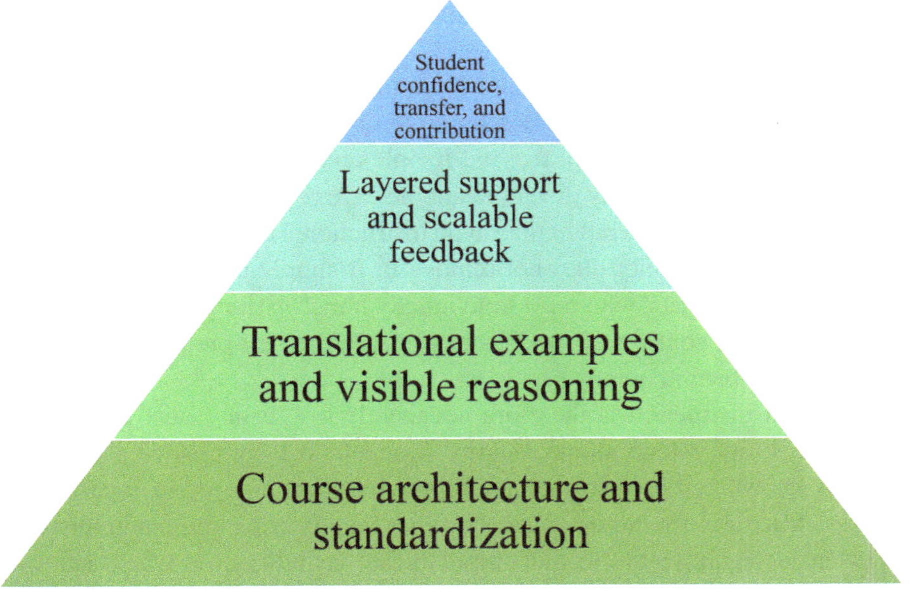

1.2 Why large classes often default to impersonal instruction

Large classes often drift toward impersonal instruction not because teachers lack care, but because scale changes what feels feasible. When class enrollment rises, instructors quickly face several pressures: limited time for individual feedback, heavy marking loads, more administrative coordination, larger volumes of student email and consultation, increased variability in student readiness, and the practical difficulty of noticing who is confused. Under these pressures, it is common for courses to become more standardized, more lecture-heavy, and more dependent on efficiency mechanisms. In itself, that is not problematic; some standardization is necessary for fairness and coherence. The problem emerges when efficiency becomes the dominant design principle and pedagogy follows behind.

In such situations, large classes tend to develop several familiar features. Explanations become more generalized. Assessment becomes more summative and less developmental. Feedback becomes shorter, delayed, or automated. Support becomes available but difficult to personalize. Students are expected to self-advocate, yet many are too unsure to do so. In mixed cohorts, confident students continue to cope while quieter or less prepared students disappear into the statistical middle. The course may run smoothly in operational terms while still leaving many students cognitively or emotionally unserved.

This problem is exacerbated in interdisciplinary computing education because students do not all hear the same lecture in the same way. A loop, a data structure, or an operating system concept may be legible and even familiar to one student while remaining conceptually distant to another. Large classes make it tempting to treat heterogeneity as noise rather than as an instructional reality requiring response. Yet ignoring heterogeneity does not remove it. It simply relocates the burden of adaptation onto students, who must individually translate the course into their own disciplinary terms, confidence levels, and goals. Those best prepared to do so succeed; others fall behind quietly.

Impersonal instruction is therefore not merely a stylistic issue. It is a risk to educational equity, retention, and quality. Students in large classes need not feel personally known by the instructor at all times, but they do need to experience the course as structured for human learning rather than only for mass administration. This means designing systems that communicate visibility even when one-to-one contact is limited: visible reasoning, regular concept checks, varied examples, layered support, clear routines, accessible help channels, and opportunities for meaningful progression.

1.3 Can translational pedagogy scale?

The short answer is yes, but only partially and deliberately. Translational pedagogy does not scale by reproducing every individualized teaching move at mass level. It scales by identifying which parts of instruction must remain consistent, which parts can be varied efficiently, and which parts require layered rather than individualized forms of support. In other words, scalable translational pedagogy is not personalized teaching for every student in the strongest sense; it is a principled combination of shared structures and targeted flexibility.

At small scale, translational pedagogy might involve highly responsive conversation, spontaneous analogy shifts, and close real-time mentoring. At larger scale, these same goals must be pursued differently. Instead of purely improvisational adaptation, the instructor designs lectures with multiple disciplinary entry points, builds repeatable pedagogical routines, equips teaching assistants with common response frameworks, uses low-stakes data to detect common confusion, and creates support channels that allow students to access help at different intensities. This is not a lesser form of pedagogy. It is a different one, requiring design intelligence rather than simply more effort.

There is good reason to believe such scaling is possible. Research on active learning, structured feedback, and inclusive design in STEM suggests that even in large classes, carefully designed pedagogy can improve engagement and learning compared to passive, transmission-heavy approaches (Freeman et al., 2014; Hattie, 2009; Prince, 2004). Work on course design and constructive alignment also indicates that large classes benefit when learning outcomes, teaching activities, and assessment are deliberately coordinated rather than left to accumulate piecemeal (Biggs & Tang, 2011). Similarly, studies on student persistence and belonging show that structure, visibility, and support can meaningfully affect retention and engagement even at scale (Kuh, 2008; Tinto, 2012).

The more difficult question is not whether translational pedagogy can scale at all, but what exactly remains difficult to scale. Some things do remain hard: deep individual mentoring for every student, intensive bespoke feedback, careful monitoring of emotional state, and nuanced adaptation to all disciplinary needs simultaneously. This chapter acknowledges those limits. Its argument is not that scale ceases to matter, but that many of its harms can be reduced through careful design.

2. UNDERSTANDING SCALE AS A PEDAGOGICAL PROBLEM

Large-enrollment teaching is often discussed as if scale were primarily numerical. Enrollment size certainly matters, but pedagogically, scale is more complex. A class of 250 homogeneous, well-prepared students is not equivalent to a class of 250 interdisciplinary learners ranging from fashion to engineering, from coding novice to experienced programmer, from confident speaker to silent struggler. To design teaching effectively, scale must be understood in multiple dimensions, which are systematically mapped alongside their corresponding mitigation strategies in Table 1.

2.1 Numerical scale

Numerical scale is the most obvious dimension. It refers simply to the number of students in a course. In practical terms, a class of 229 students differs from one of 349 students not just in seat count but in the volume of interactions, messages, assessments, attendance, troubleshooting incidents, and support needs that can arise. The difference between 30 students and 300 students is not linear; it is combinatorial. Communication load multiplies. Administrative complexity multiplies. The cost of ambiguity multiplies. Every unclear instruction, every poorly timed release, every under-specified rubric, and every unstable technical setup affects far more people.

Table 1. Challenges of Scale and Corresponding Design Responses

Challenge of scale	Typical risk	Design response	Practical example
Numerical scale	confusion multiplies	standardize core routines	weekly guidance notes
Diversity scale	some students excluded	translational example variation	multiple disciplinary analogies
Feedback scale	delayed or generic comments	feedback layering	quiz feedback + rubric comments
Assessment scale	inconsistent marking	rubric calibration	marker briefing meetings
Emotional scale	silent disengagement	low-stakes support channels	anonymous question tool

Numerical scale increases the need for clarity, consistency, and anticipation. Instructions must be written so that they survive interpretation across hundreds of learners. Tasks must be designed so that students can begin productively even when immediate staff help is unavailable. Assessment logistics must handle volume without collapsing quality. In large computing classes, technical friction is especially consequential. If software setup fails for 5% of students in a class of 331, that means around 16 students already face a barrier substantial enough to affect learning morale and support demand.

The teaching records informing this chapter include large cohorts in foundational and systems-related computing subjects such as 229 students in COMP2432, 291 students in COMP1012, 331 students in COMP1012, and 349 students in COMP1012 across different years. These numbers matter because they demonstrate that the challenge is not hypothetical. They reflect real teaching contexts where any pedagogical strategy must function under high-volume conditions.

2.2 Diversity scale

Diversity scale refers to the breadth of learner difference present in the class. In interdisciplinary computing education, this is often more pedagogically significant than enrollment alone. Students differ in prior coding knowledge, mathematical confidence, disciplinary language, motivation, self-efficacy, and assumptions about what computing is for. Some have built scripts before university; others have never opened a development environment. Some see computing as central to their goals; others see it as a required subject with unclear relevance.

Diversity scale complicates teaching because the same explanation may be too basic for some students and too abstract for others. The same assignment may feel accessible and exciting to one learner, obscure and alienating to another. In mixed cohorts, a course can accidentally optimize for the visible middle or the already confident. Beginners may become overwhelmed; stronger students may become disengaged; both outcomes reduce overall educational quality.

The challenge becomes acute when diversity intersects with identity and emotion. Students from non-technical disciplines may experience computing as culturally distant. Students with prior failure experiences may fear public error. Students with stronger backgrounds may dominate visible participation, reinforcing the illusion that others are alone in struggling. In the nomination and teaching materials informing this book, large classes included students from fashion, design, applied physics, linguistics, building sciences, engineering, data science, and applied biology, with more than ten students in one large cohort having special educational needs. This diversity is pedagogically meaningful, as a single cohort may simultaneously contain a design student intimidated by basic syntax alongside an advanced mechanical or electrical engineering student attempting to interface with real-time edge AI architectures (Aquil Mirza & Cong, 2026). This diversity is pedagogically meaningful. It demands more than a standard lecture delivered to many bodies.

2.3 Assessment scale

Assessment scale refers to the difficulty of designing, administering, grading, moderating, and returning assessment for large cohorts. In computing, this challenge is intensified by the nature of the work. Programming tasks generate varied outputs, debugging issues, and different valid solution pathways. Written explanations require interpretation, not simple answer matching. Projects produce heterogeneous artifacts that are educationally valuable but time-consuming to assess well.

Large classes often respond by simplifying assessment: more auto-graded quizzes, fewer open-ended tasks, more standardized items, and shorter feedback. Some simplification is reasonable, but there are pedagogical risks. Over-automated assessment may reward syntax or final output while neglecting reasoning, interpretation, and transfer. Large project components may become administratively overwhelming without strong rubric design and team coordination.

Assessment scale is thus not just about marking volume. It is about preserving alignment between what matters educationally and what is assessable at volume. If a course claims to teach computational reasoning, disciplinary application, and communication, its assessment system must capture more than whether code runs. Scalable assessment should therefore combine efficient formats with strategically chosen human judgment.

2.4 Feedback scale

Feedback is one of the first educational casualties of large enrollment. Personalized, timely, developmental feedback becomes harder as class size rises. Yet feedback is also one of the most powerful levers for learning improvement (Hattie & Timperley, 2007; Nicol & Macfarlane-Dick, 2006). In computing, feedback is particularly important because students often need help understanding *why* their code failed, what misconception drove the error, or how to improve structure and readability.

At scale, feedback problems take several forms. Feedback may arrive too late to matter. It may become generic and therefore less actionable. It may be inconsistent across multiple graders. It may focus on deficits rather than improvement. Or it may disappear almost entirely into marks and model answers, leaving students to infer what happened.

A scalable feedback system therefore requires redesign, not simply more effort. The goal is not always individual paragraph-level commentary for every student. Rather, it is to ensure that every student receives enough useful information, at the right time, in the right form, to improve. This may involve a combination of automated checks, common feedback banks, annotated exemplars, tutorial debriefs, rubric-linked comments, and targeted human intervention for those showing signs of difficulty.

2.5 Emotional and motivational scale

Large classes create not only administrative scale but emotional scale. When 300 students enter a room, the number of possible anxieties, silent confusions, and disengagement trajectories is substantial. Computing amplifies this because many learners associate programming with intelligence judgment, technical gatekeeping, or fear of failure. In smaller settings, instructors can often notice when a student is withdrawing psychologically. In larger classes, such signals are easier to miss.

Emotional scale matters because motivation is not self-sustaining in difficult domains. Students need reasons to persist, evidence that effort can work, and a sense that confusion is normal and recoverable. Without this, large classes can feel anonymous and unforgiving. Silence spreads easily in such environments. Students who are lost may delay asking for help because the social cost feels high, and the logistical barriers to reaching the instructor feel greater.

In interdisciplinary settings, motivational scale also includes relevance. When students from health sciences, design, civil engineering, or linguistics cannot see how computing connects to their future, large classes may intensify detachment. A student in a small seminar can ask, "Why does this matter for my field?" In a lecture hall of 300, that question may remain unasked; and unanswered.

For this reason, scalable pedagogy must address not only information delivery but emotional architecture. It must create a course climate in which students understand that struggle is expected, support is available, relevance exists, and progress is possible.

3. PRINCIPLES FOR SCALING TRANSLATIONAL PEDAGOGY

To teach computing at scale in interdisciplinary settings, it is not enough to add more teaching assistants or automate more quizzes. Scale requires a principled pedagogical model. The following four principles provide a practical foundation.

3.1 Standardization where useful, personalization where necessary

A common mistake in conversations about scalable teaching is to oppose standardization and personalization as if one must choose entirely between them. In reality, effective large-class teaching requires both. Standardization provides clarity, fairness, consistency, and operational manageability. Personalization ensures that students with different backgrounds can meaningfully enter and progress through the learning experience.

The key is to standardize what benefits from consistency and personalize what affects access. For example, learning outcomes, core task structures, assessment criteria, submission processes, and key teaching routines should usually be standardized. These create predictability and reduce confusion at scale. By contrast, examples, explanatory framings, support pathways, extension tasks, and project topics often benefit from selective personalization. These are the points where interdisciplinary translation can occur without sacrificing course coherence.

In practice, this might mean that all students complete the same conceptual milestone on loops or file handling, but examples vary: one lecture references environmental sensor readings, another social data processing, another repeated design patterns. Or all students submit a project aligned with common rubric criteria, but they may choose from discipline-relevant pathways. This form of managed variability is more scalable than attempting bespoke instruction for each learner, while still respecting heterogeneity.

3.2 Layered support systems

No single support channel can serve 300 students effectively. Large classes require layered support systems, meaning multiple support routes with different intensities, purposes, and entry thresholds. Some students need quick clarification. Some need repeated low-stakes practice. Some need human reassurance. Some need detailed help with debugging. Some need challenge extension rather than remediation.

A layered support architecture typically includes several elements: in-class concept checks, clear written guides, discussion boards, tutorial/lab help, consultation hours, FAQ updates, peer support, and targeted intervention for students showing risk indicators. The advantage of layering is that it distributes support efficiently. Students can access lower-intensity resources for common issues, preserving higher-intensity human time for more complex needs.

This is especially important in interdisciplinary computing. Students vary not only in technical need but also in willingness to seek help publicly. Anonymous question channels, structured office hours, and community discussion spaces can reduce help-seeking stigma. When support exists in multiple forms, students are more likely to find an entry point that suits them, navigating through the tiered resource allocation framework modeled in Figure 2.

Figure 2. Layered Support Architecture for Large Classes

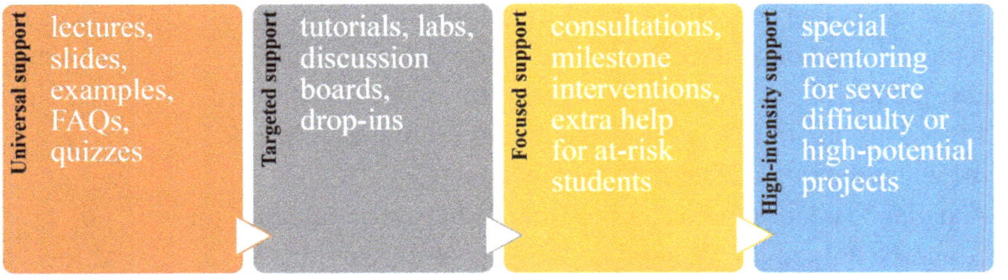

Note: Different students need different intensities of support; not all need one-to-one intervention.

3.3 Repeatable pedagogical routines

Large classes benefit from routines because routines lower cognitive overhead. When students know how lectures work, how tutorials unfold, how feedback is structured, and what happens when confusion arises, they can focus more energy on learning the content itself. Repeatable routines also help teaching teams coordinate. They reduce inconsistency across multiple tutors or lab groups.

Examples of repeatable pedagogical routines include:

- begin each lecture with a brief recap and common misconception correction;
- embed concept checks at planned intervals;
- use a predictable explain-trace-apply sequence in practical teaching;
- close each week with a summary of common errors;
- structure labs around guided work followed by one independent extension task;
- release a weekly "what students struggled with" note.

Such routines may seem simple, but at scale they are powerful. They create a stable learning rhythm that helps heterogeneous students know what is expected. Research on teaching presence and structure suggests that predictability supports engagement and self-regulation, especially in demanding learning environments (Ambrose et al., 2010; Zimmerman, 2002).

3.4 Technology-enabled but pedagogy-led scale

Technology can help large classes function, but technology should not determine pedagogy. Large-enrollment teaching often turns too quickly to tools; learning management systems, polling software, auto-graders, dashboards, recorded videos; as if these automatically solve pedagogical problems. They do not. They are only useful when serving a clear educational design.

A pedagogy-led approach asks first: What must students understand, experience, and be able to do? Where are they likely to struggle? What kind of feedback is necessary? What support forms are equitable and efficient? Only then does the instructor ask which technologies can help enact those purposes at scale.

In practical terms, this means using tools to:

- surface misconceptions quickly through polls or quizzes;
- provide immediate checks on basic syntax or logic where appropriate;
- organize communication and FAQs;
- support repeated access to explanations;
- monitor participation patterns;
- streamline rubric-based marking.

It does **not** mean replacing pedagogical judgment with automation. Especially in interdisciplinary classes, human interpretation remains essential for understanding whether students are merely completing tasks or actually making sense of computing in relation to their own fields.

4. DESIGNING LARGE INTERDISCIPLINARY COURSES

4.1 Course architecture and modularization

At scale, course architecture matters enormously. A large interdisciplinary computing subject cannot rely on week-to-week improvisation. It requires an intentional modular structure in which concepts are sequenced logically, prerequisite dependencies are managed carefully, and each component of the course supports the others.

Modularization helps in several ways. First, it breaks a potentially overwhelming course into meaningful learning units. This is especially important for beginners who may otherwise experience computing as an accumulating mass of disconnected syntax and tasks. Second, modularization facilitates pacing and checkpoint design. Third, it helps teaching teams align lectures, labs, assessments, and support around shared weekly goals.

A strong course architecture typically includes:

- a clear conceptual spine, identifying the few core ideas students must truly understand;
- modules organized around coherent skill-concept clusters;
- formative checkpoints embedded within modules;
- assessment tasks aligned with cumulative but manageable progression;
- explicit bridging between modules so students can see continuity.

For example, a foundational programming course may organize around modules such as variables and state, conditions and logic, iteration, functions, data structures, file handling, and project integration. Each module should not merely present content, but create a learning arc: introduction, visible reasoning, guided practice, formative check, and extension. In large classes, this architectural discipline reduces the risk that students will survive isolated weeks while failing to build cumulative understanding.

4.2 Lecture-tutorial-lab alignment

One of the most common weaknesses in large computing courses is misalignment between lectures, tutorials, and labs. Lectures may introduce concepts abstractly, tutorials may assume greater understanding than students have, and labs may ask for independent performance before students are ready. In large interdisciplinary classes, such misalignment is especially damaging because weaker students often depend on structural coherence to remain engaged.

Alignment means that each course component has a distinct role but connects clearly to the others. Lectures should introduce and model concepts, with visible reasoning and conceptual framing. Tutorials should consolidate understanding through discussion, worked problems, misconception clarification, and short guided tasks. Labs should provide hands-on application, first in supported form and then with some independent extension. Assessments should draw from these experiences coherently rather than surprising students with task types they have not practiced.

In scalable course design, this alignment must be visible not only to instructors but to students and teaching assistants. Weekly guides, staff briefings, shared teaching notes, and clearly labeled learning outcomes help ensure that lecture-tutorial-lab sequencing remains coherent. If lecture week 4 covers loops conceptually, tutorials should revisit loop reasoning explicitly, and labs should allow students to enact that logic before any significant assessed use.

4.3 Designing for beginner access and advanced extension

Interdisciplinary classes are typically heterogeneous not only in discipline but in skill. Some students are complete beginners; others have prior coding experience. If the course is designed only for the middle, it risks simultaneously overwhelming novices and underchallenging advanced learners. Scalable design must therefore create dual access: beginner access and advanced extension.

Beginner access involves features such as:

- low-barrier examples;
- explicit explanation of assumptions;
- guided starter code where appropriate;
- progressive tasks rather than immediate blank-page assignments;
- repeated conceptual reinforcement;
- normalized debugging and help-seeking.

Advanced extension involves:

- optional challenge tasks;
- project pathways that allow more sophisticated implementation;
- extension prompts in labs;
- opportunities to connect coursework to research, competition, or innovation;
- invitations to mentor peers or contribute in near-peer roles.

The goal is not to split the class into separate tracks unless curriculum design specifically permits that. Rather, it is to design assignments and activities with expandable depth. A beginner can meet the core outcomes through scaffolded work; a more advanced student can go further without needing a separate course. This is an important sustainability strategy because it respects heterogeneity without multiplying administrative structures excessively, providing a balanced instructional ecosystem as detailed in the dual-access layout in Table 2.

Table 2. Resource Map for Large-Enrollment Delivery

Resource type	Purpose	Reusable?	Staff owner	Timing of use
quiz bank	concept checks	yes	instructor/TA	weekly
annotated exemplars	clarify standards	yes	instructor	before assignments
FAQ sheet	reduce repeated questions	yes, updated	teaching team	ongoing
tutor briefing notes	align teaching	yes, revised	instructor	weekly
milestone templates	structure projects	yes	instructor	project phase

4.4 Scheduling and pacing for heterogeneous cohorts

Pacing is one of the most difficult design questions in large interdisciplinary computing teaching. Move too quickly and beginners disengage or panic. Move too slowly and stronger students disconnect. Poor pacing also interacts with motivation: students who repeatedly feel left behind often stop attempting tasks sincerely, while students who feel perpetually unchallenged may reduce attendance and attention.

Good pacing begins with realistic assumptions about entry knowledge. In mixed cohorts, it is safer to assume uneven preparation than hidden readiness. This does not mean lowering standards. It means sequencing challenge so that students can build toward those standards. Early overload is costly because it often shapes students' beliefs about whether they can succeed at all.

Several practical pacing strategies help:

- front-load orientation and setup support;
- keep early tasks conceptually narrow but confidence-building;
- revisit core ideas multiple times in different forms;
- delay heavy open-endedness until students have handled guided tasks;
- use low-stakes quizzes to maintain distributed engagement;
- avoid clustering major deadlines too tightly.

Importantly, pacing decisions should be informed by evidence, not only instructor instinct. If consultation spikes repeatedly at the same week, if formative quiz performance drops sharply on a concept, or if large numbers of students report falling behind, pacing may need revision.

4.5 Coordinating TAs and teaching teams

Large classes are rarely taught by a single person in practice, even when one instructor leads the subject. Teaching assistants, tutors, lab demonstrators, and support staff often shape much of the student experience. In scalable translational pedagogy, the teaching team is not just logistical support. It is part of the pedagogical mechanism.

Without coordination, large teaching teams can create inconsistency. Students may receive different explanations, contradictory debugging advice, or uneven feedback standards across lab groups. This inconsistency is especially harmful in beginner computing, where students are already uncertain about what counts as understanding. Therefore, TA coordination is a major design task.

Effective team coordination includes:

- pre-semester briefing on course philosophy and common student barriers;
- weekly tutor notes highlighting learning goals, typical misconceptions, and desired response approaches;
- clear rubric interpretation and moderation discussions;
- shared logs of frequently asked questions;
- agreed protocols for escalation when students show significant struggle;
- regular debriefing after labs to identify recurring issues.

In courses involving 200–350 students, tutors often become the first line of pedagogical sensing. They notice where students freeze, what questions recur, and how classroom climate feels in practice. Their observations are valuable evidence and should feed back into course adjustment.

5. SCALABLE TEACHING PRACTICES

5.1 Visible reasoning in large lectures

One misconception about large lectures is that they must be fundamentally passive. While interaction is more difficult in a room of 300 than in a seminar, large lectures can still make reasoning visible. This is crucial in computing because students often misunderstand not only *what* to do but *how thinking unfolds* when solving a problem.

Visible reasoning in large lectures can be achieved through several repeatable moves:

- live coding with explicit verbalization of decisions;
- intentional pause points where students predict outputs;
- paper-based or slide-based tracing of variable changes;
- visual flow representations before full code;
- showing and debugging intentional errors;
- explaining why one approach is preferable to another.

These practices are scalable because they do not require one-to-one interaction. They require disciplined lecture design. The point is to externalize expert cognition so that students are not merely watching a finished solution appear. In a large room, many students will not speak, but they can still think, predict, compare, and recognize misconception when the explanation is structured accordingly.

Such visible reasoning is especially important for interdisciplinary learners because it reduces the "polished solution fallacy," the idea that experts simply produce correct code instantly while novices fail because they lack talent. When students watch an instructor reason, hesitate, debug, or explain trade-offs, the learning process becomes more human and more learnable.

5.2 Efficient concept checks

Concept checks are one of the most effective scalable teaching practices in large classes. They provide fast information to students and instructors about whether key ideas are being understood. In computing, concept checks can focus on output prediction, logic tracing, conceptual distinctions, debugging interpretation, or transfer to a new context.

Efficient concept checks may take the form of:

- multiple-choice clicker or polling questions;
- short code output predictions;
- mini whiteboard or paper responses in smaller tutorial groups;
- one-minute explanations of what a code segment does;
- short pre- or post-lecture quizzes.

Their value lies in frequency and purpose. Concept checks should not be mere attendance substitutes. They should identify misunderstandings early enough to correct them. They are also motivational: they give students regular moments to test their own understanding rather than discovering confusion only at assessment time.

At scale, efficient concept checks also act as a feedback loop for instructors. If a large proportion of students choose an incorrect answer that reflects a common misconception, the instructor can address it immediately. This prevents hidden misunderstanding from spreading unnoticed through the cohort.

5.3 Mass personalization through example variation

True individual personalization is difficult in large classes. However, a useful form of "mass personalization" can be achieved through example variation. This involves teaching the same core concept using multiple contextual frames so that students from different disciplines can find an accessible entry point.

For instance, a loop can be illustrated through sensor sampling in engineering, repeated pattern generation in design, survey response processing in social science, or repeated rule application in linguistics. The conceptual structure remains stable, but the examples distribute relevance more widely. An instructor can demonstrate how conditional logic gates handle predictive risk data inside heavy infrastructure or intelligent construction monitoring systems (Mohammed & Zangana, 2026), immediately offering a civil engineering student a visible, domain-specific application.

Over time, students begin to see computing not as belonging to one discipline but as a transferable way of thinking.

Mass personalization through example variation is scalable because it occurs at the level of planned teaching materials. It does not require separate lesson plans for every disciplinary group. Instead, it requires the deliberate inclusion of diverse examples, alternate analogies, and occasionally varied task options. This is especially effective in foundational courses with 250–350 students because it helps different groups feel that the subject recognizes their world.

5.4 Discussion boards, feedback channels, and consultation structures

Large classes need structured communication systems. Otherwise, the instructor becomes the bottleneck for every question, and students receive uneven access depending on how assertive they are. Discussion boards, FAQ spaces, anonymous question tools, and well-defined consultation routes are essential components of scalable pedagogy.

A good discussion structure has several characteristics:

- questions and answers are visible to the cohort where appropriate;
- repeated questions are consolidated into FAQ updates;
- norms for posting are clear and low-stigma;
- teaching assistants contribute under shared guidance;
- escalation routes exist for unresolved issues.

Consultation structures also need design. If office hours are offered informally without scheduling, demand may peak chaotically before assessments. More scalable models include themed drop-ins, booked short slots, extra sessions before deadlines, and targeted outreach to students who appear disengaged.

Anonymous feedback or question channels can be especially valuable in interdisciplinary computing because many students fear asking "basic" questions publicly. Such channels reduce social risk and help instructors see where confusion is concentrated.

5.5 Peer support and near-peer mentoring

Peer support is often framed as a substitute for instructor time, but when designed well, it is pedagogically valuable in its own right. Students often learn effectively from peers who are closer to their own level of expertise and therefore remember what novice confusion feels like. Near-peer mentors; students who have completed the course successfully or who are slightly more advanced; can provide both technical help and identity modeling.

In large interdisciplinary computing classes, peer support can take several forms:

- tutorial pair or small-group problem solving;
- student discussion channels with tutor moderation;
- peer explanation activities in class;
- structured near-peer mentoring sessions;
- advanced students serving as project guides or exemplars.

The value of near-peer support goes beyond efficiency. It helps normalize difficulty and makes success seem attainable. A beginner may find it easier to believe "I can do this" when hearing it from someone who struggled similarly a year earlier. This is especially useful in courses serving non-technical majors or mixed-ability cohorts.

6. SCALABLE ASSESSMENT AND FEEDBACK SYSTEMS

6.1 Automated support with human oversight

Large classes often need automation, but automation must remain accountable to educational purpose. In computing, automated support is especially useful for immediate checking of syntax, basic logic, formatting, or test-case outcomes. Low-stakes quizzes can be auto-marked. Simple code checks can provide rapid response. Online submission systems can manage logistics efficiently.

However, automated support should be combined with human oversight for at least three reasons. First, students need help interpreting why an answer is wrong, not merely being told that it is wrong. Second, some learning goals; reasoning, explanation, domain interpretation, design quality; cannot be fully captured by automation. Third, automated systems can mislead if students optimize for passing hidden tests rather than understanding concepts.

A scalable model therefore uses automation for what it does best; speed, consistency, immediate response; and preserves human judgment for conceptual, interpretive, or developmental elements. For example, weekly quizzes may be automated, while project reflections and code explanations receive human review through rubrics and sampled commentary. This balance helps maintain rigor without overwhelming teaching teams.

6.2 Rubric design for consistency

In large classes with multiple graders, rubric quality is central. Poor rubrics increase inconsistency, student confusion, and marking disputes. Good rubrics function as pedagogical tools as well as assessment tools. They clarify expectations, support fairness, and make feedback more legible.

For scalable interdisciplinary computing courses, rubrics should:

- align closely with learning outcomes;
- distinguish between technical correctness, reasoning, documentation, and application;
- use descriptors that are concrete enough for consistent interpretation;
- support partial achievement rather than binary success/failure;
- be accompanied by exemplars or calibration discussions for markers.

Rubrics are especially important for projects because project diversity is often educationally desirable. If students are allowed to choose contexts or design pathways, the rubric becomes the shared standard that preserves fairness while permitting variation. In such cases, the rubric should assess what is common across projects; clarity of problem framing, correctness of implementation, quality of explanation, evidence of testing, and relevance of interpretation; rather than forcing identical outputs.

6.3 Scalable project supervision models

Projects are valuable in interdisciplinary computing because they support ownership, relevance, and transfer. Yet project supervision becomes difficult at scale. If every group requires intensive bespoke mentoring, the workload quickly becomes unsustainable. This bottleneck is particularly severe when advanced groups pivot toward highly sensitive environments, such as optimizing multi-threaded data transfers or ensuring zero-loss streams across web-syncing sensor platforms (Mohammed, 2026). Scalable project supervision therefore needs structure.

Useful models include:

- standardized project milestones with staged submissions;
- project pathway menus rather than fully open topics for all;
- group-based consultations instead of repeated individual troubleshooting;
- milestone-specific templates and checklists;
- shared exemplar archives;
- triage systems for identifying projects needing extra support.

A milestone model is especially effective. Students submit a proposal, then a progress check, then a draft or demo, then a final product. At each stage, feedback can be focused and efficient. Because the same milestone structure applies across the cohort, staff can anticipate common issues. Stronger projects can be identified early for extension opportunities; struggling projects can be redirected before failure becomes likely.

6.4 Monitoring participation and intervention needs

At scale, teaching teams cannot rely solely on visible classroom impression to know who is thriving or at risk. Participation monitoring is therefore important; but it must be used supportively rather than punitively. Relevant indicators may include quiz non-completion, missed submissions, sharp drops in engagement, repeated requests for extension, absence from labs, or patterns of support-seeking that indicate persistent struggle.

The aim is not surveillance for its own sake. It is early intervention. If a student has stopped attempting low-stakes tasks, the course should have mechanisms to notice and respond. A short outreach message, reminder of support options, or targeted tutorial invitation can make a substantial difference, especially before assessment crises develop.

In large interdisciplinary courses, participation monitoring is also useful at the cohort level. If one topic generates a widespread drop in quiz performance or a flood of help requests, that is pedagogical information. It suggests the need for whole-class clarification, not just individual remediation.

7. EVIDENCE FROM LARGE-CLASS IMPLEMENTATION

7.1 Course data from 250–350 student cohorts

The practical claims in this chapter are grounded in large-enrollment implementation contexts rather than hypothetical design. Recent teaching records include classes such as COMP1012 Programming Fundamentals and Applications with enrollments of 291, 349, and 331 students across different academic years, and COMP2432 Operating Systems with 229 and 240 students. Across courses taught since 2023, more than 2,091 students were reached in settings spanning 10 or more disciplines. These figures matter because they show that the pedagogical issues discussed here arise in real, repeated, high-volume teaching contexts.

Large cohorts create sustained stress tests for pedagogy. A method that feels effective with 30 students may fail operationally with 300. The evidence presented in the nomination and teaching materials suggests that several strategies retained value at scale: low-stakes quizzes, scaffolded assignments, visible reasoning practices, translational examples, consultation structures, and project pathways. The course evaluations also indicate strong student perception of teaching quality, with reported eSFQ scores in the range of 4.6 to 4.9 out of 5, compared with a departmental average around 4.2.

Such student evaluation data should not be overinterpreted. Satisfaction alone is not proof of learning. However, in large classes where students frequently complain when instruction feels inaccessible or unsupported, consistently strong feedback can at least suggest that the course did not collapse into anonymity. When paired with outcome data, it becomes more meaningful.

7.2 Impact on pass rates, withdrawal, and engagement

The available teaching evidence indicates several positive trends associated with the large-class implementation of translational and scaffolded computing pedagogy. Reported figures include a reduction in withdrawal rate from approximately 5% to 0%, an improvement in pass rate from 90% to 100%, and an increase in A-range attainment from 20% to 25%. While such figures always require contextual interpretation, they are notable because large classes often struggle with exactly these issues: silent withdrawal, failure clustering, and uneven attainment.

The zero-withdrawal figure is especially significant in light of the diverse and beginner-heavy cohorts involved. In a large foundational computing course, retaining all enrolled students is not a trivial outcome. It suggests that students experienced sufficient support, structure, and possibility to remain engaged. It does not mean all difficulty vanished. Rather, it implies that the course climate and design reduced the likelihood that students would conclude they had no place in the subject.

Engagement evidence also appears in student comments and performance patterns. Students repeatedly highlighted the value of line-by-line tracing, low-pressure but firm insistence on fundamentals, structured project scaffolding, regular quizzes, and adaptable examples. In large classes, such comments matter because they indicate that students did not experience the subject as a generic content dump. Instead, they noticed design choices intended to support learning.

7.3 Student perceptions in large-class settings

Student perceptions in large-class settings are particularly important because large enrollment often breeds the assumption that students will inevitably feel lost or depersonalized. Yet the available testimonials suggest a more nuanced picture. Students from civil engineering, applied mathematics, applied physics, data science, fashion and textiles, biology, and linguistics described experiences of increased confidence, clearer understanding, and stronger connection to computing.

One student from civil engineering reflected that tracing loops line by line on paper before typing "forced me to see where variables actually change, not just guess." This suggests that visible reasoning practices remained effective even in a large cohort. Another student from applied mathematics praised the structured project framework, noting that full main code was provided so that novices could focus on understanding and modifying key sections before writing complete programs independently. This indicates that scaffolded challenge was perceived as enabling rather than patronizing.

A student from applied physics emphasized that Python became useful in later courses such as data analysis and machine learning, and that quizzes helped reinforce concepts. This points to transfer beyond the immediate subject. Meanwhile, a linguistics student reported being close to dropping the course but later earning an A+, with a transformed sense of confidence in computing. Such comments suggest that even in large classes, students may experience significant identity shifts when pedagogy makes struggle normal, support accessible, and progress visible.

One brief testimony adapted for this chapter captures the large-class paradox well:

"I expected a class this big to feel anonymous, but the structure made it feel like there were always ways to check if I was understanding and places to get help if I was not."

This does not mean the student felt individually mentored at all times. Rather, it means the course felt pedagogically present despite numerical scale. That is a realistic and important goal for scalable teaching.

7.4 Constraints and what still does not scale easily

It is important not to romanticize large-class pedagogy. Some things remain difficult to scale, even in well-designed courses. Intensive individual feedback for every student is one. Deep one-to-one mentoring for all projects is another. Rapid emotional sensing; knowing who is silently discouraged before any data signal appears; is also difficult. So is customizing examples perfectly for every disciplinary identity in every lesson.

Consultation load is another real limit. As cohorts grow, even efficient structures can be strained during peak periods. Discussion boards can become noisy. Teaching assistants vary in quality despite training. Project moderation remains labor-intensive. Technical issues affecting a small percentage of students still generate significant support burdens because the absolute numbers are larger.

Scalable pedagogy therefore involves trade-offs. The aim is not to eliminate all limitations but to reduce avoidable failure points and preserve educational quality where it matters most. A realistic account of scale must admit that some aspects of excellent teaching remain expensive in human terms. This is why sustainability and workload deserve explicit attention.

8. SUSTAINABILITY AND FACULTY WORKLOAD

8.1 Instructor workload and burnout risks

Large, interdisciplinary, high-care teaching can be deeply rewarding, but it can also be exhausting. Instructors in such settings often face a dangerous combination of expectations: be inclusive, be responsive, maintain rigor, innovate continuously, provide timely feedback, supervise projects, support struggling students, and do all this for 200–350 learners at a time. Without sustainable structures, such work can quickly become burnout-inducing.

Burnout risks arise from several sources:

- constant email and consultation demand;
- repeated emotional labor supporting anxious students;
- pressure to maintain high teaching quality across large cohorts;
- heavy assessment oversight;
- coordination of TAs and logistics;
- expectation of continual redesign based on feedback.

In computing, these risks are intensified by the frequency of technical troubleshooting and the possibility of deadline crises when students encounter coding problems late. If instructors try to personally solve every issue, scale becomes unsustainable.

Recognizing burnout risk is not a sign of weak commitment. It is part of responsible pedagogy. Unsustainable heroics may work temporarily, but they do not create stable teaching quality over time. Scalable translational pedagogy therefore requires workload-conscious design.

8.2 Reusable resources and teaching assets

One major sustainability strategy is the development of reusable teaching assets. These include annotated slides, example banks, debugging demonstrations, FAQ documents, quiz pools, walkthrough videos, rubric libraries, project templates, exemplar submissions, and weekly tutor notes. Reusability does not mean stagnation;

resources can and should be refined. But starting from an evolving asset base each semester reduces unnecessary reinvention.

Reusable assets are especially valuable in large interdisciplinary courses because they preserve pedagogical quality across repetition. A carefully designed example that translates a concept effectively for mixed audiences can be reused and adapted. A well-constructed rubric can stabilize marking quality across years. A strong FAQ on software setup can prevent the same problems consuming staff time repeatedly.

Resource development should therefore be seen not as optional extra labor but as core sustainability work. Over time, a well-asseted course becomes more teachable at scale without becoming less humane.

8.3 Team-based delivery models

No instructor should be the sole pedagogical engine of a 300-student interdisciplinary computing course. Team-based delivery is essential for sustainability. This does not merely mean having assistants present. It means distributing responsibility intelligently: tutors handle immediate lab support, coordinators manage logistics, markers use shared rubrics, and staff meetings align pedagogical response.

Strong team-based delivery also allows specialization. One tutor may become especially effective at supporting novices. Another may help with extension tasks. Another may monitor discussion boards. Such distribution does not eliminate the instructor's leadership role, but it prevents all functions collapsing onto one person.

For team-based models to work pedagogically rather than only administratively, the team needs shared language and shared values. Tutors should understand not only what tasks students are doing, but why the course emphasizes visible reasoning, scaffolded challenge, and translational explanation. Otherwise, the frontline teaching experience may drift away from the course design philosophy.

8.4 Institutional support needed for sustainable scale

Although this chapter intentionally avoids broad institution-wide ecosystem questions reserved for later discussion, some immediate forms of institutional support are necessary to mention because large-class sustainability cannot be solved purely at subject level. Teaching 229, 291, 331, or 349 students well requires more than personal commitment. It requires sufficient TA allocation, stable technical infrastructure, administrative coordination, and recognition that large-enrollment teaching is complex scholarly work.

Institutions should support sustainable scale by ensuring:

- appropriate staffing ratios for labs and tutorials;

- technical reliability of software platforms and computer labs;
- access to learning design assistance where possible;
- realistic recognition of preparation and coordination workload;
- support for resource development and reuse;
- moderation and assessment systems that do not overload single instructors.

Without such support, even strong pedagogical models can become fragile. The instructor may still produce good outcomes for a time, but the system depends too much on personal overextension.

9. CONCLUSION

9.1 What scalable translational teaching requires

Teaching computing at scale in interdisciplinary settings is not simply a matter of enlarging a small-class model. It requires redesign. Large classes create numerical, cognitive, emotional, and logistical challenges that can easily push courses toward impersonality and blunt standardization. Yet scale does not inevitably destroy teaching quality. When treated as a pedagogical design problem, scale can be managed in ways that preserve rigor, support heterogeneity, and maintain meaningful student learning.

This chapter has argued that scalable translational teaching requires several things: strategic standardization combined with selective personalization; layered support systems rather than single-point help; repeatable pedagogical routines; technology used in service of pedagogy; coherent course architecture; careful lecture-tutorial-lab alignment; differentiated access and extension; coordinated teaching teams; scalable assessment with human oversight; and sustainability practices that protect instructors from burnout.

Evidence from large-class implementation contexts; classes of 229, 291, 331, and 349 students, more than 2,091 students taught across 10 or more disciplines, strong eSFQ scores around 4.6–4.9 compared with a departmental average of 4.2, reduced withdrawal from 5% to 0%, pass improvement from 90% to 100%, and increased A-range attainment from 20% to 25%; suggests that such an approach can work. Students in large cohorts can still feel supported, challenged, and able to connect computing with their own fields. Large classes need not be anonymous by design, even if they cannot offer identical intimacy to small-group teaching.

9.2 Transition beyond computing

The lessons of scalable translational teaching extend beyond computing. Many contemporary subjects now face the same challenge: how to teach large, diverse cohorts in ways that preserve access, depth, and dignity. The principles discussed here; visible reasoning, structured support, managed variation, feedback architecture, and sustainable teamwork; are relevant wherever disciplines are expanding into broader student populations. The next chapter therefore moves beyond computing itself to consider how the pedagogical insights developed in this book may transfer into wider interdisciplinary teaching contexts.

REFERENCES

Ambrose, S. A., Bridges, M. W., DiPietro, M., Lovett, M. C., & Norman, M. K. (2010). *How learning works: Seven research-based principles for smart teaching*. Jossey-Bass.

Aquil Mirza, M., & Cong, W. (Eds.). (2026). *Real-Time Robotics With IoT and Edge AI: Methods, Metrics, and Applications*. IGI Global Scientific Publishing., DOI: 10.4018/979-8-2600-0701-3

Banta, T. W., & Palomba, C. A. (2015). *Assessment essentials: Planning, implementing, and improving assessment in higher education* (2nd ed.). Jossey-Bass.

Biggs, J., & Tang, C. (2011). *Teaching for quality learning at university* (4th ed.). Open University Press.

Brookfield, S. D. (2017). *Becoming a critically reflective teacher* (2nd ed.). Jossey-Bass.

Freeman, S., Eddy, S. L., McDonough, M., Smith, M. K., Okoroafor, N., Jordt, H., & Wenderoth, M. P. (2014). Active learning increases student performance in science, engineering, and mathematics. *Proceedings of the National Academy of Sciences of the United States of America*, *111*(23), 8410–8415. DOI: 10.1073/pnas.1319030111 PMID: 24821756

Gibbs, G., & Jenkins, A. (Eds.). (2014). *Teaching large classes in higher education: How to maintain quality with reduced resources*. Routledge. DOI: 10.4324/9781315041384

Gibbs, G., & Simpson, C. (2004). Conditions under which assessment supports students' learning. *Learning and Teaching in Higher Education*, *1*, 3–31.

Hattie, J. (2009). *Visible learning: A synthesis of over 800 meta-analyses relating to achievement*. Routledge.

Hattie, J., & Timperley, H. (2007). The power of feedback. *Review of Educational Research*, *77*(1), 81–112. DOI: 10.3102/003465430298487

Kuh, G. D. (2008). *High-impact educational practices: What they are, who has access to them, and why they matter*. Association of American Colleges and Universities.

Mohammed, A. (Ed.). (2026). *Advanced Concurrency, Buffering, and Web-Sync in Sensor Platforms: Zero-Loss Streams*. IGI Global Scientific Publishing., DOI: 10.4018/979-8-2600-1101-0

Mohammed, A., & Zangana, H. (Eds.). (2026). *Intelligent Construction Monitoring Systems: Real-Time Safety, Environmental Prediction, and Risk Management*. IGI Global Scientific Publishing., DOI: 10.4018/979-8-3373-9245-5

Nicol, D. J., & Macfarlane-Dick, D. (2006). Formative assessment and self-regulated learning: A model and seven principles of good feedback practice. *Studies in Higher Education*, *31*(2), 199–218. DOI: 10.1080/03075070600572090

Prince, M. (2004). Does active learning work? A review of the research. *Journal of Engineering Education*, *93*(3), 223–231. DOI: 10.1002/j.2168-9830.2004.tb00809.x

Tinto, V. (2012). *Completing college: Rethinking institutional action*. University of Chicago Press. DOI: 10.7208/chicago/9780226804545.001.0001

Vygotsky, L. S. (1978). *Mind in society: The development of higher psychological processes*. Harvard University Press.

Wenger, E. (1998). *Communities of practice: Learning, meaning, and identity*. Cambridge University Press. DOI: 10.1017/CBO9780511803932

Woolf, B. P. (2021). *Building intelligent interactive tutors: Student-centered strategies for revolutionizing e-learning* (2nd ed.). Morgan Kaufmann.

Zepke, N., & Leach, L. (2010). Improving student engagement: Ten proposals for action. *Active Learning in Higher Education*, *11*(3), 167–177. DOI: 10.1177/1469787410379680

Zimmerman, B. J. (2002). Becoming a self-regulated learner: An overview. *Theory into Practice*, *41*(2), 64–70. DOI: 10.1207/s15430421tip4102_2

Chapter 11
Beyond Computing:
Generalizing Translational Pedagogy Across Disciplines

Haozhe Ruan
http://orcid.org/0009-0001-1771-5243
Department of Applied Physics, The Hong Kong Polytechnic University, Hong Kong

Hewa Majeed Zangana
http://orcid.org/0000-0001-7909-254X
Department of Information Technology, Duhok Polytechnic University, Iraq

ABSTRACT

This chapter argues that translational pedagogy, developed in computing education, offers a broadly applicable model for higher education. Its core principles are making expert reasoning visible, translating abstract concepts into learner-accessible forms, scaffolding challenge without lowering standards, converting coursework into authentic outputs, and refining teaching through evidence. The chapter shows how these principles can be adapted in engineering, design, health sciences, business, the built environment, and the social sciences and humanities, while preserving disciplinary integrity. It frames computing as a pedagogical laboratory for broader educational problems and concludes that effective transfer depends on identifying hidden barriers, aligning assessment with teaching, and redesigning learning environments to support participation, identity, and meaningful contribution.

DOI: 10.4018/979-8-2600-1811-8.ch011

1. INTRODUCTION

1.1 Why this pedagogy matters beyond computing

Although this book has focused primarily on computing education, the pedagogical challenges it addresses are not unique to computing. Across higher education, instructors face similar patterns of hidden learner struggle, uneven confidence, disciplinary alienation, and the gap between performing tasks and genuinely understanding them. In engineering, students may solve equations procedurally without grasping physical meaning. In design, students may produce polished artifacts without being able to articulate design logic. In health sciences, learners may memorize clinical protocols without understanding decision pathways. In business and management, students may repeat frameworks without knowing when and why to apply them. In architecture and construction, students may complete project submissions while still lacking integrated systems thinking. In the social sciences and humanities, students may reproduce theory terminology without being able to transfer concepts into analysis, argument, or real-world interpretation.

For this reason, the pedagogical model developed in this book should not be treated as a niche response to coding instruction. Its central concerns; making expert reasoning visible, translating abstract concepts into learner-accessible forms, scaffolding challenge without reducing rigor, converting learning into authentic contribution, and refining teaching through evidence; speak to broader conditions of contemporary higher education. Universities increasingly teach students across disciplinary boundaries, widened participation contexts, and diverse academic identities. Learners often enter programs with varying prior preparation, uneven confidence, and unclear understanding of relevance. Under such conditions, pedagogical success depends less on content transmission alone and more on how learning is mediated, interpreted, and made possible.

What computing does provide is an especially clear test case. Because computing exposes hidden thinking so starkly; through syntax, logic, error, debugging, and visible performance; it reveals pedagogical problems in concentrated form. Students can often appear to "follow" a lecture while understanding very little. They may copy polished solutions without being able to reproduce reasoning independently. They may assume that visible failure indicates lack of ability rather than part of the learning process. These same dynamics exist elsewhere, even if less visibly. In this sense, computing has functioned in this book as a pedagogical laboratory for broader educational problems.

The argument of this chapter is that translational pedagogy has significance beyond computing because it addresses a general educational challenge: how to help diverse learners cross from disciplinary distance to meaningful participation. This chapter therefore extends the model outward. It asks what is generalizable, what remains domain-specific, how the core pillars can be translated into other fields, and what kinds of adaptation are needed to avoid superficial adoption. The aim is not to claim that all disciplines should be taught identically, nor that one model can replace the epistemic integrity of specific fields. Rather, the claim is more modest and more useful: a set of pedagogical principles developed in one demanding interdisciplinary domain can be reconstructed to support learning, identity, and transfer across many others.

1.2 Translational pedagogy as a general higher education model

The term *translational pedagogy* in this book refers to more than simply "explaining things clearly." It denotes a way of teaching that recognizes the distance between expert knowledge structures and student learning realities, especially when learners do not already share the assumptions, language, or identity of the field. Translation here is both cognitive and social. It involves re-representing core concepts in forms students can enter, while preserving disciplinary rigor and enabling eventual participation in more authentic forms of practice.

As a general higher education model, translational pedagogy rests on five interconnected commitments. First, it assumes that expert thinking is often too compressed to be visible to novices; therefore, teaching must externalize reasoning processes (Chi et al., 1989; Collins et al., 1989). Second, it assumes that students learn more effectively when new concepts can be attached to familiar frames, disciplinary analogies, or prior experiences (Ambrose et al., 2010; Bransford et al., 2000). Third, it assumes that challenge must be scaffolded so that students are stretched without being abandoned (Vygotsky, 1978). Fourth, it assumes that learning deepens when students produce authentic outputs that matter beyond assessment alone, whether in research, practice, presentation, innovation, or community contribution (Kuh, 2008). Fifth, it assumes that teaching quality improves through evidence-informed refinement, not intuition alone (Biggs & Tang, 2011; Hattie, 2009).

These commitments are not unique to any single field. Indeed, they resonate strongly with broader scholarship on constructive alignment, cognitive apprenticeship, active learning, self-regulation, and disciplinary teaching (Biggs & Tang, 2011; Lave & Wenger, 1991; Nicol & Macfarlane-Dick, 2006; Prince, 2004). What this book contributes is a coherent synthesis of those ideas through the lens of interdisciplinary teaching practice, especially in contexts where students may otherwise become invisible, intimidated, or disconnected from the relevance of the subject.

To call translational pedagogy a general higher education model does not mean it is fully universal in application. Different disciplines differ in how they define evidence, what they value as authentic practice, how tightly concepts are sequenced, and what counts as novice versus advanced performance. Yet many teaching failures across disciplines share similar roots: invisible expertise, premature abstraction, unsupported challenge, weak transfer pathways, and lack of iterative redesign. A pedagogical model that addresses these roots has wide potential relevance.

1.3 Scope of cross-disciplinary extension

The scope of this chapter is deliberately broad but not infinite. It focuses on fields in which the pedagogical model can be meaningfully illustrated through recognizable teaching problems and plausible adaptation. These include engineering education, design and creative disciplines, health sciences and medical education, business and management, the built environment and construction, and selected areas of the social sciences and humanities. These fields were chosen for several reasons. First, they already intersect with computing in many institutions, making them natural sites of cross-disciplinary teaching. Second, they contain visible differences in epistemology and practice, allowing the chapter to test the elasticity of the model. Third, there is at least some evidence base and practical experience suggesting that translational approaches, scaffolded challenge, visible reasoning, authentic outputs, and evidence-informed teaching are valued in these domains.

The discussion is also informed by practical educational outreach and mentoring activities beyond formal computing classrooms. These include service-learning and international educational engagement, mentoring secondary-school students through junior research programs, invited faculty development work in physiotherapy and higher education pedagogy, applied AI and healthcare educational talks, and interdisciplinary project supervision involving health, robotics, construction, and design-related applications. These activities do not amount to a comprehensive cross-disciplinary implementation study, but they do provide credible practical grounding for the generalization argument.

This chapter does not attempt to provide complete domain-specific curriculum designs for every field discussed. Nor does it move into broad institutional culture or ecosystem-building; those wider questions are reserved for the next chapter. Instead, the purpose here is conceptual-practical: to show which elements of the model travel, how they might be re-expressed, and what educators should attend to when adapting them.

2. WHAT IS GENERALIZABLE AND WHAT IS DOMAIN-SPECIFIC?

2.1 Core transferable principles

A useful way to begin generalization is to separate principles from manifestations. The transferable part of translational pedagogy lies primarily in its principles. These can travel across fields because they describe relationships between learners, knowledge, and teaching rather than prescribing one disciplinary method.

The first transferable principle is cognitive visibility. In nearly every discipline, expert performance compresses reasoning into forms that novices cannot yet see. A clinician recognizes patterns and excludes diagnoses quickly; a civil engineer scans a problem and identifies load conditions almost immediately; a designer makes compositional judgments that appear intuitive; a management expert frames an organizational dilemma using tacit strategic categories. In all such cases, students may witness outcomes without understanding the thought process that generated them. Teaching therefore benefits from making expert cognition visible through modeling, decomposition, explanation, annotated examples, or deliberate think-alouds (Chi et al., 1989; Collins et al., 1989).

The second transferable principle is translational explanation. Students understand difficult material better when it is linked to concepts, experiences, or representational systems already available to them. Translation may involve analogy, contextualization, disciplinary bridging, plain-language unpacking, or multiple representations. The principle is not simplification for its own sake. It is meaningful access. In any field with abstract terminology or threshold concepts, translation matters.

The third transferable principle is scaffolded challenge. Learners need challenge to grow, but unsupported challenge often produces avoidance, mimicry, or collapse. Scaffolding can include staged tasks, worked examples, guided practice, low-stakes checkpoints, structured feedback, and progressive independence. This principle travels particularly well because most disciplines require students to move from supported participation toward autonomous performance (Vygotsky, 1978; Zimmerman, 2002).

The fourth transferable principle is output conversion. Learning becomes more powerful when students can convert coursework into authentic outputs: presentations, prototypes, design exhibitions, clinical communication products, policy briefs, research posters, startup concepts, simulations, or community solutions. Authenticity of output strengthens ownership, motivation, and professional identity (Kuh, 2008).

The fifth transferable principle is evidence-informed refinement. Teaching should improve through triangulated evidence, not anecdote alone. This principle applies across fields because all educators need to understand whether students are learning what they intend, where barriers recur, and how redesign affects outcomes (Banta & Palomba, 2015; Hattie, 2009).

Together, these principles form the generalizable core of translational pedagogy. They are not content-specific. They are teaching logics.

2.2 Discipline-specific manifestations

While the principles transfer, their manifestations do not transfer mechanically. Each discipline embodies its own epistemic habits, representational forms, thresholds, values, and authentic outputs. As Shulman's notion of pedagogical content knowledge reminds us, good teaching depends on understanding how particular subject matter is best represented and learned (Shulman, 1986, 1987). Therefore, translational pedagogy must become discipline-sensitive if it is to remain effective.

For example, cognitive visibility in computing may involve line-by-line code tracing and debugging. In physiotherapy, it may involve verbalizing clinical reasoning during patient assessment. In architecture, it may involve making design decision pathways explicit through annotated sketches and model iterations. In business education, it may involve unpacking how a strategic diagnosis is built from ambiguous market information. In literary studies, it may involve showing how close reading moves from textual observation to interpretive claim. The principle is the same; the enactment differs.

Likewise, scaffolded challenge in engineering may involve staged problem sets moving from idealized systems to real constraints, while in design it may involve iterative critique and prototype refinement. Output conversion in health education may produce simulated care plans or patient education materials rather than conference papers. Evidence-informed refinement in social science methods may use different indicators than in applied lab teaching. The discipline shapes the concrete form of pedagogy, acting as an adaptive architectural core that radiates into domain-specific expressions as visually mapped in Figure 1.

This distinction matters because broad educational models often fail when they ignore domain specificity. If translational pedagogy is generalized merely as a set of slogans; "be student-centered", "use authentic learning", "scaffold tasks"; it risks becoming too thin to guide action. Its value depends on reconstruction within disciplinary realities, establishing a divergent system of practice where identical core logics dictate entirely unique instructional workflows, as structurally contrasted in Table 1.

Figure 1. Generalizability Map of Translational Pedagogy

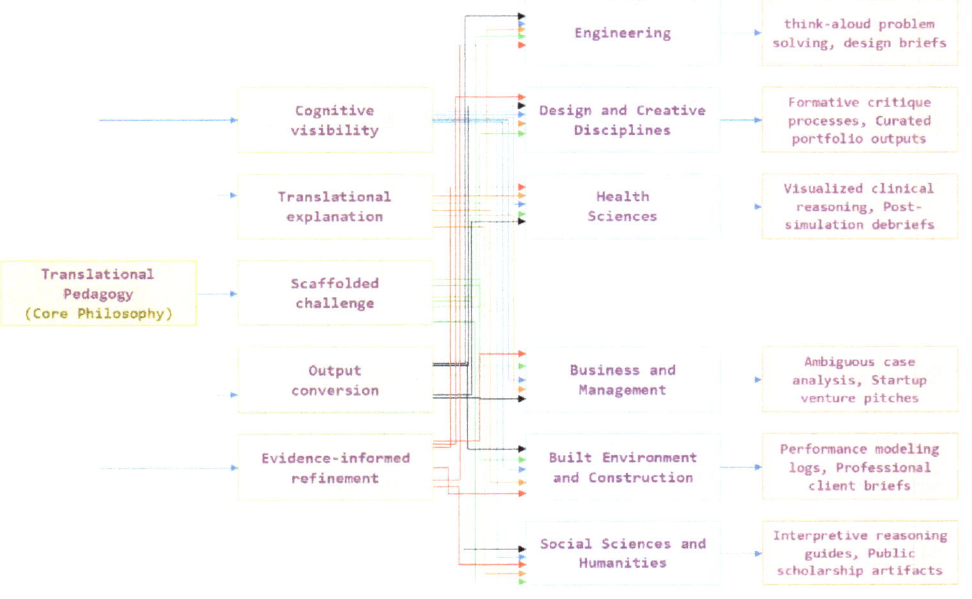

Table 1. Core Principles and Discipline-Specific Expressions

Core principle	General pedagogical meaning	Example in computing	Example in another discipline
Cognitive visibility	making expert thinking explicit	code tracing	clinical reasoning think-aloud
Translational explanation	connecting concepts to learner frames	disciplinary analogies for loops	real-world scenarios for management theory
Scaffolded challenge	staged support toward independence	starter code and milestones	guided case analysis or prototype stages
Output conversion	coursework to authentic contribution	conference paper or competition	patient brief, design show, consulting pitch
Evidence-informed refinement	improve through triangulated evidence	quiz and project trends	OSCE errors, critique themes, case performance

2.3 Conditions for successful transfer

Not every teaching context will automatically benefit from adopting the language of translational pedagogy. Successful transfer requires certain conditions.

First, educators must be willing to examine hidden disciplinary assumptions. Many teaching problems arise because instructors forget how much tacit knowledge students do not yet possess. Transfer works only when teachers can identify where expertise has become invisible.

Second, there must be a meaningful understanding of learner backgrounds. Translation depends on knowing what students already understand, fear, value, and hope to do. In interdisciplinary or professionally oriented programs, this includes knowing how students' home disciplines shape their expectations and sense of relevance.

Third, successful transfer requires alignment between pedagogy and assessment. It is not enough to teach through visible reasoning and authentic practice if assessment rewards only rote reproduction. Students quickly learn what the system actually values (Biggs & Tang, 2011).

Fourth, transfer requires sufficient flexibility in course design. If curricula are overloaded, rigidly sequenced, or excessively exam-driven, pedagogical reconstruction becomes harder. It is still possible, but more constrained.

Fifth, successful adaptation depends on evidence and reflection. Educators need to gather data on what happens after adaptation, rather than assuming that a borrowed strategy works simply because it sounds progressive. To assist educators in systematically evaluating these conditions and operationalizing the transition, the core reflective inquiries and their corresponding action prompts are organized into the diagnostic framework presented in Table 2.

Table 2. Cross-Disciplinary Adaptation Checklist

Adaptation question	Why it matters	Evidence/source to examine	Action prompt
What hidden assumptions do experts make?	Reveals biases that may exclude diverse learners	Expert interviews, curriculum docs, prior assessments	Identify and surface at least three assumptions; reframe with inclusive alternatives
Where do students become confused or silent?	Pinpoints learning bottlenecks and participation gaps	Student questions, exit tickets, discussion transcripts	Design targeted clarifications or prompts to elicit input from quiet students
What examples would feel familiar to this cohort?	Increases relevance and engagement	student surveys, prior course artifacts, disciplinary analogies	Curate 4–6 cohort-appropriate examples across sub-disciplines

continued on following page

Table 2. Continued

Adaptation question	Why it matters	Evidence/source to examine	Action prompt
What tasks are too open too early?	Prevents overwhelm and startup-friction	timing of assignments, task rubrics, pilot feedback	Scaffold tasks progressively; add scaffolds or exemplars
What counts as authentic output in this discipline?	Aligns assessment with real-world practice	portfolio artifacts, capstone projects, industry benchmarks	Define clear authentic outputs and provide rubrics
What evidence will show whether the redesign worked?	Guides evaluation and continuous improvement	learning analytics, pre/post assessments, qualitative feedback	Specify metrics, data collection plan, and review cycles

2.4 Risks of superficial adoption

There are also real risks. The first is surface contextualization without conceptual translation. An instructor may add a few domain-specific examples to slides but leave the underlying explanation structure unchanged. Students may enjoy the examples but still fail to grasp the concept. Translation is not decoration; it must connect to reasoning.

A second risk is over-scaffolding. In trying to widen access, educators may unintentionally protect students from complexity for too long, delaying the transition to independence. Effective scaffolding should be temporary and developmental, not permanent simplification.

A third risk is authenticity inflation. Not every assignment needs to become a startup, publication, or societal intervention. If output conversion is pursued indiscriminately, it can become performative rather than educational. Authentic outputs should emerge where appropriate and pedagogically meaningful.

A fourth risk is generic importation across incompatible epistemologies. What works in an applied engineering lab may not translate neatly into philosophy or fine arts without major reinterpretation. The deeper logic may still be useful, but the form must change substantially.

Finally, there is the risk of assuming transfer without evidence. Generalization is strongest when tested carefully. Educators should resist claiming broad applicability on conceptual enthusiasm alone.

3. TRANSLATIONAL PEDAGOGY IN OTHER FIELDS

3.1 Engineering education

Engineering education is perhaps one of the most natural settings for extending translational pedagogy. Engineering programs frequently teach abstract concepts with high procedural demands, strong threshold concepts, and significant novice anxiety. Students may be able to manipulate formulas without understanding system behavior, or complete calculations without appreciating design trade-offs. They often struggle to connect mathematics, physics, and application. This makes engineering a strong candidate for pedagogies that emphasize visible reasoning, translational explanation, scaffolded challenge, and authentic output.

Cognitive visibility in engineering can take the form of structured think-aloud problem solving, annotated derivations, failure analysis walkthroughs, and explicit modeling of engineering judgment. Rather than presenting a polished solution to a statics or control problem, the educator can show how assumptions are chosen, where approximations matter, and why one representation is preferable to another. This aligns with research suggesting that novices benefit when expert problem-solving processes are made explicit rather than hidden behind final equations (Ambrose et al., 2010; Prince & Felder, 2006).

Translational explanation in engineering often involves connecting abstract representations to physical systems students recognize. A differential equation becomes not just symbolic manipulation, but a story about motion, temperature, load, or signal response. For interdisciplinary engineering programs, examples can also be drawn from sectors students care about; transport, energy, healthcare devices, environmental systems, robotics, or infrastructure resilience.

Scaffolded challenge is especially important because engineering curricula can become front-loaded with mathematically dense material that discourages students before they see relevance. Worked examples, staged design tasks, simulation-supported exploration, and low-stakes conceptual checks can make rigor more accessible without reducing standards. Capstone design already offers a natural site for output conversion, but the principle can be introduced earlier through mini design briefs, posters, industry-linked problem statements, or prototype demonstrations.

For example, a civil engineering course on structural systems might apply translational pedagogy by making load-path reasoning visible through diagrammed walkthroughs, using building failures as accessible contextual entry points, staging design tasks from idealized beams to more realistic constraints, and converting student work into public design critiques or sustainability proposals. The model fits because engineering is fundamentally about making invisible forces, assumptions, and trade-offs intelligible.

3.2 Design and creative disciplines

At first glance, design and creative disciplines may seem distant from the model because they already value iteration, critique, and authentic making. Yet translational pedagogy remains highly relevant. Creative fields also contain invisible expertise, tacit criteria, threshold judgments, and confidence barriers. Students may produce artifacts without understanding why they work, or may experience critique as personal judgment rather than developmental feedback. In studio contexts, some learners appear naturally expressive while others become hesitant, especially when design language feels culturally coded or professionally opaque.

Cognitive visibility in design means making creative decision-making explicit. Educators can model how they move from brief to concept, how they evaluate alternatives, how constraints shape form, and how iteration responds to feedback. Annotated exemplars, process logs, critique reasoning, and visible revision histories can help students see that design excellence is not spontaneous inspiration alone but structured thinking-in-making.

Translational explanation in design may involve connecting abstract principles; contrast, hierarchy, rhythm, affordance, narrative, or spatial sequence; to familiar sensory, cultural, or embodied experiences. For interdisciplinary design learners, examples may be linked to fashion, digital interfaces, exhibition environments, service experiences, or public space. This helps students understand principles as tools rather than mystical aesthetic categories.

Scaffolded challenge is crucial in creative education because fully open briefs can overwhelm novices. Beginners often benefit from constrained tasks that foreground one or two principles before moving into larger open-ended projects. Safe-to-fail environments are also important, since critique cultures can unintentionally privilege confident students and silence others. Structured peer review, critique protocols, milestone-based development, and reflective commentary can support more equitable participation.

Output conversion is already common in design through exhibitions, portfolios, public showcases, and competitions. Translational pedagogy strengthens this by making output pathways more intentional and developmental. Students can be guided to understand not only how to produce an artifact, but how to document process, justify decisions, and connect their work to users, communities, or broader design conversations.

In design, then, the model does not import engineering-style instruction. It helps clarify, democratize, and scaffold what can otherwise remain tacit and confidence-dependent.

3.3 Health sciences and medical education

Health sciences and medical education provide another strong domain for generalization because they combine abstract knowledge, procedural skill, ethical judgment, and high-stakes application. Students often face information overload, intense performance anxiety, and difficulty integrating theory with practice. Clinical reasoning, in particular, is a classic site of hidden expertise. Experienced practitioners rapidly identify relevant signs, weigh possibilities, and make decisions in ways that seem intuitive but are actually highly structured.

Cognitive visibility in health education can involve think-aloud clinical reasoning, structured debriefs after simulation, visual decision trees, annotated patient cases, and explicit comparison of novice and expert approaches. Rather than presenting diagnosis or intervention as a finished answer, educators can model the reasoning chain: what clues matter, how uncertainty is managed, and why one path is chosen over another. This is especially useful in fields such as physiotherapy, nursing, rehabilitation, or medical education, where students must integrate knowledge with action.

Translational explanation matters because health concepts are often taught through specialized terminology long before students have fully internalized underlying mechanisms. Learners benefit when physiological, biomechanical, or diagnostic concepts are linked to lived bodily experience, patient narratives, or common clinical scenarios. In diverse health cohorts, translation also includes making explicit how theory relates to practice settings students may actually encounter.

Scaffolded challenge is central in simulation, clinical skills training, and case-based learning. Students need repeated low-risk opportunities to practice before facing real patients or high-stakes assessments. Safe-to-fail environments are therefore not optional; they are ethical necessities. Simulation-based education already embodies this in part, but translational pedagogy pushes further by asking whether the reasoning process itself is visible enough and whether students understand why they are making particular decisions (Issenberg et al., 2005).

Output conversion in health education need not mean publications only. It may include patient education resources, case presentations, interdisciplinary care plans, quality-improvement proposals, community health interventions, poster presentations, or clinical innovation ideas. Such outputs help students develop professional identity and communicate that their learning has practical value.

This generalization is also supported by practical engagement in faculty development and health-related educational outreach, including invited pedagogical exchange in physiotherapy and AI-for-healthcare education. These experiences suggest that the core issues of invisible reasoning, learner anxiety, and the need for context-sensitive explanation are strongly shared across computing and health professions education.

3.4 Business and management

Business and management education is sometimes misread as less dependent on translational pedagogy because it already uses case studies and real-world examples extensively. Yet business education also suffers from hidden expertise and formulaic learning. Students may memorize strategic frameworks, organizational theories, or accounting procedures without understanding when to apply them, how to adapt them, or what assumptions they rest upon. They may perform competency in presentations while lacking analytic depth.

Cognitive visibility in business education means unpacking managerial judgment. How does an experienced practitioner read a case? How are competing priorities weighed? How is a market problem framed? How does one move from data to decision under uncertainty? Think-aloud strategic analysis, annotated cases, and comparison of superficial versus deep reasoning can help students see what expert application looks like.

Translational explanation is especially important in business programs with mixed student backgrounds or international cohorts. Management terminology can be deceptively familiar while remaining conceptually vague. Translating concepts into workplace, entrepreneurial, or community examples students recognize helps prevent jargon without understanding.

Scaffolded challenge can be implemented through progressively more ambiguous case work, role-play, simulations, and structured team tasks. Novices may begin with guided analysis templates before moving into more open strategic diagnosis. Safe-to-fail conditions matter here too, especially because many students are uncomfortable with ambiguity and public speaking.

Output conversion in business may include startup pitches, consulting briefs, market analyses for local organizations, policy recommendations, innovation proposals, entrepreneurship competitions, or investor-style presentations. Such outputs align naturally with the model's emphasis on moving from coursework to contribution.

Because business and management are often taught to broad student populations, including those from non-business disciplines, translational pedagogy can be particularly useful in making concepts less formulaic and more decision-oriented.

3.5 Built environment and construction

Built environment disciplines; including architecture, building science, surveying, urban systems, and construction management; are fertile ground for translational pedagogy because they sit at the intersection of technical knowledge, spatial reasoning, regulation, sustainability, and human use. Students frequently struggle to integrate material from multiple domains: structures, services, design, safety, environmental performance, cost, and user needs. They may complete assignments by following templates without grasping system interdependence.

Cognitive visibility in the built environment can involve making design and construction reasoning explicit: why one material system is chosen over another, how sequencing decisions affect safety and cost, how environmental considerations shape form, or how conflicting constraints are negotiated. Visual process mapping, annotated project reviews, clash analysis, and staged critique can help students see integrated reasoning rather than isolated outputs.

Translational explanation is essential because students often learn from drawings, technical language, regulations, and digital tools that can feel disconnected from lived environments. Linking concepts to actual buildings, construction cases, failure examples, or site processes makes learning more concrete. Students from architecture may need help understanding systems performance; students from construction may need help entering design rationale. Translation helps bridge such differences. This grounding is particularly effective when students explore how predictive risk data and safety protocols are modeled within real-world intelligent construction monitoring systems (Mohammed & Zangana, 2026).

Scaffolded challenge is especially important in project-based teaching, where open briefs and complex software tools can overwhelm learners. Milestone-based development, partial templates, collaborative review, and iterative feedback can support progress without oversimplifying practice. Safe-to-fail environments are also valuable because mistakes in design reasoning are educational opportunities when handled before professional contexts.

Output conversion may include building performance reports, sustainability proposals, site safety innovations, digital twins, public design reviews, community plans, or interdisciplinary project showcases. In construction-related fields, the model can also connect strongly to industry-linked problem solving.

This domain is particularly relevant because several examples in the broader teaching portfolio already connect computing with building science, smart monitoring, damage detection, modular design, and AIoT-related construction applications. These intersections suggest that translational pedagogy can bridge technical systems and applied built-environment thinking effectively.

3.6 Social sciences and humanities

The social sciences and humanities may seem less obviously aligned with a model developed partly through technical teaching, yet many of the same pedagogical needs appear here in different form. Students in these fields often grapple with abstract theory, methodological language, interpretive reasoning, evidence use, and writing as a mode of thinking. They may memorize theorists or methods without knowing how to mobilize them analytically. They may fear that their interpretations are "wrong" because criteria feel tacit.

Cognitive visibility in these fields involves making interpretation and argumentation explicit. For example, a sociology instructor can show how a concept is moved from theory into analysis of a case. A literature teacher can model the progression from textual detail to interpretive claim. A political science educator can unpack how evidence is selected and weighted in policy analysis. In all these cases, experts often perform analytical moves too quickly for novices to notice.

Translational explanation may involve connecting abstract theory to contemporary issues, media texts, historical analogies, lived experience, or disciplinary neighboring concepts. This is particularly useful for students who perceive theory as detached or obscure.

Scaffolded challenge can include structured response papers, guided source analysis, staged essay development, debate protocols, method workshops, and iterative drafts. Safe-to-fail environments matter because many students in these fields fear speaking before, they feel intellectually ready.

Output conversion may take the form of policy briefs, public humanities projects, digital exhibitions, podcasts, research posters, community reports, archives, or student conference presentations. Such outputs can strengthen identity by showing that humanities and social science work also contributes beyond the essay submitted to one lecturer.

The point is not to force technical pedagogies onto non-technical subjects. It is to recognize that translation, visibility, scaffolding, and authentic contribution are just as important where the invisible work is interpretive rather than computational.

4. TRANSLATING THE PILLARS ACROSS DISCIPLINES

4.1 Cognitive visibility beyond computing

Of the model's pillars, cognitive visibility may be the most broadly transferable. It addresses a universal educational problem: expert performance is often too compressed, automated, or embodied for novices to decode. In almost any discipline, students are shown outcomes, products, or conclusions more often than they are shown how those outcomes were produced. Teaching improves when that hidden process becomes visible.

In engineering, cognitive visibility may involve narrating assumptions, boundary conditions, and approximation choices. In physiotherapy, it may involve verbalizing why a particular assessment maneuver is chosen and what evidence would alter the interpretation. In architecture, it may involve drawing through the evolution of a concept rather than presenting only final boards. In management, it may involve showing how competing data points are prioritized in a strategic decision. In history, it may involve modeling how primary sources are read critically rather than simply cited. In law, it may involve unpacking how a legal argument is built from precedent and principle.

Practical strategies for cognitive visibility include worked examples, think-alouds, annotated exemplars, error analysis, comparison of strong and weak reasoning, process journals, and staged debriefs. The exact mode varies by field, but the goal is constant: reduce the distance between expert performance and learner access.

This pillar is particularly important for students who are less likely to infer hidden disciplinary rules on their own. Learners with less prior cultural or academic familiarity often suffer most when expectations remain tacit. Making reasoning visible is therefore not only cognitively helpful but also equity-relevant.

4.2 Translational explanation in other knowledge domains

Translational explanation is often mistaken for simplification, but its deeper purpose is representational alignment. Good translational teaching does not dilute complexity; it changes the route by which students approach it. This may involve analogy, multiple representations, field-specific examples, embodied demonstration, or sequencing from familiar to unfamiliar.

In health sciences, translational explanation may link anatomy or pathology to movement, sensation, patient stories, or simulation scenarios. In business, it may connect abstract frameworks to lived organizational dilemmas. In humanities, it may connect theory to current events, cultural products, or ordinary social practices. In architecture, it may connect environmental systems to sensations of heat, light, airflow, and comfort before moving into technical modeling.

Effective translational explanation often requires more than one representation. A concept may need a diagram, a story, a case, a formula, and a practical application before it becomes robustly graspable. This aligns with research showing that students benefit when knowledge is encountered through varied forms that support integration rather than isolated memorization (Bransford et al., 2000).

Translation also matters in interdisciplinary programs where students from different homes disciplines sit together. A one-language pedagogy often privileges those already closest to the field. Translational explanation widens the circle of entry.

4.3 Scaffolded challenge and safe-to-fail environments

Scaffolded challenge is a necessary bridge between access and rigor. Without challenge, students may remain comfortable but shallow. Without scaffolding, many capable learners misread temporary difficulty as permanent inability. This is true in laboratories, studios, clinics, seminars, and workshops alike.

Across disciplines, scaffolding can include:

- sequencing from guided to open tasks;
- using exemplars before independent production;
- breaking large assignments into milestones;
- offering formative checks before summative evaluation;
- creating templates for early attempts;
- using peer or tutor support before fully autonomous performance.

A safe-to-fail environment does not mean absence of standards. It means that early mistakes are treated as information rather than identity verdicts. In clinical simulation, this is ethically essential. In design critique, it protects experimentation. In engineering labs, it promotes conceptual correction before dangerous assumptions harden. In writing-intensive humanities teaching, it encourages drafting rather than defensive perfectionism.

The phrase "safe-to-fail" must still be handled carefully. Some students experience any public exposure as risky, particularly in hierarchic or highly evaluative settings. Therefore, safe-to-fail design may also require anonymous question channels, draft submissions, structured discussion formats, and clear signaling that confusion is normal.

4.4 Output conversion in non-computing programs

One of the more distinctive pillars of this book's model is output conversion: the belief that coursework can become something more than a graded endpoint. While the examples in earlier chapters included conference papers, competitions, and startup pathways linked to computing projects, the principle extends naturally beyond computing.

In engineering, output conversion may lead to design showcases, competition entries, patent exploration, or industry-facing prototypes. In design, it may become exhibition, portfolio curation, client presentation, or community installation. In health sciences, it may become patient education resources, simulation portfolios, quality-improvement posters, or interdisciplinary case presentations. In business, it may become consulting reports, venture pitches, or organizational analysis briefs. In humanities and social sciences, it may become public scholarship, digital humanities projects, policy briefs, podcasts, or undergraduate conference papers.

The educational significance of output conversion lies not only in external recognition but in identity and ownership. When students see that their work has use value beyond passing a course, their relationship to learning shifts. They begin to think about audience, quality, communication, and purpose differently. They may also begin to see themselves as participants in professional or scholarly communities rather than merely recipients of instruction (Lave & Wenger, 1991; Wenger, 1998).

Not every course requires this, and not every student output must leave the classroom. But where feasible, output conversion can be a powerful bridge from novice participation to contributor identity.

4.5 Evidence-informed refinement across contexts

The final pillar, evidence-informed refinement, may be the least glamorous but the most necessary for responsible transfer. A pedagogical idea should not be generalized because it sounds attractive. It should be adapted, implemented, and studied. This means gathering quantitative, qualitative, process, and output-based evidence to see whether the adaptation actually helps students.

Across disciplines, evidence sources may vary. In a physiotherapy course, one might track simulation performance, reflective confidence, and error patterns. In design, one might examine critique engagement, project development, and portfolio quality. In business, one might analyze case reasoning quality and presentation effectiveness. In social science methods, one might compare conceptual understanding before and after scaffolded redesign. The same triangulation logic applies even if the indicators differ.

Evidence-informed refinement also protects against superficial adoption. It forces educators to ask whether students are merely enjoying a new method or actually learning better, transferring more, or feeling more able to participate.

5. FRAMEWORK FOR CROSS-DISCIPLINARY ADAPTATION

To make the model practically usable beyond computing, it is helpful to outline a staged adaptation framework.

5.1 Identifying hidden disciplinary barriers

The first step is diagnostic. Educators should ask: What hidden barriers prevent students from entering this field effectively? These barriers may be conceptual, emotional, linguistic, cultural, or procedural. Examples include unfamiliar notation, tacit criteria, confidence collapse, fear of critique, inability to connect theory to practice, or overreliance on memorization.

Useful questions include:

- What do experts in this field do automatically that students cannot yet see?
- Which concepts are threshold points where many students stall?
- What prior assumptions are built into teaching but not shared by all learners?
- Where do students become silent, compliant, or disengaged rather than openly confused?
- Which forms of assessment reveal recurring misunderstanding?

This phase should be evidence-based where possible: student comments, assessment analysis, observation, consultation patterns, and teacher reflection all help.

5.2 Mapping core concepts to learner backgrounds

Once barriers are identified, the next step is mapping. Here the educator examines the relationship between core disciplinary concepts and the backgrounds, motivations, and prior knowledge of the learners. The goal is to identify where translational explanation and contextual entry points are needed.

For example:

- In physiotherapy, how can anatomy and movement science be connected to bodily experience and clinical observation?
- In architecture, how can environmental systems be linked to lived space before technical modeling?
- In management, how can theory be linked to recognizable organizational situations?
- In humanities, how can abstract theory be connected to public discourse or cultural forms students already encounter?

Mapping is especially important in interdisciplinary or service-oriented programs where students may not self-identify with the dominant discourse of the course.

5.3 Reconstructing pedagogy for transfer

The third step is reconstruction. Based on the diagnostic and mapping work, the educator redesigns teaching activities using the translational pillars:

- make reasoning visible;
- translate concepts through multiple representations;
- scaffold challenge;
- create safe-to-fail participation structures;
- build possible authentic output routes;

- plan evidence collection.

This does not require rebuilding an entire course at once. Often the most effective strategy is to redesign one or two bottleneck areas first. For example, an instructor may rework how a difficult threshold concept is taught, or restructure a major assignment into staged milestones. Successful adaptation often grows iteratively.

5.4 Building discipline-appropriate outcomes

Finally, the adapted pedagogy must be connected to appropriate outcomes. These outcomes should be discipline-specific, not generic. For instance, the desired result in a health education course may be better clinical reasoning, not merely "confidence." In a design course it may be more articulate process justification. In an engineering subject it may be stronger transfer from theory to system modeling. In business it may be more nuanced strategic analysis. In humanities it may be deeper analytical writing or more confident interpretive discussion.

At the same time, broader outcomes such as belonging, self-efficacy, transfer, and contributor identity may also be relevant. The key is not to impose a single output model on all fields, but to ensure that the pedagogical design points toward outcomes the discipline genuinely values.

6. ILLUSTRATIVE APPLICATIONS AND MINI-MODELS

This section offers brief illustrative mini-models rather than full case studies. Their purpose is to show how adaptation might look in practice.

6.1 Example in physiotherapy or health education

Consider an introductory physiotherapy module on musculoskeletal assessment. Students often memorize assessment steps and special tests without understanding the reasoning behind test selection, interpretation, and sequencing. Novices may perform techniques mechanically and fear making mistakes publicly during practical sessions.

A translational adaptation might work as follows:

- Cognitive visibility: The instructor performs a think-aloud assessment of a simulated patient, verbalizing hypotheses, why one test is chosen over another, and what findings would alter the clinical pathway.

- Translational explanation: Anatomical and biomechanical concepts are linked to everyday movement patterns students can feel or observe directly.
- Scaffolded challenge: Students begin with guided observation sheets, then work in pairs using structured checklists before progressing to more independent case reasoning.
- Safe-to-fail design: Early practicals are formative, with debriefs framed around reasoning improvement rather than competence judgment.
- Output conversion: Students develop a patient-facing explanation sheet or a short clinical reasoning presentation rather than only sitting a practical exam.
- Evidence-informed refinement: Instructors analyze where students make recurrent reasoning errors and redesign subsequent demonstrations accordingly.

This model aligns strongly with simulation-based learning literature while adding a sharper emphasis on visible reasoning and translation (Issenberg et al., 2005).

6.2 Example in architecture or building science

In a building science course on environmental performance, students may struggle to relate formulas, simulation outputs, and building systems to lived spatial experience. Some architecture-oriented students may avoid technical reasoning; some technical students may neglect user experience and design integration.

A translational adaptation might include:

- Cognitive visibility: Walk through a building case, narrating how environmental decisions are made, what trade-offs matter, and how climate, material, orientation, and occupancy interact.
- Translational explanation: Connect heat transfer, daylighting, and ventilation principles to sensations of comfort, glare, airflow, and usability.
- Scaffolded challenge: Begin with analysis of existing buildings, then progress to guided simulation exercises, then to redesign recommendations.
- Safe-to-fail structures: Use iterative studio-style feedback before final submission.
- Output conversion: Students produce a building performance brief for a hypothetical client or community stakeholder. This output can challenge advanced students to outline data streaming architectures, drawing inspiration from zero-loss telemetry layouts used in web-syncing sensor platforms (Mohammed, 2026).
- Evidence refinement: Compare whether students can interpret performance data more effectively after contextual redesign.

This mini-model demonstrates how translational pedagogy can bridge technical and design cultures within the built environment.

6.3 Example in AI for healthcare education

AI for healthcare is a strongly interdisciplinary teaching area involving computing, medicine, ethics, data, and clinical interpretation. Students often come from diverse backgrounds: some understand machine learning but not healthcare; others understand health but not AI. This makes it an ideal site for translational pedagogy.

A possible mini-model:

- Cognitive visibility: Show how an AI healthcare decision pipeline works step by step, including data preprocessing, model output, uncertainty, and clinical interpretation.
- Translational explanation: Explain machine learning concepts using healthcare scenarios and explain healthcare constraints in language accessible to technical students.
- Scaffolded challenge: Start with curated datasets and guided interpretation before asking students to evaluate or design models critically.
- Safe-to-fail environment: Encourage debate around model bias, error, and ethics without requiring immediate expert-level certainty.
- Output conversion: Students produce an interdisciplinary poster, prototype evaluation report, or translational briefing for clinicians.
- Evidence-informed refinement: Gather feedback on where students from each background felt lost and adjust examples accordingly.

This area illustrates perhaps most clearly why translational pedagogy matters: no single disciplinary language is sufficient.

6.4 Example in robotics, AIoT, or applied lab teaching

Applied laboratory teaching in robotics or AIoT often attracts students from multiple engineering and science backgrounds, with highly varied confidence in coding, hardware integration, and systems thinking. This learning environment sits at the intersection of modern methods and metrics required for real-time robotics with IoT and edge AI (Aquil Mirza & Cong, 2026). Students may either become overwhelmed by complexity or focus narrowly on getting a system to "work" without understanding architecture and constraints.

A translational mini-model might involve:

- Cognitive visibility: Demonstrating debugging of sensor-actuator systems live, including intentional failure points and troubleshooting logic.
- Translational explanation: Using physical metaphors, system diagrams, and real application scenarios to explain integration.
- Scaffolded challenge: Providing starter frameworks and milestone tasks before open project work.
- Safe-to-fail structures: Framing hardware errors and unexpected outputs as normal data for learning rather than embarrassment.
- Output conversion: Students develop showcase prototypes, competition entries, or industry-facing demonstrations.
- Evidence-informed refinement: Monitor recurring lab bottlenecks, consultation spikes, and project pathway choices.

This mini-model reflects practical experience in AIoT-related teaching and broader interdisciplinary project supervision, where translational support and visible troubleshooting significantly affect student persistence and quality of output.

7. IMPLICATIONS FOR FUTURE EDUCATIONAL RESEARCH

7.1 Comparative pedagogical studies

If translational pedagogy is to become more than a locally persuasive idea, it requires stronger comparative research. One important direction is comparative pedagogical study across disciplines. For example, researchers might compare how visible reasoning practices function in computing, engineering, and health simulation. Do they improve conceptual retention similarly? Do they affect confidence differently? Which forms of representation are most effective in each domain?

Such comparative work would help distinguish genuinely transferable mechanisms from context-bound techniques. It would also contribute to the scholarship of teaching and learning by encouraging cross-disciplinary dialogue rather than isolated pedagogical silos (Felten, 2013).

7.2 Cross-disciplinary adaptation research

A second direction is focused adaptation research. Rather than merely testing whether a strategy "works," researchers should study how pedagogical models are reconstructed when moving across fields. What gets preserved? What must change? Which disciplinary cultures resist or reshape the model? Such studies would be especially valuable in hybrid areas like design computing, digital humanities, clinical AI, smart construction, or sustainability education, where multiple epistemologies meet.

Cross-disciplinary adaptation research should use mixed methods where possible, combining learning outcomes with qualitative evidence about student identity, relevance, and transfer. This would align well with the triangulation framework discussed in earlier chapters.

7.3 Transferability metrics

A third research need concerns metrics. If educators claim that a pedagogy is transferable, how should transferability be measured? Potential dimensions include:

- conceptual gain across diverse cohorts;
- student perception of relevance;
- confidence or belonging shifts;
- ability to transfer learning into later contexts;
- quality of authentic outputs;
- adaptability of teaching assets across disciplines;
- sustainability of implementation.

Developing transferability metrics would strengthen the evidence base for generalization. It would also help avoid vague claims that a pedagogy is "applicable everywhere" without showing in what sense.

7.4 Toward a broader translational pedagogy scholarship

Finally, there is scope for a broader scholarship of translational pedagogy. This would bring together research on cognitive apprenticeship, threshold concepts, interdisciplinary teaching, authentic assessment, simulation, design-based learning, and educational translation. The term "translational pedagogy" could become a useful umbrella for studying how difficult disciplinary knowledge is made accessible without loss of rigor in diverse higher education settings.

Such a scholarship would be especially timely given current pressures in higher education: widened participation, interdisciplinary curricula, AI-mediated learning, demand for authentic outcomes, and concern about student belonging and mental load. The educational question is no longer only how to transmit disciplinary knowledge efficiently, but how to design conditions in which diverse students can enter, engage, and contribute. Translational pedagogy offers one coherent response to that challenge.

8. CONCLUSION

8.1 The book's model as a general pedagogical contribution

This chapter has argued that the model developed through cross-disciplinary computing education has significance far beyond computing itself. Its generalizable contribution lies not in any one technical method, but in a pedagogical orientation: make expert reasoning visible, translate difficult concepts through learner-accessible representations, scaffold challenge without weakening standards, create authentic output pathways, and refine teaching through systematic evidence.

These principles can be adapted meaningfully in engineering, design, health sciences, business, the built environment, and the social sciences and humanities. Their concrete forms differ by discipline, but the underlying educational logic remains consistent. In every field, some students are prevented from full participation not because they lack potential, but because teaching leaves too much tacit, too much unsupported, or too much disconnected from relevance. Translational pedagogy addresses those gaps.

The model therefore constitutes a broader pedagogical contribution of this book. It offers a way of thinking about teaching that is simultaneously inclusive and ambitious. It does not lower the ceiling in order to widen the door. Instead, it widens the door by redesigning the path to high-level participation.

8.2 Transition to institutional culture and ecosystems

If this chapter has shown that translational pedagogy can travel across disciplines, the next question is how such pedagogical work becomes sustainable beyond individual courses or educators. How are supportive structures built? How do departments, programs, and institutions create environments in which evidence-informed, translational, and student-transformative teaching can flourish rather than depend on isolated commitment? The next chapter turns to those ecosystem questions: culture, leadership, support structures, and the institutional conditions needed for pedagogical models like this to endure and spread.

REFERENCES

Ambrose, S. A., Bridges, M. W., DiPietro, M., Lovett, M. C., & Norman, M. K. (2010). *How learning works: Seven research-based principles for smart teaching*. Jossey-Bass.

Aquil Mirza, M., & Cong, W. (Eds.). (2026). *Real-Time Robotics With IoT and Edge AI: Methods, Metrics, and Applications*. IGI Global Scientific Publishing., DOI: 10.4018/979-8-2600-0701-3

Banta, T. W., & Palomba, C. A. (2015). *Assessment essentials: Planning, implementing, and improving assessment in higher education* (2nd ed.). Jossey-Bass.

Biggs, J., & Tang, C. (2011). *Teaching for quality learning at university* (4th ed.). Open University Press.

Bransford, J. D., Brown, A. L., & Cocking, R. R. (Eds.). (2000). *How people learn: Brain, mind, experience, and school* (Expanded ed.). National Academy Press.

Chi, M. T. H., Bassok, M., Lewis, M. W., Reimann, P., & Glaser, R. (1989). Self-explanations: How students study and use examples in learning to solve problems. *Cognitive Science*, *13*(2), 145–182. DOI: 10.1207/s15516709cog1302_1 PMID: 34983624

Collins, A., Brown, J. S., & Newman, S. E. (1989). Cognitive apprenticeship: Teaching the craft of reading, writing, and mathematics. In Resnick, L. B. (Ed.), *Knowing, learning, and instruction: Essays in honor of Robert Glaser* (pp. 453–494). Lawrence Erlbaum.

Felten, P. (2013). Principles of good practice in SoTL. *Teaching & Learning Inquiry*, *1*(1), 121–125. DOI: 10.20343/teachlearninqu.1.1.121

Hattie, J. (2009). *Visible learning: A synthesis of over 800 meta-analyses relating to achievement*. Routledge.

Issenberg, S. B., McGaghie, W. C., Petrusa, E. R., Gordon, D. L., & Scalese, R. J. (2005). Features and uses of high-fidelity medical simulations that lead to effective learning: A BEME systematic review. *Medical Teacher*, *27*(1), 10–28. DOI: 10.1080/01421590500046924 PMID: 16147767

Kuh, G. D. (2008). *High-impact educational practices: What they are, who has access to them, and why they matter*. Association of American Colleges and Universities.

Lave, J., & Wenger, E. (1991). *Situated learning: Legitimate peripheral participation*. Cambridge University Press. DOI: 10.1017/CBO9780511815355

Mohammed, A. (Ed.). (2026). *Advanced Concurrency, Buffering, and Web-Sync in Sensor Platforms: Zero-Loss Streams*. IGI Global Scientific Publishing., DOI: 10.4018/979-8-2600-1101-0

Mohammed, A., & Zangana, H. (Eds.). (2026). *Intelligent Construction Monitoring Systems: Real-Time Safety, Environmental Prediction, and Risk Management*. IGI Global Scientific Publishing., DOI: 10.4018/979-8-3373-9245-5

Nicol, D. J., & Macfarlane-Dick, D. (2006). Formative assessment and self-regulated learning: A model and seven principles of good feedback practice. *Studies in Higher Education, 31*(2), 199–218. DOI: 10.1080/03075070600572090

Prince, M. (2004). Does active learning work? A review of the research. *Journal of Engineering Education, 93*(3), 223–231. DOI: 10.1002/j.2168-9830.2004.tb00809.x

Prince, M. J., & Felder, R. M. (2006). Inductive teaching and learning methods: Definitions, comparisons, and research bases. *Journal of Engineering Education, 95*(2), 123–138. DOI: 10.1002/j.2168-9830.2006.tb00884.x

Shulman, L. S. (1986). Those who understand: Knowledge growth in teaching. *Educational Researcher, 15*(2), 4–14. DOI: 10.3102/0013189X015002004

Shulman, L. S. (1987). Knowledge and teaching: Foundations of the new reform. *Harvard Educational Review, 57*(1), 1–23. DOI: 10.17763/haer.57.1.j463w79r56455411

Vygotsky, L. S. (1978). *Mind in society: The development of higher psychological processes*. Harvard University Press.

Wenger, E. (1998). *Communities of practice: Learning, meaning, and identity*. Cambridge University Press. DOI: 10.1017/CBO9780511803932

Zimmerman, B. J. (2002). Becoming a self-regulated learner: An overview. *Theory into Practice, 41*(2), 64–70. DOI: 10.1207/s15430421tip4102_2

Chapter 12
Cultivating a Creation-Oriented Culture in Higher Education:
Institutional Ecosystems for Translational and Interdisciplinary Learning

Aquil Mirza Mohammed
http://orcid.org/0000-0001-7756-4363
Department of Computing, The Hong Kong Polytechnic University, Hong Kong

ABSTRACT

This chapter argues for expanding translational and interdisciplinary learning from classroom practice to a university-wide ecosystem that supports scalable, impactful pedagogy. It outlines how translation of expert cognition into accessible explanations, combined with a creation-oriented culture, can surface student thinking, foster belonging, and promote transfer across disciplines. The discussion centers on design principles for scale, including governance, staffing, space, funding, and evaluation, and presents a cohesive framework linking pedagogy, curriculum, assessment, and policy. Drawing on theoretical foundations and illustrative contexts, the chapter examines how institutional structures can reward, sustain, and extend classroom innovations while addressing equity, sustainability, and stakeholder alignment. The text integrates perspectives from leadership and organizational change to articulate actionable implications for policy-makers, academics, and practitioners seeking to cultivate lasting, interdisciplinary learning ecosystems.

DOI: 10.4018/979-8-2600-1811-8.ch012

1. INTRODUCTION

1.1 Why pedagogy alone is not enough

This book has argued that teaching can be redesigned so that students in complex, interdisciplinary, and often intimidating learning environments do not remain passive recipients of information. Through translational pedagogy, difficult knowledge can be made more accessible without diluting rigor; hidden reasoning can be made visible; challenge can be scaffolded; and student work can be converted into outputs that matter beyond the classroom. Yet if the book ended there, it would leave an important problem unresolved. Good pedagogy, however innovative, remains vulnerable when it depends primarily on the commitment, creativity, and stamina of individual teachers. Classroom innovation can transform students, but unless institutions build environments that sustain, reward, and extend such work, its effects may remain local, fragile, and uneven.

Pedagogy alone is not enough because education does not occur in a vacuum. Teaching is shaped by curriculum structures, assessment systems, staffing, reward models, student support arrangements, space design, funding opportunities, research access, innovation pathways, and the cultural signals institutions send about what they truly value. A teacher may invite students to think, create, and contribute, but if the wider institution values only content coverage, exam throughput, or narrow publication metrics, that invitation has limited reach. Conversely, when institutions align policy, infrastructure, and culture around student development as contribution, teaching becomes more powerful. Students begin to encounter a coherent message: your learning is not only about acquiring knowledge but about becoming capable of using it, shaping with it, and creating from it. A teacher may invite students to think, create, and contribute, but if the wider institution values only content coverage, exam throughput, or narrow publication metrics, that invitation has limited reach. Conversely, when institutions align policy, infrastructure, and culture around student development as contribution, teaching becomes more powerful. Students begin to encounter a coherent message: your learning is not only about acquiring knowledge but about becoming capable of using it, shaping with it, and creating from it. This multi-layered, non-linear network of structural drivers and their ultimate external vectors is mapped as a cohesive operational blueprint in the systems model illustrated in Figure 1.

This matters especially in contemporary higher education, where universities face multiple, overlapping demands. They must widen participation while maintaining standards. They must prepare students for uncertain futures shaped by artificial intelligence, automation, climate crisis, health challenges, and social fragmentation. They must support interdisciplinarity while preserving disciplinary depth. They must foster innovation without becoming performative or purely market-driven. They must also respond to growing student concern about relevance, belonging, and the meaning of university learning. Under these conditions, a purely transmission-oriented model of higher education becomes increasingly inadequate. Students need more than access to content. They need access to pathways through which knowledge becomes action, authorship, contribution, and responsible participation in society.

The need, then, is not only for better teaching methods but for a broader institutional culture that makes creation possible and normal. This final chapter therefore widens the lens from pedagogy to ecosystem. It explores how universities can cultivate a **creation-oriented culture** in which translational and interdisciplinary learning are not isolated exceptions but supported practices. The chapter considers what creation-oriented higher education means, what ecosystem components are required, how faculty leadership matters, what institutional supports are necessary, how pathways from coursework to creation can be built, how policy and quality assurance can align with these goals, what tensions must be confronted, and what strategic roadmap institutions might follow.

Figure 1. Creation-Oriented Institutional Ecosystem

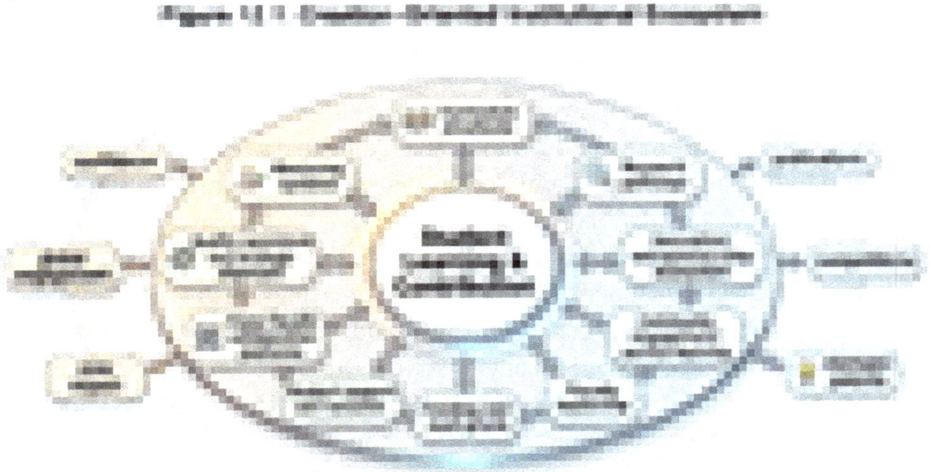

1.2 From classroom innovation to institutional culture

There is a familiar pattern in higher education reform. A talented educator builds an innovative course. Students respond strongly. Outcomes improve. Some projects gain external recognition. The course becomes an admired example. Yet after a few years, one of several things happens. The educator is overloaded, promoted away from teaching-intensive work, or simply exhausted. The innovation remains dependent on one person's invisible labor. Colleagues appreciate it but do not fully adopt it. Institutional systems admire the outcome but do not redesign around the conditions that made it possible. In time, the example survives as a story rather than a norm.

This pattern reveals a basic truth: the distance between classroom innovation and institutional culture is substantial. To cross it, universities must do more than celebrate excellent teachers. They must understand what excellent, translational, and creation-oriented teaching requires structurally. They must ask which policies inhibit it, which incentives neglect it, which forms of student support enable it, and which collaborative infrastructures make it sustainable.

Institutional culture matters because it shapes educational possibility in subtle but pervasive ways. It determines whether interdisciplinary work is administratively easy or difficult. It influences whether faculty see teaching innovation as risky or valued. It affects whether students perceive creation as a privilege for the already exceptional or as an invitation available to many. It sets the conditions under which coursework can connect to research, entrepreneurship, service-learning, publication, community partnership, or public engagement.

Moving from classroom innovation to institutional culture also requires reframing what universities believe students are for. In a strongly transmission-oriented culture, students are expected to absorb knowledge, perform competence, and proceed toward credential completion. In a creation-oriented culture, students are expected to learn deeply enough to produce something: an argument, design, prototype, insight, intervention, performance, study, tool, social contribution, or informed critique. This is not a rejection of foundational learning; rather, it is a reorientation of purpose. Foundational learning becomes the basis for meaningful output and contribution.

The practical evidence supporting this shift is increasingly visible. In the teaching context informing this book, more than 2,091 students across over 10 disciplines have been reached since 2023. Students mentored through courses and follow-on supervision have contributed to more than 40 conference papers, earned more than 10 external awards, reached more than 10 startup finalist teams, and generated more than 5 patent or startup initiatives. Those outcomes are not simply evidence of individual student talent. They indicate what becomes possible when pedagogy invites students into creation and when mentoring extends learning beyond course completion. The institutional question is how to make such trajectories more widely available.

1.3 Defining a creation-oriented culture in higher education

A **creation-oriented culture** in higher education is an institutional environment in which students are systematically supported to move beyond acquisition toward contribution. It does not assume that every student must become an entrepreneur, inventor, or published scholar in the narrow sense. Rather, it assumes that learning reaches fuller educational value when students use disciplinary knowledge to create meaningful outputs, engage real audiences, solve authentic problems, communicate insights, or contribute to communities.

Creation in this sense should be defined broadly. It includes research creation, technical creation, design creation, social creation, civic creation, entrepreneurial creation, and reflective-intellectual creation. A student may create a software tool, a clinical resource, a policy brief, a design installation, a robotics prototype, a sustainability proposal, an educational intervention, a performance, a data analysis, a scholarly poster, or a community-centered service solution. Such technical artifacts often mirror cutting-edge industrial demands, such as designing smart infrastructure layouts or intelligent construction monitoring systems (Mohammed & Zangana, 2026). What matters is not novelty in the absolute sense, but meaningful production grounded in learning and connected to purpose.

A creation-oriented culture also differs from a purely innovation-driven or commercialization-driven culture. While innovation, startups, and patents can be valuable parts of it, creation-oriented higher education is broader and ethically more grounded. It includes civic responsibility, inclusion, social contribution, and developmental access. It asks not only whether students can produce marketable outputs, but whether they can become thoughtful contributors, researchers, collaborators, and public-minded professionals.

This definition therefore rests on four premises:

1. **Knowledge is not complete until it can be used, interpreted, communicated, or transformed.**
2. **Students should be positioned as capable contributors, not merely future contributors.**
3. **Creation opportunities should be educationally structured and broadly accessible, not confined to elite enclaves.**
4. **Institutional ecosystems must support the movement from coursework to contribution through curriculum, mentoring, policy, and infrastructure.**

The rest of this chapter develops these premises in detail.

2. THE MEANING OF CREATION-ORIENTED HIGHER EDUCATION

2.1 From content acquisition to contribution

For much of modern higher education, the central educational script has been acquisition. Students are admitted, taught, assessed, and awarded degrees based largely on their capacity to absorb and reproduce disciplinary knowledge. This model is not useless; foundational knowledge matters and cannot be bypassed. However, a university system centered exclusively on acquisition increasingly fails to respond to the educational and societal demands of the present. In knowledge-rich but rapidly changing environments, what matters is not only what students know, but what they can do with what they know, how they integrate it, how they communicate it, and how they apply it responsibly in uncertain contexts (Barnett, 2004; Kuh, 2008).

A creation-oriented model therefore reframes the purpose of higher education from acquisition alone toward contribution. This does not mean content no longer matters. It means content is treated as the beginning of capability rather than its endpoint. Students are asked to understand knowledge deeply enough to generate outputs, interpretations, solutions, performances, or interventions. Learning becomes productive, not merely consumptive.

The shift from acquisition to contribution is also psychologically important. Students who experience university primarily as an endless sequence of requirements often focus on compliance, survival, and grade management. Students who experience university as a site of emerging contribution begin to see stronger reasons for effort. Relevance increases. Ownership increases. Professional identity strengthens. Confidence becomes anchored not only in marks but in evidence that one can produce something of value.

The educational literature supports this broader shift. High-impact practices such as undergraduate research, collaborative projects, service-learning, capstones, and authentic assessment are associated with stronger engagement and developmental gains because they situate knowledge in meaningful activity (Kuh, 2008). Similarly, constructivist and socio-cultural traditions emphasize that learning becomes deeper when students participate in disciplinary or quasi-disciplinary practices rather than merely observing them from a distance (Lave & Wenger, 1991; Wenger, 1998). To clarify how these overarching theoretical shifts manifest across target disciplines, Table 1 contrasts each core translational logic against specific computing and cross-disciplinary workflows.

Table 1. Institutional Enablers and Barriers

Domain	Enablers	Common barriers	Strategic response
Curriculum	authentic assessments, capstones	overloaded content	redesign for milestone-based outputs
Mentoring	faculty and peer mentors	informal or unequal access	formal mentoring schemes
Funding	seed grants, travel funds	no early-stage support	mini-grant mechanisms
Recognition	teaching awards, promotion value	innovation not rewarded	revise criteria
Inclusion	advising, accessibility, outreach	hidden curriculum	proactive access pathways

2.2 Student as creator, researcher, innovator, and civic actor

A creation-oriented culture asks institutions to reimagine who the student is. The student is not only a learner in the narrow sense, nor only a future employee, nor only an exam-taker. The student is also a potential creator, researcher, innovator, and civic actor. These roles are overlapping, not mutually exclusive.

To see students as **creators** means recognizing that they can produce meaningful work even before they are fully formed experts. Undergraduates can build prototypes, compose arguments, design systems, create exhibitions, produce analyses, and generate useful artifacts. Their outputs may not always be professional-grade in every respect, but they can still be educationally and socially meaningful.

To see students as **researchers** means giving them entry into inquiry, uncertainty, evidence evaluation, and knowledge generation. Undergraduate research need not be confined to elite pathways. It can be integrated through course-based inquiry, poster conferences, mentored projects, lab participation, and publication opportunities where appropriate.

To see students as **innovators** means acknowledging that learning can lead to practical invention, process improvement, or entrepreneurial activity. This should be pursued carefully and inclusively, but it is a legitimate extension of higher education, especially when linked to disciplinary and social needs.

To see students as **civic actors** means understanding that creation is not only personal or commercial. Students can use knowledge in service of communities, public needs, and ethical concerns. Service-learning, community-based research, outreach, educational mentoring, sustainability work, and social innovation are all part of a creation-oriented vision.

These expanded student roles are especially significant for learners who have not historically been encouraged to see themselves as knowledge producers. Students from non-technical backgrounds, first-generation students, multilingual learners, and those outside elite pathways often underestimate what they might contribute. A creation-oriented culture can therefore act as an equity intervention as well as an excellence agenda.

2.3 Output conversion as institutional value

Earlier chapters used the term **output conversion** to describe the process by which coursework or learning activity becomes something more: a conference paper, competition entry, prototype, patent pathway, startup concept, public-facing artifact, or social contribution. At institutional level, output conversion should be understood not merely as a teaching tactic but as a value orientation.

When output conversion becomes institutionally valued, universities begin asking different questions:

- How many student assignments become meaningful outputs?
- What pathways exist for students to extend promising work?
- Are there bridges between curriculum, research, innovation, and community engagement?
- Do students know that their projects can travel beyond grading?
- Are faculty supported to mentor this transition?

Treating output conversion as an institutional value shifts attention from terminal assessment to developmental trajectory. It encourages universities to create structures through which strong student work can be recognized, mentored, refined, and connected outward. It also counters the waste built into many educational systems, where substantial student effort disappears into archived submissions after marking.

Importantly, output conversion does not require every student to produce externally celebrated work. The institutional goal is not mass spectacle. Rather, it is to make meaningful extension possible, visible, and educationally legitimate. Some outputs may remain internal but still authentic, such as interdisciplinary showcases, teaching expos, or community briefings. Others may progress outward into publication, competition, service, or innovation. The structural parameters governing these outward extensions, alongside their field-specific blindspots and conversion entry points, are systematically organized in Table 2.

Table 2. Strategic Roadmap for Universities

Time horizon	Priority actions	Responsible actors	Indicators of success
Short-term (1 year)	Launch translational redesign pilots; develop milestone-based outputs; initiate inclusion and creation pathways	Provost, deans, department heads; teaching and learning centers	Number of pilot courses; faculty trained in translational redesign; early creation-pathway enrollments
Medium-term (2–4 years)	Scale across departments; strengthen interdisciplinary collaboration; expand student projects beyond coursework	Faculty leads; interdisciplinary program directors; IT and analytics teams	Increase in interdisciplinary outputs; growth in student projects extending beyond coursework; broader faculty participation
Long-term (5+ years)	Embed adaptive pedagogy university-wide; align incentives with creation culture; sustain ongoing assessment and improvement	Senior leadership; academic senate; accreditation/ compliance offices	Diversity of students accessing creation pathways; sustained faculty engagement; student perceptions of agency and belonging

2.4 Ethical and inclusive dimensions of creation

A creation-oriented culture can be misunderstood if it is interpreted simply as productivity pressure under another name. There is a risk that "creation" becomes another elite currency, available mainly to students who already possess confidence, social capital, and spare time. There is also a risk that institutions overemphasize marketable outcomes and neglect ethical reflection, care, and access. For these reasons, the ethical and inclusive dimensions of creation must be explicit.

First, access matters. Creation opportunities should not depend entirely on informal invitation, hidden networks, or faculty favoritism. Institutions should design visible, low-threshold entry points so that more students can participate.

Second, ethics matters. Not all creation is inherently good. Students need guidance around responsible innovation, research integrity, social implications, inclusion, sustainability, and public accountability. A startup mentality without ethical literacy is not educationally sufficient.

Third, developmental proportionality matters. Students should not be pushed into premature performance of "innovation" before they have built enough understanding to create responsibly. Creation-oriented education must still respect developmental stages.

Fourth, recognition matters. Institutions must value not only commercially visible outputs but also civic, scholarly, artistic, and community-oriented creation. Otherwise, important forms of contribution become marginalized.

A student comment adapted from mentoring records captures the human significance of this culture:

"What mattered most was not just being told my project was good. It was being shown that it could become something useful and that someone believed it was worth taking further."

That sense of worthiness is educationally powerful. Ethical creation-oriented institutions build it carefully rather than leaving it to chance.

3. ECOSYSTEM COMPONENTS OF A CREATION-ORIENTED CULTURE

Creation-oriented higher education does not arise from aspiration alone. It requires an ecosystem—interlocking structures that allow learning to move outward into contribution.

3.1 Curriculum structures

Curriculum is the first and most obvious ecosystem component. If curricula are tightly overloaded with content and narrowly exam-driven, students and faculty have little space for creation. A creation-oriented curriculum does not abandon disciplinary foundations, but it deliberately includes structures that support inquiry, design, reflection, and output development.

Such curriculum structures may include:

- project-based modules;
- capstone experiences;
- inquiry-led assignments;
- authentic assessment formats;
- interdisciplinary electives;
- embedded communication and reflection components;
- progressive milestone tasks;
- opportunities for revision and extension.

The key is alignment. Students should encounter a developmental arc across the curriculum rather than isolated "special" opportunities. Early modules may focus on foundational understanding and confidence. Middle stages may include authentic application and small-scale creation. Later stages may support public output, research dissemination, entrepreneurship, or community engagement. This developmental sequencing helps prevent creation from becoming either too late or too elite.

Curriculum structures also matter in interdisciplinary teaching. Where students cross disciplinary boundaries, explicit bridges are needed so that knowledge from one field can be translated into another. Without those bridges, interdisciplinary ambition often results in confusion rather than innovation.

3.2 Mentoring systems

Mentoring is one of the most important but unevenly available elements of a creation-oriented ecosystem. Students rarely move from coursework to meaningful contribution entirely alone. They need guidance in identifying potential, improving quality, understanding venues, managing revision, and imagining next steps. This is especially true for students who do not already know how universities work beyond formal classes.

Mentoring systems should therefore not be left entirely to informal goodwill. Institutions can support creation-oriented cultures by building mentoring at multiple levels:

- faculty mentoring for advanced projects;
- structured undergraduate research mentoring;
- near-peer mentoring by senior students;
- cross-disciplinary mentoring teams;
- innovation mentoring through incubators or project labs;
- community or industry mentoring for applied work.

Near-peer mentoring deserves special emphasis. In the educational contexts informing this book, undergraduates have not only created outputs themselves but also mentored secondary students and peers. This creates a virtuous cycle: students strengthen their own identity by helping others enter the same learning pathways. Creation-oriented institutions should treat such mentoring as a valued form of contribution, not merely voluntary extra work.

3.3 Research and innovation pathways

A major institutional differentiator is whether students can see a path from classroom learning into research and innovation. In many universities, research exists in one silo and undergraduate teaching in another. Creation-oriented ecosystems deliberately connect them.

Research pathways for students may include:

- course-based undergraduate research experiences;

- summer research schemes;
- student research conferences;
- faculty-supervised project continuation;
- undergraduate journal or proceedings opportunities;
- interdisciplinary research clusters with student roles.

Innovation pathways may include:

- ideation schemes;
- prototype funding;
- hackathons or challenge-based events;
- startup incubators;
- maker spaces;
- patent advisory support;
- industry-linked innovation calls.

The practical evidence cited in this book points to the power of such pathways. Students mentored through courses and subsequent supervision contributed to 40+ conference papers, 10+ startup finalist teams, and 5+ patent or startup initiatives. Such outcomes become more likely when research and innovation routes are institutionally visible rather than dependent on exceptional discovery. This continuous pipeline, tracking a student's iterative progress through structural milestones, feedback loops, and baseline enabling supports, is illustrated in Figure 2.

Figure 2. Pathway from Classroom to Contribution

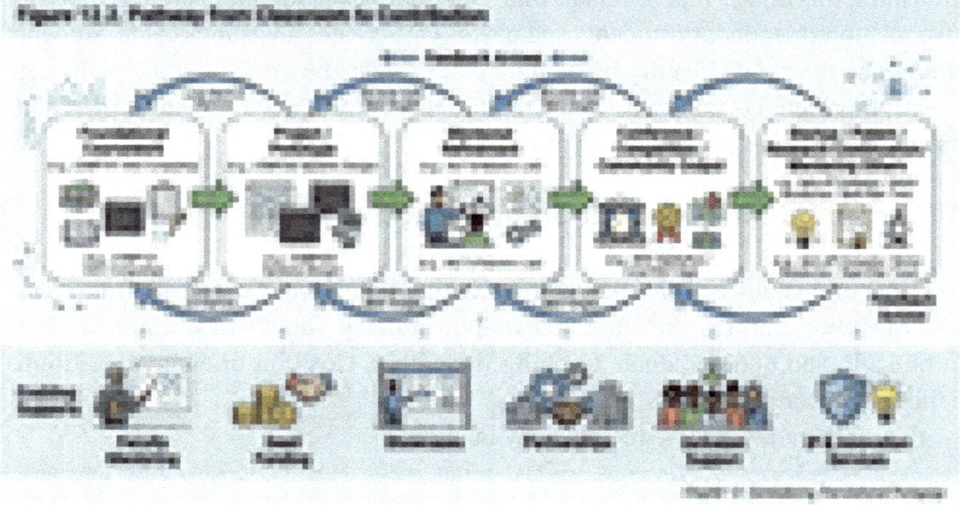

3.4 Competition, entrepreneurship, and publication ecosystems

Competitions, entrepreneurship programs, and publication ecosystems can serve as highly motivating forms of outward-facing engagement when handled well. They provide deadlines, audiences, standards, and validation beyond the classroom. They also help students understand the social life of knowledge: work can be reviewed, compared, showcased, funded, or contested.

However, these ecosystems must be structured educationally rather than theatrically. Competitions should not simply reward already advantaged teams without developmental support. Entrepreneurship should not become a thin proxy for educational value. Publication support should not pressure students into premature output for institutional prestige. Instead, the ecosystem should offer preparation, mentoring, ethics guidance, and reflective framing.

In contexts relevant to this book, students have achieved notable external recognition, including best paper and best student paper awards, international competition distinctions, and startup finalist status. These examples demonstrate possibility, but the institutional lesson is broader: universities should create ladders that help more students understand how to move from good coursework to external participation if they choose.

3.5 Community engagement and service-learning pathways

Creation-oriented higher education must extend beyond academic and commercial outputs to include social contribution. Community engagement and service-learning are therefore essential ecosystem components. They allow students to apply knowledge in response to public needs, develop empathy and civic responsibility, and learn from contexts that challenge university assumptions (Bringle & Hatcher, 1995; Eyler & Giles, 1999).

Service-learning pathways may include:

- community-based projects embedded in modules;
- outreach teaching and mentoring;
- health, engineering, or design interventions for local partners;
- international service-learning experiences;
- co-created projects with schools, NGOs, or community organizations;
- reflective components connecting service and disciplinary learning.

Such pathways are especially powerful in a creation-oriented culture because they broaden the meaning of output. Contribution is not only a startup or publication. It can also be a teaching resource, health tool, environmental design suggestion, digital access support, or educational outreach activity. Service-learning also grounds creation ethically by placing student work in relation to real people and communities rather than abstract performance metrics.

4. ROLE OF FACULTY AND TEACHING LEADERSHIP

4.1 Faculty as translational mentors

Faculty are central to creation-oriented ecosystems, but their role changes. They are not only content experts or course deliverers; they become **translational mentors**. This means they help students cross boundaries: between novice and practitioner, classroom and world, one discipline and another, idea and output, uncertainty and contribution.

A translational mentor does several things. They interpret disciplinary knowledge in accessible ways. They identify hidden student potential. They normalize struggle while preserving high expectations. They connect coursework to wider opportunities. They help students understand what quality means in authentic contexts. They also model responsible, ethical, and reflective practice.

In interdisciplinary settings, translational mentorship is particularly important because students often lack a clear map of where their learning can lead. A faculty member who can bridge design and computation, engineering and health, business and analytics, or humanities and digital methods helps students imagine pathways they may not discover alone.

The mentoring dimension should not be romanticized. It requires time, care, and institutional support. But it is one of the strongest levers for moving from educational possibility to actual student contribution.

4.2 Leadership in curriculum redesign

Faculty leadership also matters at the level of curriculum redesign. Creation-oriented cultures do not emerge only from extracurricular opportunities. They require curricular architecture that makes such pathways educationally coherent. Faculty leaders therefore need to ask difficult questions about sequencing, assessment, space, interdisciplinarity, and progression.

Leadership in curriculum redesign involves:

- identifying where curricula are too crowded for meaningful creation;
- redesigning assessments toward authentic tasks;

- building milestone structures for project development;
- integrating interdisciplinary or applied opportunities;
- ensuring that foundational learning supports later output pathways;
- reviewing where students repeatedly fail to connect knowledge to use.

This form of leadership is often underrecognized because it is neither purely managerial nor purely research-driven. Yet it is crucial if institutions want creation-oriented cultures that are more than isolated co-curricular enrichment.

4.3 Building communities of practice

No individual faculty member can sustain institutional transformation alone. Communities of practice are therefore essential. These communities allow educators to share strategies, compare evidence, co-mentor students, align standards, and reduce isolation around teaching innovation (Wenger, 1998). They also help prevent pedagogical breakthroughs from remaining private craft knowledge.

In translational and interdisciplinary teaching, communities of practice are especially important because problems often exceed a single discipline's expertise. A computing educator may need input from clinicians, designers, business mentors, or community partners. Likewise, a physiotherapy educator exploring translational simulation may benefit from dialogue with engineering faculty working on visible reasoning or project scaffolding.

Communities of practice can be formal or informal: teaching circles, interdisciplinary design groups, innovation mentoring collectives, scholarship-of-teaching seminars, project review panels, or cross-faculty learning labs. What matters is that educators have spaces where teaching as creation-oriented work can be discussed seriously and collaboratively.

4.4 Recognizing and rewarding teaching innovation

Institutional culture is shaped powerfully by reward systems. If faculty are expected to build translational, interdisciplinary, creation-oriented learning environments but such work is poorly recognized in promotion, workload, or prestige structures, it will remain difficult to sustain. Recognition does not need to be limited to awards, though awards matter symbolically. It should include workload recognition, funding access, visibility in leadership pathways, and credible weight in academic advancement.

Teaching innovation is especially vulnerable to undervaluation because it often produces diffuse outcomes: student growth, confidence, contribution, and cross-boundary collaboration. Yet these outcomes are central to higher education's public mission. Universities serious about creation-oriented culture should therefore reward faculty who build mentoring pathways, connect curriculum to research or community engagement, create inclusive access to contribution, and document educational impact rigorously.

5. INSTITUTIONAL SUPPORTS AND INFRASTRUCTURES

5.1 Funding schemes and seed grants

Creation often needs early resources. Small amounts of targeted funding can have disproportionate impact when they allow student ideas to become prototypes, posters, pilot studies, outreach projects, or competition entries. Seed grants also signal institutional seriousness. They tell students and faculty that the university believes promising work deserves developmental support.

Useful funding mechanisms include:

- mini-grants for student projects;
- prototype and maker funds;
- undergraduate research bursaries;
- travel grants for conferences or competitions;
- interdisciplinary challenge funds;
- teaching innovation grants that include student output components;
- seed support for social impact or community partnership projects.

The teaching and mentoring context behind this book includes participation in funding-supported ideation schemes and educational grant activity, showing how even modest support can create pathways from coursework to wider outcomes. Universities should design such schemes to be accessible, transparent, and educationally scaffolded rather than purely competitive.

5.2 Teaching and learning centers

Teaching and learning centers can play a crucial role in cultivating creation-oriented cultures, especially when they move beyond generic workshops and become active partners in pedagogical redesign. They can support faculty with curriculum design, authentic assessment, educational research, inclusive pedagogy, learning analytics interpretation, and faculty development around translational teaching.

They can also serve as institutional memory. When successful pedagogical models emerge, centers can help document, adapt, and disseminate them rather than letting them remain isolated successes. In creation-oriented ecosystems, centers may coordinate undergraduate research showcases, teaching innovation forums, or interdisciplinary pedagogical exchanges.

The key is to align these centers with actual educational practice rather than treating them as compliance or training units only. Their most powerful role is developmental: helping institutions convert local teaching innovations into broader capability.

5.3 Adaptive learning infrastructure

Although this chapter intentionally avoids reteaching technical systems in detail, some infrastructure matters for ecosystem-building. Adaptive and data-informed learning infrastructure can support creation-oriented and translational education when used carefully. Such infrastructure includes platforms for low-stakes diagnostics, feedback systems, dashboarding of participation patterns, and tools that allow differentiated pathways at scale.

The point is not technological determinism. Technology should support access, feedback, and responsiveness, not replace human teaching. But in large and diverse institutions, some infrastructure is necessary if educators are to monitor learning patterns, identify bottlenecks, and manage pathways effectively. Adaptive support tools can help institutions move closer to mass personalization without losing coherence.

5.4 Cross-faculty collaboration platforms

Creation-oriented interdisciplinary learning requires spaces where faculties can meet. Too many universities expect interdisciplinarity without providing mechanisms for it. Cross-faculty collaboration platforms may include challenge-based programs, thematic institutes, interdisciplinary minors, innovation hubs, faculty-student project networks, shared labs, and internal partnership databases.

Such platforms are especially important when student work might bridge domains like AI and healthcare, construction and sustainability, robotics and rehabilitation, or design and data. Without institutional connectors, these possibilities remain dependent on accidental personal networks. Platforms make it easier for faculty to find collaborators, for students to identify opportunities, and for projects to move across silo boundaries. For example, a dedicated cross-faculty framework allows engineering and computer science students to collaborate on complex network telemetry problems, such as managing zero-loss data streams across web-syncing sensor platforms (Mohammed, 2026).

5.5 Student support and inclusion systems

No creation-oriented culture can be sustainable if it assumes all students can participate on equal terms without support. Student support and inclusion systems must therefore be part of the ecosystem. This includes academic advising, disability support, financial support, mental health services, learning development, language support, and proactive inclusion practices.

Creation opportunities often require extra time, confidence, and access to informal knowledge. Students with heavier work commitments, care responsibilities, lower confidence, or less social capital may be excluded unless institutions intervene. Support systems should therefore connect not only to deficit remediation but also to opportunity access. Students should know how to enter research, innovation, service, and showcase pathways—and should receive practical help when barriers exist.

6. PATHWAYS FROM COURSEWORK TO CREATION

A creation-oriented institution needs visible pathways. Students should not have to guess how a class assignment might become something more.

6.1 Course project to prototype

The first and most immediate pathway begins within the course itself. Coursework should be designed so that some tasks have the potential to become prototypes, demonstrations, policy products, or public-facing artifacts. This does not require all courses to become project courses, but it does require faculty to consider whether assignments produce disposable work or developmental work.

A project becomes prototypical when students are encouraged to refine beyond minimum compliance, when assessment includes dimensions such as usability, relevance, communication, or application, and when the course allows some iteration. In technical and design fields this is obvious, but similar logic applies elsewhere: a policy memo can become an advocacy brief, a historical archive project can become a digital exhibition, a simulation case can become a training resource.

The educational value of prototype pathways lies in changed student orientation. Students start asking not only "How do I complete this?" but also "Could this become something others use or see?" That question often deepens quality.

6.2 Prototype to conference or competition

The next pathway involves public validation. Promising work can be refined into a conference poster, student symposium paper, design showcase, innovation challenge submission, or competition entry. This step is educationally transformative because it introduces students to audience, review, and standard beyond classroom grading.

Institutions can support this step by hosting internal showcase events, offering mentoring on abstract writing or pitching, providing travel support, and building calendars of opportunities. They can also ensure that such pathways are not confined to research-intensive or elite students only.

The cumulative teaching evidence relevant to this book includes more than 40 conference papers and over 10 external awards connected to mentored student work. These outcomes illustrate the power of prototype-to-public pathways when they are actively supported.

6.3 Conference output to startup or patent

Not all public outputs lead toward entrepreneurship or intellectual property, nor should they. But some do. A strong prototype or published idea may reveal practical promise, user demand, or technical novelty. Institutions should therefore provide guidance for students who wish to explore startup formation, patent routes, or product development.

This stage requires particular care. Students need ethical guidance, legal literacy, IP support, market realism, and mentoring that protects rather than exploits them. Universities should avoid turning every promising student project into premature commercialization theater. Nonetheless, where appropriate, this pathway can be powerful. In the educational record underlying this chapter, more than 10 startup finalist teams and over 5 patent/startup initiatives emerged from student-linked work. Many of these high-level student trajectories originate from projects that successfully integrate hardware and software components to optimize real-time robotics with IoT and edge AI (Aquil Mirza & Cong, 2026). Those numbers suggest that creation-oriented cultures can generate real downstream possibilities when the ecosystem exists.

6.4 Undergraduates as mentors and ambassadors

A mature creation-oriented ecosystem closes the loop by allowing students who have benefited from these pathways to become mentors and ambassadors themselves.

This is one of the most sustainable forms of educational culture-building because it multiplies support and normalizes contribution.

Undergraduate mentors can:

- support junior students in project work;
- speak at orientation or showcase events;
- mentor school students;
- assist in community outreach;
- help peers imagine wider possibilities;
- model that contribution is not reserved for a distant elite.

This role is especially powerful for widening participation. Students often believe possibilities when they see someone like themselves enact them. The teacher's encouragement matters, but peer exemplars can make aspiration feel more attainable.

6.5 Local-to-global educational impact

Creation-oriented pathways can also extend from local learning contexts into global educational and collaborative networks. Student outputs may connect to international conferences, cross-border research teams, community partnerships abroad, or educational exchanges. Faculty development and pedagogical outreach across countries can further amplify these effects.

The broader teaching and professional engagement context informing this book includes collaboration and outreach touching Hong Kong, India, Finland, China, the Philippines, Taiwan, the United States, Uzbekistan, Brazil, South Korea, and other contexts. Such connections matter not only for prestige but for imagination. They show students that learning can travel, that interdisciplinary work has global relevance, and that the university can be a launch point into wider scholarly and civic networks.

7. POLICY, QUALITY ASSURANCE, AND STRATEGIC ALIGNMENT

7.1 Alignment with institutional mission

Institutional culture becomes durable when it aligns with mission rather than operating as a peripheral enthusiasm. Many universities express aspirations around innovation, societal impact, interdisciplinary learning, or "learning and applying for the benefit of humankind." A creation-oriented culture gives such mission language educational substance. It translates mission into structures and expectations for student learning.

Alignment with mission matters because it legitimizes resource allocation, policy change, and leadership attention. If student creation is treated as central to the institution's public identity, then curricula, grants, support systems, and recognition schemes can be oriented accordingly. If it is treated as optional enrichment, it remains vulnerable.

Strategic alignment should also protect breadth. Institutions should define creation in ways consistent with their mission and diversity. A university committed to public service, for example, should ensure that civic and community outputs are valued alongside entrepreneurial ones. A research-intensive university should integrate undergraduate inquiry rather than reserving creation for graduate study.

7.2 Measuring creation-oriented outcomes

What institutions measure shapes what they value. Traditional metrics such as completion rates, grades, graduate employment, and research income remain relevant, but they are insufficient for a creation-oriented culture. Universities need broader indicators that capture student contribution and ecosystem strength.

Possible creation-oriented outcome measures include:

- proportion of modules with authentic or project-based outputs;
- student participation in research, showcase, service-learning, or innovation schemes;
- number and diversity of student outputs beyond coursework;
- conference papers, posters, performances, exhibitions, community outputs, competitions, or prototypes;
- student progression from course project to external engagement;
- mentoring participation and near-peer activity;
- student perception of belonging, agency, and relevance;
- evidence of interdisciplinary collaboration;
- equity of access to creation opportunities across groups.

Measurement should be used developmentally, not punitively. The goal is not to force every department into output production quotas. Rather, it is to make visible whether the ecosystem is functioning and for whom.

7.3 Governance models for interdisciplinary teaching

Creation-oriented cultures often depend on interdisciplinary teaching, yet governance for interdisciplinary work is often weak. Questions arise about ownership, staffing, credit, budget, assessment, and quality assurance. If these are left unresolved, interdisciplinary and translational education remains administratively fragile.

Institutions therefore need governance models that support:

- co-taught or cross-listed courses;
- shared funding and staffing responsibilities;
- transparent workload distribution;
- joint quality review processes;
- student progression across faculties;
- recognition of interdisciplinary outputs in departmental systems.

Governance should make collaboration easier rather than requiring heroic negotiation every time. This is especially important for creation pathways involving AI and health, design and engineering, construction and sustainability, or humanities and digital methods.

7.4 Scaling innovation responsibly

One of the great temptations in higher education is to scale innovation too quickly and symbolically. A promising pilot is announced as a model for all. A successful project becomes a branding device. Staff are told to "embed innovation" without support. Students are invited into visible programs while deeper inequalities remain unaddressed. Responsible scaling requires restraint and design.

To scale creation-oriented innovation responsibly, institutions should:

- pilot carefully and gather evidence;
- identify which components are essential and which are local adaptations;
- invest in support and training before mandate;
- preserve quality rather than multiplying low-support opportunities;
- attend to workload and inclusion;
- allow disciplines to adapt forms of creation appropriately.

Responsible scaling means cultural deepening, not superficial replication.

8. CHALLENGES AND TENSIONS

8.1 Equity in access to creation opportunities

One of the most significant challenges is equity. Even when institutions create rich opportunities, not all students can access them equally. Time poverty, financial pressure, disability, language barriers, confidence, social capital, and hidden curriculum effects all shape participation. Without care, creation-oriented cultures may reward the already visible and mobile.

Equity requires intentional design:

- paid rather than purely voluntary student roles where possible;
- transparent application processes;
- multiple forms of creation, not only those linked to extroversion or entrepreneurship;
- scheduling that considers student constraints;
- support for travel, materials, and communication;
- proactive outreach to underrepresented students.

Creation-oriented education should widen opportunity, not merely rename advantage.

8.2 Faculty workload and reward structures

A second challenge concerns faculty workload. Mentoring outputs, running showcases, developing project pathways, collaborating across faculties, and supporting student dissemination all take time. If institutions celebrate outcomes without adjusting workload or reward structures, faculty may burn out or retreat. Earlier chapters discussed this problem at course level; here it becomes institutional.

Creation-oriented cultures therefore require honest workload models, recognition in promotion, seed support, and administrative assistance. Otherwise, innovation remains dependent on invisible labor and is hard to sustain.

8.3 Risk of performative innovation

A third tension is performativity. Universities increasingly like the language of innovation, entrepreneurship, and impact because it aligns with reputation, rankings, and external visibility. Yet there is a danger that creation becomes a performance culture in which students are pushed to generate showcase outputs regardless of developmental readiness or genuine value.

Performative innovation tends to produce:

- superficial startup rhetoric;
- overloaded students;
- symbolic competitions without mentoring;
- overclaiming of impact;
- neglect of non-visible but important learning;
- devaluation of reflective, ethical, or civic forms of contribution.

Institutions must therefore ask continually whether their creation agenda serves student development or public branding first. The former is educational; the latter can become exploitative.

8.4 Maintaining rigor with inclusion

Finally, there is an enduring tension between widening access and maintaining rigor. Some educators worry that making learning more accessible, scaffolded, or translational will dilute standards. Others worry that insisting on rigor will reproduce exclusion. A creation-oriented culture must reject this false binary. The challenge is to widen pathways to excellence, not reduce expectations to preserve comfort.

Maintaining rigor with inclusion means:

- clarifying standards rather than hiding them;
- scaffolding toward authentic performance rather than replacing it;
- using evidence to judge learning, not assumptions about who belongs;
- supporting students into challenge rather than selecting them out too early;
- ensuring that authentic outputs still require quality, revision, and accountability.

This book has repeatedly argued that inclusion and high achievement are not opposites. The institutional task is to make that argument structurally credible.

9. A STRATEGIC FRAMEWORK FOR INSTITUTIONS

This section offers a practical roadmap for institutions seeking to cultivate a creation-oriented culture grounded in translational and interdisciplinary learning.

9.1 Short-term actions

In the short term, institutions can take actions that are visible, feasible, and catalytic.

1. **Map existing creation pathways.**

Identify where student projects already become outputs, where mentoring exists, and where interdisciplinary connections are already functioning.

2. **Create visible entry points.**

Establish student showcases, mini-grants, undergraduate research calls, or innovation seed schemes that are easy to understand and apply for.

3. **Support faculty pilots.**

Fund small experiments in authentic assessment, translational redesign, community-engaged projects, or interdisciplinary capstones.

4. **Document and share examples.**

Build internal repositories of student outputs, mentoring stories, and pedagogical approaches so that possibility becomes visible.

5. **Recognize educational creation.**

Use awards, communications, and local recognition to signal that student contribution and teaching innovation matter.

These short-term actions are useful because they build momentum without requiring immediate structural overhaul.

9.2 Medium-term system building

Medium-term work involves building more coherent systems.

1. **Embed creation pathways in curricula.**

Ensure that modules, programs, and capstones contain authentic tasks and progression routes rather than relying only on extracurricular options.

2. **Develop mentoring infrastructure.**

Formalize faculty-student and near-peer mentoring with support, training, and recognition.

3. **Strengthen interdisciplinary governance.**

Create mechanisms for shared ownership of cross-faculty courses, labs, and projects.

4. **Integrate support services with opportunity pathways.**

Connect advising, inclusion, language support, and learning development to student participation in research, innovation, and service.

5. **Refine measurement.**

Develop indicators for student contribution, equity of access, and pedagogical impact.

At this stage, institutions begin moving from isolated opportunity to ecosystem capability.

9.3 Long-term cultural transformation

Long-term transformation is deeper and slower. It involves changing what the institution believes university education is for.

1. **Align mission, policy, and reward structures.**

Promotion criteria, strategic plans, quality assurance processes, and funding decisions should reflect creation-oriented values.

2. **Normalize students as contributors.**

Across communications, curriculum, leadership speech, and student support, the idea that students can create and contribute should become part of the institution's identity.

3. **Build durable cross-boundary communities.**

Sustain communities of practice among faculty, students, researchers, and partners so that translational and creation-oriented work continues evolving.

4. **Protect breadth and ethics.**

Ensure that creation includes civic, scholarly, artistic, and social forms, not only commercial innovation.

5. **Sustain evidence-informed improvement.**

Treat the ecosystem itself as something to be studied, refined, and ethically governed.

Cultural transformation occurs when these commitments become ordinary rather than exceptional.

9.4 A roadmap for translational higher education

A translational higher education roadmap can be summarized in four sequential but overlapping movements:

Movement 1: Make learning accessible.

Use translational pedagogy to help diverse students enter difficult knowledge domains.

Movement 2: Make learning visible.

Externalize reasoning, support feedback, and scaffold challenge so students can build confidence and competence.

Movement 3: Make learning productive.

Connect coursework to authentic outputs, research, innovation, and civic engagement.

Movement 4: Make creation cultural.

Build institutional systems that reward, sustain, and expand these pathways across programs and cohorts.

This roadmap captures the arc of the entire book. It begins in the classroom, but it ends in culture.

10. CONCLUSION

10.1 Synthesis of the whole book

This book began with a pedagogical concern: in large, diverse, interdisciplinary learning environments, many students risk becoming invisible. They may follow polished demonstrations without understanding. They may copy without reasoning. They may remain silent because they fear asking basic questions. They may conclude that difficult subjects are for other kinds of people. In response, the book developed a model of translational pedagogy centered on cognitive visibility, translational explanation, scaffolded challenge, output conversion, and evidence-informed refinement.

Across the chapters, this model was explored in relation to teaching design, student transformation, evidence use, large-class implementation, cross-disciplinary generalization, and finally institutional culture. Several central claims emerged.

First, pedagogical access and rigor need not be opposites. Students from varied backgrounds can achieve strong outcomes when teaching reveals reasoning, connects to meaningful contexts, and supports struggle productively.

Second, transformation in higher education extends beyond grades. It includes confidence, belonging, identity, transfer, and contribution.

Third, student work should not be treated as disposable. With mentoring and pathway design, coursework can become prototypes, papers, presentations, community resources, competition entries, startup ideas, or public scholarship.

Fourth, large-scale and interdisciplinary teaching require design, not just effort. Quality at scale depends on routines, support architecture, feedback systems, and pedagogically led use of technology.

Fifth, the model extends beyond computing. Its core principles are transferable across fields when adapted thoughtfully.

Finally, pedagogy reaches fuller power only when institutions build ecosystems that sustain it.

10.2 Vision for future higher education

The future of higher education should not be imagined as a race between automation and credentialing, nor as a choice between elite rigor and widened access. A more hopeful and demanding vision is possible: universities as places where diverse students are taught so well, supported so thoughtfully, and challenged so meaningfully that they become capable creators, contributors, and responsible actors.

In such a future, foundational learning remains indispensable, but it is no longer the endpoint. Students do not merely pass through subjects; they begin to inhabit disciplines and connect them. They build things, question things, improve things, communicate things, and offer things back to society. Teachers are not mere transmitters but translational mentors. Institutions are not credential factories but ecosystems of capability.

This vision is ambitious, but it is not abstract. The practical evidence throughout this book suggests that even within a relatively short period, one can reach 2,091+ students across diverse disciplines, maintain high teaching effectiveness scores around 4.6–4.9 against a departmental average of about 4.2, reduce withdrawal from 5% to 0%, improve pass rates from 90% to 100%, and support students in producing 40+ conference papers, 10+ external awards, 10+ startup finalist teams, and 5+ patent/startup initiatives. These figures should not be read triumphalistically. They should be read as indicators of what becomes possible when educational design and institutional opportunity begin to align.

10.3 Final reflections on translational and creation-oriented pedagogy

The deepest argument of this book is ultimately a moral one as much as a pedagogical one. Education should not leave students feeling that knowledge belongs elsewhere, that contribution is for others, or that their role is only to consume what experts have already made. A humane and rigorous university invites students into the difficult work of understanding, then accompanies them toward the difficult work of creating.

Translational pedagogy matters because it makes that invitation intelligible. Creation-oriented culture matters because it makes that invitation sustainable. Together, they offer a way of rethinking higher education not as the management of learner throughput, but as the cultivation of human capability in forms that matter.

If universities can make hidden reasoning visible, if they can widen access without lowering aspiration, if they can support students from uncertainty to authorship, and if they can build ecosystems where learning naturally seeks expression in contribution, then higher education can remain not only relevant but transformative. That is the hope with which this book closes.

REFERENCES

Aquil Mirza, M., & Cong, W. (Eds.). (2026). *Real-Time Robotics With IoT and Edge AI: Methods, Metrics, and Applications*. IGI Global Scientific Publishing., DOI: 10.4018/979-8-2600-0701-3

Barnett, R. (2004). *Learning for an unknown future*. Higher Education Research and Development Society of Australasia.

Bringle, R. G., & Hatcher, J. A. (1995). A service-learning curriculum for faculty. *Michigan Journal of Community Service Learning*, *2*(1), 112–122.

Eyler, J., & Giles, D. E.Jr. (1999). *Where's the learning in service-learning?* Jossey-Bass.

Kuh, G. D. (2008). *High-impact educational practices: What they are, who has access to them, and why they matter*. Association of American Colleges and Universities.

Lave, J., & Wenger, E. (1991). *Situated learning: Legitimate peripheral participation*. Cambridge University Press.

Mohammed, A. (Ed.). (2026). *Advanced Concurrency, Buffering, and Web-Sync in Sensor Platforms: Zero-Loss Streams*. IGI Global Scientific Publishing., DOI: 10.4018/979-8-2600-1101-0

Mohammed, A., & Zangana, H. (Eds.). (2026). *Intelligent Construction Monitoring Systems: Real-Time Safety, Environmental Prediction, and Risk Management*. IGI Global Scientific Publishing., DOI: 10.4018/979-8-3373-9245-5

Wenger, E. (1998). *Communities of practice: Learning, meaning, and identity*. Cambridge University Press.

Compilation of References

Agarwal, P. K., & Bain, P. M. (2019). *Powerful teaching: Unleash the science of learning*. Jossey-Bass. DOI: 10.1002/9781119549031

Akkerman, S. F., & Bakker, A. (2011). Boundary crossing and boundary objects. *Review of Educational Research*, *81*(2), 132–169. DOI: 10.3102/0034654311404435

Ambrose, S. A., Bridges, M. W., DiPietro, M., Lovett, M. C., & Norman, M. K. (2010). *How learning works: Seven research-based principles for smart teaching*. Jossey-Bass.

Anderson, J. R. (1984). *The architecture of cognition*. Harvard University Press.

Anderson, J. R., Corbett, A. T., Koedinger, K. R., & Pelletier, R. (1995). Cognitive tutors: Lessons learned. *Journal of the Learning Sciences*, *4*(2), 167–207. DOI: 10.1207/s15327809jls0402_2

Aquil Mirza, M., & Cong, W. (Eds.). (2026). *Real-Time Robotics With IoT and Edge AI: Methods, Metrics, and Applications*. IGI Global Scientific Publishing., DOI: 10.4018/979-8-2600-0701-3

Atkinson, R. K., Derry, S. J., Renkl, A., & Wortham, D. (2000). Learning from examples: Instructional principles from the worked examples research. *Review of Educational Research*, *70*(2), 181–214. DOI: 10.3102/00346543070002181

Ausubel, D. P. (1968). *Educational psychology: A cognitive view*. Holt, Rinehart and Winston.

Bandura, A. (1997). *Self-efficacy: The exercise of control*. W. H. Freeman.

Banta, T. W., & Palomba, C. A. (2015). *Assessment essentials: Planning, implementing, and improving assessment in higher education* (2nd ed.). Jossey-Bass.

Barker, L. J., Garvin-Doxas, K., & Roberts, E. M. (2009). What can computer science learn from a fine arts approach to teaching? *SIGCSE Bulletin*, *41*(1), 421–425. DOI: 10.1145/1047124.1047482

Barker, L. J., McDowell, C., & Kalahar, K. (2009). Exploring factors that influence computer science introductory course students to persist in the major. *SIGCSE Bulletin*, *41*(1), 153–157. DOI: 10.1145/1539024.1508923

Barnett, R. (2004). *Learning for an unknown future*. Higher Education Research and Development Society of Australasia. DOI: 10.1080/0729436042000235382

Barnett, S. M., & Ceci, S. J. (2002). When and where do we apply what we learn? A taxonomy for far transfer. *Psychological Bulletin*, *128*(4), 612–637. DOI: 10.1037/0033-2909.128.4.612 PMID: 12081085

Baxter Magolda, M. B. (2009). Authoring your life: Developing an internal voice to navigate life's challenges. *Stylus (Rio de Janeiro)*.

Bers, M. U. (2020). *Coding as a playground: Programming and computational thinking in the early childhood classroom*. Routledge. DOI: 10.4324/9781003022602

Biggs, J., & Tang, C. (2011). *Teaching for quality learning at university* (4th ed.). Open University Press.

Black, P., & Wiliam, D. (1998). Assessment and classroom learning. *Assessment in Education: Principles, Policy & Practice*, *5*(1), 7–74. DOI: 10.1080/0969595980050102

Boud, D., & Falchikov, N. (2006). Aligning assessment with long-term learning. *Assessment & Evaluation in Higher Education*, *31*(4), 399–413. DOI: 10.1080/02602930600679050

Bransford, J. D., Brown, A. L., & Cocking, R. R. (Eds.). (2000). *How people learn: Brain, mind, experience, and school* (Expanded ed.). National Academy Press.

Braun, V., & Clarke, V. (2006). Using thematic analysis in psychology. *Qualitative Research in Psychology*, *3*(2), 77–101. DOI: 10.1191/1478088706qp063oa

Bringle, R. G., & Hatcher, J. A. (1995). A service-learning curriculum for faculty. *Michigan Journal of Community Service Learning*, *2*(1), 112–122.

Brookfield, S. D. (2017). *Becoming a critically reflective teacher* (2nd ed.). Jossey-Bass.

Brusilovsky, P., & Millán, E. (2007). User models for adaptive hypermedia and adaptive educational systems. In P. Brusilovsky, A. Kobsa, & W. Nejdl (Eds.), *The adaptive web* (pp. 3–53). Springer. https://doi.org/DOI: 10.1007/978-3-540-72079-9_1

Carlone, H. B., & Johnson, A. (2007). Understanding the science experiences of successful women of color: Science identity as an analytic lens. *Journal of Research in Science Teaching*, *44*(8), 1187–1218. DOI: 10.1002/tea.20237

CAST. (2018). *Universal design for learning guidelines version 2.2*. http://udlguidelines.cast.org

Chi, M. T. H. (2008). Three types of conceptual change: Belief revision, mental model transformation, and categorical shift. In Vosniadou, S. (Ed.), *International handbook of research on conceptual change* (pp. 61–82). Routledge.

Chi, M. T. H., Bassok, M., Lewis, M. W., Reimann, P., & Glaser, R. (1989). Self-explanations: How students study and use examples in learning to solve problems. *Cognitive Science*, *13*(2), 145–182. DOI: 10.1207/s15516709cog1302_1 PMID: 34983624

Chi, M. T. H., de Leeuw, N., Chiu, M.-H., & LaVancher, C. (1994). Eliciting self-explanations improves understanding. *Cognitive Science*, *18*(3), 439–477. DOI: 10.1207/s15516709cog1803_3

Cohen, G. L., & Steele, C. M. (2002). A barrier of mistrust: How negative stereotypes affect cross-race mentoring. In Aronson, J. (Ed.), *Improving academic achievement: Impact of psychological factors on education* (pp. 303–327). Academic Press. DOI: 10.1016/B978-012064455-1/50018-X

Collins, A., Brown, J. S., & Newman, S. E. (1989). Cognitive apprenticeship: Teaching the craft of reading, writing, and mathematics. In Resnick, L. B. (Ed.), *Knowing, learning, and instruction: Essays in honor of Robert Glaser* (pp. 453–494). Lawrence Erlbaum.

Cooper, K. M., Gin, L. E., Akeeh, B., Clark, C. E., Hunter, J. S., Roderick, T. B., Elliott, D. B., Gutierrez, L. A., & Brownell, S. E. (2019). Factors that predict life sciences student persistence in undergraduate research experiences. *PLoS One*, *14*(8), e0220186. Advance online publication. DOI: 10.1371/journal.pone.0220186 PMID: 31412071

Corbett, A. T., & Anderson, J. R. (1994). Knowledge tracing: Modeling the acquisition of procedural knowledge. *User Modeling and User-Adapted Interaction*, *4*(4), 253–278. DOI: 10.1007/BF01099821

Deming, W. E. (1986). *Out of the crisis*. MIT Press.

Denning, P. J. (2017). Remaining trouble spots with computational thinking. *Communications of the ACM*, *60*(6), 33–39. DOI: 10.1145/2998438

Denzin, N. K. (1978). *The research act: A theoretical introduction to sociological methods* (2nd ed.). McGraw-Hill.

Deslauriers, L., McCarty, L. S., Miller, K., Callaghan, K., & Kestin, G. (2019). Measuring actual learning versus feeling of learning in response to being actively engaged in the classroom. *Proceedings of the National Academy of Sciences of the United States of America, 116*(39), 19251–19257. DOI: 10.1073/pnas.1821936116 PMID: 31484770

Duit, R., & Treagust, D. F. (2003). Conceptual change: A powerful framework for improving science teaching and learning. *International Journal of Science Education, 25*(6), 671–688. DOI: 10.1080/09500690305016

Dweck, C. S. (2006). *Mindset: The new psychology of success*. Random House.

Eccles, J. S., & Wigfield, A. (2002). Motivational beliefs, values, and goals. *Annual Review of Psychology, 53*(1), 109–132. DOI: 10.1146/annurev.psych.53.100901.135153 PMID: 11752481

Eccles, J. S., & Wigfield, A. (2020). From expectancy-value theory to situated expectancy-value theory: A developmental, social cognitive, and sociocultural perspective on motivation. *Contemporary Educational Psychology, 61*, 101859. DOI: 10.1016/j.cedpsych.2020.101859

Edmondson, A. (1999). Psychological safety and learning behavior in work teams. *Administrative Science Quarterly, 44*(2), 350–383. DOI: 10.2307/2666999

Eyler, J., & Giles, D. E.Jr. (1999). *Where's the learning in service-learning?* Jossey-Bass.

Felten, P. (2013). Principles of good practice in SoTL. *Teaching & Learning Inquiry, 1*(1), 121–125. DOI: 10.20343/teachlearninqu.1.1.121

Fisher, D., & Frey, N. (2014). *Better learning through structured teaching: A framework for the gradual release of responsibility* (2nd ed.). ASCD.

Freeman, S., Eddy, S. L., McDonough, M., Smith, M. K., Okoroafor, N., Jordt, H., & Wenderoth, M. P. (2014). Active learning increases student performance in science, engineering, and mathematics. *Proceedings of the National Academy of Sciences of the United States of America, 111*(23), 8410–8415. DOI: 10.1073/pnas.1319030111 PMID: 24821756

Freeman, T. M., Anderman, L. H., & Jensen, J. M. (2007). Sense of belonging in college freshmen at the classroom and campus levels. *Journal of Experimental Education, 75*(3), 203–220. DOI: 10.3200/JEXE.75.3.203-220

Gentner, D. (1983). Structure-mapping: A theoretical framework for analogy. *Cognitive Science*, *7*(2), 155–170. DOI: 10.1207/s15516709cog0702_3

Gibbs, G., & Jenkins, A. (Eds.). (2014). *Teaching large classes in higher education: How to maintain quality with reduced resources*. Routledge. DOI: 10.4324/9781315041384

Gibbs, G., & Simpson, C. (2004). Conditions under which assessment supports students' learning. *Learning and Teaching in Higher Education*, *1*, 3–31.

Glynn, S. M. (2008). Making science concepts meaningful to students: Teaching with analogies. In Mikelskis-Seifert, S., Ringelband, U., & Brückmann, M. (Eds.), *Four decades of research in science education; From curriculum development to quality improvement* (pp. 113–125). Waxmann.

Gulikers, J. T. M., Bastiaens, T. J., & Kirschner, P. A. (2004). A five-dimensional framework for authentic assessment. *Educational Technology Research and Development*, *52*(3), 67–86. DOI: 10.1007/BF02504676

Guzdial, M. (2008). Education: Paving the way for computational thinking. *Communications of the ACM*, *51*(8), 25–27. DOI: 10.1145/1378704.1378713

Guzdial, M. (2015). Learner-centered design of computing education: Research on computing for everyone. *Synthesis Lectures on Human-Centered Informatics*, *8*(6), 1–165. DOI: 10.1007/978-3-031-02216-6

Hammer, D., Goldberg, F., & Fargason, S. (2012). Responsive teaching and the beginnings of energy in a third grade classroom. *Review of Science. Mathematics and ICT Education*, *6*(1), 51–72.

Hattie, J. (2009). *Visible learning: A synthesis of over 800 meta-analyses relating to achievement*. Routledge.

Hattie, J., & Timperley, H. (2007). The power of feedback. *Review of Educational Research*, *77*(1), 81–112. DOI: 10.3102/003465430298487

Henderson, C., Beach, A., & Finkelstein, N. (2011). Facilitating change in undergraduate STEM instructional practices: An analytic review of the literature. *Journal of Research in Science Teaching*, *48*(8), 952–984. DOI: 10.1002/tea.20439

Hiebert, J., & Grouws, D. A. (2007). The effects of classroom mathematics teaching on students' learning. In Lester, F. K.Jr., (Ed.), *Second handbook of research on mathematics teaching and learning* (pp. 371–404). Information Age. DOI: 10.1108/978-1-28141-200-320251013

Hundhausen, C. D., Douglas, S. A., & Stasko, J. T. (2002). A meta-study of algorithm visualization effectiveness. *Journal of Visual Languages and Computing*, *13*(3), 259–290. DOI: 10.1006/jvlc.2002.0237

Issenberg, S. B., McGaghie, W. C., Petrusa, E. R., Gordon, D. L., & Scalese, R. J. (2005). Features and uses of high-fidelity medical simulations that lead to effective learning: A BEME systematic review. *Medical Teacher*, *27*(1), 10–28. DOI: 10.1080/01421590500046924 PMID: 16147767

Jasanoff, S., Hüsing, B., Jochem, E., Lösch, A., Mikhailova, E., & Scheer, D. (2021). *Digital transformations and their social implications*. Springer.

Kapur, M. (2008). Productive failure. *Cognition and Instruction*, *26*(3), 379–424. DOI: 10.1080/07370000802212669

Kolb, D. A. (1984). *Experiential learning: Experience as the source of learning and development*. Prentice Hall.

Kuh, G. D. (2008). *High-impact educational practices: What they are, who has access to them, and why they matter*. Association of American Colleges and Universities.

Lattuca, L. R., Knight, D. B., & Bergom, I. (2017). Developing a measure of interdisciplinary competence for engineers. *Proceedings of the ASEE Annual Conference & Exposition*.

Lave, J., & Wenger, E. (1991). *Situated learning: Legitimate peripheral participation*. Cambridge University Press. DOI: 10.1017/CBO9780511815355

Lawrence Erlbaum. du Boulay, B. (1986). Some difficulties of learning to program. *Journal of Educational Computing Research*, *2*(1), 57–73. DOI: 10.2190/3LFX-9RRF-67T8-UVK9

Lewis, C. M. (2011). Is pair programming more effective than other forms of collaboration for young students? *Computer Science Education*, *21*(2), 105–134. DOI: 10.1080/08993408.2011.579805

Lister, R., Adams, E. S., Fitzgerald, S., Fone, W., Hamer, J., Lindholm, M., McCartney, R., Moström, J. E., Sanders, K., Seppälä, O., Simon, B., & Thomas, L. (2004). A multi-national study of reading and tracing skills in novice programmers. *SIGCSE Bulletin*, *36*(4), 119–150. DOI: 10.1145/1041624.1041673

Lister, R., Simon, B., Thompson, E., Whalley, J. L., & Prasad, C. (2006). Not seeing the forest for the trees: Novice programmers and the SOLO taxonomy. *SIGCSE Bulletin*, *38*(3), 118–122. DOI: 10.1145/1140123.1140157

Margolis, J., & Fisher, A. (2003). *Unlocking the clubhouse: Women in computing*. MIT Press.

Marsh, H. W. (1987). Students' evaluations of university teaching: Research findings, methodological issues, and directions for future research. *International Journal of Educational Research, 11*(3), 253–388. DOI: 10.1016/0883-0355(87)90001-2

Maton, K. (2013). Making semantic waves: A key to cumulative knowledge-building. *Linguistics and Education, 24*(1), 8–22. DOI: 10.1016/j.linged.2012.11.005

Mayer, R. E. (2004). Should there be a three-strikes rule against pure discovery learning? *The American Psychologist, 59*(1), 14–19. DOI: 10.1037/0003-066X.59.1.14 PMID: 14736316

Mayer, R. E. (2021). *Multimedia learning* (3rd ed.). Cambridge University Press.

Merriam, S. B., & Tisdell, E. J. (2016). *Qualitative research: A guide to design and implementation* (4th ed.). Jossey-Bass.

Meyer, J. H. F., & Land, R. (2003). Threshold concepts and troublesome knowledge: Linkages to ways of thinking and practising. In Rust, C. (Ed.), *Improving student learning: Theory and practice ten years on* (pp. 412–424). Oxford Centre for Staff and Learning Development.

Mishra, P., & Koehler, M. J. (2006). Technological pedagogical content knowledge: A framework for teacher knowledge. *Teachers College Record, 108*(6), 1017–1054. DOI: 10.1111/j.1467-9620.2006.00684.x

Mohammed, A. (Ed.). (2026). *Advanced Concurrency, Buffering, and Web-Sync in Sensor Platforms: Zero-Loss Streams*. IGI Global Scientific Publishing., DOI: 10.4018/979-8-2600-1101-0

Mohammed, A., & Zangana, H. (Eds.). (2026). *Intelligent Construction Monitoring Systems: Real-Time Safety, Environmental Prediction, and Risk Management*. IGI Global Scientific Publishing., DOI: 10.4018/979-8-3373-9245-5

Morrow, W. (2009). *Bounds of democracy: Epistemological access in higher education*. HSRC Press.

Nathan, M. J., & Petrosino, A. J. (2003). Expert blind spots in the education of preservice teachers. *American Educational Research Journal, 40*(4), 905–928. DOI: 10.3102/00028312040004905

National Academies of Sciences, Engineering, and Medicine. (2018). *How people learn II: Learners, contexts, and cultures*. National Academies Press. https://doi.org/DOI: 10.17226/24783

Nicol, D. J., & Macfarlane-Dick, D. (2006). Formative assessment and self-regulated learning: A model and seven principles of good feedback practice. *Studies in Higher Education, 31*(2), 199–218. DOI: 10.1080/03075070600572090

Ohlsson, S. (1996). Learning from performance errors. *Psychological Review, 103*(2), 241–262. DOI: 10.1037/0033-295X.103.2.241

Paivio, A. (1986). *Mental representations: A dual coding approach*. Oxford University Press.

Patton, M. Q. (1999). Enhancing the quality and credibility of qualitative analysis. *Health Services Research, 34*(5 Pt 2), 1189–1208. PMID: 10591279

Pea, R. D. (1986). Language-independent conceptual "bugs" in novice programming. *Journal of Educational Computing Research, 2*(1), 25–36. DOI: 10.2190/689T-1R2A-X4W4-29J2

Perkins, D. N., & Salomon, G. (1992). Transfer of learning. In Postlethwaite, T. N., & Husen, T. (Eds.), *International encyclopedia of education* (2nd ed., pp. 6452–6457). Pergamon Press.

Perkins, D. N., & Salomon, G. (1992). Transfer of learning. In Postlethwaite, T. N., & Husen, T. (Eds.), *The international encyclopedia of education* (2nd ed., pp. 6452–6457). Pergamon Press.

Piaget, J. (1970). *Science of education and the psychology of the child*. Orion Press.

Prince, M. (2004). Does active learning work? A review of the research. *Journal of Engineering Education, 93*(3), 223–231. DOI: 10.1002/j.2168-9830.2004.tb00809.x

Prince, M. J., & Felder, R. M. (2006). Inductive teaching and learning methods: Definitions, comparisons, and research bases. *Journal of Engineering Education, 95*(2), 123–138. DOI: 10.1002/j.2168-9830.2006.tb00884.x

Renkl, A. (2014). Toward an instructionally oriented theory of example-based learning. *Cognitive Science, 38*(1), 1–37. DOI: 10.1111/cogs.12086 PMID: 24070563

Ritchhart, R., Church, M., & Morrison, K. (2011). *Making thinking visible: How to promote engagement, understanding, and independence for all learners*. Jossey-Bass.

Robins, A., Rountree, J., & Rountree, N. (2003). Learning and teaching programming: A review and discussion. *Computer Science Education, 13*(2), 137–172. DOI: 10.1076/csed.13.2.137.14200

Roediger, H. L. III, & Karpicke, J. D. (2006). Test-enhanced learning: Taking memory tests improves long-term retention. *Psychological Science*, *17*(3), 249–255. DOI: 10.1111/j.1467-9280.2006.01693.x PMID: 16507066

Rumelhart, D. E. (1980). Schemata: The building blocks of cognition. In Spiro, R. J., Bruce, B. C., & Brewer, W. F. (Eds.), *Theoretical issues in reading comprehension* (pp. 33–58). Lawrence Erlbaum.

Sax, L. J., Lehman, K. J., Jacobs, J. A., Kanny, M. A., Lim, G., Monje-Paulson, L., & Zimmerman, H. B. (2018). Anatomy of an enduring gender gap: The evolution of women's participation in computer science. *The Journal of Higher Education*, *88*(2), 258–293. DOI: 10.1080/00221546.2016.1257306

Schraw, G. (1998). Promoting general metacognitive awareness. *Instructional Science*, *26*(1–2), 113–125. DOI: 10.1023/A:1003044231033

Shanahan, T., & Shanahan, C. (2008). Teaching disciplinary literacy to adolescents: Rethinking content-area literacy. *Harvard Educational Review*, *78*(1), 40–59. DOI: 10.17763/haer.78.1.v62444321p602101

Shulman, L. S. (1986). Those who understand: Knowledge growth in teaching. *Educational Researcher*, *15*(2), 4–14. DOI: 10.3102/0013189X015002004

Shulman, L. S. (1987). Knowledge and teaching: Foundations of the new reform. *Harvard Educational Review*, *57*(1), 1–23. DOI: 10.17763/haer.57.1.j463w79r56455411

Sorva, J. (2013). Notional machines and introductory programming education. *ACM Transactions on Computing Education*, *13*(2), 8. Advance online publication. DOI: 10.1145/2483710.2483713

Stake, R. E. (1995). The art of case study research. *Sage (Atlanta, Ga.)*.

Sweller, J. (1988). Cognitive load during problem solving: Effects on learning. *Cognitive Science*, *12*(2), 257–285. DOI: 10.1207/s15516709cog1202_4

Sweller, J., van Merriënboer, J. J. G., & Paas, F. (2019). Cognitive architecture and instructional design: 20 years later. *Educational Psychology Review*, *31*(2), 261–292. DOI: 10.1007/s10648-019-09465-5

Theobald, E. J., Hill, M. J., Tran, E., Agrawal, S., Arroyo, E. N., Behling, S., Chambwe, N., Cintrón, D. L., Cooper, J. D., Dunster, G., Grummer, J. A., Hennessey, K., Hsiao, J., Iranon, N., Jones, L.II, Jordt, H., Keller, M., Lacey, M. E., Littlefield, C. E., & Freeman, S. (2020). Active learning narrows achievement gaps for underrepresented students in undergraduate science, technology, engineering, and math. *Proceedings of the National Academy of Sciences of the United States of America, 117*(12), 6476–6483. DOI: 10.1073/pnas.1916903117 PMID: 32152114

Tinto, V. (2012). *Completing college: Rethinking institutional action*. University of Chicago Press. DOI: 10.7208/chicago/9780226804545.001.0001

Uttl, B., White, C. A., & Gonzalez, D. W. (2017). Meta-analysis of faculty's teaching effectiveness: Student evaluation of teaching ratings and student learning are not related. *Studies in Educational Evaluation, 54*, 22–42. DOI: 10.1016/j.stueduc.2016.08.007

van Merriënboer, J. J. G., & Kirschner, P. A. (2018). *Ten steps to complex learning: A systematic approach to four-component instructional design* (3rd ed.). Routledge.

Van Merriënboer, J. J. G., & Sweller, J. (2005). Cognitive load theory and complex learning: Recent developments and future directions. *Educational Psychology Review, 17*(2), 147–177. DOI: 10.1007/s10648-005-3951-0

Vosniadou, S. (1994). Capturing and modeling the process of conceptual change. *Learning and Instruction, 4*(1), 45–69. https://doi.org/Vygotsky, L. S. (1978). *Mind in society: The development of higher psychological processes*. Harvard University Press.DOI: 10.1016/0959-4752(94)90018-3

Vygotsky, L. S. (1978). *Mind in society: The development of higher psychological processes*. Harvard University Press.

Wainer, H. (2000). *Computerized adaptive testing: A primer* (2nd ed.). Lawrence Erlbaum. DOI: 10.4324/9781410605931

Weiss, D. J., & Kingsbury, G. G. (1984). Application of computerized adaptive testing to educational problems. *Journal of Educational Measurement, 21*(4), 361–375. DOI: 10.1111/j.1745-3984.1984.tb01040.x

Wenger, E. (1998). *Communities of practice: Learning, meaning, and identity*. Cambridge University Press. DOI: 10.1017/CBO9780511803932

Wiggins, G. (1998). *Educative assessment: Designing assessments to inform and improve student performance*. Jossey-Bass.

Wing, J. M. (2006). Computational thinking. *Communications of the ACM*, *49*(3), 33–35. DOI: 10.1145/1118178.1118215

Winslow, L. E. (1996). Programming pedagogy; A psychological overview. *SIGCSE Bulletin*, *28*(3), 17–22. DOI: 10.1145/234867.234872

Wood, D., Bruner, J. S., & Ross, G. (1976). The role of tutoring in problem solving. *Journal of Child Psychology and Psychiatry, and Allied Disciplines*, *17*(2), 89–100. DOI: 10.1111/j.1469-7610.1976.tb00381.x PMID: 932126

Woolf, B. P. (2021). *Building intelligent interactive tutors: Student-centered strategies for revolutionizing e-learning* (2nd ed.). Morgan Kaufmann.

Yin, R. K. (2018). *Case study research and applications: Design and methods* (6th ed.). Sage.

Zepke, N., & Leach, L. (2010). Improving student engagement: Ten proposals for action. *Active Learning in Higher Education*, *11*(3), 167–177. DOI: 10.1177/1469787410379680

Zimmerman, B. J. (2002). Becoming a self-regulated learner: An overview. *Theory into Practice*, *41*(2), 64–70. DOI: 10.1207/s15430421tip4102_2

About the Contributors

Mohammed Aquil Mirza is a senior member of IEEE, a researcher and educator specializing in AI, AIoT, robotics, sensor networks, and medical imaging. He is a Dean and Professor at Liaoning Technical University, China and a Senior Lecturer at The Hong Kong Polytechnic University, Hong Kong. His research has been funded by major grants, and his work has earned several national and international awards such as the IEEE Best Student Paper awards, Young Investigator Award, etc. With a strong academic background and innovative research, he continues to inspire future engineers.

***

Huahua Chen is an incoming graduate student in the Department of Statistics at The Chinese University of Hong Kong (CUHK). She holds a Bachelor's degree with First Class Honours from the Faculty of Humanities at The Hong Kong Polytechnic University (PolyU). Her academic background bridges the humanities and quantitative disciplines, reflecting a broad intellectual commitment to interdisciplinary inquiry.

Ka Chung Lai is an undergraduate student at The Hong Kong Polytechnic University, majoring in Computing and Artificial Intelligence. His research interests lie primarily in Computer Vision and robotics, with a specific focus on image deblurring algorithms and the integration of the Robot Operating System (ROS/ROS2). He was a research exchange student at the Shibaura Institute of Technology, where he contributed to international collaborative research projects. His technical work includes the development and optimization of models such as CAR-Net, aimed at enhancing real-time motion estimation in mobile robotics.

Zeyuan Ren received his BEng (Hons) degree in Industrial and Systems Engineering from The Hong Kong Polytechnic University with First Class Honours.

His research interests include dexterous robotic manipulation, human-in-the-loop shared control, imitation learning, and robot learning for industrial applications.

Kam Yung Yang is an undergraduate student pursuing a BA in Fashion at the School of Fashion and Textiles, The Hong Kong Polytechnic University. Her academic and creative focuses center on the innovative fusion between textile materials and fashion design. She is dedicated to exploring how advanced material properties can enhance contemporary garment design, structural aesthetics, and sustainability within the fashion industry.

Hewa Majeed Zangana is an Assistant Professor currently affiliated with Duhok Polytechnic University (DPU) in Iraq. He holds a Doctorate in Philosophy (PhD) degree in ITM, which he is currently pursuing at DPU. He has also held administrative positions such as Curriculum Division Director - Presidency of DPU, Head of the Computer Science Department at Nawroz University, and Acting Dean of the College of Computer and IT at Nawroz University. Hewa Majeed Zangana's research interests span a wide range of topics in computer science, including network systems, information security, mobile communication, data communication, and intelligent systems. He has published extensively in peer-reviewed journals and has published many academic books with IGI Global, several of which are indexed in Scopus and Web of Science (Clarivate). In addition to his research contributions, Hewa Majeed Zangana has been actively involved in editorial roles. He has also been a member of various scientific committees and administrative bodies at Nawroz University.

Index

A

B

C

D

E

F

H

I

L

M

N

O

P

S

T

V

www.ingramcontent.com/pod-product-compliance
Lightning Source LLC
LaVergne TN
LVHW081532300926
849161LV00006B/1397
9798260018118